RESEARCH HANDBOOK ON THE ECONOMICS OF CRIMINAL LAW

RESEARCH HANDBOOKS IN LAW AND ECONOMICS

Series Editors: Richard A. Posner, *Judge, United States Court of Appeals for the Seventh Circuit and Senior Lecturer, University of Chicago Law School, USA* and Francesco Parisi, *Oppenheimer Wolff and Donnelly Professor of Law, University of Minnesota, USA and Professor of Economics, University of Bologna, Italy*

Edited by highly distinguished scholars, the landmark reference works in this series offer advanced treatments of specific topics that reflect the state-of-the-art of research in law and economics, while also expanding the law and economics debate. Each volume's accessible yet sophisticated contributions from top international researchers make it an indispensable resource for students and scholars alike.

Titles in this series include:

Research Handbook on the Economics of Criminal Law

Edited by

Alon Harel

Boston University, USA, Hebrew University of Jersualem, Israel

Keith N. Hylton

Boston University, USA

RESEARCH HANDBOOKS IN LAW AND ECONOMICS

Edward Elgar

Cheltenham, UK • Northampton, MA, USA

Published by
Edward Elgar Publishing Limited
The Lypiatts
15 Lansdown Road
Cheltenham
Glos GL50 2JA
UK

Edward Elgar Publishing, Inc.
William Pratt House
9 Dewey Court
Northampton
Massachusetts 01060
USA

A catalogue record for this book
is available from the British Library

Library of Congress Control Number: 2012935266

MIX
Paper from
responsible sources
FSC® C018575

ISBN 978 1 84844 374 7 (cased)

Typeset by Servis Filmsetting Ltd, Stockport, Cheshire
Printed and bound by MPG Books Group, UK

Contents

Figures

Tables

Contributors

Jennifer Arlen, Norma Z. Paige Professor of Law, New York University School of Law, USA

Nuno Garoupa, Professor of Law, H. Ross and Helen Workman Research Scholar, Co-Director, Illinois Program on Law, Behavior and Social Science, University of Illinois College of Law, USA

Michael D. Guttentag, Professor of Law, Loyola Law School, USA

Alon Harel, Phillip and Estelle Mizock Professor of Law, Hebrew University of Jerusalem, Israel, Boston University, USA

Keith N. Hylton, Honorable Paul J. Liacos Professor of Law, Boston University, USA

Jonathan Klick, Professor of Law, University of Pennsylvania Law School, USA

John MacDonald, Chair, Department of Criminology, Associate Professor of Criminology, University of Pennsylvania, USA

Thomas J. Miceli, Professor of Economics, Department of Economics, University of Connecticut, USA

Robert A. Mikos, Professor of Law, Director, Program in Law and Government, Vanderbilt Law School, USA

Murat C. Mungan, Visiting Assistant Professor of Law, Florida State University College of Law, USA

Thomas Stratmann, University Professor of Economics and Law, George Mason University, USA

Avraham D. Tabbach, Senior Lecturer, Faculty of Law, Tel Aviv University, Israel

Introduction

Economic analysis of criminal law exploits social science methodologies (economics, behavioral economics, psychology and even sociology) to examine and evaluate the role of criminal law in society; the nature, and optimal size, of criminal sanctions; and the doctrines governing criminal law such as *actus reus*, *mens rea* and the nature of criminal law defenses. Further, economic analysis of criminal law is also concerned with issues that traditionally are not classified as criminal law questions: law enforcement policy, evidence law and procedural law.

Criminal law sanctions are perceived by law and economics theorists as incentives for individuals to behave in a way that is socially optimal. In contrast to the retributive tradition, which views the primary goal of criminal law as the punishment of wrongdoers for past actions, economic analysis considers the most effective incentives for achieving socially optimal conditions in the future. Thus, under the economic view of criminal law, the primary role of criminal sanctions is to influence future behavior (typically by deterring and sometimes also by incapacitating criminals). Under this view, the punishment is a necessary but unavoidable evil (given its costs to society and to the criminal). We ought to use criminal law sanctions only when they reduce the costs of anti-social behavior. These costs include the direct costs of crime as well as the costs of precautionary measures against crime.

This collection is by no means an exhaustive survey aimed at representing all scholarly traditions of economic analysis of criminal law. However, it includes chapters representing different traditions and approaches, including theoretical economic models, behavioral findings and empirical research. Designing an optimal system of criminal law requires delineating what wrongs ought to be criminalized and what wrongs ought to be regulated by tort law or administrative law (Harel, Mungan, Hylton). It also requires determining the size of sanctions on the basis of a complex balance between deterrence-based and incapacitation considerations (Harel, Miceli). The size and nature of optimal sanctions may differ in accordance with the identity of the victims (Mikos) or the identity of the perpetrators (Arlen). Extrinsic societal circumstances, such as technology (Klick, MacDonald and Stratmann) and even distribution of wealth (Tabbach), may be relevant to criminal law policy or impact its effectiveness (or both). It is not sufficient, however, to discern the optimal policy; it is also crucial to design institutions in a way that incentivizes officials to implement the optimal policies (Garoupa) and even recruit the help of private actors (Arlen). Further, effective criminal law policy cannot presuppose the rationality of perpetrators; it ought to be informed by behavioral studies and by a nuanced understanding of human psychology (Guttentag).

Chapter 1 (Harel)

This chapter is a survey of criminal law and economics. It examines three main traditions in law and economics. First, it examines traditional economic analysis of criminal law, which is based on the premise that criminals are rational (and, consequently, react to incentives provided by the legal system). Second, it explores the social norms tradition and the behavioral law and economics tradition, which question the assumption of rationality and are inclined to exploit psychological and sociological findings in designing criminal law prohibitions. Last, it discusses the "happiness" research founded on the recent work by Daniel Kahneman.

The traditional economic analysis of law is based on the premise that the criminal is rational, and it aims at designing incentives that minimize the sum of the costs of crime and the costs of precautions against crime. This section of the survey starts by identifying the anti-social behavior that ought to be deterred by using legal sanctions. Next, it examines what type of legal sanctions ought to be used: civil liability, administrative sanctions, criminal sanctions or others. It investigates the size of the optimal expected sanction and its optimal composition. It also explores the economic rationale of the rules governing criminal law doctrine: *actus reus, mens rea*, the optimal scope of defenses, etc.

The second section of the survey examines theories aimed at complementing economic theory by exploiting sociological, psychological or behavioral observations. This enterprise requires using empirical and experimental methodologies. Criminal law influences individuals by influencing their beliefs and preferences. If there are systematic biases that distort the judgments of individuals and their choices, such biases change individual behavior. Given that these biases and distortions are systematic and predictable, legislatures and policy-makers can make use of these biases and distortions in a way that is socially beneficial.

The final section of the survey examines the literature on happiness and criminal law. Jeremy Bentham believed that happiness has non-instrumental (intrinsic) value and that maximizing happiness ought to guide legislatures and policy-makers. This position has enjoyed a revival in recent years due to the work of psychologists, in particular the recent work by Daniel Kahneman. Kahneman distinguishes between two conceptions of utility: decision utility and experienced utility. Decision utility is based on the subjective evaluation of the individual with respect to the future utility derived from his decision. It therefore guides the actual decisions of individuals. Experienced utility, on the other hand, is the contemporary incarnation of Benthamite hedonic utilitarianism; it refers to the happiness that is experienced by the individual. Kahneman believes that experienced utility often differs from decision utility in ways that can be predicted and measured.

Both retributivists and utilitarian theorists should be interested in happiness research. Some retributivists (subjective retributivists) believe that the size of a sanction should be determined on the basis of the subjective disutility experienced by the criminal. Subjective retributivists call for equal (un)happiness for identical crimes (rather than equal sanctions for identical crimes). Deterrence theorists believe that we ought to deter crime, which requires the imposition of a sufficiently large sanction. Such a sanction ought to be sensitive to the expectations of the criminal with respect to the disutility resulting from the sanction. The two approaches focus on different types of happiness: retributivists care about experienced utility (the mental state of the person who is sentenced) while deterrence theorists focus on expected utility (based on the predictions of individuals concerning their future happiness) because of its deterrent effects.

Chapter 2 (Mungan)

This chapter explores the boundaries between criminal law and other fields of the law. Law uses various mechanisms to regulate behavior: tort law, administrative law, criminal law, etc. To evaluate the desirability of these mechanisms, Mungan first identifies the consequences of the criminalization of an act. These consequences include both doctrinal consequences (i.e., consequences resulting from the nature of the criminal law and criminal procedure) and social consequences (in particular, the stigma attached to criminal conviction). One important (doctrinal) consequence of criminalizing an act is the stringent standard of proof required in criminal law. A second (doctrinal) consequence is the detachment of the criminal sanction from the size of harm resulting from the crime. Typically, criminal sanctions (unlike tort law sanctions) impose much greater costs on criminals than the harms caused by the crime. A third (social) consequence of criminalizing an act is the negative attitude towards the perpetrator of the criminal act (stigma effects). The challenge of the legal theorist is to establish when these consequences are congenial to efficiency and why.

It is well established in the literature that intentional acts resulting in grave harms ought to be criminalized. This is primarily because of the need to impose harsh sanctions that reflect the gravity of the harms resulting from such crimes. Such sanctions ought to be particularly high given the typically low probability of detection of the criminals committing such acts.

High sanctions of the type required to deter intentional wrongs resulting in grave harms cannot be monetary sanctions, because offenders' wealth will not suffice to pay fines of the necessary magnitude. The problem of judgment-proof offenders necessitates the use of non-monetary sanctions such as imprisonment to deter judgment-proof offenders. Hence, it is necessary to resort to non-monetary sanctions of the type characterizing criminal law, e.g., imprisonment.

But why should the procedure in criminal trials be so stringent? Mungan identifies an important consideration justifying the stringency of criminal procedure. Criminal conviction provides information concerning a convict's criminal dispositions. This information is useful for third parties such as potential employers. The stringent procedural requirements used in criminal trials are necessary to guarantee the reliability of such information. Yet Mungan does not consider the fact that stigma attached to criminal conviction also imposes costs on third parties, as some third parties who could benefit from interaction with the criminal are pressured against their will to distance themselves from criminals.

Criminal law is also used in cases of intentional wrongs that result in smaller harms. Why could not such behavior be governed by non-criminal norms? After all, the sanctions required in order to deter such behavior typically do not result in insolvency. Mungan believes that non-criminal norms may fail to deter such wrongs because of the relatively small benefits resulting from civil litigation. Tort law remedies may fail to deter because the expected litigation costs are too high and there are psychic costs to the litigation that deter potential plaintiffs from pursuing the litigation. Punitive damages may remedy such defects but they suffer from other defects, e.g., grave risks of fraudulent litigation.

Mungan also explains why criminal law does not typically regulate unintentional harms. In the case of unintentional harms, the probability of detection is high, and consequently the sanctions necessary to deter such behavior need not be as large. It follows that monetary sanctions (characterizing tort law) may suffice to deter such behavior. Furthermore, in cases of unintentional harms there is a concern that the criminalization of unintentional acts would deter desirable activities. If inadvertently taking the umbrella of another may result in criminal conviction, I may be deterred from using umbrellas. Last, Mungan believes that unintentional behavior does not provide information concerning the anti-social dispositions of individuals. Hence, conviction for unintentional acts does not benefit third parties in the same way as conviction for intentional acts. This last point could be challenged on the grounds that it is often as desirable for third parties to know that a person is negligent as it is to know that he is inclined to commit intentional crimes. When I want to hire a cab, I may be very keen to know if the cabdriver is negligent.

Mungan analyses numerous considerations relevant to the criminalization of certain activities. What is particularly challenging is to balance the conflicting considerations and evaluate their relative weights. It seems to us that at the end of the day a careful analysis may expose the fact that there is a greater mismatch of economic considerations and existing criminal law doctrine and legal practices than envisaged by Mungan.

Chapter 3 (Hylton)

This chapter, like the preceding chapter by Mungan, explores the boundary between criminal law and other areas of law, such as tort law. One basic feature that separates criminal law from tort law is that the sanctions applied by the state – or, alternatively, the remedies sought by victims – are different and have different goals. Criminal law imposes penalties (fines, imprisonment or execution) that are designed to deter completely the offensive conduct at issue. Tort law, in contrast, imposes damage remedies: court awards that require the offender to compensate the victim by the amount of some estimate of the monetary value of the harm imposed by the offender on the victim. As Bentham urged, criminal law seeks to eliminate any prospect of gain on the part of the offender. Tort law seeks merely to require the offender to compensate the victim for his harm. Thus, if an offender gains $100 from committing an offense, and the victim suffers a loss of $50, the criminal sanction should be no less than $100 while the tort damages award will be $50.

What this difference in approach to sanctions reveals is that criminal law applies "property rules", in the language of Calabresi and Melamed (1972), while tort law applies "liability rules". It follows that the theory of property rules, as developed by Calabresi and Melamed as well as later writers, should provide the basis for a positive theory of criminal law. Although this is a reasonable conjecture, it has been challenged recently by critiques of the property rules framework. The most important of these modern critiques is the argument by Kaplow and Shavell (1996) that property rules and liability rules are equivalent in terms of their welfare implications (in low transaction cost settings), a thesis which Hylton refers to as the "Indifference Proposition". Hylton uses a simple example involving an actor who has a choice to take or to purchase a bicycle to explore the welfare implications of property and liability rules in a setting where transaction costs are low. He finds that when bounded rationality, predatory behavior and defensive behavior are incorporated into the analysis, property rules are unambiguously superior to liability rules in terms of welfare effects. He concludes that the Indifference

Proposition is invalid when applied to a richer description of the low transaction cost environment – a description that incorporates predatory and defensive conduct, as well as bounded rationality. The upshot is a more complicated but sturdier defense of the property rules framework as a positive theory of the boundaries of criminal law (separating criminal law from other areas of law), and of specific criminal law doctrines.

Chapter 4 (Mikos)

In this chapter, Mikos re-examines the question of the size of the optimal sanction taking into account the differential vulnerability of different victims. Under the traditional view of law and economics theorists, the (expected) size of the criminal sanction should be equal to the size of the (expected) harm caused by the crime. If the sanction is set appropriately, the potential criminal would commit the crime if and only if the benefits to the criminal are larger than the size of the harm. It follows that only "efficient crimes", namely crimes that benefit criminals more than they harm victims, will be committed.

Yet, Mikos reminds us, designing sanctions calibrated to achieve efficient deterrence is difficult because the harms resulting from a crime depend on the identity of the victim: some victims are particularly vulnerable while others are not. The variance in the level of harm of different victims is a challenge to the legal system; there are great difficulties in calibrating the size of the criminal sanction in accordance with the vulnerability of the particular victim. Given these difficulties, criminal law often imposes a sanction that is not sufficiently sensitive to the harm borne by the particular victim. Instead of individualizing the sanction in accordance with the resulting harm to the particular victim, criminal law uses the average harm as a basic measure.

Mikos also demonstrates that the failure to differentiate between different victims may be inefficient as it may over-deter some crimes and under-deter others. In the last part of the chapter, Mikos examines some strategies designed to ameliorate these difficulties. He concludes by arguing that investment on the part of victims in precautions can guarantee an efficient scheme of incentives. It is victims who know better than the state how vulnerable they are; consequently, their investment in precautions could ameliorate the difficulties resulting from the differential vulnerability of victims. Vulnerable victims would take more precautions while less vulnerable ones would take fewer precautions. Another desirable byproduct of the differential investment in precautions is that crime would be directed toward less vulnerable victims as they invest less in precautions.

Unfortunately, given the large externalities (both positive and negative) of precautions it is often difficult to know whether the investment in precautions is conducive to efficiency. Some investments are desirable because they may serve to differentiate between more and less vulnerable victims. Others, however, are not desirable because they are motivated by the desire to displace crime from one victim to another. Furthermore, vulnerable victims may be the precise individuals for whom it is particularly costly to invest in precautions.

Chapter 5 (Tabbach)

Mungan and Mikos examined the optimal scope of criminal law and the optimal sanction, assuming a certain fixed distribution of wealth. Distribution of wealth constrains the type of sanctions that can be imposed on criminals, because monetary sanctions can be imposed only on those who can pay them. In this chapter, Tabbach examines the effects of the distribution of wealth on the costs of crime and law enforcement. Tabbach's model establishes that in a broad set of circumstances, progressive redistribution of resources reduces the cumulative costs of crime and law enforcement. Yet there are circumstances under which the opposite is true, namely, it is regressive redistribution that reduces the cumulative costs of crime and law enforcement. Tabbach formally specifies the circumstances under which progressive/regressive redistribution is efficient. His conclusion is that "the social desirability of wealth redistribution is contingent on a trade-off between the social costs of enforcing the law upon the poor and those costs vis-à-vis the rich."

It is generally cheaper to enforce the law with respect to the rich than with respect to the poor for two cumulative reasons. First, monetary sanctions are superior to non-monetary sanctions such as imprisonment, because they merely involve transferring money from one person to another (rather than imposing suffering on a person without benefiting anybody else). Second, monetary sanctions are limited in their size; they cannot exceed the wealth of the offender. Hence it is often the case that a monetary sanction S deters effectively those whose wealth is larger than S ("the rich") but fails to deter those whose wealth is smaller than S ("the poor").

The distribution of wealth is essential to facilitate the effective imposition of monetary sanctions. If the efficient sanction is $1000, then redistribution – which guarantees that all offenders can pay $1000 – reduces the costs of crime enforcement because it facilitates imposing effective monetary sanctions on the poor. If the poor's wealth is $500 and the optimal sanction is $1000, it is necessary to supplement the monetary sanction with a non-monetary one.

If, on the other hand, the redistribution reduces the wealth of the rich below the optimal sanction, redistribution is inefficient. At times, regressive redistribution may reduce the costs of crime enforcement. This happens when redistribution guarantees that (at least) the rich can pay the optimal fine and therefore can be effectively deterred by monetary sanctions. If the optimal fine is $10000 and the richest person has only $9000, it may be efficient to transfer $1000 to him.

While many authors have explored the optimal probability and severity of punishment where wealth varies across individuals, Tabbach is the first to consider the social desirability of wealth distribution in reducing the social costs of crime and law enforcement. Yet, as he concedes, there are many efficiency-based considerations relevant to the distribution of wealth. The solvency of offenders seems a marginal consideration; our redistributive practices would not be greatly influenced by the fact that redistribution reduces the cumulative costs of crime and crime prevention.

Chapter 6 (Miceli)

Previous chapters relied exclusively on the deterrence model. Yet even traditional sentencing theorists identify incapacitation as a major consideration. Miceli develops "the hybrid model", designed to determine the optimal length of imprisonment where imprisonment serves both to deter and to incapacitate individuals. Under the traditional deterrence theory, the optimal expected sanction could be set at a level that is sometimes larger or smaller than the expected harm. As imprisonment is costly, it is sometimes efficient to under-deter criminals; consequently, the expected gain of criminals resulting from the crime is less than the social harms they cause. In such a case, criminals commit inefficient crimes. Miceli demonstrates that, under such circumstances, incapacitation results in longer optimal prison terms than those required by the pure deterrence theory, because longer sentences prevent offenders from committing further inefficient acts. In contrast, if it is efficient to over-deter individuals under the pure deterrence model, the expected gains for offenders who commit crimes is larger than the harms they impose. In this case, criminals may fail to commit efficient crimes. If this is the case, incapacitation considerations result in shorter optimal prison terms than those required by the pure deterrence theory. Miceli refines the model by adding the possibility of having monetary sanctions and also extending the model to address new and more complicated assumptions.

Chapter 7 (Arlen)

Previous chapters did not differentiate between different perpetrators of crime. This chapter focuses its attention on a special sub-set of perpetrators of crime – corporations – and argues that law enforcement policy should apply differently to individuals and corporations. The differences are attributable to the fact that corporate liability is not designed merely to deter crime but also to induce firms to invest in "policing" measures that increase the probability of corporate crimes being detected and sanctioned. Hence, the state must ensure that firms benefit from investing in such measures. Arlen praises the existing practice of offering leniency from prosecution to firms that fully cooperate with the state, coupled with residual sanctions imposed on such firms. In her view, such a scheme potentially enhances deterrence by increasing corporate cooperation while still providing firms with a financial incentive to prevent wrongdoing. The chapter examines the scheme governing corporate liability and evaluates its economic desirability.

Chapter 8 (Guttentag)

All previous chapters were premised on the assumption of rationality of criminals. In this chapter, Guttentag exploits behavioral and experimental research to challenge the premise that fraudulent accounting practices are rational and can be effectively deterred by using traditional economic methodology. In fact, he maintains that fraudulent accounting is "the unforeseen consequence of minor and seemingly innocuous transgressions rather than a product of planning and forethought." This conclusion results from various behavioral findings. For instance, it was found that cheating is self-limited and situationally contingent. The frequency of cheating is not always sensitive to its expected benefits. Changes in economic incentives do not have significant effects on the propensity to commit frauds. In sum, the decision to commit frauds is not typically the product of a rational calculation.

Guttentag argues that stochastic modeling can better explain the dynamics within a firm that may lead to accounting fraud. Stochastic process models are designed to capture the case in which "observable macroscopic behavior is produced by the cumulative effects of numerous 'microscopic' events."

Two types of data support Guttentag's hypothesis: psychological and sociological. Psychological data establishes that many cheaters are "honest cheaters". Such cheaters constrain the scope of their own cheating; they are inclined to limit the nature and the size of cheating. Further, changes in the potential gains resulting from cheating do not seem to have significant effect on the propensity to cheat. Sociological data indicates that circumstances in an agent's environment and the behavior and expectations of others have a great influence on the propensity to cheat.

Guttentag exploits these findings and develops models that describe mathematically the behavior of a system that undergoes a series of relatively small changes at random. These models establish the possibility that such a series of small changes may result in fraud. One interesting policy implication is that the sanction for fraud ought not depend on the motives of managers. This is because, under Guttentag's view, many accounting frauds are not motivated primarily by personal gain. Instead, managers stumble upon fraud rather than plan it in a rational manner. Although Guttentag's main interest is in examining accounting practices, his proposal may have implications concerning the use of motives in general and their relevance to criminal law and to sentencing practices.

Chapter 9 (Garoupa)

Previous chapters examined the optimal policy for combatting crime. Yet, combatting crime effectively presupposes that officials' incentives converge with the social good. Garoupa examines the set of incentives that influence prosecutors' behavior – in particular, their behavior under different institutional schemes. Under the classic model developed by Landes, prosecutors seek maximization of convictions weighted by sentences. In contrast, Garoupa suggests that American systems and European systems differ in the type of incentives provided to prosecutors and in the composition of the officials choosing to serve as officials (selection effects). Consequently, the two systems generate different behavior on the part of officials. Garoupa develops a typology of prosecutorial bodies. Some prosecutorial bodies (e.g., the American system) are "hierarchical", i.e., they have a lot of power, particularly with respect to their investigative resources and tactics; others (primarily European systems) are "coordinative", i.e., they have limited ability to influence the investigative process. The amount of control over investigative resources and tactics attracts different people to serve as prosecutors and generates different behavior on the part of prosecutors. The more powerful the prosecutor is, the more the result of the trial can be attributed to the prosecutor and, thus, the more the prosecutor is willing to take risks. Garoupa shows that evaluating the institutional environment is crucial for evaluating the efficacy of different legal systems.

Chapter 10 (Klick, MacDonald, and Stratmann)

This chapter re-examines a question that has puzzled many theorists of crimes: the dramatic reduction of crime rates in the United States in the 1990s. Numerous economists have investigated the reduction in crime rates. One of the most famous hypotheses is the controversial claim that the decline in crime rates can be explained by the legalization of abortion. Klick, MacDonald and Stratmann provide a new explanation, supported by empirical tools. They rely on the simple intuition that mobile phones provide opportunities for victims to report crimes to the police in real time and also allow bystanders to provide details of crimes at a very low cost. Mobile phones often facilitate the transmission of photographic information and help the police to locate the precise location of the victim. To establish this conjecture, this chapter provides empirical data concerning the correlation between the number of mobile phones and crime rates. The data shows that all of the violent crime measures exhibit a negative relationship with the number of mobile phones, whereas property crime rates do not exhibit such correlation. The findings of the chapter highlight the importance of private precautions against crime and their role in preventing crime, which is often overlooked.

Let us warn the readers that the law and economics of criminal law is merely one perspective relevant to evaluating criminal law practices. It is evident that citizens have strong reactions to crimes and they wish that criminal law and law enforcement policy reflect their sentiments and moral convictions. Nothing here should be understood as precluding the importance of the urge that criminal law mirrors such sentiments to some extent (subject to constitutional limitations). Criminal law is probably the field most influenced by popular sentiment. This book explores just one aspect of the complex considerations bearing on criminal law. But, as this volume establishes, even this narrow aspect is sufficiently rich to merit scholarly attention.

REFERENCES

Calabresi, Guido and Douglas Melamed (1972) "Property Rules, Liability Rules, and Inalienability: One View of the Cathedral", 85 *Harvard L. Rev.* 1089

Kaplow, Louis and Steven Shavell (1996) "Property Rules versus Liability Rules: An Economic Analysis", 109 *Harvard L. Rev.* 713

1 Economic analysis of criminal law: a survey
Alon Harel

I. HISTORICAL AND PHILOSOPHICAL BACKGROUND

1. Introduction

Economic analysis of criminal law exploits social science methodologies (economics, behavioral economics, psychology and even sociology) to examine the role of criminal law in society, the nature of criminal sanctions and the optimal size of those sanctions. Furthermore, given the nature of the relevant methodologies, economic analysis of criminal law is bound also to deal with issues that traditionally are not classified as criminal law questions: enforcement policy and issues involving evidence law and procedural law.

Criminal law sanctions are perceived by law and economics theorists as incentives for individuals to behave in a way that is socially optimal. In contrast to the retributive tradition, which views the primary goal of criminal law as the punishment of wrongdoers for past behavior, economic analysis considers the most effective incentives for achieving socially optimal behavior in the future. Thus, under the economic view of criminal law, the primary role of criminal sanctions is to influence future behavior (typically by deterring and sometimes also by incapacitating criminals). Under this view, the punishment is a necessary but unavoidable evil (given its costs to society and to the criminal). We ought to minimize the use of punishment and use it only when it limits the scope of anti-social behavior.

The classical criminal law doctrine is based on retributive values. The traditional legal theorist believes that the criminal law sanction ought to be imposed only on the guilty and that its severity ought to reflect the degree of wrongfulness of the act and the culpability of the actor.[1] Furthermore some retributivists oppose the use of criminal law for the sake of deterrence, as such a use violates the basic Kantian principle under which one ought not use a person as a means (not even as a means to deter crimes).[2] By regarding deterrence as the primary (or even exclusive) consideration of criminal law, economic analysis has the potential to challenge fundamental principles of traditional criminal law. Even basic premises of criminal law, such as punishing the guilty and imposing similar sanctions for similar crimes, need new justifications, as punishing the innocent can be as effective as, and perhaps cheaper than, punishing the guilty, and imposing different sanctions for similar crimes may at times be efficient.

Regarding criminal sanctions as negative incentives designed to prevent future crimes is not unique to the economic analysis of law. Traditional utilitarianism is based on the premise that criminal law is nothing but an incentive designed to deter future crimes; indeed, there are many similarities between the utilitarian analysis of criminal law envisioned by the utilitarian philosopher Jeremy Bentham and contemporary economic analysis. Yet contemporary economic analysis rejects the utilitarian principle of maximizing happiness defined in hedonic terms (pain and pleasure). In contrast to Bentham, economists believe that pain and pleasure are not operative concepts that can be measured and used in policy-making. Instead, economists use the term "preference" and aim at designing legal norms to satisfy preferences. Recently, however, psychologists revived the old utilitarian concepts of pain and pleasure in attempting to measure them scientifically and use them to design policy.

2.   Historical Evolution of the Economic Study of Criminal Law

In his monumental book, *An Introduction to the Principles of Morals and Legislation*, Bentham examines the norms of criminal law and analyses their desirability in terms of social utility. Under Bentham's view, only happiness (based on the aggregate pain and pleasure) has intrinsic value. This view is labeled "normative hedonism".[3] Bentham also believed that moral and legal norms ought to be designed in such a way that maximizes the aggregate pleasure in society. Criminal law is a branch of law that is defined as such:

> The business of the government is to promote the happiness of the society by punishing and rewarding. That part of its business which consists in punishing is more particularly the subject of penal law.[4]

Despite the dominance of the utilitarian tradition, the effect of Bentham's vision on the development of the practice of criminal law and even on the theory of criminal law was limited. The next primary step in the formation of the economic analysis of criminal law was the publication of the seminal article by Gary Becker, "Crime and Punishment: An Economic Approach", in 1968.[5] Unlike Bentham, Becker analyses criminal law not in terms of happiness but in terms of preferences, using the tools of neo-classical economics. Becker starts with the premise that the criminal is a rational maximizer of utility: he calculates the utility resulting from the crime and compares it to the expected costs of committing the crime. The role of the criminal law is to minimize the expected costs of the crime and the expected costs of precautions against crime. This article forms part of a broader project of Gary Becker: to analyse phenomena that traditionally were part of sociology (racial discrimination, family, drug addiction) in formal, rigorous terms. Becker's writings were followed by other theorists of law and economics. Richard Posner, Steven Shavell and many others have developed and explored the implications and limitations of Becker's economic approach to criminal law.

During the 1990s, two new schools of thought developed: one examines the law from the perspective of social norms and the other (labeled behavioral law and economics) uses psychology to investigate the optimal content of legal norms. The first school is based on sociological insights, and it explores the relationship between social norms and legal norms.[6] With the rise of behavioral economics in the 1990s, many works explored criminal law from a behavioral and psychological perspective.[7] The seminal works by Tversky and Kahneman (labelled prospect theory) provided new ways of thinking about law in general and criminal law in particular. Unlike Becker's tradition, these works are based not on *a priori* premises concerning the rationality of individuals but on empirical and experimental methodologies. More recently, law and economics theorists additionally have used insights from the psychological studies of happiness.[8] The tradition of law and economics turns back to the early hedonic Benthamite tradition.

3.   Purposes of the Economic Study of Criminal Law

The traditional economic analysis of criminal law is primarily a normative analysis. Criminal law under this view is designed to minimize the sum of the expected costs of crime and enforcement (or, more generally, precautions against crime). This starting point is used to address such questions as what constitutes a criminal offense, what are the optimal sanctions against criminal offenses, what is the optimal probability of detection, and what is the mental state required for conviction. Yet the economic methodology need not endorse this particular normative ideal. There is nothing which prevents the economist from endorsing the view that criminal law ought to give priority to the utility of victims over the utility of criminals, or that there are costs or benefits that ought not be taken into account for the purposes of criminal law policy. Furthermore, concerns of equality and distributive justice are not irrelevant to economic analysis. Even if we accept the goal of minimizing the costs of crime and the enforcement costs, one need not regard this as the only goal guiding criminal law. Perhaps one ought to limit the severity of criminal sanctions for justice-based reasons even where such limitation cannot be justified in terms of utility.[9] In addition to the normative approach of economic analysis of criminal law, there is literature that tries to predict and describe the behavior of criminals or potential criminals and the effect that changes to criminal law policy have on their behavior.

As economic analysis of criminal law ultimately is concerned with incentives, it deals not only with criminal law as such (the content of the prohibitions and the size of the sanctions) but also enforcement policy, evidence and procedure. Indeed, the traditional separation between punishment, enforcement and procedural or evidence law is perceived by law and economics theorists as an artificial separation. The willingness of a criminal to commit a crime depends not only on the punishment but also on the probability of detection (which, in turn, depends on the enforcement policy) and the probability of conviction (which itself depends on procedural and evidence law). Hence this chapter must deal not only with questions that are traditionally classified as "criminal law" but also with questions of enforcement policy, evidence and procedure.

4.   Structure of the Survey

Part II examines the traditional economic analysis of law based on neo-classical economics. This theory, which is based on the premise that the criminal is rational, aims to design incentives that minimize the sum of all the costs of crime (direct costs of crime and costs of precautions against crime). Part III explores the attempt to enrich or sometimes challenge the traditional, classical economic analysis by using tools from social norms theory and behavioral law and economics. Part IV explores the study of happiness and its bearings on criminal law. Part V raises several conjectures concerning the future of economic analysis of criminal law.

II.   THE RATIONAL CRIMINAL IN A UTILITY-MAXIMIZING SOCIETY: CLASSICAL ECONMIC ANALYSIS OF CRIMINAL LAW

1.   Introduction

Classical economic analysis is based on the premise that the criminal is maximizing his own utility. The criminal (like everyone else) is calculating the expected utility that he derives from the criminal act and compares the expected costs and expected benefits of his behavior. The utility can be monetary gain, sadistic pleasure or sexual satisfaction. The costs can be monetary (fine) or imprisonment or even stigma or lost wages or feelings of guilt. Sometimes the utility or the cost is a probabilistic utility or cost. Assume that Derek considers whether to steal a good worth $100. Assume also that the probability that he succeeds is 50% and that there is a fine of $200, which is imposed in 50% of cases of theft (regardless whether successful). In such a case the expected utility of the theft is 50% x 100 = $50 and the expected cost of the theft is 200 x 50% = $100. Given that the expected costs are larger than the expected benefits, Derek will not perform the theft.

This chapter looks at criminal law (and enforcement policy) from the perspective of the social planner who wishes to use criminal law for the sake of promoting the social good. Let us specify, therefore, the questions that the social planner has to examine. First, the social planner ought to identify the anti-social behavior that ought to be deterred by using legal sanctions. After identifying this anti-social behavior, the social planner ought to decide the appropriate type of legal sanction: civil, administrative or criminal. Given that the social planner will deem criminal sanctions appropriate, he must also determine the size of the expected sanction.

The size of the expected sanction is determined by the probability of detection and the size of the sanction (i.e., the size of the fine or the length of the imprisonment). The social planner has to determine the size of these two parameters. Finally, the social planner has to determine the rules governing the details of criminal law doctrine: the *actus reus*, the *mens rea*, the nature and the optimal scope of defenses, etc. After examining these questions in the following sections, we examine the way rational legislators operate and the sub-optimal consequences of such rational legislators' behavior.

2.   What is Anti-social Behavior?

Criminal law is designed to deter anti-social behavior. Although of course not all anti-social behavior is criminal, it seems that only anti-social behavior ought to be criminalized. Differentiating between anti-social behavior and socially desirable behavior is at times difficult; in these situations, sometimes it is appropriate to criminalize socially desirable behavior. For instance, it is often difficult to differentiate between necessary and unnecessary speeding. The law may prohibit and impose sanctions on speeding even where speeding is justified, because of the difficulties and the costs involved in differentiating between justified and unjustified speeding.

One way to describe anti-social behavior is as behavior that causes negative externalities. When an individual decides what to do, he takes into account only *his* expected costs and benefits. He does not take into account the costs and benefits his behavior imposes on others. When the behavior harms others and the expected harm to others is larger than the expected benefits to the actor, the behavior is anti-social; to the extent that the costs of deterring it are not too high, it ought to be deterred.

Note that the claim that the individual acts in order to promote his own utility is correct also when the behavior is altruistic (aimed to benefit others) or sadistic (aimed to harm others). Under the traditional view of law and economics, in both cases the individual derives utility from changing the utility of others. The altruist derives pleasure from increasing the well-being of others while the sadist derives pleasure from decreasing the well-being of others.

Although most criminal prohibitions are designed to prevent negative externalities (i.e., deter harmful behavior), one ought not preclude the possibility of criminal law prohibitions designed to induce behavior that has positive externalities (i.e., induce beneficial behavior). Yet sanctions designed to induce beneficial behavior are relatively rare. One challenge is to understand the reasons for this scarcity.

As we argued earlier, not every behavior that results in negative externalities is anti-social. Sometimes the utility derived by the perpetrator is larger than the disutility borne by others. In such cases, there is no efficiency-based justification for legal intervention. Legal intervention is necessary when the utility derived by the perpetrator is smaller than the disutility borne by others. Thus, for instance, it is necessary to intervene in the case in which I build a factory that produces goods worth $100 but imposes harms worth $200. The harm resulting from the behavior includes not only direct harms such as pollution or noise but also indirect harms such as enforcement costs and litigation costs.

Sometimes the social planner does not know whether an act increases or decreases social utility. For instance, the social planner may not know whether the costs of pollution are smaller or larger than the benefits resulting from the production. In such cases the social planner can impose a sanction, not because the behavior is anti-social, but in order to guarantee optimal incentives. If the social planner imposes on the factory owner costs equal to the costs the factory imposes, the factory will operate only if the utility to the owner is larger than the harm caused to others.

3.   Boundaries of Criminal Law

Criminal sanctions are nothing but negative incentives designed to deter individuals from engaging in anti-social behavior. But criminal law is not the only mechanism designed to produce such incentives. Administrative law and tort law are also designed to deter individuals from perpetrating anti-social behavior. For the purposes of this chapter it is important to identify the economic justification for using one type of sanction rather than another. Furthermore, the social planner can use two or more parallel systems, all of which are designed to create negative incentives.

To see the efficiency-based reasons for choosing one type of sanction rather than another let us identify two primary differences between criminal law and tort law. One difference is that criminal sanctions are often non-monetary (e.g., imprisonment, capital punishment or, in ancient legal systems, exile or torture). Furthermore, criminal sanctions are typically much more severe than the harms resulting from the wrong. In contrast, tort law sanctions are typically based on the size of the harm (with the exception of punitive damages). The second primary difference is the identity of the agent in charge of imposing the sanction. Typically, victims of a tort are in charge of bringing suit against a wrongdoer while criminal sanctions are initiated and controlled by the state. This is because legal theorists believe that the criminal offense (unlike the civil wrong) harms not only the victim but also the society or the public as a whole. With the rare exception of private criminal prosecution, contemporary criminal law grants the victim of a criminal act no control over the process; in general, the victim cannot initiate criminal prosecution or end it.

Monetary sanctions (characterizing tort law) have two advantages over non-monetary sanctions. First, monetary sanctions involve nothing but transferring money from one person (the wrongdoer) to another (the victim).[10] The typical criminal sanction (imprisonment) imposes costs on the criminal but (excluding satisfying sentiments of revenge and hatred) it does not promote the well-being of the victim (or anyone else) and it also imposes great costs on society. The only utilitarian advantage of prisons is that they prevent perpetrators from committing additional offenses (incapacitation). In contrast, monetary sanctions (either criminal or civil) impose costs on perpetrators but also benefit victims (in the case of compensation) or society (in the case of fines). Secondly, there is an advantage in victims' greater participation in the civil legal process, as victims often have information concerning the nature of the act committed and the size of the harm. This is the economic reason why victims of civil wrongs receive compensation; without such compensation, victims would have no incentive to cooperate and invest effort in providing information to the courts.[11] The criminal law process provides victims fewer incentives to cooperate than the civil law, as typically victims receive no benefit from cooperation. Perhaps the recent legal developments providing victims of crimes greater control over the criminal law process can be rationalized as means designed to encourage participation and cooperation on the part of victims.

This analysis implies that it is preferable, if possible, to use civil law sanctions. First, because they are monetary, such sanctions have direct benefits; the civil sanction is a mere transfer of money from one person to another. Second, the greater involvement of victims of civil wrongs in the legal process (and the fact that they are the potential beneficiaries of the process) is desirable, as this provides victims with an incentive to share information.

But, as Polinsky and Shavell have shown, civil sanctions are not always effective for several reasons. The primary reason is the risk that the wrongdoer is insolvent.[12] If the wrongdoer cannot compensate the victim, civil law can provide no incentives, as monetary sanctions hinge on the solvency of the wrongdoer. Furthermore, tort law sanctions may require an overly lengthy and expensive process and therefore may fail to incentivize victims to seek remedy. Sometimes, the wrongdoer harms many victims and the harm caused to each victim is too small to incentivize any one victim to seek remedy. Sometimes, the victim does not have the relevant information required to demonstrate harm. Sometimes, victims do not know about the harm (e.g., pollution). Finally, there are offenses such as bribes that harm society as a whole but for which the harms are dispersed and no single person has an incentive to seek remedy. The choice between using criminal law norms or tort law norms depends on the relative costs of the legal process for the victim, on the one hand, and the state, on the other.[13]

Let us turn our attention to the primary difficulty of monetary sanctions: the risk of insolvency. The monetary sanction characterizing tort law is limited to the value of the property of the wrongdoer. If the expected benefits resulting from the wrong are higher than the property of the wrongdoer, the wrongdoer is likely to commit the offense even if the monetary sanction imposed is larger than his expected benefit, simply because a monetary sanction cannot be imposed. The poorer the person is, the less effective monetary sanctions become. In order to guarantee effective deterrence in such cases, the legal system resorts to non-monetary sanctions (such as imprisonment).

This fact does not explain why the state ought to control the legal process. Arguably one could grant the victim control over the process even when the sanction is not a monetary sanction. But such a scheme is not effective. If the sanctions are non-monetary, the state must control the legal process, as the victim does not have sufficient incentives to sue in such cases. Criminal law is used in such cases only because civil law sanctions are monetary, and such sanctions are not effective when they are larger than the size of the wealth of the wrongdoer.

Theoretically, this difficulty could be overcome if the state paid the victim to participate in the legal process. The state could pay the victim compensation that is proportional to the severity of the punishment imposed on the wrongdoer. In such a case, the victim would have an incentive to participate in the process and provide the necessary information. Given that the sanction imposed on the victim is a non-monetary sanction, this solution would also overcome the problem of insolvency. Yet this solution has serious negative implications as people may manufacture crimes or exaggerate their seriousness in order to get paid.

Naturally, the question of whether insolvency is a problem depends on the resources of the particular wrongdoer. One unintuitive result of this analysis is that monetary sanctions (criminal or civil) ought to be used in cases where the wrongdoer is wealthy, while imprisonment ought to be used only where monetary sanctions cannot be used due to insolvency of the wrongdoer, i.e., where the wrongdoer is poor.[14]

The need to impose harsh sanctions (which are more likely to result in insolvency in cases where sanctions are monetary) exists in particular in cases where the probability of detection is low. To understand this, assume that committing the wrong results in a benefit of $100 to the wrongdoer. If the probability of detection is 100%, it is sufficient to impose a sanction of $100 to guarantee deterrence. If, however, the probability of detection is 1%, an expected sanction of $100 requires imposing a sanction of $10,000.[15] But such a high sanction is more likely to result in insolvency. From this analysis, it follows that the lower the probability of detection, the greater the need to use non-monetary sanctions such as imprisonment and, consequently, the greater the need that the state controls the process (as the victim has no sufficient incentives to do so). The lower the probability of detection, the greater the need to impose criminal, rather than tort law, sanctions.

This analysis is based on the assumption that one can impose either a criminal sanction or a tort law sanction. In fact we can deploy both. Theoretically, we could allow the victim to sue the wrongdoer for the harm and, in cases where the harm exceeds the wealth of the wrongdoer, impose non-monetary sanction. If, for some reason, the victim cannot sue, a fine could be imposed. If it is necessary to increase the fine above the monetary value of the wealth of the wrongdoer, the state could impose a non-monetary sanction equal to the difference between the optimal sanction and the monetary value of the wealth of the wrongdoer.[16]

Currently, the legal system does not operate in such a way. Typically, many criminal offenses are also civil wrongs and the imposition of a criminal sanction is independent of the wealth of the wrongdoer. It is certainly possible that the co-existence of criminal and tort law sanctions leads to too much deterrence.

4. Size of the Expected Criminal Sanction

The discussion in the previous section identified the nature of anti-social behavior and the circumstances under which such behavior ought to trigger the use of criminal sanctions. Criminal law sanctions ought to be imposed where tort law sanctions are not effective due to the absence of sufficient incentives for victims to sue. As a general rule, monetary sanctions are preferable to non-monetary sanctions as long as there is no insolvency problem.

Assuming that a criminal sanction is preferable (on the grounds mentioned above) the policy-maker ought to determine the size of the criminal sanction. In examining this question, we ought to differentiate between the actual and the expected size of the sanction. The expected sanction for a crime is calculated by multiplying the size of the sanction by the probability of detection and conviction; these two parameters determine the deterrent effects of the sanction. The larger the sanction, and the larger the probability of detection and conviction, the greater the deterrent effect of the sanction.

But what is the optimal expected criminal sanction? Theorists answer this question in two ways. Under the view of Gary Becker (the internalization theory), the role of criminal sanctions is to internalize the expected harms of crimes. The expected sanction ought to be equal to the expected harm resulting from an offense.[17] If the expected sanction and the expected harm caused by the offense are equal, the potential criminal would commit the offense only if the expected utility he derives from the crime is greater than the expected sanction. Under Becker's view, the expected sanction ought to be determined in a similar way as tort law remedy, i.e., by guaranteeing that the perpetrator "internalizes" the costs of the criminal behavior. The only difference between criminal sanctions and tort law remedies is that the probability of detection and conviction influences the size of the expected sanction. If the sanction is calibrated properly, the criminal would offend if and only if the expected benefits resulting from the behavior are higher than the expected harms resulting from the behavior. Under the view developed by Richard Posner (the prevention theory), the sanction ought to guarantee that the crime would not be perpetrated; therefore, the sanction ought to be higher than the expected utility resulting from the crime.[18]

The difference between the internalization theory and the prevention theory can be described by using the famous distinction between liability rules and property rules.[19] Liability rules are designed to guarantee that a person performs an action if and only if the expected utility resulting from the action is higher than the expected costs of the action. The sanctions attached to these norms are determined on the basis of the harms resulting from the act (independent of the expected utility that the perpetrator derives from the act). Tort law norms constitute the paradigmatic case of liability rules. The economic logic of norms protected by liability rules is straightforward. If the expected harm from the behavior is $100, the legal system ought to impose sanctions that will guarantee the wrongdoer internalizes the harm. If the expected benefit the perpetrator derives from the behavior is more than $100, he will perform the act (and thus maximize aggregate utility). If the expected utility is lower than $100, however, he will not perform the act (and thus maximize social utility). In identifying the social utility, one ought to take into account the direct harms of the victim as well as the indirect harms, including the costs of enforcement and private precautions taken by victims.

In contrast to norms protected by liability rules, norms protected by property rules are designed not only to impose costs on an act but also to deter the act (as long as the victim does not consent). Thus, property rules determine the expected sanction on the basis of the expected utility that the perpetrator derives from the act, independent of the expected harms resulting from the behavior. If the expected sanction for an act is higher than the *expected utility a perpetrator derives from the act*, the perpetrator will not perform the act.

The question addressed here is what the optimal size of criminal sanctions is. Should sanctions internalize harm (such that if the benefits exceed the harms, the perpetrator would perform the act) or should they deter the act altogether? Before we examine the economic logic underlying the internalization and prevention theories, let us examine first the intuitive, common-sense answer to the problem. The fundamental intuition of the lawyer is that the primary purpose of criminal law is to prevent acts such as murder, theft or rape, independent of the resulting benefits to the perpetrator. Criminal law is designed to deter also the "utility monster" (the person who derives huge pleasure from consuming resources such that her utility always exceeds the utility of other persons). The legal system ought to deter the utility monster from eating the flesh of another person, even if this cannibalistic practice maximizes social utility.[20] But there are other criminal offenses, which seem to be different and are more properly understood as designed to internalize the harms. Thus, the fine imposed on loitering or parking offenses or speeding offenses is perceived as a fine designed to guarantee that persons do not commit the harmful act *unless* they have good reasons to do so. An overly high sanction may deter individuals from committing such offenses even when it is socially desirable to commit them, e.g., deter people from speeding even in cases where speeding may save human life. Let us examine now what the efficiency-based considerations dictate.[21]

The internalization theory views the criminal sanction as a norm protected by liability rules. The sanction ought to guarantee that the criminal commits the offense only if the utility derived from the crime is higher than the harms he caused. Assume that Arthur owns a bicycle, worth $100 to him. Betty sells bicycles for $200 each. The probability of detection of theft is 10%. If Betty is risk neutral, the sanction that internalizes the harms caused by the theft of Arthur's bicycle is $1000. If such a sanction is imposed, Betty will steal the bicycles. As a matter of fact she would steal the bicycle in every case where the expected utility of the theft is equal to or greater than $1000 \times 10\% = \$100$. This is precisely the cost that the theft inflicts on Arthur. If the value of Arthur's bicycle for Betty is $200, the utility resulting from the theft is $100 = \$200$ (the value of the bicycles to Betty) $- \$100$ (the value of the bicycle to Arthur). The theft is therefore "an efficient theft". Imposing a sanction of $3000 would deter the theft as the expected utility of stealing is negative: $\$200 - 3000 \times 10\% = -\$100$. Yet such a high fine seems to be inefficient, as it prevents Betty from performing an "efficient theft". A similar analysis can be applied to violent crimes and rape.

How can this result be reconciled with the intuition that criminal law is often designed to prevent the act rather than to internalize the harm? One traditional response is to say that there are utilities that ought not be taken into account in the utilitarian calculus. For example, the utility derived by Marquis De Sade from torturing his victims ought not to be taken into account in the utilitarian calculus. John Stuart Mill famously differentiated between "high pleasures" (those resulting from art, music, etc.) and "low pleasures" (those resulting from eating or sex), assigning greater weight to "higher pleasures" in the utilitarian calculus.[22] But there are theorists such as Richard Posner who are faithful to the basic premises of Benthamite maximization and resist the idea that policy-makers ought to differentiate between higher and lower pleasures. Despite his opposition, Posner believes that it is possible to explain why criminal law norms ought sometimes to be protected by property rules, i.e., ought to guarantee that the criminal will not commit the offense even where the expected utility he derives from committing the offense is higher than the expected harms to the criminal.

Posner believes that often the best way to transfer goods or services is the market; therefore, the role of criminal sanctions is to guarantee that individuals do not evade the market.[23] Even if the criminal act increases social utility, it does not maximize social utility because there is a better way of increasing social utility. Under Posner's view, the legal system ought to be designed to incentivize individuals to bring about the transfer of goods in the most efficient way possible. In the bicycle theft case, the optimal way to transfer the bicycles from Arthur to Betty is to use the market and not to use theft.

The following numerical example illustrates this argument.[24] Assume that Arthur has bicycles worth $100 to Arthur and $200 to Betty. The cost (to the state) of detection and conviction of Betty (in case she steals the bicycles) is $20. The social gain from the theft is $200 - 100 - 20 = \$80$. The overall social cost resulting from the theft is $100 + 20 = \$120$. The sanction that internalizes the social costs is $120. Assume also the costs of negotiation between Arthur and Betty is $10, and that Arthur and Betty each bear the equal cost of $5. The social gain from a market transaction is $200 - 100 - 10 = \$90$. It is evident on the basis of these assumptions that theft (increasing social benefits by $80) is less efficient than a voluntary transaction (increasing social benefits by $90).

But Betty may prefer theft to a voluntary transaction. If Betty decides to buy the bicycle she will have to pay at least $105 (as Arthur will not be willing to sell the bicycle for less than $105) but not more than $195 (as Betty will not be willing to pay more for the bicycle). Betty may predict that in negotiations the price will be $150. The net gain to Betty in such a case will be only $200 - 150 - 5 = \$45$, while the gain resulting from theft under a system of internalization will be $80.

In fact, Betty will prefer to steal the bicycle in every case in which she predicts the price of the bicycle is higher than $115. If the price of the bicycles is $115, Betty will gain $200 - 115 - 5 = \$80$, which is precisely the benefit she would derive from theft (under a scheme of criminal law that internalizes the harms). Every price higher than $115 will incentivize Betty to steal the bicycle rather than buy it. But a market transaction is more efficient. Hence, the criminal law norm ought to force Betty to use the market, by deterring the theft altogether, rather than merely internalizing the costs resulting from the theft. To do so, the criminal law ought to impose a fine of at least $200. In such a case, even if Betty believes that the price of the bicycle is $195 (and therefore the gains from a voluntary transaction for Betty provides the lowest possible gains), Betty would not perpetrate the theft. This example illustrates that sometimes criminal law ought to reject the internalizing scheme and instead use preventive sanctions even where the theft increases social utility. Only such a sanction assures us that the potential offender will use the free market to purchase the goods or services instead of resorting to theft or violence.

We examined two primary conflicting economic conjectures concerning the size of the expected sanction. Under one view, the criminal sanction ought to internalize the expected harm, while under the second view, the optimal sanction is a preventive sanction designed to prevent the behavior. Which one is better from an economic perspective?

The answer is not fundamentally different from the intuitive, common-sense answer: namely, it all depends. Sometimes criminal law ought to use an internalizing sanction (protecting criminal law norms by using liability rules) and sometimes the law ought to use a preventive sanction (protecting criminal law norms by using property rules). Where there are efficient markets, through which the transfer of rights can occur, it is more desirable to use a preventive sanction (to guarantee that individuals do not "evade the market"). In contrast, where there are no efficient markets and transaction costs are high, an internalizing sanction is more efficient. The example of Arthur and Betty is an example in which preventive sanctions are more efficient (because the transaction costs are low). But it is not too difficult to imagine cases where it is more desirable to use internalizing sanctions. While walking through the desert and dying of thirst, it is not always possible to negotiate with the owner of water – the transaction costs are too high. An internalizing sanction that guarantees that she steals water only if the utility derived from the water is greater than the costs she imposed on the owner seems reasonable. A less dramatic example involves parking offenses. If I desperately need to park, negotiations with the authorities are too costly. It is better simply to park illegally and pay the fine. My willingness to pay the fine indicates that my need is sufficiently great and exceeds the social harm.

In sum, the optimal expected criminal sanction is sometimes equal to the expected harms caused by the act (in cases where the transaction costs are high and the internalizing norm is better). In other cases, the criminal sanction ought to be preventive, i.e., a sanction that prevents the crime and incentivizes the potential offender to resort to the market (the case of the bicycle theft).

There are still many questions left open. Sometimes the size of the internalizing sanction depends on the identity of the victim (as the harm caused by the act may change from one victim to another). Additionally, the size of the preventive sanction depends on the identity of the perpetrator (as the utility from the act differs from one perpetrator to another). Criminal law cannot fully accommodate these different factors (e.g., by imposing different sanctions for the same crime depending on the identity of the victim and offender) and instead ought to use approximations. Thus, even if criminal law chooses to impose a preventive sanction, there still will be individuals who perpetrate the act (because the utility they derive from the act is particularly high). Inevitably, the implementation of these principles requires many speculations. In practice, it will be very difficult to calibrate the sanctions in accordance with economic rationales.

5.   Components of the Expected Sanction: The Size of the Sanction and the Probability of Detection

Even after following our instructions in section II.4 and calibrating the size of the expected sanction, a policy-maker must decide on the size of the two main components of the expected sanction: the probability of detection and conviction, and the size of the sanction.

Doctrinal discussions of criminal law differentiate sharply between the size of the sanction and the probability of detection and conviction. The size of the criminal sanction ought to reflect the seriousness of the crime. The more hideous the crime, the greater the sanction ought to be. Murder is a more serious wrong than burglary, and burglary is more serious than theft. The punishments for these offenses should reflect their hierarchy of gravity. There is no relation between the probability of detection and conviction, and the size of the sanction. Empirical studies indicate that the strict separation between these two questions reflects the moral intuitions of most people.[25]

Economic analysis rejects this view. The primary purpose of criminal sanctions is to deter individuals from anti-social behavior. Increasing the probability of detection and conviction, and increasing the size of the sanction, are both congenial to deterrence. Both the probability of detection and conviction, P, and the size of the sanction, S, determine the size of the expected sanction. The higher the sanction, the lesser the probability of detection and conviction ought to be, and vice versa. Thus, an expected sanction of $100 can be imposed by imposing either (1) a sanction of $100 with a 100% probability of detection and conviction; (2) a sanction of $1000 with a 10% probability of detection and conviction; or (3) a sanction of $10,000 with a 1% probability of detection and conviction. The legal system ought to determine not only the size of the expected sanction but also the size of the expected sanction's relevant components: the probability of detection and conviction, on the one hand, and the size of the sanction, on the other.

This observation explains the otherwise counterintuitive claim made in the introduction, namely, that economic analysis cannot adopt a sharp differentiation between criminal law and the components of procedure, evidence and law enforcement policy. In addition to the size of the criminal sanction, evidence law and investment in enforcement (both of which determine the probability of conviction) influence the expected sanction. In turn, the expected sanction determines the deterrent effects of the criminal law norms. There is therefore an intimate connection between the size of the sanction and the probability of detection. We need to turn our attention to the question of what the optimal size of these two factors is.

In his seminal article, Gary Becker provides a simple and compelling answer to this question.[26] In his view, it all depends on the costs of increasing the size of the sanction, on the one hand, and the probability of detection, on the other. Typically, increasing the size of the sanction is much less costly than increasing the probability of detection. Hence, Becker makes a very provocative proposal: efficiency requires the imposition of a very harsh sanction (e.g., capital punishment, administered by boiling the offender in oil, for parking offenses) with a very low probability of detection.

Becker's conclusion illustrates the radical potential of economic analysis of law. Even law and economics theorists disfavor such conclusions; they seem to deviate too radically not only from our contemporary practices but also from our moral intuitions. If the conclusion of economic analysis of criminal law is that parking offenders ought to be executed (admittedly with a low probability of detection) something must have gone wrong.

Some theorists have argued that harsh sanctions may have negative implications as they induce offenders to increase their investment in precautions and therefore it may have negative effects on the probability of detection and conviction. Harsh sanctions may lead offenders to resist far more fiercely at the time of arrest or trial.[27]

Another relevant observation, which at least provides some rationale for our contemporary practices, is that individuals may be much more influenced by the probability of detection than by the size of the sanction. To clarify this point, let us define the concepts of risk neutral, risk averse and risk loving individuals. An individual is risk neutral if he is indifferent as to two sanctions with equal expected value. A fine of $10,000 with a 1% probability of detection deters such an individual to the same degree as a fine of $100 with a 100% probability of detection. An individual is risk averse if he is deterred more by a harsh sanction with a low probability of detection (e.g., $10,000 with a 1% probability of detection) than by a light sanction with a high probability of detection (e.g., $100 with a 100% probability of detection). A risk loving individual is deterred more by a light sanction with a high probability of detection (e.g., $100 with a 100% probability of detection) than by a harsh sanction with a low probability of detection (e.g., $10,000 with a 1% probability of detection). If individuals are risk averse, the policy-maker can increase deterrence by imposing harsh sanctions with low probabilities of detection; if individuals are risk loving, the policy-maker can increase deterrence by imposing light sanctions with high probabilities of detection.

Criminology research establishes that increasing the probability of detection has much greater effects on crime than increasing the size of criminal sanctions. Increasing the size of a sanction has a marginal effect (if any) on deterrence. It seems that individuals are risk loving; they are deterred more by low sanctions with high probabilities of detection than by harsh sanctions with low probabilities of detection. How can this phenomenon be explained?

Increasing the size of a sanction from a one-year prison term to a two-year prison term does not double the deterrent effects of the sanction, because of a psychological phenomenon called discounting of the future.[28] Compare Arthur, who expects to go to the dentist tomorrow and have a painful treatment, with Betty, who expects to go to the dentist next month. Arthur is anxious and wakes up at night while Betty has no anxiety at this point. Individuals tend to discount the significance of distant future events. It follows that a second year of imprisonment (which starts only after the end of the first year) has a lesser deterrent effect than the first year (which starts immediately after conviction). A prison term of one year with a 2% probability of detection has a greater deterrent effect than two years with a 1% probability.

Furthermore, legal sanctions are only part of the overall sanctions imposed on criminals. The criminal also suffers from stigma, which in turn often has economic effects on the criminal. Conviction exposes the criminal to both legal and social sanctions. Assume that conviction exposes the criminal to a legal sanction of $100 and to a social sanction worth $100 to him. The sanction is effectively $200. Assume also that the probability of detection is 1% and the expected overall sanction (consisting of the legal and non-legal sanction) is therefore $2. If the state increases the legal sanction from $100 to $200, the overall sanction increases from $200 to $300 and the expected sanction increases as a result to $3. Doubling the size of the (legal) fine in this case from $100 to $200 does not double the overall sanction. Yet doubling the probability from 1% to 2% would double the expected sanction from \$2 to \$4. Increasing the probability of detection has a greater effect on deterrence than increasing the sanction.

It seems therefore that part of the answer to Becker's challenge is based on the fact that increasing the probability of detection has much greater deterrent effects than increasing the size of sanctions. But this may not be sufficient to explain why efficiency does not dictate imposing the harshest sanctions possible with the lowest possible probability of detection. Increasing the sanction is arguably almost costless. After we catch and convict a criminal, it costs almost nothing to impose a harsh sanction on him. Hence, even if increasing a sanction has very little deterrent effect, it is always desirable to increase the sanction and decrease the probability of detection. To address this challenge, economists provide two additional explanations.

First, economic theory ought to examine not deterrence as such but "marginal deterrence". The legal sanction ought to deter marginally, i.e., it ought to deter a person from committing a second offense if he has already committed one offense. If a parking offender is boiled slowly in oil, the offender will have a strong incentive not to park illegally, but once he has parked illegally, he also will have a strong incentive to kill any witnesses. It is essential that there will be a range of punishments such that the parking offender will have a strong incentive not to commit additional offenses. The light sanctions for parking offenders enables the legislator to fix a range of punishments for different crimes and facilitates the marginal deterrence of offenders.[29] A second answer is based on risk aversiveness. Large sanctions with low probabilities impose costs on risk averse criminals. The costs of risk aversiveness are socially wasted. While society benefits from fines imposed on parking offenders, it does not benefit from the risk to which risk averse offenders are exposed. The conclusion of Polinsky and Shavell is that, if offenders are risk averse, the optimal fine is lower and the probability of detection higher than if offenders are risk neutral or risk loving.[30] For this reason, Becker's proposal to impose harsh sanctions may deter individuals from socially desirable activity. Given that the legal system is not perfect, some innocent people may be convicted. Further, risk averse individuals may be deterred from legal activities, as such activities increase the probability of being convicted for a crime they did not commit. In a system in which a parking violation is a capital offense, individuals may be deterred from driving cars because doing so may increase the probability of conviction for illegal parking.

Although there is a rich body of literature exploring the deterrent effects of criminal law,[31] most of this survey is theoretical and thus it does not explore the empirical aspects of the question. Economists examining the empirical findings use sophisticated econometric models to examine the effects of changing the sanction or increasing the investment in detection of crime. Such research is often complicated, given the difficulty of differentiating between the deterrent effects of punishment and other effects such as incapacitation. Furthermore, identifying the causal relations between severe punishments and low crime rates is not easy. It seems plausible that increasing the size of the sanction reduces the rate of crime but reducing the rate of crime also influences the sanction (as it may change the stigma attached to the crime) or the probability of detection (as it may reduce the burden on the police and facilitate better investigation).[32] These problems challenge the empirical study of the deterrent effects of criminal law.

6.   Criminal Law Doctrine

Criminal law consists of numerous legal principles that are traditionally perceived to serve the interests of retributive justice. For instance, it is a basic premise of criminal law that criminal activity must be defined clearly and precisely by rules, instead of by vague principles or norms such as "good faith" or "negligence". Criminal law also requires performing an act, which is sometimes defined as "bodily movement". This is the famous requirement of *actus reus*; the law does not punish thoughts or intentions that do not have a behavioral component. Furthermore, criminal law typically requires *mens rea* ("guilty mind") and does not punish individuals for negligence or strict liability. Punishment for negligent acts is an exception that is used rarely. Criminal law also includes defenses such as necessity, self-defense, insanity, etc. Economic analysis of criminal law explores the economic rationale of these doctrines. Let us see how this is done.

6.1   Specificity of criminal law norms
Criminal law norms are typically rules rather than standards; they define precisely what the prohibited activity is. Such norms enable the agent to know precisely what the prohibited behavior is and act accordingly.

Theorists distinguish between rules and standards. The difference between rules and standards can be conceptualized as a difference in the stage in which the norm is created. A rule is created *ex ante* by the legislator or the regulator. The use of a rule by judges is mechanical and (at least in the ideal case) does not require the use of discretion. A standard, in contrast, is applied *ex post* by judges (or juries), such as negligence in tort law. Determining what constitutes negligence is ultimately a judicial decision. Theorists of law and economics have examined carefully the choice between rules and standards.[33] The primary purpose of selecting a rule or a standard is to minimize the costs of creating the norms in the first place (by the legislature or regulator) and the costs of applying or implementing these norms by judges (and also by those who are subject to these norms). The investment at the stage of creating rules is relatively high, but once they are created, the costs of implementing rules is low because judges can apply the norms mechanically and citizens can know when they apply. In contrast, the investment in standards is relatively low at the early stage (the stage of creating the norms), but the use of standards imposes high costs on the judicial system, as it requires judges to determine whether the standard applies to the case at hand. Similarly it imposes higher costs on citizens who cannot be guided by these norms. The question of whether a contract violates "the good faith" standard is a complicated question that requires costly effort on the part of judges.

Criminal law is rule-based. In some legal systems, there is a constitutional requirement that criminal law norms be specific and precise. In the United States, for instance, penal standards may be unconstitutional on the basis of the "void for vagueness" doctrine.

To understand the reasons for criminal law's preference for rules over standards, consider the following hypothetical penal norm: any person who causes unreasonable harm to others is subject to two years of imprisonment. Assume that the legal system makes no mistakes and convicts only people who cause unreasonable harm to others, where reasonableness is measured by the costs and benefits of the activity. Under this hypothetical standard, individuals could make costly mistakes as to whether the harms they inflict on others are unreasonable.

Assume that I consider whether to play the violin knowing that there is some probability that playing the violin will cause unreasonable harm to my neighbors. There are two possible mistakes I can make: (1) playing the violin too much and causing unreasonable harm to my neighbors, or (2) playing the violin too little. Both mistakes are socially costly mistakes. In the first case, I cause unreasonable harm to my neighbors, and in the second case I fail to act in a way that is beneficial to me only because of the unjustified concern that I may cause unreasonable harm to others.

Assume that I believe playing the violin for two hours is most likely to be optimal, because the benefits resulting from playing the violin exceed the costs I impose on my neighbors. Playing for longer than two hours would impose larger costs on my neighbors than the benefits I derive from it. How many hours will I play the violin?

The answer is that I will play for less than two hours. While I believe that if I play for two hours I will not be convicted of a crime, I am aware that I may be mistaken. The consequences of the two possible mistakes are not symmetrical. If playing the violin for two and a half hours does not harm unreasonably my neighbor I am mistaken in my judgment but the cost of such a mistake is only the loss resulting from failing to play for an additional half an hour. On the other hand, if playing for two hours is unreasonable, a mistaken judgment on my part would lead to criminal conviction. In such a case, I would be disposed to act in a way that is overly cautious because of the asymmetrical consequences of the two mistakes. For instance, I may play for an hour and a half rather than two hours, despite my judgment that playing for two hours is optimal. Similar results follow in the case where I know what unreasonable behavior is but I also know that judges make mistakes with respect to it. Even if the mistakes cancel each other out (such that sometimes judges find unreasonable behavior to be reasonable and at other times reasonable behavior to be unreasonable), individuals will be over-cautious. The criminal law standard (as opposed to the criminal law rule) is paralyzing; it deters people from engaging in socially desirable activities because of the uncertainty resulting from the standard. The decision to use only rules in criminal law is based not merely on considerations of justice but also on considerations of efficiency.[34]

6.2   Actus reus

Criminal law typically requires *actus reus*, namely an act on the part of the perpetrator. There is a fierce debate among doctrinal lawyers as to the tests necessary to satisfy the *actus reus* requirement. But all agree that to convict someone, it is not sufficient to prove an intent to commit a crime; some behavioral manifestation of the intention is necessary for conviction. Criminal law doctrine distinguishes between preparation (which is not punishable), attempt (which is punishable, though the sanction is sometimes lower than the sanction imposed for the complete offense), and a complete offense. The boundaries between non-punishable preparation and punishable criminal attempt are blurred; there is a list of complicated (and controversial) tests designed to draw the boundaries between the two. Can these distinctions be justified on efficiency-based grounds?

On the one hand, imposing criminal responsibility for an attempt reduces the size of the optimal expected sanction imposed on criminals.[35] To see why, assume that a person commits an offense that, if completed successfully, would generate a benefit of $100 to the criminal. The probability of success is 50% and the expected benefit is therefore $50. Compare the status of a criminal in a legal system that punishes criminal attempts with the status of a criminal in a legal system that does not punish attempts. Assume that in both systems, the probability of detection of both successful and unsuccessful criminals is 50%. In a system that does not punish attempts, only 25% of the criminals are punished, because half of the criminals (those who did not complete the offense) are not punished and, among those who completed the crime, only 50% are caught. To deter criminals from committing the offense, the sanction ought to be $200. If the fine is $200, the expected sanction is $50, which is equal to the expected utility derived from committing the crime. If, on the other hand, the system chooses to impose a sanction on criminal attempts, it is enough to impose a sanction of $100 to guarantee complete deterrence. Under such a system, half of the criminals are punished (all criminals who are detected are punished), and therefore a sanction of $100 is sufficient: the expected sanction under such a scheme is $50, which is equal to the expected benefit from the crime. It follows that in a system in which attempts are punishable, the optimal sanction for criminals is lower than the optimal sanction in a system in which criminal attempts are not punishable.

Reducing the size of sanctions has positive effects for the reasons discussed earlier. First, smaller sanctions facilitate the use of fines, because the risk of insolvency is smaller. As shown above, fines are better than non-monetary sanctions. Second, with smaller sanctions, there is less investment of risk averse individuals in precautions against wrongful conviction. Third, lower sanctions facilitate differentiating the sanctions for different offenses, resulting in more efficient marginal deterrence.

But there are also disadvantages to the criminalization of attempt. The criminal law process is costly. Criminalization of attempt results in increasing the volume of litigation. Furthermore, prosecuting criminal attempts is more costly and also raises the risks of wrongful conviction.[36] Criminal attempts, as a whole, leave fewer evidential tracks than complete crimes. These considerations explain the reluctance of the criminal law system to convict a person for preparation. Preparation is a very early stage of the criminal act and it leaves few and weak evidential manifestations.

Lastly, there are efficiency-based considerations that justify differentiating between criminal attempts and the complete crime for reasons that have to do with marginal deterrence. If criminal attempts are punished in the same way as complete crimes, criminals have an incentive to try again. Deterring such criminals requires imposing smaller sanctions on criminal attempts than on complete crimes. Although officially, many legal systems (including the Model Penal Code) do not differentiate between the sanctions imposed for criminal attempts and those imposed for the complete crimes, judges use their discretion to differentiate between the two. Furthermore, some legal systems exempt perpetrators of attempts from criminal responsibility when they voluntarily decide not to complete the offense. The potential regret on the part of the criminal may also explain why the legal system does not punish preparation. Preparation consists of early stages of the commission of the offense and thus it is likely that the perpetrator of preparation eventually changes his mind.

6.3   Mens rea
Typically, the mental requirements required for conviction of a criminal offense is significant relative, for instance, to the mental requirements for liability in tort law. The attribution of criminal responsibility requires "*mens rea*", i.e., awareness of not only one's own behavior but also the existence of the relevant circumstances and the possibility that

harmful outcomes can result from the behavior. With few exceptions, criminal law does not criminalize negligent behavior. Can this requirement be rationalized?

One answer is that criminal sanctions typically are harsh. The attribution of responsibility for negligent acts may incentivize individuals to take overly costly precautions. Compare the situation of an innocent person who mistakenly takes someone else's umbrella. Under the current system, such a person cannot be convicted of theft, because he does not have the required *mens rea*. Attributing criminal responsibility for "negligent theft" would impose great costs on individuals, because individuals will invest too much in precautions designed to prevent the possibility that they would be convicted for "negligent theft". At the same time, the requirement of *mens rea* imposes costs on the legal system, because proving *mens rea* could be difficult and requires costly investment on the part of the prosecution. Finally, it is more likely that manipulative criminals abuse the current system because of the evidential difficulties in establishing *mens rea*.

The *mens rea* requirement has exceptions. One exception includes light offenses of a regulatory type. The fact that some regulatory offenses do not require *mens rea* supports the rationale mentioned above, because the risk of over-investment in precautions is significant in serious crimes involving severe sanctions.

One often cited exception to the *mens rea* requirement is the case of statutory rape (intercourse with a minor). This is a very serious crime in all legal systems and yet in many legal systems there is no need to prove that the defendant knew or suspected that the victim was a minor. Posner believes that, in such a case, the costs of precautions are not too high. The defendant could be more cautious in selecting his sexual partners. The costs of a mistake resulting from not having sex with an adult because of a false belief that she is a minor are not too high.[37]

Typically, *mens rea* is considered by lawyers as a requirement grounded in justice-based considerations, in particular, the injustice of convicting a person in the absence of *mens rea*. But the statutory rape exception raises difficulties. If indeed the only consideration is the injustice, why should these considerations not apply to the case of intercourse with a minor?

One of the primary disadvantages of the *mens rea* requirement is the incentive that it provides to individuals not to search out or acquire relevant information. If the legal system requires *mens rea* for the sake of conviction, a person who considers whether to engage in intercourse would have no incentive to determine a sexual partner's age, as failing to search for this information would lead to exculpation. Another example is the case of a person who sells alcohol to minors. Such an offense typically does not require *mens rea*. Without attributing responsibility to such a person independently of her knowledge of the age of the buyer, the seller would have no incentive to inquire about the age of her clients. Under such a regime, ignorance is bliss, as it would exempt perpetrators from criminal responsibility.[38]

The claim is not free of difficulties, as *mens rea* does not require knowledge; it is sufficient that the perpetrator is aware of the mere possibility that the relevant circumstances apply or the mere possibility that the relevant harmful outcome may be caused by her behavior to guarantee conviction. Hence, ignorance is not sufficient for exculpation. Yet, even if ignorance is not sufficient for acquittal, searching for the information may indicate that the defendant was aware of the possibility that the act is criminal and consequently lead to his conviction in a system that requires *mens rea*.

This claim raises an additional and intriguing possible explanation for why the legal system ought not always to require *mens rea*. Perhaps requiring *mens rea* in cases such as statutory rape or selling alcohol to minors may deter the perpetrator from searching for relevant information not because such a search may result in acquiring information but because searching for the information provides evidence that the perpetrator was aware of the circumstances or the possible harms resulting from his behavior. If the person inquires about the age of his partner, this provides evidence that he may have suspected that she may be underage. Hence, if *mens rea* is required, a perpetrator may fail to inquire about the age of his sexual partner even if he suspects she may be underage.

But is this argument too strong and broad in its implications? Perhaps it implies that we ought not to require *mens rea*. After all, the challenge is to explain not only why *mens rea* is sometimes not required but also why, in most cases, it is required.

The economic explanation is that, in many cases, the perpetrator has sufficient incentives to acquire the information independently of the exemption from criminal liability resulting from ignorance. In other cases, the perpetrator has no such incentives but there are no reasons to impose a duty to search, because search is too costly.[39] Let us illustrate both cases.

In the American case *United States v. Ahmad*, the owner of a gasoline station was charged with polluting because he discharged gasoline in a sewer system.[40] The defendant argued that he believed the liquid discharged was water rather than gasoline. The court found the defendant not guilty on the grounds that *mens rea* is required in this offence. The economic rationale is simple. Given that gasoline is much more expensive than water, the owner has a strong incentive to differentiate between the two. There is no reason to believe that the owner will not invest in acquiring this information independently of whether *mens rea* is required or not.

In other cases, the *mens rea* requirement induces perpetrators not to invest in searching for information but at the same time there is no efficiency-based reason to induce individuals to acquire the information. The legal system does not convict a person who possesses or uses forged money if he does not know or suspect that the money is forged. The *mens rea* requirement induces individuals not to investigate whether the money is forged. But there is no economic justification for incentivizing individuals to verify the authenticity of the money they use. Imposing such a duty is simply too costly. The conclusion is that imposing strict liability in criminal law is justified on efficiency-based grounds only if the following two conditions are satisfied: (1) the *mens rea* requirement induces individuals not to invest in acquiring information; and (2) acquiring information is efficient and consequently the law ought to encourage it.

Sometimes the legal system differentiates between offenses that require *mens rea* and those that have an even more demanding mental requirement, such as "malice aforethought". The classic case is the distinction drawn between murder and homicide. Can this requirement be justified?

One rationale is that a person who kills another with malice aforethought (i.e., murders) typically plans his act more systematically than one who kills without malice aforethought (i.e., commits homicide) and, as a result, the probability of detection is much lower. An enhanced sanction is required to guarantee the same expected sanction for murder as for homicide. Furthermore, impulsive killing is often unavoidable and the effort to deter it is simply a waste. An impulsive killing is not characterized by a detailed calculation of costs and benefits and an attempt to deter such killings is wasteful. If this is the case, then perhaps impulsive killings ought to be decriminalized. Alternatively, these findings may lead to the opposite conclusion that impulsive killings deserve particularly harsh sanctions, as the person who kills with malice aforethought calculates his acts more carefully than the person who commits an impulsive killing (who may miscalculate and kill even where the expected sanction is higher than the expected benefits of the killing). A particularly harsh sanction may induce the person who commits homicide not to commit the act.[41]

6.4   Defenses

Criminal law recognizes a long list of defenses, divided into two types: justifications and excuses. A criminal law justification is a defense based on the premise that the act is justified under the circumstances. A criminal law excuse is a defense based on the premise that, although the act is unjustified, the perpetrator ought to be excused given the difficult circumstances in which the act was done. A classic case of justification is a necessity defense where the expected costs of the harms resulting from the act are lower than the expected harms resulting from failing to perform it. In the famous case of *Dudley and Stephens*, the defendants (sailors of a boat) killed a member of the crew to feed on his body and avoid starving to death.[42] It was also claimed that the victim would have died anyways, because he was suffering from extreme malnourishment. In such a case, it seems that a simple cost-benefit analysis would require exempting the perpetrators from liability. Similarly, it seems that such an analysis would also justify exempting a starving individual from criminal liability for having stolen a loaf of bread. Yet criminal law refuses to grant thieves such a defense. One way of explaining why common law refuses to exculpate in such cases is that sometimes the costs of examining the evidence are too high. Furthermore, a necessity defense in the *Dudley* case opens the possibility of manipulation by defendants and raises the need to invest in costly factual investigation. In deciding to grant a justificatory defense such costs ought to be taken into account.

Criminal law excuses apply to defendants who perpetrate an act under difficult circumstances so that it would be unreasonable to expect them to comply with a legal prohibition. Is it justified to exempt such defendants from responsibility?

To explore this question let us examine the insanity defense that is often characterized as an excuse. The economic justification for such an excuse is that, in such cases, the criminal law sanction does not deter. There is no economic rationale to impose a sanction where it does not have a deterrent effect. Yet there are also costs to the legal recognition of excuses. Excuses may provide opportunities for perpetrators to deceive the court, and such opportunities may weaken the deterrent effects of criminal law. Furthermore, excuses impose procedural costs on the legal system, because judges need to investigate whether they apply to the particular case at hand.

6.5   The criminal sanction

Criminal sanctions can be fines or imprisonment, and they often result in a social sanction (stigma). We pointed out that fines have great advantages over imprisonment. A fine is merely transferring resources from the criminal to the state. Imprisonment, on the other hand, requires investing state resources, and it provides no benefits other than deterrence and sometimes also incapacitation.

During the 1990s, courts started making use of old-new sanctions: shame penalties based on social stigma. Shame penalties were used extensively in the Middle Ages. Unlike today, the public manifestation of the justice system in the Middle Ages was not the trial but the imposition of the sanction. Among the most feared outcome of conviction was the social stigma that attached to the person who was publically shamed. Shame penalties have gradually disappeared but in the last two decades became fashionable again. Often shame penalties involve publicizing the names of the criminals and their pictures on the Internet. The result is public exposure that naturally triggers hostility against the criminals, social isolation and monetary losses. Shame penalties presuppose some degree of cooperation between the state and its citizens. The state publicizes the names and pictures of criminals, and citizens react by distancing themselves from the criminals. Given this cooperation by citizens, social sanctions can replace wholly or partly the classic legal sanctions, fines or imprisonment.

One advantage of shame penalties is the low cost of imposing them. In comparison to imprisonment, the cost of shame penalties is negligible. A state merely has to publicize the names of criminals in a way that triggers hostility toward them. Furthermore, unlike the case of fines, there are no problems of insolvency. But shame penalties also have some costs. First, the effect of shame penalties hinges on social reaction, and such a reaction need not be proportional to the gravity of the offense. Some social reactions may be too harsh and impose grave costs that are disproportional to the gravity of the offense. Other reactions may be too lenient. It is difficult, therefore, for the state to calibrate optimally the size of shame penalties.[43]

Furthermore, shame penalties impose disproportional costs on citizens who are required to bear the costs of punishment. Some citizens bear these costs voluntarily and gain utility because they prefer on moral, ideological and even pragmatic grounds to distance themselves from criminals. The crimes may be ones that trigger disgust and resentment or they may indicate lack of reliability on the part of criminals (such as in cases of fraud, or driving under the influence of alcohol). But in other cases, individuals are not inclined to bear such costs and they do so only because of social pressure and the fear of being identified with the crimes. In such cases one ought to take into account the costs borne by such individuals, as they are relevant to determining whether shame penalties are efficient.[44]

7. Duty of Rescue and Positive Duties

The common law is very reluctant to impose positive duties. Positive duties exist in criminal law, but they typically hinge on the existence of prior relationships (such as the parent-child relationship) or special circumstances (such as drivers who observe a traffic accident). A classic case illustrating the common law's reluctance to impose positive duties is its refusal to embrace so-called "good Samaritan" duties, i.e., duties to rescue. Other legal systems, such as Jewish law or civil law, recognize broad duties to rescue.

Traditionally, the absence of positive duties is justified on grounds of autonomy or "negative liberty". Richard Posner thinks that legal responsibility for failing to rescue characterizes communist or fascist legal systems, because the imposition of responsibility is a form of "conscription for the social service".[45] Under this view, individuals ought not cause harm to others but they have no (legal) obligation whatsoever to help others. Can the absence of positive duties in the common law be justified?

Arguably, it is very difficult to explain the absence of positive duties on economic grounds. The utilitarian tradition, which provides the normative foundations for economic analysis of law, imposes very demanding duties on individuals. Maximizing utility requires one individual to help another as long as the marginal utility resulting from one's efforts is greater than the costs. My duty is to serve the beggars of Jerusalem instead of sitting in my air-conditioned office and writing this text.[46] Naturally, it does not follow that the legal system ought always to impose such duties, as sometimes there are grave costs to such an imposition. Yet it is quite difficult to explain why, if I sit on the beach watching the birds while my desperate friend is struggling in the water, the law ought not impose a legal duty to interrupt my favorite hobby and throw a rope to save him.

One explanation, provided by Posner and Landes, is based on the conjecture that imposing such a duty would deter individuals from visiting areas where accidents may occur and, consequently, reduce the probability of rescue.[47] This explanation seems speculative. Another explanation is grounded in behavioral conjectures (many of which will be examined in the next chapter) and especially on the thesis of Richard Titmuss in his famous book, *The Gift Relationship from Human Blood to Social Policy*.[48] In this book, Titmuss identifies a psychological phenomenon that he labels "crowding out". Titmuss explores the practice of blood donations, comparing the American practice (in which blood donors receive monetary compensation) with the British practice (in which blood donors get no such compensation). Titmuss found that the willingness to donate blood in Britain is greater than the willingness to donate blood in the United States despite the absence of monetary compensation in Britain. His claim (which is highly controversial) is that monetary compensation reduces or annuls altruistic incentives, and therefore, the blood supply in a society in which blood donors receive monetary compensation may be lower than in a society in which blood donors receive no such compensation.

Titmuss focuses his attention on monetary incentives "crowding out" altruistic motivations, but his hypothesis can apply also to legal sanctions "crowding out" the same altruistic motivations. Under this view, by imposing a criminal law duty, law may weaken rather than strengthen the disposition of individuals to invest in rescue. Individuals may invest in rescuing precisely because they perceive it as a moral duty. Imposing legal responsibility for failing to rescue may turn the act from an act of charity, indicating the virtues of the rescuer, into an act that is merely done out of compliance with the law. Hence, legal sanctions may "crowd out" the altruistic motivations and thus reduce the willing to rescue.

8. The Mouse is Not the Thief – The Hole is the Thief[49]

Traditionally theorists of criminal law argue that criminal law does not recognize the comparative fault of victims. The mere fact that a victim invested too little or too much in precautions should not influence the criminal responsibility of a perpetrator.[50] But a more careful investigation of criminal law doctrines reveals that precautions may influence criminal responsibility. Thus, reducing the charge from murder to homicide in cases of provocation can be described as a comparative fault defense. The criminal law declines to protect the provoker as much as it protects non-provokers, because the provoker contributed in his behavior to the killing. Furthermore, if I leave my property on the street corner, a person who takes the property may be convicted of failing to return lost property but not of theft. If, on the other hand, I leave the property at home and lock it, a person who takes the property would be convicted of the more serious offense of burglary. The precautions taken by the victim (locking the property at home) influence the size of the sanction imposed by the criminal law system. The distinction between sanctions imposed for theft and burglary, for instance, benefit (even if inadvertently) victims who invest in precautions. Is this efficient? If so, when?

To explore this question think of the following case: John has left the keys to his apartment in the door and somebody has stolen his property. Is there an efficiency-based reason to mitigate the sanctions against the thief given the "comparative fault" of John?

It seems that there is no such efficiency-based reason for mitigating criminal sanctions. First, it is unclear why imposing a lighter sanction on the criminal increases John's incentives to take precautions. Unlike in tort law, where comparative fault reduces the compensation of the victim (and therefore induces him to take precautions), it is unclear why mitigating criminal sanctions induces victims to take precautions. Furthermore, it is unclear why there is an efficiency-based reason to increase the investment of the victim in precautions. After all, John's negligence already causes harm to himself. Traditional economic analysis would maintain that as long as taking precautions (or failing to take them) affects only the victim, there is no reason to induce John to take more precautions. His behavior is based on his preferences. The cost of taking precautions (in our case, taking the keys) is higher than the expected cost resulting from the increase in the probability of theft. There is no reason to induce John to invest more in precautions, because his investment has no external effects and we may assume it is efficient.

But a more thorough exploration exposes some deficiencies in this argument.[51] First, very often there are externalities (both positive and negative) to the investment in precautions. In such cases, there are reasons to induce victims to take more precautions (in cases of positive externalities) or less precautions (in cases of negative externalities). To see why, think of the irritations caused by car alarms. Another important case of negative externalities is the case of installing bars on apartment buildings. Installing bars typically does not reduce the rate of crime but merely displaces the crime from one victim to another. The investment in precautions on the part of one person increases the probability that others will become victims of burglary.

Displacement of crime resulting from investment in precautions may result in suboptimal results. The neighbor who has not installed bars will install them, as she knows that the investment of her neighbors in bars exposes her to higher risks of burglary. This is only because other neighbors installed the bars and the result is that the rate of crime in society may remain constant despite the large investment in precautions. This explains perhaps the opposition to the establishment of gated communities. Such communities protect residents living inside the gated community at the expense of their neighbors, who become more vulnerable to crime.

In other cases, precautions have positive externalities on potential victims. Installing LoJacks in a car benefits not only the particular car owner but also cars owners in general.[52] LoJacks are hidden instruments installed in cars that enable police to locate the car in cases of theft. Because LoJacks are hidden, criminals cannot identify their existence; thus, installing LoJacks reduces the incentives to steal cars in general (not just the incentives to steal cars in which a LoJack is installed).

The conclusions from these observations can be generalized as follows: observable precautions (such as window bars) typically create negative externalities, because they merely shift the crime from one victim to another. In contrast, unobservable precautions (as LoJacks) may generate positive externalities, because they deter criminals from committing the crime.[53] The social planner ought to deter potential victims from investing in observable precautions and instead induce them to invest in unobservable precautions.

We have established so far that potential victims may over-invest or under-invest in precautions. Yet one still ought to establish that comparative fault can indeed influence the investment of potential victims in precautions. Even if we want to encourage or discourage investment in precautions why would a doctrine of comparative fault incentivize victims to invest efficiently? To see how, let us return to provocation. Under the doctrine of provocation, killing triggered by provocation is homicide rather than murder. How does this doctrine affect the inclination of individuals to kill?

The answer is complicated, because the doctrine of provocation has two conflicting effects and its aggregate effect on the rate of killing depends on the size of these conflicting effects. On the one hand, given that a provocation has been already perpetrated by the victim, recognizing provocation as a partial defense increases the willingness to kill, because it reduces the expected sanction. The expected sanction of the potential provoked killer is lower in a system that recognizes provocation as a defense than in a system that does not recognize provocation as a defense. But precisely for this reason, the doctrine reduces the inclination of potential victims to provoke, because a person who considers whether to provoke knows that the probability that the provocation endangers her life is not insignificant. Therefore, the doctrine reduces a potential victim's willingness to commit provocation. The aggregate effects of these conflicting effects depend on contingent factors. But it is certainly possible that the overall rate of killings is lower in a system that recognizes provocation as a defense than in a system that does not recognize such a defense.

Another relevant example is the American controversy concerning the regulation of weapons. This debate is typically framed in terms of a political debate between conservatives and liberals. Economic analysis, however, may provide a new rationale for the relevant considerations. On the one hand, regulation of weapons reduces the cost of committing crimes, because potential victims cannot arm themselves and therefore cannot adequately protect themselves against crimes. On the other hand, the regulation of weapons increases the cost of committing crimes, because it is more costly for criminals to acquire weapons.[54]

One may argue that provocation, or killings resulting from provocation, are not subjected to rational calculation. Criminal behavior in such cases is impulsive and cannot be analysed in terms of costs and benefits. The example was provided only to illustrate how a doctrine of comparative fault may influence the incentives of victims to use precautions. Mitigating the sanctions of a criminal who perpetrated a crime directed at a victim who invested either too much in precautions (e.g., installed bars or an alarm in his apartment) or too little (e.g., left his car keys in the door) induces criminals to target such a victim. Thus, this mitigation increases the cost of victims' behavior and induces them to invest efficiently.

The economic analysis of private precautions raises many questions concerning the effectiveness of investment in crime prevention. Some would say that such an investment is wasteful. Governmental investment that is too large reduces the incentives of victims to invest in crime prevention or in precautions. The aggregate effects of increasing public investment and the resulting reduction in private investment may fail to affect the overall rate of crime. Yet one ought to remember that public investment may have desirable distributive effects. Even if the rate of crime is not affected, the distribution of the crime may change.

9.   The Criminal at the Garden of My Neighbor is Greener: The Political Economy of Criminal Law Legislation

Our assumption so far has been that a good faith legislature passes legislation that affects both potential criminals and potential victims. Because it is subject to elections, the legislative body has an incentive to serve its community by enacting efficient policies.

But in a global world the legislature affects not only the political unit of the legislature but also other political units. Often the combined rational behavior on the part of different legislatures is sub-optimal. In the language of game theory, the situation gives rise to a prisoner's dilemma. Each political unit acts to serve its own interests, and the resulting outcome is bad for all.

One way to illustrate this hypothesis is to examine the process that led to increasing criminal sanctions in the United States. Many theorists believe that US criminal sanctions are much higher than those dictated by efficiency-based considerations. But why would legislators be inclined to inflict harsh sanctions that result in high costs of incarceration without a resulting decrease in the crime rate?

To understand why, recall that criminal legislation in the United States is primarily based in state, rather than federal, law. Each state is responsible for criminal law legislation in its own territory, and has an incentive to reduce the crime rate in that territory. Reducing the crime rate reduces the cost of crime to the residents of the state while increasing the willingness to invest in the state (as a crime-free environment is congenial to investment). One way to reduce crime is to increase the size of sanctions or the probability of detection. Increasing the size of sanctions and increasing the probability of detection have two results: some potential criminals may decide not to commit the crime, while others may decide to shift their activity to another territory.[55]

Shifting the activity to another territory is analogous to the case discussed in the last section, namely, displacement of crime. In the last section, we showed that an increase in a potential victim's investment in precautions may often result not in preventing the crime but in shifting the crime to another victim. Likewise, increasing criminal sanctions in one state may lead not to reducing the crime rate overall but to shifting (or exporting) the crime from one territory to another.

Needless to say, from the perspective of the state legislator (who wishes to reduce the crime rate in her own territory) the decision of a criminal to shift his activity is desirable. In fact, such a decision is more desirable than the case where a criminal is detected and punished, because punishment results in high costs while shifting the crimes from one territory to another has no costs for the state legislator. But the new territory where the criminal resides is not indifferent to this decision. Pennsylvania is no more willing to absorb New York criminals than New York is willing to absorb New Jersey criminals. The rational reaction on the part of Pennsylvania's legislature is to increase sanctions for criminal offenses and thus to induce the criminal to shift to yet another territory. It is easy to see that the result of the process is an inefficient increase in the size of the criminal sanctions leading to over-investment in prisons. For the same reason that installing precautions such as window bars leads to a displacement of crime from one victim to another, increasing sanctions in one political unit leads to shifting crime from one jurisdiction to another without necessarily influencing the overall crime rate. Perhaps the popularity of exiling criminals from Britain to colonies such as Australia was based on this effect. If Australia could send its criminals back to Britain, both Australia and Britain would invest resources in extraditing their criminals without influencing the resulting crime rate.

The foregoing analysis is applicable not only to the United States but also throughout the international sphere. The more globalized the world becomes, and the lower the cost of moving from one jurisdiction to another, the more criminal law can be used not to reduce the crime rate but to export crime from one territory to another. The way to solve this problem is to increase cooperation among the different jurisdictions. For example, the constitutional procedural guarantees given to defendants in the United States guarantee that inter-state competition would not lead to an excessive encroachment on criminals' procedural rights. Perhaps a stricter supervision of the size of sanctions (based perhaps on the Eighth Amendment of the US Constitution) could mitigate the disastrous effects of inter-state competition.

10.   Summary and Qualifications

Traditional economic analysis is based on assumptions concerning the rationality of criminals. On the basis of these assumptions, theorists explore the optimal norms governing criminal law, including the optimal expected sanction, the optimal size of the components of the expected sanction (probability of detection and the size of the sanction), the content of criminal law norms, and the optimal scope of defenses. One of the most important observations of law and economics is that over-reliance on harsh sanctions is less effective than expected. Increasing the duration of imprisonment is less effective because of discounting in the future. We also saw that legislators may have perverse incentives to increase sanctions beyond the optimal level.

Yet traditional law and economics has weaknesses, which were exploited by its critics. The field's propensity for over-abstraction; over-reliance on theory at the expense of empirical or experimental research; and, finally, the formation of strong assumptions about the rationality of criminals, are criticized by those who are less prone to abstraction and more inclined to observe human behavior rather than merely to speculate about it. None of these objections undermines the value of traditional economic analysis of law. Yet it seems that the traditional economic analysis ought to be supplemented by behavioral and experimental research and it ought to take into account psychological and sociological findings. Among the primary critics of economic analysis are also theorists who believe that preferences are less stable than traditionally assumed and that criminal law influences preferences. Criminal law is not merely a tool to punish individuals; it is also a tool to shape their preferences. The next section explores the ways in which empirical and experimental findings can enrich and challenge traditional economic analysis of criminal law.

III.   SOCIAL NORMS THEORY AND BEHAVIORAL CRIMINAL LAW AND ECONOMICS

1.   Introduction

This chapter examines theories that reject traditional abstract, rationality-based analysis of criminal law and rely instead on sociological, psychological or behavioral observations on the ways individuals (especially criminals) behave in practice. This requires exploiting empirical and experimental methodology. In this chapter we examine two main movements, both of which reject the traditional economic analysis of law: the social norms theory (based on sociological research) and the behavioral law and economics movement (based on psychological observations). The chapter will be divided accordingly into two sections.

Traditional economic analysis of criminal law explains human behavior as grounded in the probability of detection, the size of the sanction, the attitudes of individuals towards risk, the expected costs of the sanctions, etc. The basic premise of this analysis is that individuals make rational judgments of these parameters and guide their behavior accordingly. But there is a hidden premise, namely, that individuals can acquire information concerning the size of these parameters and that they act in accordance with such information.

The theories examined in this chapter challenge this claim. The expected sanctions do not guide people's behavior in mechanical ways. Criminal law influences individuals by influencing their beliefs and preferences. If there are systematic biases that distort the judgments of individuals, such biases alter, in predictable ways, individual behavior. Policy-makers can benefit from a better understanding of such biases. Both social norms theory and behavioral law and economics maintain that biases, distortions and irrational beliefs play important roles in understanding human behavior.[56] Furthermore, these biases and distortions are systematic and their influence predictable; often theses biases and distortions are even amenable to manipulation by policy-makers or legislators.

There is an important sense in which the theories we examine below are parasitic to traditional law and economics. Even the basic concepts used by behavioral law and economics (such as biases) are defined as deviations from the predictions of traditional economic analysis of law. The writings we examine in this chapter are often described by their advocates as revisions or challenges to traditional law and economics, not only because traditional economic analysis is a dominant movement and, therefore, an attractive target for critics but also because the movements we explore here take as a starting point the traditional law and economics observations and endeavor to revisit some of their assumptions. There is a strong affinity between these different methodologies. Theorists belonging to the social norms tradition or to behavioral law and economics use traditional law and economics as a starting point; in turn, the more reflective traditional law and economics theorists exploit the findings of social norms theory and behavioral law and economics in order to shed light on the nature of individual preferences. The conviction that social norms theory and behavioral law and economics are necessarily opponents of traditional law and economics is false.

Social Norms Theory is based on the conjecture that there is an interaction between law and social norms. This view rejects the equation of criminal law sanctions as costs that decrease the inclination of criminal behavior. Instead, the legal sanction itself influences individual preferences, and much of the influence of criminal law hinges on social pressures and stigma.

One branch of the social norms movement maintains that criminal behavior is not determined primarily by the size of sanctions or the probability of detection. A person's criminal behavior is influenced to a larger extent by the behavior of other members of the person's social group, the rate of compliance in the society as a whole, perceptions of the justness of the legal system, etc.[57] The view under which law is merely an external incentive whose size is determined by legal sanctions does not reflect reality. In fact, there is an ongoing interaction between legal norms and social norms. The legal norms and the size of the sanctions inflicted on violators influence one's inclinations to perform the act and one's perception as to whether such an act is morally appropriate.

A famous example identified with the social norms movement can illustrate these conjectures. The "broken windows" metaphor is used to convey the idea that the willingness of individuals to obey the law depends on the environment. In particular, the theory posits that minor violations (graffiti, abandoned buildings, garbage, etc.) regularly encourage criminal activity.[58] This conjecture led the former mayor of New York City, Rudy Giuliani, to strictly punish such minor violations, as he believed that individuals adjust their behavior not to the expected sanction but to the norms of behavior of their neighbors and friends.[59]

In a famous experiment, the psychologist Phillip Zimbardo left a car with a broken window unattended and documented the resulting vandalism. Zimbardo found that the car had a negative effect on the behavior of individuals.[60] The influence of social norms has different explanations, some of which can be accommodated within the frame of neo-classical economics. One explanation is the "signaling" theory. Under this theory, individuals gain information from their environment with respect to the level of enforcement. Thus, minor violations (such as graffiti or broken windows) signal to individuals that the social order has collapsed and the probability of detection is low; therefore, crime is beneficial. Another explanation is based on the stigma effects of minor violations. If stigma is affected by the crime rate, a high rate of a crime indicates that there is no stigma attached to the crime.

Behavioral Law and Economics uses insights from psychology to complement and sometimes to challenge the classical economic analysis of law based on the rationality of individuals.[61] Sometimes behavioral law and economics complements traditional economic analysis, e.g., when it identifies certain preferences individuals have. Behavioral law and economics often predicts when individuals are risk averse or risk loving, when they discount the future and by how much, etc. At other times, behavioral law and economics challenges traditional law and economics when it identifies contexts in which individuals act irrationally, form false beliefs concerning the state of the world, make decisions in ways that do not maximize their utility, make decisions based not on the way the world actually is but on the way the world is described (framing), etc.

In the criminal law context, the relevance of behavioral studies is evident, because it challenges the assumption that criminals are rational. We shall examine below some cognitive biases, their effects on behavior and the ways in which policy-makers or legislators can use biases to increase deterrence. One intuitive example can clarify the nature of behavioral law and economics. In section II we examined the influence of the size of sanctions and the probability of detection on deterrence. But deterrence is not a byproduct of the actual size of a sanction or the probability of detection but a byproduct of the *beliefs* concerning the size of the sanction and the probability of detection. Can we examine how these beliefs are formed and shaped? Can we affect these beliefs?

Some (and perhaps most) readers of this chapter have considered once or twice in their life whether to speed or to park illegally. In such cases those readers also thought of the potential risks of such behavior: the risk of being fined. But (with the exception of the fine for illegal parking) it is likely that the readers did not know the precise sanctions for such behavior and certainly did not know the probability of detection.

How did those who decided to speed (or not to speed) or to park illegally and risk a fine (or drive again around the block and look for a legal parking space) form their decision? There is perhaps one parameter that influences greatly such a decision. If on the evening before the event, one of your friends complained about getting a speeding ticket or you read in the paper a report on a police campaign against speeding, you are more likely to comply with the law. Psychologists call this phenomenon availability. The term "availability" denotes the disposition of individuals to form their beliefs on the basis of anecdotal information, which they can easily recall from memory. Thus, our beliefs concerning detection are not formed by the annual statistics collected by the police; instead they are formed by a story we read in the news or an anecdote told by your neighbor.[62] Some theorists proposed to use this bias to reduce the rate of illegal parking by using colorful and visible parking tickets. The argument is that neighbors and pedestrians will remember such tickets, thus creating great deterrent effects.[63] This observation suggests that the public punishment used in the Middle Ages (e.g., public flogging or public execution) was congenial to deterrence not because it provided information concerning the probability of detection but because it provided a memorable and salient reminder to individuals of the risks of conviction.

Unlike traditional economic analysis, both the social norms theory and behavioral law and economics are eclectic fields. They are based on different hypotheses and not on a single, axiomatic set of assumptions. This often provides the basis for the accusation that behavioral analysis is not "a theory". At the foundations of the neo-classical economics, there is a set of clear and defined principles that give rise to predictions concerning human behavior. Advocates of behavioral law and economics maintain that irrespective of whether neo-classical economics is a "theory", it fails to predict human behavior. The crucial issue is not whether behavioral law and economics is a theory. What is crucial is its superior ability to predict (and provide tools to control) human behavior.

Before we start our exploration we wish to add a warning. Many of the behavioral observations are based on experiments and most of the experiments use students as subjects. One ought to be cautious in extending behavioral findings to the population as a whole.

2. Law, Justice, and Efficiency: Social Norms Theory and Criminal Law

In section II we identified anti-social behavior as behavior that has negative externalities. One way to prevent anti-social behavior is to increase expected sanctions (either by increasing the probability of detection or by increasing the size of sanctions). One important insight raised by advocates of social norms theory is that this ignores one important factor: the attitudes of individuals toward the law and, in particular, their beliefs concerning the justness of the legal system. Under this view there is an intimate relation between the belief that the law is just and the willingness to obey it. Perceptions concerning the justness of the law have motivational effects. The more a person believes that the law is just, the greater her willingness to obey the law. Justice Brandeis voiced this conviction when he said, "If the Government becomes a lawbreaker, it breeds contempt for law, it invites every man to become a law unto himself".[64] This is perhaps why some people also believe that justice should not only be done but also be seen to be done.

Some of the advocates of the social norms theory believe that these claims can be empirically substantiated. In one experiment, researchers found that there is a correlation between an encounter that subjects had with a victim of injustice of the tax authorities and the willingness to evade taxes. In another experimental work, some of the subjects were exposed to stories of injustice of the legal system while others were exposed to stories that present the legal system as considerate and just. The first group showed much greater willingness to violate the law than the latter group.[65]

This observation may have operative results. The decision to criminalize must take into account not only the negative externalities of the behavior but also the concern that criminalization undermines trust in the law. Criminalizing behavior that is perceived to be just may weaken the willingness of subjects to obey legal norms.

3. Behavioral Law and Economics

Unlike the discussion of traditional law and economics, our discussion in this sub-section is inevitably eclectic and consists of an examination of several different cognitive biases. Behavioral law and economics is not a unified, coherent field; it is a field that contains numerous different psychological observations.

3.1 How to enrich the state by using prospect theory

Tax evasion is among the most common criminal offenses and many resources are invested in an effort to reduce its scope. Behavioral scientists believe that prospect theory, developed by Tversky and Kahneman, may be used to reduce the scope of tax evasion.[66]

Among the most important findings of prospect theory is the finding that individuals have differential attitudes towards risk. Risk attitudes are different in cases in which the risks involve gains and in cases in which they involve losses. While individuals are risk averse with respect to gains, they are often risk loving with respect to losses. Thus, if individuals face a choice between an 80% probability of gaining $100 or receiving (for certain) $80 they would prefer to receive $80. In contrast, if individuals face a choice between an 80% probability of losing $100 or losing (for certain) $80, they would prefer the lottery to the loss.

Tax evasion can be described as a lottery. The individual faces the choice to pay his taxes or to pay a smaller amount but to face a risk that, if caught, he would be subject to a large fine. Given that the inclination to take risks hinges on the question of whether individuals perceive the lottery as a lottery designed to increase their gains or to reduce their losses and given (as we show below) that the state can control whether the lottery is perceived as minimizing losses or maximizing gains, the state can control the risk attitudes of individuals and manipulate them to promote its ends.

One instrument used by the state is advance tax payment. The state deducts money during the year and at the end of the year the taxpayer is required to provide an annual report of his income. If the income is larger than the evaluation on the basis of which the advance payment was made, the taxpayer pays the difference to the state. If the income is lower than the evaluation on the basis of which the advance payment was made, the tax authorities pay back the difference to the taxpayer. Should the state make a high evaluation of the income (and therefore most likely return money to the taxpayer at the end of the year) or should it make a low evaluation of the income (and charge the difference from the taxpayer at the end of the year)?

Prospect theory would recommend that the state make a high evaluation. High advance tax payments mean that tax evasion is a lottery over gains rather than losses. To see why, assume that the state imposes a fine of $80 on tax evasion which, if successful, will generate $20 to the taxpayer, and assume also that the probability of detection is 20%. The individual can choose between receiving $80 (if he reports his income accurately) or to participate in a lottery in which he has an 80% chance of receiving $100 (if he is not detected) and a 20% chance of receiving no return at all (if he is detected). If the taxpayer expects to get the money from the state, he perceives it as a gain and prospect theory would predict therefore that he would prefer $80 over a lottery with the same expected value. If, on the other hand, the advance payment is low, tax evasion is a lottery over losses because the individual predicts that at the end of the year he would have to pay the difference between taxes on his actual income and the taxes paid in the advance payment (based on the low evaluation of his income). Given the prediction of prospect theory that individuals are risk loving with respect to losses, one may expect that individuals would be more inclined to engage in tax evasion under such a scheme. The state therefore ought to prefer a system in which advance payments are high over a system in which advance payments are low, as high advance payments will result in better compliance with the law.

It is easy to think of other applications of prospect theory to criminal law. Some have used prospect theory to examine the willingness of defendants to accept or reject plea bargains. Prospect theory predicts that defendants who face criminal sanctions would be risk loving and reject bargains where the sanction offered in the bargain is equal to the expected sanction at trial. Thus, a defendant is expected to reject an $80 fine offered in a bargain if he predicts that, at trial, he has a 50% probability of paying $160.[67]

3.2   Behavioral effects of uncertainty: the punishment and the detection roulettes

One of the puzzles of criminal law is its seemingly inconsistent attitude toward uncertainty. On the one hand, there is a commitment to certainty with respect to the size of sanctions. Such certainty is required by principles of the rule of law. On the other hand, there is no attempt on the part of the social planner to guarantee certainty with respect to the probability of detection or conviction.

To illustrate this, consider the following example. Arnold and Betty commit an identical offense under similar circumstances. Arnold is sentenced to 10 years, while Betty is sentenced to 5 years. This gap seems unjust and perhaps may provide grounds for appeal. Under the common view, there is no reason why different sanctions are imposed on individuals who committed identical offenses under identical circumstances. In contrast, assume that when Arnold commits the offense, police invest little in enforcement and, consequently, the probability of detection is low. For various reasons, the police increase the investment in detection, and when Betty commits the offense, she is caught as a result of this special effort by the police. It is difficult to claim in such a case that Betty was discriminated against even if she could not have known when she committed the offense that the police would increase its investment in detection and even if she can prove that she would not have been caught unless the police changed their enforcement policy.

Another indication of the difference between uncertainty with respect to the size of the sanction and uncertainty with respect to the probability of detection can be found in the information given to individuals. Criminal law provides information with respect to the size of criminal sanctions; it does not provide such information with respect to the probability of detection. Criminal law doctrine guarantees that the sanction meted out would not be more severe than the one in force when the offense was committed, but it does not guarantee that the probability of detection remains fixed. It is a basic principle of criminal law that increasing a sanction for a criminal offense does not apply retroactively. A criminal can "rely" on the size of a sanction at the time she commits the offense. On the other hand, no legal system allows a criminal to argue that the probability of detection increased after the offense was committed.

More generally, different legal ethos govern the size of legal sanctions and the probability of detection. The severity of the sanction reflects the seriousness of the offense; hence, the legal system is committed to consistency in inflicting sanctions. Most importantly, it is committed to providing "fair warning" to criminals with respect to the size of the criminal sanctions. The Sentencing Guidelines are perhaps the most evident manifestation of the commitment to provide a fair and precise warning. On the other hand, the probability of detection is a function of pragmatic considerations, which change from time to time. The legal system rejects punishment roulettes and tries to provide certainty and predictability with respect to the size of the sanction. It does not, however, oppose detection roulettes where the probability of detection is subject to uncertainty.

The differential treatment of punishment, on the one hand, and probability of detection, on the other hand, appears puzzling. Economic analysis of law regards both punishment and probability of detection as components with a similar function: determining the expected sanction (which ultimately determines the deterrent effect). Why should there be such a major difference between the treatment of the size of the sanction and the probability of detection?

One natural way to explain this differential treatment is to explain it on behavioral grounds, based on the expected reaction of a criminal to punishment roulette, on the one hand, and probability of detection roulette, on the other hand.[68] To illustrate, compare the two following legal systems. Under the first system, every convicted thief is sentenced to two years in prison. Under the second system, there is a sentencing roulette that inflicts a sanction of three years in prison on 50% of thieves and one year in prison on the other 50% of thieves. The expected sanction is two years in prison. Which system is better?

The answer to this question depends on the deterrent effects of each one of these systems. If thieves were risk averse, they would prefer the first system to the second system, and consequently sentencing roulette would have greater deterrent effects. If, on the other hand, thieves are risk loving they would prefer sentencing roulette, and therefore the deterrent effects of a certain sanction would be greater. Similar observations can be made with respect to the probability of detection roulette. If criminals prefer probability of detection roulette over a known probability (e.g., 50% of the criminals are caught with a probability of 1% and 50% with a probability of 3%), the deterrent effect of probability of detection roulette would be lower than the deterrent effect of a known probability (2%) and vice versa.

We can now evaluate the desirability of sentencing roulette, on the one hand, and probability of detection roulette, on the other. Behavioral findings concerning the risk attitudes of individuals can aid us in deciding whether to adopt fixed sanctions or sentencing roulettes, and fixed probability of detection or probability of detection roulette.

As we saw earlier, the existing legal system rejects sentencing roulette but endorses probability of detection roulette. The current system is justified only if criminals are risk loving with respect to sentences but risk averse with respect to the probability of detection.

There are indeed good reasons to believe so. Criminals are risk loving with respect to the size of sentences, because sentences impose a cost. Consequently, under prospect theory one would expect criminals to be risk loving with respect to a sentencing lottery. Empirical research also suggests that individuals hate uncertainty with respect to probabilities (ambiguity aversion); consequently, uncertainty with respect to the probability of detection may have deterrent effects. These observations therefore support the existing legal regulation of uncertainty.

3.3   Prediction and postdiction

Much of the discussion so far has focused on uncertainty. Psychological research has exposed the ways in which individuals react to uncertainty. One of the interesting findings is the differential treatment of future versus past uncertainty.[69] Psychological research suggests that individuals are less willing to bet on past events than on future events.

Assume that you have to bet on the result of tossing a dice. In one case the dice has already been tossed while in a second case the experimenter is going to toss it. It seems as if there is no difference between the cases. The probability of guessing correctly in both cases is identical. However, experimental research indicates that individuals react differently in these cases. In another famous experiment, subjects were asked to choose between two possible bets: one involved guessing whether a particular stock had increased or decreased in value on the day *prior* to the experiment and the second involved guessing whether a particular stock would increase or decrease in value on the day *after* the experiment. The results indicated that 70% of individuals preferred the second bet. I show below that the social planner can use the differential attitudes toward the past and future in order to increase the deterrent effects of criminal law.

Precautions against crime are divided into two types. Some precautions operate before the crime is committed (e.g., cameras and LoJacks). Other precautions operate after the crime is committed (e.g., police patrols). The empirical findings concerning uncertainty indicate that precautions of the first type are more effective than precautions of the second type. In the case of the first type of precautions, the criminal bets on precautions, which operate at the time *the offense is committed.* He is asked therefore to bet on a dice that has already been tossed, e.g., on the question of whether a camera documents his behavior. In the case of the second type of precautions, the criminal is asked to guess the probability of a future event, e.g., a police patrol. The differential treatment of prediction and postdiction suggests that criminals are more likely to bet in the second case than in the first. Consequently, the first type of precautions is more effective.

One way to illustrate this point is to re-examine the operation of tax enforcement authorities. Typically, tax authorities use samples of individuals who are selected randomly. The sample is selected at the end of year. Taxpayers who consider committing fraud bet on the future; they bet that their names will not come up in the sample. It is easy to see how the system can change such that taxpayers bet on the past rather than on the future. If the lottery takes place not at the end of the year but at the beginning of the year, the taxpayer bets not on the question of whether their names *will* come up on the sample but whether their names *already appear* in the sample. This latter bet has greater deterrent effects.

4. Summary: Social Norms Theory and Behavioral Law and Economics

We ended section II by challenging traditional law and economics theories on the grounds that these theories often blinded themselves to the realities of crime and criminality. These theories viewed crime as a phenomenon that can be understood in mathematical terms. Their critics argue that criminals are not economists and do not operate in the ways attributed to them by economists. At best, we ought to complement traditional law and economics by examining what the real preferences of criminals are. At worst, we ought to reject some of the foundational premises of economic models.

This chapter described the theoretical literature that developed these views. Yet this literature is subject to criticisms of two types: internal and external. Among the internal criticisms, one ought to include the absence of a distinct, coherent theoretical foundation for behavioral theories. The absence of such a foundation makes it particularly difficult to make any predictions concerning the behavior of individuals. Often the effects observed by behavioral economists are too context-dependent to facilitate any reliable predictions. For instance, the concept of framing used by prospect theory is difficult to apply, because the question of how individuals behave hinges on whether an individual frames a decision as one involving gains or losses. But this last question depends on the context and surrounding circumstances, and on the individual's perception of the "status quo". It follows that the prediction as to what the individual ultimately does is fragile and manipulative.

Beyond these internal objections, there is a sense that both social norms theory and behavioral law and economics treat individuals mechanistically. Punishment is designed to "train" the criminal. Concepts such as autonomy or choice, which are so central to criminal law, do not have a place within the social norms theory or within the tradition of behavioral law and economics. Furthermore, some criminal law theorists believe that punishment is designed to cause pain to individuals and not only to deter them. Punishment is about retributive justice and it seems that retributivism has no place in the classical law and economics tradition, social norms theory or behavioral law and economics. The next section discusses the recent research on happiness and examines its ambition to provide a better understanding of retributive justice.

IV.   HAPPINESS AND CRIMINAL LAW

In section I we discussed the views of Jeremy Bentham, the pre-eminent representative of the position that happiness has non-instrumental (intrinsic) value and that maximizing happiness ought to guide legislatures and policy-makers. This position has enjoyed a revival in recent years due to the work of psychologists, in particular the recent work by Daniel Kahneman.[70] Kahneman distinguishes between two conceptions of utility: decision utility and experienced utility. Decision utility is based on the subjective evaluation of the individual with respect to the future utility derived from his decision. Experienced utility, on the other hand, is the contemporary incarnation of the Benthamite hedonic utilitarianism discussed earlier. Economists have long since abandoned experienced utility, as they believe it cannot be measured and used for policy-making.[71]

Research on happiness has shown that this last accusation is flawed and that happiness can be measured. One can simply ask individuals how happy they are and their reports can indicate their experienced utility. More importantly, the happiness research indicates that individuals do not always choose the course of action that maximizes their happiness. The experienced utility in "real time" differs from the predictions or beliefs of individuals concerning what is likely to bring them happiness; it also differs from individuals' memories concerning the happiness they experienced in the past. A hungry client entering a food shop may purchase more food than he needs for the week simply because he is hungry.[72] The actual utility derived from the food differs from the utility that the client predicts will be derived from the food. Individuals also over-estimate the effects that changes in one's life have on their experienced utility. As Schkade and Kahneman claim, "Nothing in life matters quite as much as you think it does while you are thinking about it".[73] Thus, when students from the Midwest and in California were asked questions about the happiness expected from living in these places, students tended to believe that life in California is much better than life in the Midwest. But when they were asked to indicate how happy they are in their own lives, it became evident that there is no gap between the happiness of students in California (as reported by them) and the happiness of students in the Midwest (as reported by them).

Happiness research may be especially relevant to criminal law theorists. Bentham well understood one reason for this. Criminal law is a means of causing pain. But different people suffer differently from similar sanctions. Bentham, therefore, writes:

> [O]wing to different manners and degrees in which persons under different circumstances are affected by the same exciting cause, a punishment which is the same in name will not always either really produce, or even so much as appear to others to produce, in two different persons the same degree of pain.[74]

Both retributivists and utilitarian theorists should take account of this fact. Arguably, retributivists believe that the size of a sanction should be determined on the basis of the subjective disutility experienced by the criminal; if this subjective disutility differs from one person to another, the sanction should also be different. The deterrence theorist believes that we ought to deter crime and that deterrence requires the imposition of a sufficiently large sanction. Such a sanction ought to be sensitive to the expectations of the criminal with respect to the disutility resulting from the sanction. It seems, therefore, that happiness research is relevant to both retributivists and deterrence theorists. Yet the two approaches focus on different types of utility: the retributivists care about experienced utility (the mental states experienced by the person who is sentenced) while the deterrence theorists focus on expected utility (based on the predictions of the individuals) because the expected utility determines the deterrent effects of the sanction.

Let us explore first the retributive analysis. Traditionally the economic analysis of criminal law did not account for retributive considerations. Economists are not interested in whether criminals "deserve" sanctions, as they are interested exclusively in the future and not in the past. It follows that what economists care about is which sanctions deter or, more broadly, prevent crime. But psychological research can provide new insights with respect to retributivism. Under the subjective understanding of retributivism (offered by Adam Kolber), retributivism should focus not on the objective size of the sanction (the size of the fine or the duration of the imprisonment) but on the subjective experiences of prisoners.[75]

Assume that Mr. Sensitive and Ms. Non-Sensitive are convicted of a crime and are sentenced to four years in prison. But Mr. Sensitive suffers in prison while Ms. Non-Sensitive prefers freedom but is well-adjusted to prison life. The fences, locks and the prison-guards provide her with a sense of security and comfort, which she lacks when she is out of prison. In Kolber's view, retributivism ought to take into account the differences in their subjective experiences of imprisonment. Happiness research can contribute to the understanding and measuring of the subjective experiences of criminals and consequently also to calibrating sanctions in accordance with retributive justice considerations. For instance, Kolber believes that the finding that rich people suffer more in prison than poor people requires (given retributivist assumptions) imposing harsher sanctions on poor people than on the rich. While this position, as we saw, is shared also by traditional law and economics theorists,[76] the reasoning underlying it is different. Kolber cares about the experienced utility of criminals rather than expected utility.

The retributivist hedonic view seems radical, but despite its radicalism, it has already some manifestations in contemporary legal practices. Some legal systems impose differential fines based on a criminal's income. The rationale could be that identical fines impose greater disutility on the poor than on the rich. Judges often take into account in their decisions an offender's personal circumstances. This consideration by judges could be understood as being based on the view that the experienced disutility of an offender resulting from a sanction is sometimes too high and disproportional to the gravity of the offense.

One of the most surprising findings of happiness research is what is labeled "hedonic adaptation," namely, the inclination of individuals to adjust to new circumstances such that dramatic changes in one's life do not radically change their happiness. Individuals expect that receiving a large amount of money would greatly increase their happiness. Yet the research indicates that this is false. Similarly, individuals predict that their lives would be ruined by a serious disease or by being paralyzed. Yet the level of reported happiness after such a catastrophic event does not differ radically from the level of happiness before such an event. The typical reaction in such cases is a dramatic increase or decrease in subjective happiness, followed by changes that bring the level of happiness to that which was reported before the event took place.[77] Hedonic theorists of criminal law inferred that once a person enters a prison, one could expect a dramatic decrease in her happiness. But in the long run, the prison would have little effect on the happiness of convicted criminals. Furthermore, sometimes release from prison causes disutility. One of the implications of this observation is that the hedonic gap between short and long imprisonment is relatively small as people adjust to prison conditions.[78]

While the hedonic analysis provided by criminal law theorists, and, in particular, its implications concerning retributivism, is intriguing, I believe that it is fundamentally flawed because it is based on a misunderstanding of retributivism. Retributivism is not based on the subjective experiences of the criminal but on the expressive significance of the sanctions as understood by the society as a whole. Punishment therefore ought to be understood objectively (on the basis of the duration of the imprisonment or the size of the fine) and not on the basis of the subjective disutility of the criminal (unless the subjective disutility could be conveyed to the public in the same way the size of the sanction can). Retributive practices are public, communicative, expressive practices designed to convey the intensity of moral disapproval as understood by society and not a practice designed to cause subjective disutility to the criminal.[79]

Needless to say, if happiness research develops to the extent that would enable us to measure disutility and create a "happiness scale," there is no principled reason why such a "happiness scale" cannot be used to determine the size of the sanction. In such a society judges could impose not ten years of imprisonment but 500 units of disutility. The directors of the prison could be in charge of enforcing this sentence, and different individuals would be subjected to different sanctions in accordance with the degree of subjective disutility resulting from the sanction. But to use such a system, what is crucial is not the subjective disutility as such but a public understanding of the retributive significance of units of disutility in the same way as the public understanding, in contemporary society, of the retributive significance of the size of fines and the length of imprisonment.

Happiness research can be relevant also to deterrence theories, as it is relevant to evaluating the effectiveness of punishment in deterring criminals. Yet here, as observed above, what is crucial is not the experienced utility but the expected utility. In fact, deterrence theorists would be pleased if punishment could be predicted by criminals to be particularly harsh, but once it is imposed causes no disutility whatsoever. Deterrence is triggered by expected rather than experienced utility. Happiness research could contribute by shedding light on the expected utility.

Happiness research is young and is expected to develop further. Yet the more traditional research described in sections II and III will not become irrelevant. To its credit, happiness research is the only attempt in the law and economics tradition to struggle seriously with what is perceived by many to be the central role of criminal law – retributive justice. While utilitarians and economists provide no account of retributivism, happiness researchers use happiness as a tool to measure the severity of sanctions. But this research is based on a flawed understanding of retributivism: retributivism is not about subjective disutility but about the communicative and expressive significance of punishment. To achieve this purpose, fines and imprisonment are useful tools even if the disutility resulting from them differs from one criminal to another.

V.   SUMMARY AND FUTURE CHALLENGES

I will not deceive the reader by denying that economic analysis of criminal law has so far had very limited effect on legal practice. There are very few fields in which economic analysis had lesser impact than in the field of criminal law. This is true both with respect to traditional economic analysis as well as behavioral economic analysis and happiness research.

Perhaps the reason is the great interest of the public in criminal law (in contrast to other more technical fields). Criminal law deals with murder, robbery, blood and love and beneath the gowns of judges one can sense intense human sentiments and emotions. Economics seems too impoverished to govern this field where death, blood, sex, love and hatred intermingle with each other. As a historical fact, it is evident that criminal law is based on retributive sentiments, which were quite dominant in shaping the law. Perhaps philosophers rightly observe that retributivism is a primitive sentiment that ought to be overcome. But nobody has yet taught us how to do this, and the public and the legislature do not pay attention to the pleadings of philosophers.

Furthermore, beyond the positive or negative effects of criminal law prohibitions on human behavior, it is still the case that the existence of criminal law prohibitions (independent of what they are or what their effects are) serves, as Durkheim observed, to reinforce social solidarity. Criminal law is not merely a means of training and inducing individuals to behave; it maintains and protects the social framework.[80] This function cannot easily be translated into the language of economics or psychology.

These observations do not imply that economic insights cannot be useful but their effects are limited to the more technical aspects of criminal law, such as regulatory or even white collar offenses. Criminal law doctrine will continue to be governed by the Freudian id rather than by the rational ideals of social scientists.

NOTES

1.   See, e.g., Duff (1990) at 103; Fletcher (1978) at 454–9; Nozick (1981) at 363–97.
2.   This is the standard interpretation of Immanuel Kant in *Metaphysics of Morals*. For a radical view which interprets Kant as endorsing a mixed position under which deterrence is the reason for punishment and retributive concerns constrain the size and the nature of the sanction, see Byrd (1989) at 151–200.
3.   See Moore (Fall 2008).
4.   Bentham [1996].
5.   Becker (1968) at 169–217.
6.   See, e.g., Posner (2000).
7.   McAdams and Ulen (2008).
8.   See Posner and Sunstein (2010).
9.   For developing a more comprehensive approach along these lines, see Zamir and Medina (2010).
10.   See, e.g., Posner (2007) at 223.
11.   See Posner (2007).
12.   Polinsky and Shavell (2007) at 403–54. See also Posner (2007) at 192.
13.   See Polinsky and Shavell (2007).
14.   Posner (2007) at 224.
15.   Posner (2007) at 221.
16.   Polinsky and Shavell (1984).
17.   See Becker (1968).

18. See Posner (2007) at 205.
19. The distinction between these two types of rules is central to economic analysis of law and was first developed in Calabresi and Melamed (1972).
20. Nozick (1974) at 41.
21. This analysis is based on Hylton (2005).
22. For a lucid description of Mill's view on this issue, see Brink (2007).
23. See Posner (2007) at 205.
24. The analysis is based on Hylton (2005).
25. See Sunstein, Schkade and Kahneman (2000).
26. Becker 1968.
27. See, e.g., Mikos (2005).
28. This explanation is developed in Harel and Segal (1999) at 295–7.
29. Posner (2007) at 222.
30. Polinsky and Shavell (2007); Posner (2007) at 221–2.
31. Levitt and Miles (2007) at 455–95.
32. For these effects, see Bar-Gill and Harel (2001) at 485–501.
33. Kaplow (1992).
34. This analysis is based on Coffee and Craswell (1984). Coffee and Craswell examine the choice between a standard of negligence and strict liability. Their interest is therefore tort law rather than criminal law but their analysis is applicable also to criminal law.
35. See Posner (2007) at 229.
36. See Posner (2007) at 229.
37. Posner (2007) at 233.
38. See Hamdani (2007).
39. The discussion is based on Hamdani (2007).
40. *United States v. Ahmad*, 101 F. 3d 386 (1997).
41. See Posner (2007) at 234.
42. *R v. Dudley and Stephens* (1884) 14 Q.B.D. 273.
43. For a discussion of the economic rationales of shame penalties, see Rasmussen (1996).
44. For this argument see Harel and Klement (2007).
45. Posner and Landes (1972).
46. This is one of the standard arguments against utilitarianism. See Hills (2010).
47. See Posner and Landes (1972).
48. Titmuss (1997). For a survey of empirical support for Titmuss' analysis, see Frey and Jergen (2001).
49. Talmud, Gittin 45a.
50. Fletcher (1993).
51. Harel (1994).
52. Ayres and Levitt (1998).
53. Although, of course, the criminals may shift their activity in such a case to commit other crimes. The frustrated car thief may specialize in such a case in committing other crimes.
54. Posner (2007) at 239.
55. This is a specific instance of a more general phenomenon analysed first in Tiebot (1956). For an application to criminal law, see Teichman (2005).
56. Note that the terminology we use here, "biases" or "distortion", is not meant to be normative but purely descriptive. It is meant to denote the fact that the behavior deviates from the one dictated by rationality.
57. For a survey of social norms theories, see Posner (2000). For an application of it to the criminal law field, see Kahan (1997).
58. See, e.g., Kahan (1997) at 369.
59. See Harcourt and Ludwig (2006) at 274. Harcourt and Ludwig dispute the effectiveness of these methods.
60. See Kahan (1997) at 356.
61. For a useful survey, see Jolls, Sunstein and Thaler (1998).
62. See Tversky and Kahneman (1973).
63. See Jolls, Sunstein and Thaler (1999) at 1538.
64. *Olmstead v. United States*, 277 U.S. 438, 485 (1928).
65. Nadler (2005).
66. For an accessible description of this proposal, see Guthrie (2002–2003) at 1142–5.
67. Birke (1999).
68. See Harel and Segal (1999).
69. See Guttel and Harel (2008).
70. See, e.g., Kahneman and Thaler (2006).

71. See "Well-Being" in *Stanford Encyclopedia of Philosophy*, sec. 4.2, available at http://plato.stanford.edu/entries/well-being/#Hed.
72. See Kahneman and Thaler (2006).
73. Schkade and Kahneman (1998).
74. Bentham [1996] chap. XIV.
75. Kolber (2009) "The Subjective Experience of Punishment"; Kolber (2009) "The Comparative Nature of Punishment."
76. Kolber (2009), "The Subjective Experience of Punishment" at 232.
77. See, e.g., Kahneman and Thaler (2006) at 229.
78. See Market (2010) at 924–9.
79. For such an account of retributivism, see, e.g., Nozick (1981).
80. For a brief presentation of Durkheim's theory, see Hart (1967).

REFERENCES

Ayres, Ian and Steven D. Levitt (1998) "Measuring Positive Externalities from Unobservable Victim Precautions: An Empirical Study of LoJack," 113 *Quarterly Journal of Economics* 43

Bar-Gill, Oren and Alon Harel (2001) "Crime Rates and Expected Sanctions: The Economics of Deterrence Revisited," 30 *Journal of Legal Studies* 485

Becker, Gary (1968) "Crime and Punishment: An Economic Approach," 76 *Journal of Political Economy* 169

Bentham, Jeremy [1996] *An Introduction to the Principles of Morals and Legislation* (J.H. Burns and H.L.A. Hart, eds.)

Birke, Richard (1999) "Reconciling Loss Aversion and Guilty Pleas," *Utah L. Rev.* 205

Brink, David (2007) "Mill's Moral and Political Philosophy," in *Stanford Encyclopedia of Philosophy* (Edward N. Zalta, ed.) sec. 2.3, available at http://philosophysother.blogspot.com/2007/10/brink-david-mills-moral-and-political.html

Byrd, Sharon (1989) "Kant's Theory of Punishment: Deterrence in Its Threat, Retribution in Its Execution," *Law and Philosophy* 151

Calabresi, Guido and Douglas Melamed (1972) "Property Rules, Liability Rules and Inalienability: One View of the Cathedral," 85 *Harvard L. Rev.* 1089

Coffee, John and Richard Craswell (1984) "Some Effects of Uncertainty on the Compliance with Legal Standards," 70 *Virginia L. Rev.* 965

Duff, R.A. (1990) *Intention Agency and Criminal Liability*

Fletcher, George (1978) *Rethinking Criminal Law*

— (1993) "Corrective Justice for Moderns," 106 *HLR* 1673 (book review)

Frey, Bruno S. and Reto Jergen (2001) "Motivation Crowding Theory," 15 *Journal of Economic Surveys* 589

Guthrie, Chris (2002–2003) "Prospect Theory, Risk Preference and the Law," 97 *Northwestern University L. Rev.* 1115

Guttel, Ehud and Alon Harel (2008) "Uncertainty Revisited: Legal Prediction and Legal Postdiction," 107 *Michigan L. Rev.* 467

Hamdani, Assaf (2007) "Mens Rea and the Cost of Ignorance," 93 *Va. L. Rev.* 415

Harcourt, Bernard E. and Jens Ludwig (2006) "Broken Windows: New Evidence from New York City and Five-City Social Experiment," 73 *U. Chicago L. Rev.* 271

Harel, Alon (1994) "Efficiency and Fairness in Criminal Law: The Case for a Criminal Law Principle of Comparative Fault," 82 *California L. Rev.* 1181

Harel, Alon and Alon Klement (2007) "The Economics of Stigma: Why More Detection of Crime May Result in Less Stigmatization," 36 *Journal of Legal Studies* 355

Harel, Alon and Uzi Segal (1999) "Criminal Law and Behavioral Law and Economics: Observations on the Neglected Role of Uncertainty in Deterring Crime," 1 *American Law and Economics Review* 295

Hart, H.L.A. (1967) "Social Solidarity and the Enforcement of Morality," 35 *University of Chicago L. Rev.* 1

Hills, Allison (2010) "Utilitarianism, Contractualism and Demandingness," 60 *The Philosophical Quarterly* 225

Hylton, Keith (2005) "The Theory of Penalties and the Economics of Criminal Law," 1 *Review of Law and Economics* 175

Jolls, Christine, Cass Sunstein and Richard Thaler (1998) "A Behavioral Approach to Law and Economics," 50 *Stanford L. Rev.* 1471

Kahan, Dan (1997) "Social Influence, Social Meaning and Deterrence," 83 *Virginia L. Rev.* 349

Kahneman, Daniel and Richard Thaler (2006) "Utility Maximization and Experienced Utility," 20 *Journal of Economic Perspectives* 221

Kaplow, Louis (1992) "Rules versus Standards," 42 *Duke L.J.* 557

Kolber, Adam J. (2009) "The Subjective Experience of Punishment," 109 *Columbia L. Rev.* 182

— Kolber, Adam J. (2009) "The Comparative Nature of Punishment," 89 *B.U.L. Rev.* 1565

Levitt, Steven D. and Thomas J. Miles (2007) "Empirical Study of Criminal Punishment," in 1 *Handbook of Law and Economics* 455

McAdams, Richard H. and Thomas S. Ulen (2008) "Behavioral Criminal Law and Economics," (SSRN) URL http://papers.ssrn.com/sol3/papers.cfm?abstract_id=1299963

Market, Dan (2010) "Bentham on Stilts: The Bare Relevance of Subjectivity to Justice," 98 *California L. Rev.* 907

Mikos, Robert (2005) "Enforcing State Law in Congress' Shadow," 90 *Cornell L. Rev.* 1411

Moore, Andrew (Fall 2008) "Hedonism," in *Stanford Encyclopedia of Philosophy*, available at http://plato.stanford.edu/entries/hedonism/

Nadler, Janice (2005) "Flouting the Law," 83 *Texas L. Rev.* 1399

Nozick, Robert (1974) *Anarchy, State and Utopia*

— (1981) *Philosophical Explanations*

— (2007) "The Theory of Public Enforcement of Law" in 1 *Handbook of Law and Economics* 403

Polinsky, Mitchell A. and Steven Shavell (1984) "Optimal Use of Fines and Imprisonment," 24 *Journal of Public Economics* 89

Posner, Eric (2000) *Law and Social Norms*

Posner, Eric and Cass Sunstein, eds. (2010) *Law and Happiness*

Posner, Richard (2007) *Economic Analysis of Law*, 7th edn

Posner, Richard and William Landes (1972) "Altruism in Law and Economics," 68 *American Economic Review* 417

Rasmussen, Eric (1996) "Stigma and Self Fulfilling Expectations of Criminality," 39 *Journal of Law and Economics* 519

Schkade, David and Daniel Kahneman (1998) "Does Living in California Make People Happier? A Focus Illusion in Life Satisfaction," 9:5 *Psychological Review* 340

Sunstein, Cass R., David Schkade and Daniel Kahneman (2000) "Do People Want Optimal Deterrence?" 29 *Journal of Legal Studies* 237

Teichman, Doron (2005) "The Market for Criminal Justice: Federalism, Crime Control, and Jurisdictional Competition," 103 *Michigan L. Rev.* 1831

Tiebot, Charles (1956) "A Pure Theory of Local Expenditure," 64 *J. Pol. Econ.* 416

Titmuss, Richard (1997) *The Gift Relationship: From Human Blood to Social Policy* (Ann Oakely and John Ashton, eds.)

Tversky, Amos and Daniel Kahneman (1973) "Availability: A Heuristic for Judging Frequency and Probability," 5 *Cognitive Psychology* 207

Zamir, Eyal and Barak Medina (2010) *Law, Economics and Morality*

2   The scope of criminal law
Murat C. Mungan

1.   INTRODUCTION

The objective of this chapter is to categorically study common and traditional acts which are punished under criminal law and compare them to others which are not defined as crimes. Studying traditional crimes such as murder, rape, theft and their attempts, and comparing them to acts which are excluded from the scope of criminal law, will allow the determination of conditions under which defining an act as a crime is normatively justifiable. These conditions can be used in future research to evaluate the desirability of extending the scope of criminal law to non-traditional fields of potential regulation. As the title of this book suggests, the analysis will be conducted by making use of economic tools, and in particular by implicitly employing a utilitarian approach to evaluating social welfare.

The main function of this chapter is to supply a guide to study the efficiency of the scope of criminal law. Although this chapter provides a structured framework to determine conditions under which there are economic rationales to regulate an act through criminal law, most ideas it contains have been expressed earlier by law and economics scholars. Of particular importance are earlier works by Richard Posner, Steven Shavell, and David Friedman, as well as recent joint works by Roger Bowles, Michael Faure, Nuno Garoupa, and Keith Hylton and Vikramaditya S. Khanna.[1] There are also related issues which have been covered by other strands of literature, such as the tort/crime distinction[2] and the study of alternative punishment mechanisms.[3] The reader who is particularly interested in studying the scope of criminal law will find these sources very valuable.

To analyse the scope of criminal law, it will be necessary to explain what is meant by criminal law, and how criminal law generally operates. This can be done by identifying important characteristics of criminal law and comparing it to other branches of law, such as tort law and administrative law. This is the goal of section 2. To form an idea of what generally distinguishes criminal law from other modes of regulation, various acts included and excluded from the scope of criminal law can be compared and contrasted. Section 3 serves this purpose by identifying relevant dimensions to compare acts. The same section provides rationales as to why certain categories of acts are best regulated through criminal law, whereas others need not be criminally sanctioned. Section 4 summarizes the findings in this chapter.

2.   CRIMINAL LAW VERSUS TORT LAW AND OTHER MODES OF REGULATION

As stated earlier, the objective of this chapter is to suggest conditions under which regulation through criminal law is likely to result in better outcomes compared to other

Table 2.1   Methods of punishment and dimensions of comparison

	Criminal law	Tort law (compensatory)	Tort law (punitive)	Civil infractions
Prosecution/ Enforcement	Public	Private	Private	Public
Standard of proof	Beyond a reasonable doubt	Preponderance of the evidence	Clear and convincing evidence / preponderance*	Preponderance of the evidence
Moral stigma	Yes	No	Yes	No
Harm necessary?	No	Yes	Yes	No
Non-monetary Sanctions possible?	Yes	No	No	No
Probability Multiplier possible?	Yes	No	Yes	Yes

Note: * See www.atra.org/show/7343, providing a list of relevant state procedures concerning punitive damages. For punitive damages most states require clear and convincing evidence, and some require preponderance of the evidence.

commonly used modes of regulation. As such, it will be useful to identify specific differences in the way various branches of law operate. This is a harder task than one may imagine.

The tort/crime distinction, for instance, has been the subject of numerous scholarly articles.[4] Despite the wide attention this issue has received, however, authors have been unable to reach a consensus as to what distinguishes a tort from a crime.[5] But this does not imply that one cannot identify general characteristics to compare how criminal law and other branches of law operate most of the time.

David D. Friedman, in a comment concerning the tort/crime distinction[6] (and in his subsequently published book[7]) has identified various dimensions of comparison between different punishment[8] methods. He considers methods available in today's modern Anglo-American legal system, as well as methods used in medieval and eighteenth century England. Here, I consider similar dimensions of comparison. But I focus only on modern Anglo-American modes of regulation, because my goal is to determine whether the scope of criminal law appears efficient, when society has to choose a method of punishment readily available. The methods of punishment and dimensions of comparison I am focusing on are summarized in Table 2.1.

I am excluding many methods of punishment which do not belong to the four categories shown in Table 2.1. Furthermore, there are cases in which Table 2.1 does not accurately describe the mode of punishment.[9] These omissions and errors should be harmless, however, given the objective of making a first approximate evaluation of the efficient scope of criminal law. Once this objective is achieved, further analysis concerning the scope of criminal law can be more easily conducted.

The dimensions of comparisons I list in Table 2.1 are the ones which I will rely on extensively to evaluate the effects and functions of criminal law and other methods of punishment. It is therefore worth briefly explaining the dimensions, which are not self-explanatory, especially for those readers who are not familiar with the relevant literature.[10]

2.1 Standard of Proof

Standard of proof refers to the level of proof necessary to find a defendant guilty or liable. In the theoretical law and economics literature, standard of proof can be modeled as a threshold probability.[11] If the fact-finder believes that the defendant is guilty or liable with a probability higher than this threshold, he should find him guilty or liable. In most tort cases, this standard is preponderance of the evidence, which corresponds to a threshold probability of $(50+\varepsilon)\%$. In criminal trials, however, the standard is beyond a reasonable doubt. Although this standard is not clearly quantifiable as a threshold probability, it is clear that it represents a much higher requirement.[12] In some, less common, civil law cases an intermediate standard of proof described as "clear and convincing evidence" is used. In most states, this standard of proof is employed when requiring the defendant to pay punitive damages.[13]

2.2 Harm Necessary?

In tort law, one must show that the defendant committed an act which resulted in harm to the plaintiff. A similar requirement does not exist in criminal law and civil infractions. A person who is speeding is not fined because he caused harm. He is fined because he is engaging in a dangerous activity which may result in harm. A similar logic applies to attempted crimes, such as attempted murder and attempted rape.

2.3 Probability Multiplier

Compensatory damages in tort law are more or less equal to the harm caused to the plaintiff. As such, damages are not obtained by multiplying harms caused to the victim. Punitive damages, however, can exceed the harm caused to the victim. Therefore, they can be calculated by multiplying harm by some meaningful number. This number can be obtained by considering how likely it is that the defendant can evade liability.[14] The availability of such probability multipliers can assist in achieving desirable levels of deterrence by increasing the expected punishment to the offender.

In a very simple framework, consider the following notation:

    h: Harm associated with act
    p: Probability that actor will be found liable
    d: Damage awards

Furthermore, assume away every other relevant issue (e.g., litigation costs, judgment-proof actors, false accusations, fraudulent claims, etc.).

In this setting, if d is chosen such that the expected penalty to the offender is exactly h (i.e., $dp = h$), then the potential actor will commit the harmful act only if his benefits from doing so are sufficiently high. In other words, such damage awards will force the actor to internalize the social costs of his actions. In symbols, if b is the benefit to the potential actor, he will commit the act only if:

$$b>h = dp$$

which, in this simple setting, is optimal. Hence, optimal damages are $d = (h/p)$. In this case, $(1/p)$ can conveniently be called the probability multiplier. This simple example certainly omits many important issues, but its purpose is to demonstrate what probability multipliers mean, and why they can potentially be useful.

Having identified and explained some important characteristics of various modes of punishment, we can explore conditions under which criminal law is likely to be superior, by focusing on how it differs from other methods of penalizing individuals.

3.   SCOPE OF CRIMINAL LAW

The main goal of this section is to comment on when the use of criminal law, as opposed to other commonly used branches of law, is desirable to regulate specific behavior.[15] To achieve this purpose it will be useful to identify specific categories of acts which are best regulated through criminal law and categories of acts where criminal law is likely to perform poorly. Furthermore, it will be helpful to focus on traditional or common fields of regulation and/or punishment, because we have more knowledge about these fields. These include common law crimes, ordinary accidents, civil infractions and conduct crimes. Categorizing and studying the regulation/punishment of acts which belong to these fields will allow the determination of factors which cause criminal law to achieve desirable outcomes.

Acts can be categorized in infinitely many ways. My main objective is to choose dimensions of characterization which will allow the construction of meaningful categories that enable the identification of trends in specifying the scope of criminal law. In particular, to categorize acts, I initially focus on three main dimensions: (i) intent, (ii) harm, and (iii) whether the act generates actual harm or only an expectation of harm. Using these three dimensions, Figure 2.1 can be generated.

The third dimension may require further explanation. Consider conduct crimes, such as reckless or drunk driving.[16] These acts do not necessarily produce harm, but people engaging in such acts can be criminally sanctioned. Therefore, it is the dangerous conduct which is being punished, and not the harmful result. Inchoate crimes and various regulations also fit this description. In the tort system, however, plaintiffs cannot be compensated unless they can demonstrate that they have been harmed. Accordingly, the domain of torts is acts which result in actual harm.

The word "intent" also requires some explanation. In the proceeding discussions and categorizations, I am referring to the intent to cause the event which harms another person. Such intent is obviously present when we speak about murder or theft. On the other hand, a person who is speeding ordinarily acts without intending to hit a pedestrian or another car. The desired goal is to get from one place to another quickly. Therefore, speeding can be called an act which may cause unintended harms.

It is also worth mentioning that intent and harm are normally non-binary variables.

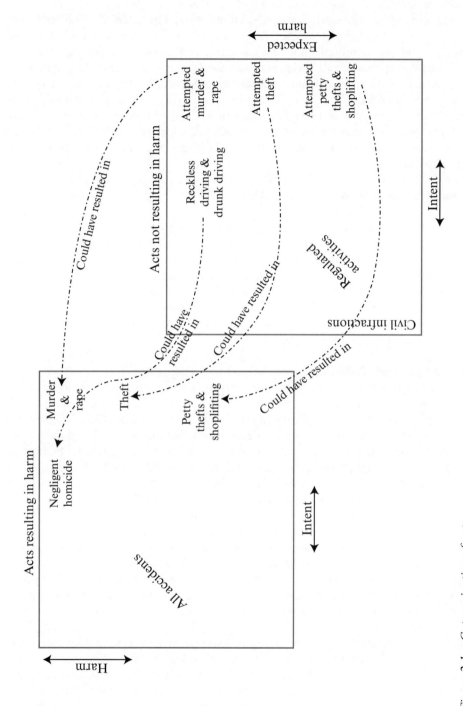

Figure 2.1   Categorization of acts

The fact that expected harms can range over a continuum does not require explanation. Similarly, intent can vary significantly. The Model Penal Code, for instance, defines four terms for culpability: negligently, recklessly, knowingly and purposefully.[17] Nevertheless, for the purposes of defining categories, I will refer to high and low expected harms, and intentional and unintentional inflictions of harm, and clarify ambiguities when they arise. Using this terminology I divide acts into the following five general categories: (1) intentional acts resulting in high harm, (2) intentional acts resulting in low harm, (3) acts resulting in unintended harms, (4) acts presumably intended to cause harm but which fail, and (5) dangerous acts presumably committed with intention to achieve harmless results. Next, I discuss typical offenses which fall under each category, and discuss whether there are utilitarian justifications to include (exclude) these acts within (from) the scope of criminal law.

3.1   Intentional Acts Resulting in High Harm

Most common law crimes fall in this category. Common examples include murder, rape, arson and theft. Victims of these crimes may, of course, seek compensation through civil actions.[18] In other words, criminal law and tort law co-exist in regulating acts which fall under this category. The presumption is that these acts result in harms to victims which offset the benefits to offenders. As such they are socially undesirable acts and complete deterrence is optimal. It is therefore not surprising that these acts are criminalized. Next, I consider specific economic rationales as to why remedies available in tort law should be complemented through criminal sanctions.[19]

3.1.1   Judgment proof offenders
When harm is inflicted intentionally, the offender may take steps to avoid detection and liability. This will lead to low probabilities of liability.[20] Accordingly, the threat of having to pay compensation for the damage he has caused will be insufficient to deter the potential offender. Therefore, to achieve deterrence, sanctions which exceed compensatory tort damages must be imposed. Moreover, given that the probability of detection is low and the harm inflicted on the victim is great, it will be necessary to impose fines which exceed many offenders' wealth. This will necessitate non-monetary sanctions, such as imprisonment, to deter judgment proof offenders.[21] Furthermore, the probability of detection can be increased through superior technology and access to information enabled through public enforcement of criminal law.[22] It should also be noted that, given high error costs associated with imprisonment, it will be desirable to impose punishment through a legal system where wrongful convictions are minimal but the consequences of being convicted are high. Typical criminal procedures satisfy these needs. High standards of proof guarantee that wrongful convictions are minimal. The presence of probability multipliers allows very severe punishments, and criminal stigma makes the cost of conviction even greater.

There is one potential problem with this reasoning. If it is the case that imprisonment is being imposed only for the sake of achieving higher deterrence, why not use monetary sanctions when exhausting a murderer's wealth is not an issue (i.e., when he is extremely rich)? Most people's first response would be that such a practice would be "unfair." For some economists, however, this is not a satisfying answer, because of the ambiguity surrounding the word "unfair". A partial answer to those who are not persuaded by the fairness approach is that the availability of collecting monetary sanctions for acts committed by murderers could induce policy-makers to design incentive programs for law enforcers which could induce them to abuse their power and frame innocent individuals to legally raise money for the government.[23]

3.1.2 Information production and stigma

Criminal law also has the function of producing information concerning a convict's attitude towards the rest of society and his preferences. This information will on average be accurate and reliable only if wrongful convictions are minimized. This objective is achieved through high standards of proof in criminal trials. Hence, criminal law may allow other members of society to alter their behavior towards the ex-convict and take low-cost targeted precautions against him. It is likely the case that these precautions are socially desirable, since they would achieve specific deterrence at relatively low costs.

Criminal law's function of producing reliable information concerning the convict's social preferences would not likely be fulfilled by alternative public law systems such as administrative law. This is because these mechanisms lack the constitutional procedural constraints imposed on criminal law, and are therefore susceptible to produce false positives more frequently.[24]

3.2 Intentional Acts Resulting in Low Harm

Petty thefts and trespass can be listed under this category. There are at least two main reasons which may provide economic justifications for the criminalization of these offenses. First, deterrence will be inadequate, because of low probabilities of conviction and lack of victims' willingness to sue under tort law.[25] Second, valuable information relating to offenders' social attitudes will not be discovered unless the act is criminalized. I have previously discussed why information production may be important when considering intentional acts resulting in high harm. Therefore, I will only discuss inadequate deterrence in detail.

3.2.1 Inadequate deterrence

As briefly discussed earlier, detection probabilities will be low when harm is inflicted intentionally. This fact alone implies that compensatory tort damages will not be sufficient for adequate deterrence.[26] Furthermore, when victims suffer small harms, it may not be in their best interest to pursue legal actions against the tortfeasors.[27] This may be because expected material litigation costs are higher than the harm suffered, or because the psychic costs of pursuing legal action might be high. Hence, compensatory damage awards through tort law alone would be inadequate in deterring potential offenders.

The use of criminal law can solve the problem of inadequate deterrence by providing a commitment mechanism where every detected crime is prosecuted. Furthermore, access to superior technology and information can increase the probability of detection. Hence, expected punishments for criminals can be increased, which would result in greater deterrence.

3.2.2   Alternative solutions

The inadequacy of compensatory damages, however, does not imply that the only solution is criminalizing these acts. Alternative solutions are to use administrative law and/or award punitive damages in tort law. Both alternatives, however, lack the accurate information production aspect of criminal law, because under neither regime is the suspect protected by standards of proof as high as beyond a reasonable doubt.

There can be economic justifications for relying on punitive damages rather than criminal sanctions when the act in question reflects slight deviances from social norms, but not great enough to warrant the imposition of criminal stigma on the offender. The fact that the plaintiff is the recipient of punitive damages suggests that such damages should be awarded only upon clear evidence supporting accusations. Otherwise, the possibility of obtaining punitive damages may be an invitation to fraudulent claims.[28] The implications of this reasoning are consistent with the clear and convincing evidence requirement for awarding punitive damages, which is adopted by most of the states in the United States.[29]

3.3   Acts Resulting in Unintended Harms

All accidents belong to this group. By definition, an accident occurs unintentionally and causes harm. Not all accidents, however, lead to legal liabilities. This is because most accidents are incidental, undesirable and functionally unavoidable consequences of other desirable activities. For instance, transportation is a socially desirable activity, which leads to very frequent and inevitable accidents. The only way to prevent all transportation related accidents is to deter transportation completely. This is, however, socially undesirable. As such, the most that can be done is to require that individuals take due care when engaging in activities which may result in accidents. Those who exercise due care can be said to be engaging in reasonable and socially desirable activity, and the opposite can be said for individuals not exercising due care.

Unreasonable acts resulting in unintended harms are usually regulated by tort law and not by criminal law. Most definitions of crimes include a *mens rea* element, which require that the offender possess a predefined level of culpability. Offenders committing acts resulting in unintentional harms (e.g., car accidents) are usually presumed to lack the level of culpability which is required by most crimes. There are important exceptions to this general trend, such as strict liability crimes, which do not include a *mens rea* requirement at all, and negligent homicide, which has a weaker *mens rea* requirement than most other crimes.

There are persuasive utilitarian arguments for restricting the scope of criminal law to intentional wrongdoings. In the context of unintentional harms, the probability of detection is expected to be high which would mitigate the inadequate deterrence problem encountered in the case of intentional wrongdoings.[30] Perhaps more importantly, the criminalization of an undesirable act can cause individuals to refrain from similar desirable acts to minimize potential wrongful convictions. Furthermore, when the harm in question is unintended, criminal law is less likely to produce accurate and valuable information concerning the offender's preferences over social interactions. Finally, imposing mandatory third-party insurance to regulate conduct may increase deterrence in low harm cases.

3.3.1 High probability of detection

When harms are inflicted unintentionally, it is more likely that the offender will be caught than in a corresponding case where he causes harm intentionally. The offender is not trying to cause harm and therefore the probability of achieving a harmful result is lower. Accordingly, in most cases it will not be worthwhile for the future offender to take steps which will allow him to avoid detection. Furthermore, in most accidents the offender simply does not have the time to conceal his offense (consider car accidents in heavy traffic). Due to these reasons, the probability of detection is usually higher for acts resulting in unintended harms.

When the probability of detection is close to unity, compensatory damages for non-trivial damages will suffice to deter non-judgment proof offenders from taking inadequate care to avoid accidents. Compensatory damages will be much lower than monetary criminal sanctions that would be required to achieve optimal deterrence in a corresponding intentional harm case. Hence, the number of judgment proof future defendants will be fewer. Accordingly, the imposition of criminal sanctions will result in lower benefits from solving the problem of judgment proof offenders.

3.3.2 Criminalization of an undesirable act can cause fear of wrongful conviction

Assume that it is undesirable that individuals drive over 65 m.p.h., because this is exactly that speed where the driver's private marginal benefit from speeding equals the marginal social expected cost of speeding. Next, imagine an extreme case where the law suggests that a person having an accident while driving over 65 m.p.h. be executed. People would presumably avoid driving at 64 m.p.h. Most people would probably even avoid driving above 60 m.p.h.[31] Such abstention from driving as fast as is socially desirable represents social costs. Although this is an unrealistic hypothetical, it demonstrates the problems associated with criminalizing certain acts causing unintentional harms.

In general, it is hard to identify the cause of an unintentionally inflicted harm, and there will necessarily be errors in the determination of such causes. Hence, when certain acts are criminalized, people can abstain from acts which are socially desirable (and legal) and similar to the criminalized act to minimize the chances of being falsely convicted. Therefore, criminalizing undesirable acts which are hard to distinguish from desirable acts will cause social costs due to unnecessary abstentions.[32] Similar problems do not exist with intentionally inflicted harms, because there are fewer desirable acts which can be mistaken as intentional acts inflicting harm (e.g., murder, rape or theft), and the high standards of proof in criminal trials make it unlikely that such mistaken determinations will be made.

This observation, however, does not preclude the possibility of punishing people who unintentionally harm others through the commission of acts which are sufficiently distinguishable from those which are socially desirable. That is to say, criminally punishing those who have accidents while driving 150 m.p.h. would not cause people to abstain from driving at 65 m.p.h., because it would be relatively easy to distinguish between two accidents which occur at these two speeds. In fact, this type of policy is consistent with what we observe in reality, which will be explored when discussing negligent homicides.

3.3.3   Less accurate and valuable information production

The fact that a person has experienced an accident provides little information about his conscious state. The accident may have happened due to unobservable factors (e.g., momentary malfunctioning of a car) which may have made it seem as if the person did not exercise due care. Furthermore, a failure to take due care to prevent future accidents represents a lesser deviation from social norms than an intention to steal, rape or kill. Hence, even if criminal law could produce accurate information concerning a person's attitude towards taking due care to prevent daily accidents, this information would not affect most social interactions. Accordingly, the benefits of supplying information about offenders' conscious state through criminal law would be low.

3.3.4   Insurance

The possibility of regulating conduct by making third party insurance mandatory alleviates the problem of inadequate deterrence. Parties have an incentive to increase their level of care, even if they do not expect their victims to bring liability claims, because they fear that their insurance premium may rise. This additional source of incentives can mitigate the problem of inadequate deterrence, especially in low expected harm cases.

3.3.5   Fewer benefits, constant costs

The benefits of imposing criminal sanctions are lower in accident cases than in intentional harm infliction cases due to the reasons explained above. However, it is likely to be the case that the administrative costs of a criminal case resolving an accident would be no lower than one resolving an intentional harm case. In other words, compared to intentional infliction of harm cases, the imposition of criminal sanctions costs the same but generates fewer benefits. Accordingly, the fact that most acts resulting in unintended harms are not regulated by criminal law can be justified on utilitarian grounds.

3.3.6   Negligent homicide

Negligent homicide seems to be an exception to the general trend of criminally punishing offenders only upon a showing of intent to cause harm. Strictly, speaking this is true, because (criminal) negligence does not require intent to harm another. However, negligence in criminal law requires that the offender display indifference or disregard for others' well-being. It is different from regular standards of negligence where it is sufficient to take less care than a reasonable person would under similar circumstances. In fact, the Model Penal Code's definition of (criminal) negligence requires "gross deviation from the standard of care that a reasonable person would observe in the actor's situation."[33]

This requirement of "gross deviation" demonstrates two economic justifications for punishing negligent homicide through criminal law. First, criminalizing such acts will not cause people to abstain from socially desirable behavior, because individuals taking due care will rarely be mistaken for people who display gross deviation from ordinary conduct. Second, criminal law will achieve its information producing function by convicting and identifying a person whose preferences greatly deviate from social norms.

3.3.7   Strict liability crimes

Strict liability crimes represent the greatest deviation from the general trend of requiring intent to criminally sanction offenders. Intent is irrelevant in determining whether a person is guilty of a strict liability crime. Strict liability is generally used either for regulatory purposes or to increase deterrence where legislators have determined that there is an exceptionally important social goal. Illegal parking is a strict liability offense, which is designed for regulatory purposes, whereas statutory rape (in some states) is a strict liability offense designed to deter people from engaging in sex with underage children. An explanation of why it makes sense to impose strict liability for regulatory purposes is provided in section 3.5. Next, I will argue that there are no apparent economic rationales to define statutory rape as a strict liability crime.

I assume that society has made the determination that people who achieve the age of 18 are autonomous and may make their own decisions. Hence, voluntary sex between two adults is not an activity that the state needs to regulate, and will occur only if there are expected social gains associated with it (i.e., both individuals expect to enjoy it, and not regret it). In this regard, sexual activity is analogous to the speeding hypothetical provided above: voluntary sex between any two adults is socially desirable, but sexual activity between two individuals at least one of whom is underage is socially undesirable. Accordingly, criminalizing sex with an underage person, based on the honest and mistaken belief that the minor is an adult, generates at least two problems. First, it causes fear of conviction, leading individuals to abstain from having sex with adults who they believe might be underage where there is only a very small probability of this. This leads to social losses, since by definition consensual sex between two adults is socially beneficial.[34] Second, inaccurate information concerning individuals' mental states can be provided through convictions. This follows because an individual who truly thought that she was having sex with a 22-year-old will be convicted, if her partner turns out to be only 17. This is true even if her partner shows her a fake identification card, and even when the jury believes the accused's statement that she believed her partner was an adult.[35]

Some states have acknowledged the problems associated with imposing strict liability in the context of statutory rape. This is evidenced by the existence of states requiring a showing of intent to convict a person who has had sex with a minor. A greater number of states provide a solution to the problem by adopting hybrid statutory rape laws, which are a cross-breed between strict liability and regimes which require a showing of intent.[36]

I will make a single speculation as to why strict liability statutory rape laws exist despite the apparent lack of utilitarian rationales justifying them. Politicians who are opposed to such laws may not be able to state their preferences openly, fearing loss of support or debates with their opponents about sensitive issues which are easily manipulatable. This may imply that once a strict liability statutory rape law is passed, it may be extremely hard to change it.

3.4   Acts Presumably Intended to Cause Harm but which Fail

Attempted crimes fall in this category. Generally, the utilitarian rationales listed in sections 3.2 and 3.3 provide justifications as to why common law crimes should be deterred through criminal law. Criminalizing attempts addresses inadequate deterrence problems identified in the context of common law crimes. Criminal sanctions for attempts achieve this purpose by raising the probability of conviction, which leads to higher expected punishments associated with criminal activity.[37] This is especially desirable in cases where an upper boundary on criminal sanctions cause the expected punishment for completed crimes to be inadequate deterrents.[38] Another reason to resort to criminal law enforcement to regulate attempts is that it offers methods to prevent crime before it occurs.[39]

The most important problem with punishing attempts is accurately identifying a person's intent to cause harm. Inferring intent is less problematic in a case where a person shoots at his victim but fails to kill him only because his victim was wearing a bullet proof vest. But showing intent in cases where law enforcers stop a person in the process necessary to commit a crime is very hard, if not impossible.[40]

3.5   Dangerous Acts Presumably Committed with Intention to Achieve Harmless Result

Conduct crimes such as reckless driving, and driving while intoxicated, fall under this category.[41] Individuals committing conduct crimes presumably do not intend to hurt others. They may, for instance, want to go from one place to another quickly, as opposed to hitting a pedestrian on the way home. Speeding and other civil infractions also belong to this category.

3.5.1   High expected harm conduct crimes

Driving intoxicated and reckless driving are associated with higher expected harms than civil infractions, such as speeding. People who engage in these types of activities are more likely to disregard the risk that they cause for others, which reflects their "gross deviation from the standard of care that a reasonable person would observe in the actor's situation."[42] One good way to think of such activities is as conduct which could have but has not resulted in negligent homicide. Accordingly, such conduct can be interpreted as the unintentional or criminally negligent analog of attempted murder. As such, the justifications for punishing attempts through criminal law are equally applicable to standard conduct crimes. Furthermore, as noted in the discussion of attempts, criminal law enforcement provides the means to prevent harm before it occurs.

3.5.2   Civil infractions

Speeding and some other traffic violations (e.g., not signaling) are associated with low expected harms. The lack of remedies through tort law necessitates an alternative mechanism to regulate these acts. This is presumably why these offenses are regulated through public prosecution. However, despite public prosecution, liabilities for civil infractions do not impose significant stigma on offenders.[43] Public enforcement of these violations causes the incentive problems identified in section 3.2 to vanish. Furthermore, the lack of intent to cause harm and the lack of gross deviations from social norms implies that criminal law is unnecessary to regulate these acts. It should also be noted that the same law enforcers who enforce crimes are employed to enforce civil infractions. This is presumably because of the existence of economies of scale and scope. Police officers who detect reckless driving and intoxicated drivers can detect civil infractions at relatively low cost.

It is also very important to note that these acts are arguably not always socially undesirable. The benefit to the offender may frequently outweigh the expected harm to society. Therefore, the optimal level of deterrence is partial as opposed to complete deterrence. To achieve optimal deterrence, forcing offenders to internalize the negative externalities they cause to society should be sufficient. This can be achieved through a pricing scheme, which is almost exactly what public prosecution of civil infractions achieve.

Criminalizing these acts would probably achieve over-deterrence due to stigmatization, which can be interpreted as a fixed cost of conviction which cannot exclusively be controlled by the government. Furthermore, criminal proceedings would come at high administrative costs, which would not be justified given the small amount of harm and risk associated with these acts. This last point also explains why certain acts are made strict liability offenses (e.g., illegal parking). Fines associated with most strict liability offenses are small. Hence, the cost to demonstrate intent is presumably higher than error costs associated with false positives.

One may still wonder why tort law would not suffice to regulate civil infractions, or why the inefficiencies of tort law in regulating these acts are not present in public prosecution. As explained, it is probably not worthwhile to require a showing of intent to regulate civil infractions. Given this constraint, under tort law individuals would have enormous incentives to bring fraudulent claims. It would be harder to punish fraudulent claims coming from many different individuals than to punish those coming from fewer and easily identifiable law enforcers.

4.   CONCLUSION

Common law crimes are socially unproductive acts. Therefore, complete deterrence is desirable. Criminal law is used to achieve this purpose, and familiar economic rationales provide justifications for criminalizing such acts. The existence of judgment proof offenders, low probabilities of detection, and (in case of small harms) victims' inadequate incentives to sue cause inadequate deterrence in the absence of sanctions complementing compensatory tort damages. Delivering these sanctions through criminal law is desirable, because it provides the necessary procedural tools to minimize wrongful convictions. Avoiding wrongful conviction in this context is necessary, because such convictions would disseminate inaccurate information about the convicted person.

Criminal sanctions are not nearly as necessary or desirable in regulating acts leading to unintended harms as they are in regulating common law crimes. Inadequate deterrence is not as great a problem in this context, because the unintentional nature of accidents leads to higher detection probabilities. Furthermore, criminalizing undesirable acts can cause individuals to refrain from similar desirable acts in fear of wrongful convictions. Another mechanism to induce some degree of additional deterrence is the use of third-party insurance in the context of accidents. Finally, criminal law is unlikely to perform its informational function when regulating accidents.

Negligent homicide and strict liability crimes do not fit the general trend of requiring intent to criminally sanction offenders. Nevertheless, criminalizing negligent homicide is justifiable on utilitarian grounds. Negligent homicide requires a state of mind which greatly deviates from the average. As such, criminalizing this act is unlikely to cause fear of wrongful conviction and abstention from socially desirable activity. Furthermore, criminal law will fulfill its informative function by convicting only those who show great deviances from social norms. Strict liability crimes, such as statutory rape, on the other hand, do not seem to be supported by economic rationales, and could perhaps be explained as an undesirable result of political processes.

When thinking of attempts, conduct crimes and civil infractions, it is useful to draw analogies with the resulting counterpart of these acts. Punishing attempts and conduct crimes is justified to mitigate the inadequate deterrence of common law crimes and negligent homicides. A potential problem with punishing attempts is the difficulty or impossibility of demonstrating that the suspect possessed the necessary intent. Civil infractions, which do not warrant the use of criminal law, are publicly prosecuted most likely because of the lack of remedies through tort law. However, their regulation does not possess most of the characteristics of criminal law.

In sum, the criminalization of most acts that traditionally fall under the scope of criminal law are consistent with what a utilitarian approach would suggest. The justifications identified for the use of criminal law in these fields may prove to be useful when considering whether criminal law should extend to other fields, such as corporate acts, medical malpractice and the regulation of other professions. When considering new fields of regulation, it may make sense to concentrate on the characteristics of acts to be regulated and determine how they are similar to and different from the common and traditional acts which have been analysed in this chapter.

NOTES

1. See Posner (1985); Shavell (1993); Friedman (2000); Bowles, Faure and Garoupa (2008); Hylton and Khanna (2007); and Hylton and Khanna (2009).
2. See, e.g., 76 *Boston University Law Review* Nos. 1 and 2, which are symposium issues almost entirely devoted to the tort/crime distinction.
3. See, e.g., Friedman (2000); Landes and Posner (1975); Becker and Stigler (1974); and Epstein (1996).
4. See *supra* note 2.
5. See David Friedman reaching this conclusion in Friedman (1996).
6. *Id.*
7. Friedman (2000).
8. I am using the word "punishment" broadly to refer to any mechanism through which an offender is required to incur losses. The word punishment in this sense does not imply that the offender will suffer from stigmatization or that the act in question is a socially undesirable one (i.e., where the harm to the victim is greater than the benefit to the offender).
9. For instance, tort cases brought by the government, in which instance the case would resemble a public prosecution.
10. For additional comments on similar tables, see Friedman (1996) and (2000).
11. See, e.g., Mungan (2011).
12. In order to provide examples, scholars have used 95% as an approximation of this threshold. See, e.g., Harel and Porat (2009). This is not to suggest that beyond a reasonable doubt corresponds exactly to this number. It should, however, provide an approximation of how high the standard of proof is for convicting a person through criminal law.
13. See, e.g., www.atra.org/show/7343, providing a list of relevant state procedures concerning punitive damages. For punitive damages most states require clear and convincing evidence, and some require preponderance of the evidence.
14. For probability multipliers in the context of punitive damages, see Polinsky and Shavell (1998).
15. To preserve the scope of this chapter, I am limiting my analysis to a comparison between criminal law and other commonly used branches of law (e.g., tort law and administrative law) and not any conceivable method of regulation. See *supra* note 3 for an analysis of whether criminal law, as we know it, could efficiently be replaced by a privately enforced legal system.
16. For references to the "result crime" versus "conduct crime" dichotomy, see Dressler (2007).
17. Model Penal Code § 2.02.

18. In cases where the victim is deceased, his close relatives may seek compensation.
19. See Bowles, Faure and Garoupa (2008), where the authors provide economic justifications for the use of public enforcement rather than private enforcement to regulate certain harmful acts, which are very similar to those proposed here.
20. See Landes and Posner (1975), Posner (1985), and Shavell (1993) where this point is made.
21. There are a considerable number of articles identifying the optimal use of imprisonment and non-monetary sanctions in law enforcement. Important articles in this field include Polinsky and Shavell (1984), Shavell (1987), and Kaplow (1990).
22. See, Bowles, Faure and Garoupa (2008), and Shavell (1993).
23. One can potentially respond to this argument by asking why it is that there are criminal monetary sanctions associated with other crimes, if it induces corruption by law enforcers. An argument for limiting criminal/administrative monetary fines to less serious offenses may have to do with fixed costs faced by law enforcers when acting in a corrupt manner. Such fixed costs can be the result of expected costs associated with loss of occupation. Hence, law enforcers may risk such losses only if the monetary sanction in question is high enough. This observation leads to the proposition that criminal monetary sanctions should only be used for less severe crimes. This explanation is also consistent with the public choice theory of criminal procedure extended by Hylton and Khanna (2007).
24. For a formal explanation as to why alternative legal mechanisms do not produce reliable information, see, Galbiati and Garoupa (2007).
25. See note 20 *supra*.
26. I am not separately analysing intermediate harms, where offenders are not judgment proof and where victims have sufficient incentives to sue. However, it should be noted that low probabilities of detection are sufficient to establish the desirability of criminal law to regulate intentional inflictions of intermediate harm. Furthermore, as long as there are potential offenders whose wealth is lower than the plaintiff's litigation costs, there will be no such category as intermediate harms as defined in this note, making the problem uninteresting.
27. This point has been identified in the existing literature by many scholars, see, e.g., Bowles, Faure and Garoupa (2008) and Friedman (2000). A variant of this problem can occur when an act inflicts small harms on multiple victims, leading to great aggregate harms. The existence of this problem alone, however, is not sufficient to imply that tort law will perform poorly. The existence of class actions can mitigate the problem of inadequate deterrence in this context. This last point is identified in Friedman (2000).
28. See Friedman (2000), where the author discusses the issue of fraud and offers anecdotal evidence from history.
29. See note 13 *supra*.
30. See note 20 *supra*.
31. A very similar example is provided in Parker (1993) at 773.
32. See Parker (1993); Craswell and Calfee (1986); and Calfee and Craswell (1984), where the authors discuss this and very similar costs.
33. Model Penal Code § 2.02.
34. Richard Posner makes a comment against this point. He states: "Again we do not care about deterring activity bordering on the activity that the basic criminal prohibition is aimed at. Because we do not count the avoidance of that activity as a social cost, it pays to reduce the costs of prosecution by eliminating the issue of intent (more precisely, an issue of intent)." See Posner (1985) at 1222. Given that we have made a determination that consensual sex among two adults is beneficial, not counting avoidance of that activity as a social cost contradicts utilitarianism.
35. This is, of course, not true in the rare event of jury nullification.
36. For a description and discussion of these regimes, see Carpenter (2003).
37. See Shavell (1990), where this point is formalized.
38. Such upper boundaries can be natural (i.e., life imprisonment or the death penalty), or due to external reasons (e.g., constitutional constraints requiring punishments to be proportional to the severity of the crime or the necessity of achieving marginal deterrence). See Shavell (1990), and Posner (1985), for brief remarks concerning upper boundaries for sanctions.
39. For a more detailed discussion of crime prevention, see Shavell (1993).
40. At what point one can infer intent from the acts already completed is an interesting question. See Dressler (2007) at ch. 10, which has a discussion concerning interesting issues about inferring intent in attempt cases.
41. See note 16 *supra*.
42. See note 33 *supra*.
43. One could, however, argue that multiple speeding tickets may cause criminal prosecution, which is similar to a stigma effect.

REFERENCES

Becker, Gary and George Stigler (1974) "Law Enforcement, Malfeasance, and the Compensation of Enforcers," 3 *Journal of Legal Studies* 1

Bowles, Roger, Michael Faure and Nuno Garoupa (2008) "The Scope of Criminal Law and Criminal Sanctions: An Economic View and Policy Implications," 35 *Journal of Law and Society* 389

Calfee, John E. and Richard Craswell (1984) "Some Effects of Uncertainty on Compliance with Legal Standards," 70 *Virginia Law Review* 965

Carpenter, Catherine L. (2003) "On Statutory Rape, Strict Liability, and the Public Welfare Offense Model," 53 *American University Law Review* 313

Craswell, Richard and John E. Calfee (1986) "Deterrence and Uncertain Legal Standards," 2 *Journal of Law, Economics, and Organization* 279

Dressler, Joshua (2007) *Cases and Materials on Criminal Law*, 4th edn, American casebook series, St. Paul, MN: Thomson/West

Epstein, Richard (1996) "The Tort/Crime Distinction a Generation Later," 76 *Boston University Law Review* 1

Friedman, David (1996) "Beyond the Tort Crime Distinction," 76 *Boston University Law Review* 103

— D. (2000) *Law's Order: What Economics Has to Do with Law and Why It Matters*, Princeton, NJ: Princeton University Press

Galbiati, Roberto and Nuno Garoupa (2007) "Keeping Stigma Out of Administrative Law: An Explanation of Consistent Beliefs," 15 *Supreme Court Economic Review* 273

Harel, Alon and Ariel Porat (2009) "Aggregating Probabilities Across Offenses in Criminal Law," 94 *Minnesota Law Review* 261

Hylton, Keith and Vikramaditya S. Khanna (2007) "A Public Choice Theory of Criminal Procedure," 15 *Supreme Court Economic Review* 61

— (2009) "Political Economy of Criminal Procedure," in *Criminal Law and Economics*, N. Garoupa, ed., Edward Elgar Publishing, 171–206

Kaplow, Louis (1990) "A Note on the Optimal Use of Nonmonetary Sanctions," 42 *Journal of Public Economics* 245

Landes, William M. and Richard A. Posner (1975) "The Independent Judiciary in an Interest-Group Perspective," 18(3) *Journal of Law and Economics* 875

Mungan, Murat C. (2011) "A Utilitarian Justification for Heightened Standards of Proof in Criminal Trials,"167 *Journal of Institutional and Theoretical Economics* 352

Parker, Jeffrey S. (1993) "The Economics of Mens Rea," 79 *Virginia Law Review* 741

Polinsky, Mitchell and Steven Shavell (1984) "The Optimal Use of Fines and Imprisonment," 24 *Journal of Public Economics* 89

— (1998) "Punitive Damages: An Economic Analysis," 111 *Harvard Law Review* 869

Posner, Richard (1985) "An Economic Theory of the Criminal Law," 85 *Columbia Law Review* 1193

Shavell, Steven (1987) "The Optimal Use of Nonmonetary Sanctions as a Deterrent," 77 *American Economic Review* 584

— (1990) "Deterrence and the Punishment of Attempts," 19 *Journal of Legal Studies* 435

— (1993) "The Optimal Structure of Law Enforcement," 36 *Journal of Law and Economics* 255

Stigler, J. (1974) "Law Enforcement, Malfeasance, and Compensation of Enforcers," 3 *Journal of Legal Studies* 1

3 Some notes on property rules, liability rules, and criminal law

Keith N. Hylton

1. INTRODUCTION

Property rules prohibit conduct and liability rules internalize costs.[1] Using this distinction, criminal law can be described as a set of property rules. The law aims to prohibit offensive activity altogether rather than regulate it to some optimal level. In other words, criminal law assumes that there is no "optimal level" of offensive activities such as fraud, rape, and robbery.

In view of this, one should expect the property-liability rules framework set out in Calabresi and Melamed (1972) to point the way toward a robust positive theory of criminal law. Posner (1985) applies the property rule theory to explain criminal law at a high level of detail. No other article has attempted such a complete survey of the criminal law grounded in positive theory.[2]

The value of the property-liability rules framework has come under attack in recent years. Kaplow and Shavell (1996) present perhaps the most troubling critique. They argue that property rules and liability rules are equivalent, in low transaction cost settings, in terms of their welfare implications.[3] The reason is that takings will not be observed under either property rules or liability rules.[4] I refer to this below as the *Indifference Proposition.*

In this chapter I re-examine the Indifference Proposition. I have argued before that even on its owns terms the Indifference Proposition does not imply that property rules and liability rules are equivalent in their welfare implications, and that the Indifference Proposition depends on rather special conditions (Hylton 2006). I argue here that the Indifference Proposition is invalid, and that, unlike property rules, takings will be observed under liability rules in low transaction cost settings.

In particular, in several plausible low transaction cost settings, takings will occur under the liability rule, violating the Indifference Proposition. The variations on the low transaction cost setting involve defensive conduct, predatory conduct, and bounded rationality.

I also explore the role of informational asymmetry in a simple model of takings. The liability rule is often ideal under informational asymmetry because it can enable efficient transfers in spite of the informational disparity.[5] But if property is more valuable to the acquiring party under the property rule than under the liability rule, because transfers occur without risk of subsequent disputes over title, then informational asymmetry can result in takings under the liability rule, even under conditions in which takings would be unlikely. This is another scenario in which the property rule is socially preferable to the liability rule.[6]

In the final part of this chapter I summarize the implications of the property and liability rules framework for criminal law. The defense offered here for property rules provides a stronger foundation for the positive economic theory of criminal law.

2.   THEORY AND ILLUSTRATION

I will use an example to illustrate my argument. The setting I consider consists of possessors and acquirers. As the labels suggest, possessors own some object that the acquirer wishes to possess. The acquirer has a choice to bargain for and purchase the object from the possessor in an arm's-length transaction, or to take the object from the possessor.

Assume the possessor has a bicycle worth $75 to him. Assume there are two types of acquirer: one values the bicycle at $100 (high-valuing acquirers) and the other type values the bicycle at $25 (low-valuing acquirers).

The state has a choice with respect to enforcement of possession rights. It can apply a liability rule, which consists of a fine that will be imposed on the acquirer. Alternatively, the state can apply a property rule which simply prohibits takings. If the acquirer takes the bicycle, the state will enforce the law (whether under the property rule or under the liability rule) at a cost of $10 for each instance of enforcement.

If the state adopts the liability rule approach, the optimal fine for taking a bicycle is equal to the sum of $75 and $10, or $85. This fine internalizes to the acquirer the social cost of taking bicycles, which consists of the monetary injury to possessors and the enforcement cost borne by the state. A policy of imposing a fine of $85 on acquirers who take bicycles will ensure that only those acquirers whose subjective valuations exceed the social cost of a taking will actually take a bicycle. In other words, only those takings that enhance society's wealth will occur.

Obviously, the state could set the fine at some level other than the optimal level. But in order to evaluate the choice between the property rule and liability rule, I will confine myself to the optimal fine. This ensures that the comparison is based on the most efficient liability rule regime. If I compare the two rules on the assumption that the state chooses a sub-optimal fine level, that obviously would bias the analysis in favor of the property rule.

If the state adopts the property rule, it can implement it through more than one approach. It can prohibit takings and incarcerate all acquirers who violate the rule. Or the state can impose a fine of at least $100 on any taking, which will remove any gain that an acquirer could enjoy as the result of a taking. Whatever approach the state takes, I will assume that it is effective in completely deterring takings. Takings will therefore not occur under the property rule.

2.1   High Transaction Cost Setting

First, consider a setting in which transaction costs are so high that no acquirer would consider bargaining for a bicycle; bargaining is too costly and time-consuming. Acquirers will obtain bicycles only through taking.

Under the liability rule only those acquirers whose valuations are equal to $100 will take bicycles. The acquirers whose valuations are equal to $25 will not take bicycles. The reason is that if such an acquirer takes a bicycle, he will have to pay a fine of $85, which results in a negative return.

Each taking by a high-valuing acquirer delivers a social dividend of $15 ($25 less the cost of enforcement $10). Thus, the liability-rule enforcement policy permits society to reap this dividend on every taking. Society has no interest in permitting takings to occur involving low-valuing acquirers because the gain they receive is less than the monetary loss imposed on the possessors.

If all of the acquirers were low-valuing types, the penalty of $85 would deter them from taking bicycles. But since the social dividend is negative for any taking involving a low-valuing acquirer, society could just as well accomplish the same outcome with a penalty set at $1 million. The important point is that society prefers to completely deter takings by low-valuing acquirers.

Now consider enforcement under the property rule. Under the property rule, no acquirers will ever take bicycles. This means that society forfeits the social dividend that is generated by the takings that occur between high-valuing acquirers and possessors.

It follows that the liability rule is preferable to the property rule when transaction costs are high. Under both rules, no takings occur between low-valuing acquirers and possessors. Takings occur between high-valuing acquirers and possessors only under the liability rule. Obviously, if we consider any less efficient liability rule regime, such as one in which the penalty is set at $1 rather than $85, the superiority of the liability rule becomes less clear.

2.2   Low Transaction Cost Setting

In the low transaction cost setting acquirers have the option of bargaining for and purchasing the bicycle rather than taking it. To simplify, I will assume that the transaction cost is zero – that is, that no resources are consumed by the act of bargaining between acquirer and possessor.

If high-valuing acquirers make deals with possessors, those deals will involve the transfer of a bicycle for some price between $75 and $100. The surplus to the acquirer will be $100 minus the price; the surplus to the possessor will be the price minus $75. The total social surplus in every such transaction will be $25.

Obviously, low-valuing acquirers will never acquire a bicycle through a voluntary bargain. They will offer a bid of $25 and the possessor will turn it down.

The outcome under bargaining (low transaction cost) is preferable to the outcome under the liability rule with high transaction costs. In the high transaction cost setting, takings occur between high-valuing acquirers and possessors, with each delivering a social dividend of $15. However, when the parties can bargain cheaply, acquirers and possessors enter into voluntary deals, and the social dividend is $25 per voluntary transaction.

But there is no guarantee that only voluntary transactions will take place. That depends on the enforcement rule.

If the state adopts the property rule, no takings will occur, and only voluntary transactions between high-valuing acquirers and possessors will be observed – again with each transaction generating a surplus of $25.

If the state adopts a liability rule, the matter is more complicated. The traditional view reflected in the Calabresi and Melamed article and in the Posner article is that takings will occur under a liability rule. Some high-valuing acquirers will take bicycles, generating a social surplus of only $15 ($25 transfer surplus − $10 enforcement cost) for each taking. Indeed, any time a possessor demands a price greater than $85 for the bicycle, the acquirer will take.

On the assumption that takings occur under the liability rule regime, the property rule is preferable to the liability rule. The reason is that voluntary transactions, which are the only transactions that occur under the property rule, generate a social dividend of $25. This is greater than the social dividend from a taking under the liability rule regime, which is $15. This is the core of the case for the property rule in Calabresi and Melamed.

3.   INDIFFERENCE PROPOSITION

Kaplow and Shavell argue that *takings will not occur* under the liability rule.[7] Reconsider the bargaining environment. The high valuing acquirer will approach the possessor and offer to purchase. The possessor will state a price. Suppose the possessor offers a take-it-or-leave-it price to the high-valuing acquirer. In order to examine the robustness of the Kaplow-Shavell argument, I will consider it first under the assumptions of the previous section, specifically, that the liability rule penalty forces the acquirer to bear the enforcement costs. Second, I will assume that the liability rule penalty does not force the acquirer to bear the enforcement costs.

3.1   Acquirer Bears Enforcement Cost

The possessor knows that he cannot set the price too high. If he sets the price at $99, the high-valuing acquirer will take. The reason is that he will get a surplus of only $1 if he purchases at $99; but if he takes the bicycle, he will get a surplus of $15 ($100 value − $85 fine). Clearly the high-valuing acquirer will take if the possessor demands $99.

Suppose instead the possessor demands only $76. Then the acquirer will reason as follows: I can purchase the bicycle for a surplus of $24 ($100 − $76), or I can take the bicycle for a surplus of $15. In this case the acquirer will purchase. If the acquirer purchases, the possessor gets a surplus $1. If the acquirer takes, the possessor gets no surplus.

The acquirer will prefer to purchase for any price less than or equal to $85, and will take when the price is higher than $85. The possessor will be better off selling at any price greater than $75 and less than or equal to $85 than he would be in the event of a taking. It follows that a transaction will take place for a price less than or equal to $85 and greater than or equal to $75. No takings will occur under the liability rule.

3.2   Acquirer Does Not Bear Enforcement Cost

The foregoing argument should be reconsidered under the assumption that the cost of enforcement is borne by the state instead of the acquirer (in the form of an addition to the fine). If the cost of enforcement is borne by the state, the liability rule fine will be $75. The only way that a transaction will take place is if the possessor is willing to sell for $75, which is the value the possessor places on the bicycle. In this case, there is a single objective transaction price.

A plausible assumption is that in this scenario, when transactions can take place only at a price at which the possessor is indifferent as between a sale and a taking, that the possessors will choose randomly; some bicycles will be sold (because the possessor set his price at $75) and some will be taken (because the possessor refuses to sell at $75). This is the approach adopted in Hylton (2006). However, suppose all possessors choose to sell at $75. In this scenario, no takings will occur, and all bicycles will sell at the $75 price.

3.3 Informational Asymmetry

Although the low transaction cost setting was assumed in Calabresi and Melamed to exclude informational asymmetry, the preceding arguments do not necessarily fall apart when informational asymmetry is introduced. The claim that no takings will occur under the liability rule may still continue to be valid in the presence of informational asymmetry.

First, consider the case where the state bears all enforcement costs. A transaction could occur at only one price, when the price is equal (in monetary value) to the liability rule penalty. In this case, informational asymmetry would not affect the outcome. Everyone knows the liability rule penalty. If the possessor sets his price above the penalty, high-valuing acquirers will take.

Second, consider the case where the acquirer bears the enforcement costs (as assumed in the example of the previous part). Informational asymmetry becomes an issue in this scenario only if there are some acquirers whose valuations fall within the contract range, between $85 and $75. If there are no acquirers of this sort, informational asymmetry is again an irrelevant factor. No takings will be observed.

3.4 Summing Up

Putting the previous subsections together leads to the following conclusions. First, as long as some portion of the enforcement cost of enforcement is borne by the acquirer, then all bicycles will be transferred through market transactions and no takings will occur. Second, even if no portion of the enforcement cost is borne by the acquirer (because the state bears the full enforcement cost), no takings will occur if the possessor, whenever indifferent between a sale and a taking, always chooses to sell. With these two conclusions accepted, the Kaplow-Shavell argument is complete.

From this argument, Kaplow and Shavell conclude that the property rule and liability rule have equivalent welfare implications in the low transaction cost setting. I will state their result as follows.

> Indifference Proposition: If transaction costs are low, takings will not occur under property rules and under liability rules. Society should therefore be indifferent as between the two rule types.

At first glance the Indifference Proposition is startling, with troubling implications. The traditional view of Calabresi and Melamed, that takings will occur under liability rules and will not occur under property rules, had been accepted in the literature. The

Indifference Proposition implies that the basis for favoring property rules in low transaction cost settings is weak, or non-existent. If that is correct, then the property-liability rule framework falls apart as a positive theory of common law.

The Indifference Proposition is an implication of the Coase Theorem (Coase 1960). If transaction costs are low, according to the Coase Theorem, parties will bargain themselves to the most efficient allocation of resources. It follows that under low transaction costs the most efficient allocation of resources will be observed whether the property rule or the liability rule is in effect. Of course, the most efficient allocation of resources would be observed in the end whether or not takings occurred. When takings occur, however, there is, in effect, a joint decision by the possessor and acquirer to "burn" money. A taking is, in the low transaction cost setting, an agreement to waste resources through the enforcement action. The most efficient transaction is the voluntary transaction. Hence, if transaction costs are low, the parties should always opt for the voluntary transaction. For the remainder of this chapter I will examine the limitations of this argument.

4.   WHY SOCIETY SHOULD NOT BE INDIFFERENT AS BETWEEN PROPERTY RULES AND LIABILITY RULES

In this part I will explore the reasons society should prefer the property rule to the liability rule in the low transaction cost setting. The general reasons can be put initially into two categories. First, even if the Indifference Proposition were valid, society should still prefer the property rule to the liability rule.[8] Second, I will discuss the reasons that the Indifference Proposition is invalid.

4.1   Preferring Property Rules When the Indifference Proposition is Valid

Under the Indifference Proposition, no takings occur under the liability rule, contradicting Calabresi and Melamed (1972). Efficient transfers occur, in the sense that the bicycle gets traded to the agent who values it the most. However, even though only "voluntary" trades occur, these are essentially trades made under duress.

There is an additional implication for the prices that will be observed in the low transaction cost setting when the liability rule is in effect. The maximum transaction price that will be observed under the liability rule regime is the liability rule penalty. The total wealth transfer from possessors to acquirers will be determined in large part by the liability rule penalty. As the penalty is set lower, more wealth is transferred from possessors to acquirers.

In the example considered in the previous part of this chapter, I assumed that acquirers consisted of two types, while the possessors simply valued their bicycle at the market value of $75. Suppose, however, that possessors have heterogeneous subjective valuations. For example, suppose there is a subgroup of possessors that values their bicycles at $90 each. In this scenario, it is still the case that no takings occur under the assumptions of the Indifference Proposition. High-valuing possessors agree to sell their bicycles for a price no greater than $85, because they would rather receive some surplus over the market value as the result of a sale, rather than no surplus at all when a taking occurs.

But even when these sales occur, the high-valuing possessor receives a price that is less than his subjective valuation. This has troubling implications.

When voluntary sales are made, as predicted by the Indifference Proposition, merely to avoid a taking under the liability rule, possessors are not compensated for losses in subjective value in these transactions. That has long-term implications for investment. A high-valuing possessor may have a large subjective valuation because he has made some sort of investment that cannot be easily valued by the market, or which may have no value in the market. For example, suppose a high-valuing possessor has painted his bicycle a special color. Some market participants would prefer to buy a bicycle of that special color, while an equal number would not prefer to buy such a bicycle. The objective market therefore places a zero value on the bicycle's color. Still, even in this case, the possessor may have an expectation of waiting and finding a buyer who prefers the special color and receiving a premium in a transaction as a result. This will not happen under the liability rule, because all acquirers know that they can simply take the bicycle whenever the asking price exceeds the liability rule penalty level.

Knowing that subjective valuations in excess of the market will not be compensated, possessors with substantial subjective valuations, or who anticipate a substantial subjective valuation arising from some future investment, will change their plans to avoid a transaction that imposes a subjective loss. Some will avoid settings in which market exchanges may be forced on them, unless compelled to enter into such an exchange by some uncontrollable change in events. Some will avoid the investment that creates the subjective valuation, since they know that the investment is unlikely to be rewarded in the future.

These actions are harmful to long run social welfare. Again, consider the simple example of the possessor who paints his bicycle a special color. Suppose he has already done so. Knowing that he might eventually find himself in a position where it is privately optimal, under the conditions, to sell his bicycle at a price that he considers beneath his subjective valuation, he may attempt to avoid all settings in which this might occur. He may decide to hide his bicycle in a secret location, and to ride it only in places where he will never run into potential acquirers. Possessors with high subjective valuations may self-segregate in order to avoid market transactions. All of this is costly and reduces welfare. Alternatively, suppose the possessor has not painted his bicycle, but is merely thinking about it. He will do so only if he can find a way to secure its possession in the future. If he cannot secure its possession, he may forgo painting even though the subjective valuation increment from painting far exceeds the cost of painting. This is harmful to social welfare too.

Conversely, consider the incentives of potential acquirers. Knowing that they can simply take a bicycle when the possessor's price exceeds the liability rule penalty, high-valuing acquirers will have every incentive to invest in technology that facilitates taking. These investments would serve no useful purpose to society; they merely facilitate the transfer of resources from one person to another. Social welfare is reduced as resources are drawn into the takings process.

These are sufficient reasons to reject the Indifference Proposition, and to prefer the property rule to the liability rule when transaction costs are low. However, I will argue below that when one looks closely at transaction costs and the takings process, the case for preferring property rules gets even stronger.

4.2   Reasons Why the Indifference Proposition Fails

In this part I will examine in more detail the transactions that are assumed to occur under the Indifference Proposition. The Indifference Proposition holds that property rules and liability rules are equivalent in terms of welfare when transaction costs are low (zero). Of course, there is no definition of precisely what is meant by low transaction costs. The definition that works best in terms of the Coase Theorem is one that is perfectly circular: low transaction costs means any setting in which there is no feature of the environment that prevents the parties from reaching the efficient agreement. The circularity approach has to be set aside to make progress on this issue.

I will break the notion of transaction costs down into different components: primary and secondary. Primary transaction costs are the cost of meeting. Secondary transaction costs are the costs of reaching agreement after meeting.

For example, consider accidents between strangers, such as automobile collisions. The parties cannot bargain *ex ante* over the allocation of risk because the cost of identifying the bargaining parties and meeting before the accident are prohibitively high. This is a case in which bargaining does not occur because primary transaction costs are too high. When the primary transaction costs are low, and the parties can meet easily, there may be secondary transaction costs that prevent them from reaching an agreement. Those costs can take the form of strategic hold out incentives, informational asymmetry, or behavioral norms that pose obstacles to agreements.

I will assume below that primary transaction costs are low. The remaining costs, secondary transaction costs, may not be low. The presence of secondary transaction costs suggest that property rules are preferable to liability rules when primary transaction costs are low.

Return to the basic story. Why do takings *not* occur under the liability rule? Because the possessor, realizing that a taking will occur if he sets his asking price too high, will set his asking price at a sufficiently low level to avoid the taking. The possessor and acquirer agree at first to bargain. When they meet to bargain, the possessor realizes that the law has given the acquirer an option to take whenever the possessor's asking price goes above the level of the liability rule penalty. The liability rule penalty is, in effect, a "strike price" that triggers a taking. Realizing this, the possessor knows to keep his asking price below the strike price set by the law.

As a description of bargaining, this is inconsistent with behavioral patterns. I will consider the implications of cognitive dissonance, bounded rationality, predation, defensive actions, and asymmetric information below. Each of these factors can easily prevent the Indifference Proposition from being valid. Of course, informational disparities have been treated as another type of transaction cost.[9] Predation and defensive actions, however, would appear to be a feature of the bargaining environment even in low transaction cost settings. The prospect of these factors indicates that the Indifference Proposition is invalid even under the most expansive non-circular definition of transaction costs.

4.3   Behavior, Cognitive Dissonance, and Bounded Rationality

When people choose to bargain, they generally commit themselves to the notion that they will bargain, and that if the bargaining fails, in the sense that no transaction takes place, they will walk away with the same endowments that they carried into the bargaining session (Hylton 2006). I am aware of no real life scenarios in which individuals engage in conditional bargaining where if the seller proposes terms that fall outside of certain parameters the prospective acquirer abandons the bargaining process and resorts to expropriation.

Perhaps the closest example of conditional bargaining in American law is observed in collective bargaining as required by the labor laws. In the union bargaining process, the parties are required by law to bargain until an impasse is reached. After an impasse, the employer is allowed under the law to make unilateral changes in working conditions. This is a case of conditional bargaining, because the employer bargains knowing that if the union demands too much, he will simply reject the demand and implement the change he prefers. But in this case, it is the employer exercising his common law property rights after the impasse stage. The law does not permit one party to take part of the common law property rights package from the other after the impasse stage.

Probably the closest examples of conditional bargaining are observed not among individuals, but among governments on the international relations stage. China wants Taiwan to reunify by becoming part of China. The Chinese government asks politely and even enters into trade agreements, but at the same time fortifies missile batteries aimed directly at Taiwan. The clear signal China sends is that this is a bargaining game that could end, at any time, with a taking. The signal is designed to pressure Taiwan not to set its terms for reunification too high. Although this is a valid example of conditional bargaining, it also illustrates how rare the conditions must be for such bargaining to be observed. The international relations stage is unique precisely because there are no property rights enforced by a super-government, while at the same time there are boundaries long recognized by custom. These conditions are unlikely to be observed among individuals within a community. If property rights are not enforced in a community, many individuals would resort to taking, without wasting any time on bargaining. Those who attempted conditional bargaining would be victimized by the many others who resorted to taking.

Bargaining is common in open air markets and in car dealerships. The norm that is uniformly followed is simple. The seller offers a price and the prospective buyer counters with lower prices. But the seller never does so with the expectation that the prospective buyer will take if the seller puts his asking price too high. The understood bargaining ritual is one in which the parties commit to the process, under the assumption that if it fails they retain their current endowments. This appears to have been the behavioral norm in all societies, at all times.

Given that bargaining is a process to which actors commit, the cognitive dissonance problem is easy to see. Suppose the possessor shows up to the bargaining table, assuming that the acquirer is committed to bargaining. The acquirer, suspecting that the possessor will not respect the trigger price limit, has no incentive to bargain. The acquirer's best move would be to take immediately, rather than waste time in a failed bargaining process. Takings rather than bargains would occur, and society would waste resources on enforcement in response to the takings. The Indifference Proposition would fail to hold, and property rules would be preferable to liability rules.

Of course, one response to this argument is that it reflects the way people have thought, given the existence of the property rule. If property rules had never existed, or had never been widespread, possessors would have no reason to enter into bargaining sessions in the belief that the acquirer was committed to bargaining. If liability rules were the norm, each possessor would anticipate a taking whenever he set his asking price above the liability rule penalty.

This is a suitable response, but it raises new issues, related to bounded rationality. Suppose one of the parties makes a mistake, and fails to learn the precise level of the liability rule penalty. If one of the parties has a mistaken understanding of the liability rule penalty level, takings will occur because of errors in the bargaining process. Specifically, the possessor will set his price at a certain level, thinking it below the liability rule penalty, and the acquirer will take because he thinks the price is above the liability rule penalty. One or both parties may be mistaken.

Is it reasonable to assume that bargaining parties will always be aware of the liability rule penalty? Probably not. At best, both sides may have rough guesses. Takings will occur because there will inevitably be instances in which at least one bargaining party does not have perfect information with respect to the liability rule penalty.

The practice of bargaining with entitlements intact appears to be the norm across societies. Why this is so is a subject worthy of study. The bounded rationality theory may be a key reason for the prevalence of property rules (Smith 2004). Imagine a mixture of property and liability rules applied in low transaction cost settings, for example, property rules for cars, liability rules for bicycles. The conditional bargaining strategy envisioned in the Indifference Proposition requires the parties to know what kind of bargaining process they have entered. This would be a costly and unworkable system of administration. The bounded rationality argument indicates that one of the key functions of property rules is to economize on the information necessary for markets to exist.

One could argue that the bounded rationality assumption takes us outside of the low transaction cost setting. But bounded rationality is such a primitive feature of the human condition that it would be strange to assert that the low transaction cost assumption requires perfect information and perfect ability to process all information. As a theoretical construct useful for analysis, the setting of low transaction costs should at least be consistent with observed human capacities. When the construct of low transaction costs is completely divorced from any notion of human capacities, it serves then only as an assumption that guarantees the efficient Coasean solution in all settings. But once reduced to that status, it no longer serves a useful purpose.

4.4   Predation

It may be rational for acquirers to create a reputation for predation (Milgrom and Roberts 1982). With such a reputation, they will be able to extract a larger share of wealth from the possessors.

Return to the bargaining scenario envisioned in the Indifference Proposition. Suppose the acquirer is a repeat actor, in the sense that he knows that he will meet with other possessors in the future and attempt to acquire bicycles from them. Or, suppose the acquirer is the member of some group or club that transacts with possessors. Under these assumptions, predation may be a rational strategy.

The possessor's reason for engaging in predation runs as follows. If he is a one-shot actor, it will always make sense for the acquirer to accept any price that is less than or equal to the liability rule penalty. Given such a price, the threat to take the bicycle will not be credible. But if he is a repeat transactor, he may reason that if he establishes a reputation as a taker, he will be able to push the possessor down to the lowest price at which the transaction still has value to the possessor. He may reason that he is better off in the long run by suffering a few losses early by taking and then paying the liability rule penalty, because that enables him to establish a reputation as a taker. Once the reputation is established, he will find that in future bargaining sessions, possessors will cut their prices to the bottom end of the bargaining range. In the long run, he profits from the reputation, which enables him to expropriate more wealth from possessors.

The same reasoning applies if the acquirer is a member of a club or from some identifiable region or population subgroup. A few unprofitable takings may be profitable in the long run by building up reputation capital for the group. Once the group is known to consist of takers, possessors will cut their prices immediately when bargaining with them.

Given the likelihood that predation would arise as a rational strategy under the liability rule, takings will occur. This implies that the property rule is preferable to the liability rule.

4.5   Defense

Another problem that the Indifference Proposition fails to take into account is defensive action by the possessor. Recall that the story behind the Indifference Proposition is a bargaining process in which the acquirer shows up to the bargaining table ready to take, and the possessor shows up ready to be victimized. But why would the possessor walk into the bargaining process expecting to be victimized? Why wouldn't the possessor take steps to avoid victimization? If the possessor could take a defensive action that cost $1 in order to avoid an expropriation of $2, he would do so.

Reconsider the bargaining story. Suppose the possessor values the bicycle at $95 and the acquirer values it at $100. The liability rule penalty is set at $85 (the sum of the bicycle's market value $75 and the enforcement cost $10). In the original Indifference Proposition scenario, the possessor realizes that he is better off setting his price at $85 and losing $10 (the difference between his reservation price and the actual transaction price) in a voluntary transfer rather than setting his price at $95 and losing the full amount. In either enforcement scenario, the possessor loses more from a taking followed by enforcement than from a voluntary transfer at the price determined by the liability rule penalty. But the possessor may be able to do better by adopting some defensive measure.

Suppose the possessor invests $1 into a technology that electrically shocks the acquirer when he attempts a taking. The shock does not prevent the taking, it merely imposes a cost. Suppose the cost of the shock, from the perspective of the acquirer, is $12. Now if the acquirer attempts a taking, he will have to "pay" $12. After he has taken the bicycle from the possessor, the acquirer will be prosecuted for the penalty of $85. Under these conditions, the acquirer will accept a voluntary transfer for any price less than or equal to $97. Again, no takings will occur, as the Indifference Proposition predicts. But neither is the possessor expropriated.

Although no taking occurs in this example, the property rule is unambiguously preferable to the liability rule. The reason is that the liability rule induces defensive expenditures that would not be observed under the property rule. Social welfare is greater under the property rule than under the liability rule.

One could argue that a Coasean solution is still possible in this scenario. Suppose the acquirer, realizing that the possessor has the option to invest in a defensive technology, approaches the possessor before the possessor obtains the defensive technology. In this setting, the acquirer can offer to share a larger part of the bargaining surplus with the possessor in exchange for the possessor forgoing the defensive technology. Under this Coasean bargain, the Indifference Proposition re-emerges, and no taking occurs.

The problem with this Coasean solution is that it requires some especially strong assumptions. After the possessor forgoes investment in defense, what would prevent the acquirer from reneging on his promise to share a larger part of the bargaining surplus? Nothing. Unless the acquirer could commit to his promise to share, the possessor would have no incentive to accept a deal in which he forgoes investment in defense. For the Indifference Proposition to be valid, some especially strong assumptions regarding commitment and trust would have to be valid also. Moreover, these assumptions would appear to violate the individual rationality assumption at the heart of this framework (Hylton 2011).

4.6   Information

Information asymmetry provides yet another basis for rejecting the Indifference Proposition. At first glance, informational asymmetry appears to be an unlikely reason for preferring property rules over liability rules. Informational asymmetry often provides a basis for preferring liability rules to property rules. More generally, informational asymmetry makes it difficult to determine whether property rules are socially preferable to liability rules.

In the story behind the Indifference Proposition, the acquirer decides whether to take the possessor's bicycle by comparing the surplus he would gain from a taking with the surplus he would gain from a voluntary transfer. The comparison is made by the possessor in deciding whether to transfer voluntarily or reject a deal.

As I argued in section 3.3, informational asymmetry does not necessarily play a role in this story. For example, consider the case where there is a single, observable, objective price at which the transaction can take place. Both parties compare their own reservation values to the objective price in order to determine whether a taking or a trade will occur. In the model considered above, the single objective price is equal to the liability rule penalty. However, I will show in this part that informational asymmetry may play a role in determining whether a taking will occur, even under assumptions that are most favorable to the no-takings conclusion (section 3.3)

Let V_a be the value that the acquirer places on the bicycle. The acquirer takes whenever

$$V_a - F > V_a - p \tag{1}$$

or when

$$p > F \tag{2}$$

Given the rule determining when the acquirer takes, the possessor will avoid a taking by setting a price equal to the penalty ($p = F$). Thus, informational asymmetry plays no role in determining whether a taking will occur.

But this model is incomplete. The value of a bicycle to the acquirer is likely to depend on the process by which it is transferred. If the bicycle is transferred voluntarily, the former possessor will relinquish all claims on the bicycle. In regimes that record ownership, the former possessor will transfer formal documents registering title to the acquirer. More importantly, the former possessor will not attempt to recapture the item.

The situation is different when the acquirer obtains the bicycle by a taking. The possessor will not relinquish all claims to ownership. He will retain formal documents proving ownership, which could cast a legal cloud over the acquirer's new possession. The possessor will attempt to recapture the item whenever the opportunity presents itself.

In light of these differences, the value of the bicycle to the acquirer should depend on whether he acquires it through a voluntary trade or through a taking. Thus, the decision to take is governed by

$$V_{al} - F > V_{ap} - p \qquad (3)$$

Where V_{al} is the value of the bicycle to the acquirer when it is taken, and V_{ap} is the value of the bicycle when it is obtained in a voluntary transaction.

This complicates matters. In the original version of the Indifference Proposition account, informational asymmetry played no role in the bargaining process because the decision to take was governed completely by the relationship between the transaction price p and the liability rule penalty F. The equilibrium was one without takings because possessors set $p = F$. If a possessor demanded $p > F$, his bicycle would be taken. If a possessor demanded $p < F$, he would be forfeiting surplus. So the possessor avoided takings by setting $p = F$, and no takings occurred. However, in this more complicated version, possessors can no longer avoid takings by setting the transaction price equal to the liability rule penalty.

I will provide an intuitive account of the bargaining process in this more complicated version. Suppose, to simplify, the value of the bicycle to the possessor when obtained through trade is related by a fixed ratio to the value when obtained through a taking:

$$V_{al} = kV_{ap} \qquad (4)$$

where k is less than 1 because the value of the bicycle is worth less when taken than when it is obtained through a voluntary trade. Takings occur when

$$kV_{ap} - F > V_{ap} - p \qquad (5)$$

or when

$$p - F > (1 - k)V_{ap} \qquad (6)$$

By keeping the price low the possessor can avoid a taking. But he has room to raise the price above the liability rule penalty because the surplus from the taking is generally less than the surplus from the voluntary trade. Indeed, the possessor can safely avoid a taking and earn a bit of the surplus by setting his price equal to the liability rule penalty plus the additional surplus gained from a voluntary trade $(1 - k)V_{ap}$. If the possessor knows the reservation valuation of each acquirer, he can set a price that extracts the additional surplus of each transaction and also avoid the taking.

In an informational asymmetry setting, the possessor will not be able to exploit the surplus differential of each acquirer. He could use the average as a basis for setting his price, though that will lead to takings.

The possessor will be able to exploit the bilateral monopoly relationship between the possessor and the acquirer. Suppose the reservation values of acquirers are unknown to the possessor, although the possessor knows the distribution of reservation values. In this case, the possessor is in the same position as a monopolist who knows the demand curve but does not know the reservation price of each counterparty. He will trade off raising the price and scooping out additional surplus from the bargain with reducing the price and suffering a taking. The price that he sets will lead to some takings.

Again, the property rule is preferable to the liability rule. Takings occur under the liability rule, but not under the property rule. The property rule avoids the welfare loss that results from takings.

5.   IMPLICATIONS FOR CRIMINAL LAW

The foregoing discussion has taken a close look at the Indifference Proposition, according to which no takings will be observed under the property rule *and* under the liability rule in the low transaction cost setting, and therefore property and liability rules are equivalent in terms of welfare implications. I have made several points.

First, the welfare implications of property and liability rules diverge once any one of many plausible variations on the low transaction cost assumption is considered. Consider, for example, predatory and defensive actions. The Indifference Proposition's validity depends on acquirers refusing to behave in a predatory fashion, and possessors allowing themselves to be victimized without taking defensive actions.

Once defensive investments are introduced, takings are avoided and expropriation reduced through the adoption of defensive measures by possessors. But the defensive measures, because they are costly, reduce social welfare. The property rule emerges as superior to the liability rule, since defensive measures are not necessary under the property rule. The relative inefficiency of the liability rule appears to be *more severe* in this setting than in the analysis of Calabresi and Melamed. Possessors will invest into the technology of defense up to the value of the property that needs to be defended. And defensive investment can spur countervailing investment into the technology of taking.

It would be difficult to argue persuasively that defensive actions should not be considered to be part of the low transaction cost setting. Some defensive actions will be taken instinctively, others after long thought. Thus, any model that examines conduct in a low transaction cost setting should at least take the possibility of defensive behavior into account.

Second, the Indifference Proposition's prediction that takings will not occur in the low transaction cost settings does not survive a close inspection. If we allow for standard behavioral bargaining patterns, takings will occur because possessors are likely to treat a decision to bargain by the acquirer as a commitment to the bargaining regime. Realizing this, acquirers will take rather than bargain. Alternatively, if we allow for uncertainty over the types of acquirers, and the fact that property obtained from a voluntary transaction is more valuable than that obtained from taking, the bargaining process will fail to generate voluntary transactions all of the time.

When predatory behavior is taken into account, takings are predictable events even in low transaction cost settings. Moreover, one need not assume irrational behavior on the part of predators; predation may be a rational reputation-building strategy than enables actors who wish to acquire property through the market to do so at lower prices. When the takings associated with rational predation occur, they will inevitably lead to costly enforcement actions by the state.

Finally, I should note that even if the Indifference Proposition were correct in its prediction that takings will not be observed, it does not follow that property rules and liability rules are equivalent in terms of welfare implications. Although the Indifference Proposition implies that takings will not occur, expropriation of wealth does occur through pressured transactions (or transactions under duress). No enforcement costs are incurred, given that all transfers are "voluntary," and for this reason social welfare is not reduced as a result of enforcement expenditures. But the expropriation of wealth is likely to have efficiency consequences in any setting in which fear of expropriation reduces market participation or investment by possessors.

In the end, this analysis provides a slightly more complicated defense of the property rule, but it is based on assumptions that are entirely plausible. The result is a more complete defense of the fundamental claim of Calabresi and Melamed: that property rules are preferable in low transaction cost settings and liability rules are preferable in high transaction cost settings.

This simple proposition provides the foundation of a positive theory of criminal law and of tort law.[10] Criminal law is based on the property rule model. Theft, for example, is flatly prohibited rather than regulated to an optimal level by a tort-law approach with compensatory damages.

There are two reasons property rules are observed in criminal law. One, as Posner (1985) argued, is that the takings prohibited by criminal law are generally the types that occur in low transaction cost settings. Theft and robbery are obvious examples. Most thieves and robbers have the option to approach their intended victim and seek a voluntary transaction. Their offenses can therefore be viewed as efforts to "bypass the market" (Posner (1985) at 1196). Although it requires a rather special perspective, battery and rape can also be described as market-bypassing offenses. Since the batterer and the rapist can find markets to satisfy their preferences, their choice of involuntary victims can be viewed as a type of taking. The victims are likely to set an infinite price in a hypothetical transaction, but that does not justify the taking; it merely shows that there is no price at which the transaction could be voluntary. Property rules prohibit such takings by directly enjoining them, or by imposing penalties that completely deter the activity rather than aiming merely to internalize the losses suffered by victims.

The second reason property rules are observed in criminal law is in order to completely deter activity that is virtually always inefficient, whether transaction costs are high or low. Reckless conduct falls into this category. Intentional driving in the wrong direction of a street is prohibited rather than regulated exclusively under the tort law model with compensatory damages.

Posner (1985) describes criminal law doctrine as largely built around the goal of prohibiting efforts to bypass the market. The positive theory set out by Posner is essentially the property rule framework of Calabresi and Melamed. The property rule framework explains why the internalization model observed in tort law should not be extended to criminal law, as urged by Becker (1968). More importantly, the property-liability rules framework provides a predictively accurate theory of the allocation of tort and criminal law rules (Hylton 2005).

The arguments offered here in defense of the property rule framework seem especially applicable to criminal law. Predation, defensive behavior, and bounded rationality are all familiar features of the criminal law enforcement process. Some of the behavior is reflexive and instinctual, or reflects deep personality traits, and therefore cannot be regulated effectively by the law. Where behavior is not based on rational calculation, the law can do little other than to incapacitate the offender by separating him from potential victims.

But this chapter has advanced the argument that criminal law can be justified in terms of its impact on rational actors. Rather than ignoring common behavioral patterns in order to examine the conduct of an ideal hypothetical rational actor, who never engages in predatory conduct, I have considered a more realistic type of rational actor who behaves in a manner familiar in the crime stories. When allowing for this type of rational actor, the property-rules-based justification of criminal law seems clearer and stronger than in earlier analyses.

6.   CONCLUSION

I have surveyed the reasons why property rules and liability rules are not equivalent in terms of their welfare implications in low transaction cost settings. The reasons emphasized here are: defensive actions, predatory actions, bounded rationality. I have also examined informational asymmetry coupled with the fact that property has a greater value under the property rule than under the liability rule.

Certainly, any model that provides a positive theory of law should take into account basic human behavior and characteristics that are relevant to the establishment of property rules. Defense and predation are clearly within the category of basic behavior that should be incorporated into the analysis of property rules. Bounded rationality is also a fundamental characteristic. Informational asymmetry arguably takes us outside of the low transaction cost assumption typically imposed in the analysis of property rules, but this a matter of context.

Because of these four reasons, I have argued in this chapter that property rules are unambiguously superior to liability rules in low transaction cost settings, supporting the main proposition of Calabresi and Melamed. This defense of property rules provides a sturdier foundation for the positive economic theory of criminal law.

NOTES

1. On the theory of property rules and liability rules, see Calabresi and Melamed (1972).
2. For an effort to formalize Posner's argument, see Hylton (2005), which also provides a general survey of substantive criminal law doctrine, though not at the same level of detail as Posner's.
3. See Kaplow and Shavell (1996) at 720 ("As Coase emphasized, if there are no obstacles to the consummation of mutually beneficial bargains, it will make no difference what the legal regime is; thus, it will be irrelevant whether property rules or liability rules apply"). One distinction noted by Kaplow and Shavell is that liability rules may result in multiple takings (or threatened takings), which in the end provides a justification in their analysis for property rules. The proposition that property rules and liability rules are equivalent in low transaction cost settings was first stated in Polinsky (1980). However, Polinsky focuses on the efficiency implications of remedies rather than the incentives for takings.
4. See, e.g., Kaplow and Shavell (1996) at 732–3.
5. Kaplow and Shavell (1996) at 725.
6. One might respond that it is well known that, under informational asymmetry, takings can occur under the liability rule. However, I make two points in the text. The first point is that informational asymmetry does not necessarily lead to takings under the liability rule. Second, I consider a setting in which the liability rule generally "works" (in accordance with the Indifference Proposition), in the sense that no takings occur under low transaction costs, even in the presence of informational asymmetry. Then I introduce the assumption that property is more valuable under the property rule than under the liability rule, and observe that takings do occur under the liability rule.
7. Kaplow and Shavell (1996) at 733 ("Consider first the case in which parties always strike mutually beneficial bargains because they have perfect information about each other. In this case there is no difference between property and liability rules: bargains leading to an optimal result will always be made").
8. The arguments in this part are drawn from Hylton (2006).
9. See Calabresi and Melamed (1972) at Part 4, text accompanying note 66.
10. For a more detailed examination of criminal law using the Calabresi-Melamed framework, see Hylton (2005).

REFERENCES

Becker, Gary S. (1968) "Crime and Punishment: An Economic Analysis," 76 *Journal of Political Economy* 169
Calabresi, Guido and Douglas Melamed (1972) "Property Rules, Liability Rules and Inalienability: One View of the Cathedral," 85 *Harvard Law Review* 1089
Coase, Ronald (1960) "The Problem of Social Cost," 3 *Journal of Law and Economics* 1
Hylton, Keith (2005) "Theory of Penalties and Economics of Criminal Law," 1 *Review of Law and Economics* 175
— (2006) "Property Rules and Liability Rules Once Again," 2 *Review of Law and Economics* 137
— (2011) "Property Rules and Defensive Conduct in Tort Law Theory," 4 *Journal of Tort Law*, Article 5, available at www.bepress.com/jtl/vol4/iss1/art5.
Kaplow, Louis and Shavell, Steven (1996) "Property Rules and Liability Rules: An Economic Analysis," 109 *Harvard Law Review* 713
Milgrom, Paul and Roberts, John (1982) "Predation, Reputation, and Entry Deterrence," 27 *Journal of Economic Theory* 253
Polinsky, A. Mitchell (1980) "Resolving Nuisance Disputes: The Simple Economics of Injunctive and Damage Remedies," 32 *Stanford Law Review* 1075
Posner, Richard (1985) "An Economic Theory of the Criminal Law," 85 *Columbia Law Review* 1193
Smith, Henry E. (2004) "Property and Property Rules," 79 *New York University Law Review* 1719

4 Accuracy in criminal sanctions
Robert A. Mikos

1. INTRODUCTION

Law and economics scholarship suggests that criminal sanctions should equal the harm caused by a crime, divided by the probability the criminal will be detected and punished (Becker 1968; Shavell 2004). The formula for optimal sanctions is thus $S_i = H_i / p$. S_i is the nominal sanction imposed and H_i is the harm caused in an individual case. When the legal sanction is fixed by this formula, it is considered accurate[1] in the sense that it reflects the exact harm caused in a particular case.[2] For example, the sanction for causing $10,000 in harm would be exactly double ($2\times$) the sanction for causing $5000 in harm, holding p constant. As scholars have shown, accurate sanctions give persons optimal incentives to engage (or not) in criminal behavior; namely, they will do so only if the private benefits of crime (b) exceed the harms.

In individual cases, however, criminal law regularly imposes sanctions that are smaller or larger than the ratio H_i / p prescribes (Mikos 2006). For example, suppose that D_1 and D_2 each commit a separate robbery involving the identical criminal act (*actus reus*); e.g., each pushes a victim and grabs a bag containing $100 cash. Suppose, however, that D_1's victim (A) dies of a heart attack triggered by the robbery, while D_2's victim (B) suffers only minor scrapes and bruises. Although D_1 and D_2 have caused dramatically different harms, they would be punished identically in many jurisdictions. In effect, the law would fix their sanctions based (largely) on the *average* harm suffered by robbery victims $(\overline{H})$, as opposed to the actual harm suffered by A or B (H_a, H_b). In algebraic terms, the law uses the formula $\overline{S} = \overline{H}/p$. In other words, in many cases, the law imposes sanctions that are not accurate – or, to be more precise, sanctions that are only accurate on average.

This chapter examines the law and economics of accuracy in criminal sanctions. It suggests that the law's ability to impose sanctions that are accurate on an individualized level is constrained by three information problems: (1) criminals' lack of information, *ex ante*, concerning victim harms; (2) courts' lack of information, *ex post*, concerning harms; and (3) courts' inability to process information concerning harms. As a result of these information problems, the law oftentimes settles for a second-best approach to sanctioning: it imposes sanctions based on the average harm caused by a type of crime (e.g., robbery), as opposed to the actual harm caused by particular episodes of that crime. This approach is second best because it under-protects certain high-harm victims – ones who suffer greater than average harms $(H_h > \overline{H})$, and over-protects low-harm victims – ones who suffer lower-than-average harms $(H_l < \overline{H})$.

We may be stuck with second-best legal sanctions, but the chapter suggests how society could (and does) correct the under-deterrence problem average sanctions generate: encourage high-harm victims to supplement law's protection by buying precautions against crime. Crime victims do not face the same information constraints that courts do. In particular, they know more about the potential harms they would suffer from crime than do criminals (*ex ante*) and courts (*ex post*). What is more, victims can act upon that information and purchase a level of protection customized to their particular needs, including their idiosyncratic harms (Mikos 2006). In fact, imposing legal sanctions based on average harms may spur high-harm victims to buy more precautions against crime, arguably moving the combined public / private criminal justice system closer to providing an optimal level of deterrence against inefficient crime.

The chapter seeks to build upon two distinct lines of research in law and economics scholarship. One line, pioneered by Steven Shavell and Louis Kaplow, analyses the value of accuracy in tort litigation (Kaplow 1994; Kaplow and Shavell 1994; Kaplow and Shavell 1996). It recognizes that the same tort may inflict different levels of harm on different victims. Yet it also recognizes that imposing accurate sanctions (damages) based on the harms caused in individual cases may not be justified, given courts' limited ability to gauge actual harms *ex post* and tortfeasors' limited awareness of them *ex ante*. The research, however, neglects the role of tort victims; namely, it ignores the impact that the accuracy of sanctions could have on victims' levels of care (e.g., Kaplow 1994). This oversight limits the value of the research in the criminal law field, both because (1) victim precautions arguably exceed public expenditures on law enforcement; and (2) individual victims are comparatively well-suited to adjust deterrence based on actual (potential) harms (Mikos 2006).

A second, seemingly unrelated body of research examines private citizens' incentives to purchase precautions against crime (e.g., Ben-Shahar and Harel 1995, 1996; Clotfelter 1977; Hylton 1996). Unlike the accuracy in tort scholarship mentioned above, this line of research puts victim precautions front and center. The research suggests victims generally spend too much (or too little) on precautions against crime because they do not internalize all of the costs and benefits precautions generate. Among other things, precautions can increase (or decrease) third parties' exposure to crime. Unlike the tort scholarship mentioned above, however, this body of criminal law research tends to ignore variance in victim harms. In other words, the research assumes that crime inflicts the same level of harm on all victims (Mikos 2006).[3] It thus proves of limited value in addressing the accuracy problem in criminal law – a problem that only arises if victim harms vary.

In sum, one line of research ignores an important problem (variance in the level of harm) while another line of research ignores a potential solution (victim precautions against harm). This chapter seeks to bridge the gap between these two lines of research. On one hand, it uses extant tort scholarship to illuminate how law should respond to disparities in the harms suffered by *crime* victims. On the other hand, it uses criminal law scholarship to illuminate how law's response – i.e., imposing sanctions based on average harms – could impact victim precautions and fine-tune society's deterrence and distribution of crime.

The chapter proceeds as follows. First, it discusses the law and economics of criminal sanctions. It elaborates upon the three information problems that help explain why the law oftentimes does not impose accurate criminal sanctions. The chapter then examines the costs of inaccurate sanctions. In particular, it suggests that imposing inaccurate sanctions results in an inefficient *level and distribution* of crime. Lastly, the chapter considers ways that society could (and does) improve the efficiency of the system by fine-tuning the protection of victims according to actual harms.

2.   THE LAW AND ECONOMICS OF CRIMINAL SANCTIONS

This section provides some background on the law and economics of criminal sanctions. Law and economics scholarship suggests that criminal sanctions should be designed to force criminals to internalize the harms caused by their behavior. Imposing sanctions based on the harm caused in individual cases (H_i) ensures that legal sanctions will be neither excessive, i.e., they will not deter efficient crimes ($b > H_i$), nor inadequate, i.e., they will deter inefficient ones (where $b < H_i$).

From an economics perspective, sanctions must also be adjusted for the probability of detection (p). Only a small portion of all criminal acts are ever detected, prosecuted, and punished.[4] When $p < 1$, imposing a sanction equal to the harm caused by a crime does not provide adequate deterrence. To provide optimal deterrence, the sanction must be multiplied by the ratio $1 / p$.

The formula for optimal sanctions can be expressed algebraically: $S_i = H_i / p$. Imposing sanctions based on this formula gives rational criminals optimal incentives to engage (or not) in proscribed behavior. Criminals will commit crimes only when the gains (b) exceed the expected sanctions ($S_i * p$), which, in turn, are equivalent to the harm caused (H_i).

In practice, however, the criminal law does not follow the simple sanctioning formula outlined above ($S_i = H_i / p$). Criminal law frequently imposes sanctions greater (or less) than H_i / p in any individual case. To a large extent, criminal law ignores the actual level of harm caused by a discrete criminal act (e.g., D's simple assault of A) and instead calculates sanctions according to the average harm ($\overline{H}$) caused by criminal acts meeting the definition of a particular crime (e.g., simple assault).

Three information problems help explain criminal law's departure from the standard formula ($S_i = H_i / p$): (1) criminals' lack of information, *ex ante*, concerning victim harms; (2) courts' lack of information, *ex post*, concerning victim harms; and (3) courts' inability to process complex information concerning harms. As I explain in more detail below, these three information problems constrain law's ability to impose accurate sanctions and thereby provide truly optimal deterrence. For now, I elaborate upon the information problems and how criminal law has adapted to them.

First, criminals cannot always foresee individualized victim harms *ex ante* (i.e., just before they commit an offense). Criminals might not anticipate a certain type of harm occurring (e.g., a physical injury); or they might not accurately foresee the degree of harm caused by an offense (e.g., the extent of the physical injury). To illustrate, suppose that D robs A of $100. Suppose that A suffers a heart attack and dies as a result of the robbery. *Ex post*, a criminal court would have no problem verifying the harm(s) caused by D. Nonetheless, D might not have foreseen that A would die during the encounter, e.g., A may have looked young and healthy. Instead, D might only have anticipated causing scrapes and bruises, i.e., the usual harms caused by robbery.

From an economic perspective, it makes sense to ignore the unforeseeable harm actually caused and to impose sanctions based only on the harm that was foreseeable *ex ante* (typically, the *average* harm). In our illustration, punishing D for homicide (on top of robbery) would not enhance law's deterrence function; after all, if D could not foresee A's death, he could not foresee the added sanction for homicide either (Kaplow 1994; Kaplow and Shavell 1994, 1996).[5]

Indeed, criminal law generally ignores unforeseeable harms for purposes of grading and sanctioning offenses (Mikos 2006). In many jurisdictions, D would *not* be held criminally liable for A's death. D would be guilty only of robbery (not homicide[6]) and D's sentence would be calculated based (largely) on the average harm caused by robbery, and not the above-average harm D actually caused (Mikos 2006).

Second, courts cannot easily gauge some harms *ex post* (i.e., at sentencing) (Kaplow 1994; Mikos 2006). Consider the loss of sentimental value caused by the theft or destruction of property. Courts have no reliable way of measuring the sentimental value that a victim attached to lost property. A victim could assist a court in measuring sentimental value, e.g., by testifying at a sentencing hearing, but victim testimony may not be availing, for at least two reasons. For one thing, a victim might have questionable motives in providing testimony concerning the magnitude of a loss; e.g., the victim might exaggerate her loss in order to exact revenge on a defendant or to extract higher compensation in restitution. In addition, some victims would not be helpful witnesses, even if they are properly motivated. Many witnesses would struggle to articulate the exact magnitude of a loss suffered. Imagine, for example, a victim trying to explain to a court the sentimental value (in dollar terms, no less) of a wedding ring, a dog, or a family home. In short, harms such as the loss of sentimental value may elude quantification.

As a result of this information problem, the law generally ignores the loss of sentimental value as well as other difficult to quantify harms for purposes of grading and sanctioning offenses (Mikos 2006). To demonstrate, suppose D_1 steals a watch from A and D_2 steals a similar watch from B. The watches are identical models and have identical market values of $1000. Suppose, however, that A was sentimentally attached to his particular copy of the watch, e.g., because it was a cherished graduation present from his father, whereas B had no particular affinity for his watch, e.g., he valued it no more than a replacement copy. A has suffered greater harm, yet D_1's and D_2's offenses would be indistinguishable under the law. D_1 and D_2 both would be sanctioned based only on the market value of the watches they took, and not on any additional sentimental value they may have destroyed. This is so even if D_1 had some prior knowledge of A's sentimental attachment to his watch. In other words, the law ignores some harms not because (or not just because) they are unforeseeable, *ex ante*, but because they are difficult to quantify *ex post* (Mikos 2006).

Third, courts are limited in how much information they can utilize at sentencing (Mikos 2006). In other words, even if courts (*ex post*) and criminals (*ex ante*) could obtain perfect information about the harms caused by a particular criminal offense, courts could not tailor sanctions accordingly. The degree of complexity that would be required to precisely tailor sanctions to all known, foreseeable harms (across more than 21 million criminal cases annually, NCSC (2008)) could easily overwhelm the criminal justice system.

Indeed, the law commonly ignores obvious and foreseeable differences in the magnitude of harm when grading and sanctioning individual criminal offenses. As I have shown elsewhere, the law does this by sorting cases into a finite set of categories, based on the monetary, physical, and psychological harms inflicted:

> In the state of Texas, for example, the criminal code sorts all theft offenses, involving losses
> that range from a few dollars to hundreds of millions of dollars, into just seven distinct grades,

escalating in seriousness from a Class C misdemeanor to a first degree felony as the amount of the pecuniary loss grows. (Mikos (2006) at 331)

Crimes sorted into different categories (e.g., a class C misdemeanor versus a first degree felony) may be punished differently, but crimes sorted into the same category (e.g., two first degree felonies) are generally punished the same (or nearly the same). Under the United States Sentencing Guidelines, for example, the theft of $400,000 carries the same recommended sentence (33–41 months imprisonment) as the theft of $1,000,000, even though the latter offense inflicts 2.5× as much harm as the former (Mikos 2006). The United States Sentencing Commission, the organization responsible for promulgating the Guidelines, has explicitly acknowledged that courts must ignore some information: "a sentencing system tailored to fit every conceivable wrinkle of each case can become unworkable."[7]

In sum, due to common information problems – (1) inability to foresee harms *ex ante*; (2) inability to gauge harms *ex post*; and (3) inability to process complex information – the law ignores variations in harms across cases. In essence, the law imposes sanctions based on the average harm caused by a category of crime, and not the actual harm caused by a particular criminal. Law's failure to impose accurate sanctions may be justified, on balance, by economic considerations (e.g., the cost of obtaining information); but inaccuracy in criminal sanctions has costs that have been minimized (or overlooked) by the law and economics literature. The sections below analyse these costs and consider what steps, if any, society can take to reduce them.

3.   COSTS OF IMPOSING SANCTIONS BASED ON AVERAGE HARM

This section examines the largely overlooked costs of imposing sanctions based on average harm. In a nutshell, it suggests that sanctions based on average harm provide (1) inadequate protection for high-harm victims and (2) excessive protection for low-harm victims. The section illustrates these costs by comparing the total (net) harm of crime under (1) the current system that imposes sanctions based on average harm and (2) a hypothetical system that imposes sanctions based on actual harm. In this hypothetical system, I assume that criminals know exactly how much harm a planned crime would cause each prospective victim. I assume further that courts could easily gauge those harms *ex post* and could also tailor sanctions accordingly on a case by case basis. In short, the system would escape the information constraints discussed above; it would impose accurate sanctions based on the precise harms inflicted in every case and criminals could also foresee those harms before committing crimes.

In a system devoid of information constraints, imposing accurate sanctions would reduce the net harms of crime in two distinct ways. First, it would provide greater protection for high-harm victims. To illustrate, suppose D can only commit one robbery and must choose between A and B. D knows that A has $25,000 in jewelry while B has only $10,000 in jewelry (both market value). The harm to each victim would equal the market value of the jewelry; suppose as well that D only gains 80% of that market value from the crime.[8] Obviously, D would prefer to rob A for a gain of $20,000 rather than B for a gain of only $8000. Under extant doctrine, the law probably would not punish D more severely if he robs A versus B.[9] Instead, it would impose a sanction based on the average harm caused by robberies; if A and B are representative of the population of victims, the average harm $(\overline{H})$ and the sanction would be $17,500 (assuming p = 1). Such a sanction, however, is not high enough to deter D from robbing A, even though the crime is clearly inefficient; D's gain ($20,000) exceeds the expected sanction ($17,500), but does not exceed A's actual loss ($25,000). Imposing accurate sanctions would deter D's crime against A and thereby reduce the net harm of crime by $5000.

Imposing accurate sanctions could also reduce the net harm of crime even if it did not reduce the overall crime rate but merely displaced crime onto lower-harm victims (Mikos 2006).[10] To illustrate, suppose our thief (D) is now entirely indifferent between A or B; e.g., suppose D values A's and B's jewelry at $18,000, even though A's jewelry has 2.5 × the market value.[11] On these facts, neither accurate sanctions nor average sanctions could deter D from robbing B (assuming D is risk-neutral); D's gain ($18,000) exceeds both the average sanction ($17,500) and the accurate sanction ($10,000) that would apply if B were the victim. However, accurate sanctions could give D an incentive to target B in the first instance; *ceteris parabis*, D would prefer a sanction of $10,000 (for B) versus $25,000 (for A). Thus, even if law did not deter D's robbery, it could reduce the net harm D causes by an expected $3500.[12]

Second, accurate sanctions could reduce protection for low-harm victims. Imposing sanctions based on average harms could deter efficient crimes, that is, crimes for which $(p * \overline{S}) > b > H_i$.[13] In the robbery example above, suppose D values A's and B's jewelry at $15,000; A and B continue to value their jewelry at market value ($25,000 and $10,000 respectively). If the legal sanction is set at $17,500, D would not rob A or B, even though robbing B is arguably a socially efficient theft.[14] To be sure, society may not care; namely, it might not count D's ill-gotten gains as part of social welfare. But assuming we count the criminal's gains, and assuming no dynamic costs to theft (a big assumption), the gains of the foregone robbery ($5000) constitute another cost of inaccurate sanctions. On these facts, imposing accurate sanctions would reduce the *net* harm of crime by $5000, even though it would increase the crime rate.

Ultimately, the total societal costs of under- and over-deterrence sketched out above could be substantial. The magnitude of these costs and, conversely, the value of imposing more accurate (individualized) sanctions, depend on the variance in the level of harms across victims. Simply put, the bigger the variance in the level of harms across victims, the more value there is to imposing accurate versus average sanctions.

To illustrate, imagine two possible distributions of the harms caused by thefts the law now would consider equivalent for sanctioning purposes:

Distribution 1: 500, 510, 490, 500, 500
Distribution 2: 100, 500, 900, 500, 500

The average harm in both distributions is identical (500), but the variance is much larger in the second distribution. Not surprisingly, imposing accurate sanctions would generate more value in the second distribution (assuming < 5 thefts). For example, if only one theft occurs, the accurate regime could reduce the harm of the crime by as much as 800 in the second distribution versus only 20 in the first.

In sum, imposing accurate sanctions on perfectly informed criminals would eliminate the costs of under- and over-deterrence that beset our current, second-best approach to sanctioning crime. In the illustration above, D would commit a robbery if – and *only* if – his gain outweighed each victim's (A's or B's) actual loss, as opposed to their average loss. The first-best approach would reduce the crime rate against high-harm victims like A. In particular, it would close a loophole that enables criminals to target high-harm / high-gain victims without risking additional sanctions. And though it might simply increase the crime rate against low-harm victims like B, doing so is arguably socially beneficial, from an economic perspective.[15]

4.   CAN WE FINE-TUNE PROTECTION BASED ON ACTUAL VICTIM HARMS?

In this section, I consider what, if anything, society could do to reduce the costs of our inaccurate sanctioning system. I first consider potential legal reforms; I then consider ways that victims could supplement law's imperfect protection.

4.1   Law Reforms

As the first section demonstrated, law-makers may have already addressed information constraints in the best way possible: by imposing sanctions based on average harms. In other words, our current approach to sanctioning may be optimal, given the information constraints facing courts and criminals. Nevertheless, this section briefly considers three reforms that might improve public law enforcement and reduce crime harms.

First, the law could strive to impose more accurate sanctions when criminals can anticipate victim harms. Indeed, recent sentencing reforms suggest that criminal law may be moving toward a more finely-tuned approach to sanctioning.[16] For example, following the Supreme Court's decision in *United States v. Booker*, judges have been granted more leeway to tailor sanctions according to the discrete circumstances of individual cases. Among other things, the reforms empower judges to impose sanctions that are based more closely on actual harms.[17] To the extent criminals can foresee the harms they cause, a more accurate sanctioning regime would give them better incentives to engage (or not) in proscribed behavior and to avoid high-harm victims.

Simply enabling judges to impose more accurate sanctions, however, does not address the information constraints discussed earlier. Whether or not they are legally obliged to do so, judges might ultimately revert to a charge-based (average) sanctioning approach because they cannot obtain and / or process the information needed to tailor sanctions perfectly according to harms done in individual cases. Granting judges new flexibility only increases the costs and complexity of sanctioning; it does nothing to ameliorate those costs. What is more, empowering judges to tailor sanctions in individual cases could greatly exacerbate a second problem: agency costs. For example, a judge might impose above or below average sanctions in a given case because she rejects the utilitarian theory of punishment, and not because she found an unusual degree of harm in the case. In any event, even if judges could gauge harms cheaply, could utilize that information, and could be properly motivated to serve utilitarian objectives, accuracy would only prove valuable to the extent criminals know something about victim harms *ex ante*.

Second, if law-makers cannot tailor nominal sanctions according to the harm actually caused in each case, they might strive to adjust the probability of detection (p) instead. In theory, police could devote more resources to protecting high-harm victims from crime. For example, the police could station a patrol near the homes of high-harm victims. Criminals would have an incentive to avoid high-harm victims because p is (presumably) higher in the presence of the police. Importantly, criminals would not need to foresee victim harms *ex ante*; they would only need to observe the added police presence. The extra police would raise the expected sanction for targeting high-harm victims, even though the nominal sanction (S) remained constant (i.e., based on average harm).[18]

As a practical matter, it is conceivable that the police could tailor protection more accurately than courts currently tailor sanctions. The reason is that police are less constrained than courts by cumbersome procedural guarantees. For example, the police could provide more protection to one potential victim based on far less than proof beyond a reasonable doubt that the victim would suffer above-average harms. In fact, the police probably already devote more protective resources to high-harm victims; e.g., the police devote far more resources patrolling school yards than they do patrolling parks frequented only by adults.

The strategy, however, has limits. It seems implausible to expect police to tailor protection on an individual victim basis. The police simply do not know (*ex ante*) how much harm A, B, or C would suffer from a crime. More realistically, police probably know that some groups (e.g., children) tend to suffer more harm than other groups from the same criminal incident. But even if they could ratchet-up protection of high-harm groups, they would still leave high-harm members of those groups under-protected and low-harm members over-protected.

Third, law-makers could calculate sanctions based on the harm suffered by high-harm victims, rather than average harm. Doing so would address the under-deterrence problem analysed above. To illustrate, suppose our thief, D, is once again choosing between two targets, A and B. As before, A has $25,000 in property, whereas B has $10,000 in property. Instead of imposing a sanction based on average harm ($17,500), suppose the law imposed a sanction based on the highest-harm case ($25,000) (assuming p = 1). Unless D gained more than $25,000 from this offense, the sanction would deter him from committing theft; it would protect high-harm victims like A as well as low-harm victims like B.

However, basing sanctions on highest harm instead of the average (or actual) harm is flawed, for two reasons. First, high-harm sanctions could undermine marginal deterrence. In our example, D might as well rob A if he gains at least $1 more than by robbing B, even though targeting A causes $15,000 more harm. Second, imposing high-harm sanctions would exacerbate the over-deterrence problem discussed above. To illustrate, suppose D values B's property at $20,000 and cannot acquire it through a voluntary transaction. The transfer would generate societal gains of $10,000; however, imposing a sanction based on the harm that A would have suffered ($25,000) would deter D.

In short, the government's power to impose accurate sanctions that shape criminal behavior is severely limited. Due to various information problems, accurate sanctions are cost-prohibitive and / or ineffective. To be sure, there is no reason to assume that the current legal regime has necessarily chosen the optimal level of accuracy. Government could probably tweak the current approach, e.g., by tailoring the probability of detection or by empowering judges to depart from lumpy grading and sentencing guidelines. But any reforms would still fall far short of the optimal sanctioning approach hypothesized above.

4.2   Victim Precautions

Governments have limited ability to fine-tune criminal sanctions and provide optimal deterrence against crime. Victims, however, are not as constrained as government officials. In a nutshell, "victims know more about their idiosyncratic losses *ex ante*" than do courts "and they can act on that information by taking more or less private precaution, as the situation dictates" (Mikos (2006) at 342).

To begin, victims do not face the same information gaps constraining government officials. A victim knows, for example, how much cash she keeps in her wallet; she knows that a particular possession, such as a diamond ring, holds sentimental value and how much; and she likely knows whether she would suffer unusually severe harms from crime due to a medical condition (such as heart arrhythmia). To be sure, victims do not always have perfect information about the harms they would suffer from crime; but in many situations, victims can gauge harms far more accurately than can criminals, police, and judges.

Just as importantly, victims can act on that knowledge. They can take a variety of precautions against crime to supplement the protection provided by government. For example, victims can lock doors, hide valuable property, install alarm systems, avoid crime-prone neighborhoods, carry concealed firearms, and so on.

Such precautions benefit potential victims in at least two ways. First, precautions can reduce the probability that a particular individual would become the victim of a crime. Precautions do this by making it more difficult for criminals to perpetrate crimes against particular victims. Suppose, for example, that a victim locks up her sentimental keepsake in a safe. Doing so would make it more difficult for a criminal to steal that particular piece of property. The thief would need safe-cracking skills or some other means by which to pry open the safe.

Second, victim precautions can increase the chances that a criminal would be caught and punished for a crime.[19] Suppose that our victim simply marks her property, e.g., by inscribing her name on it. A simple precaution such as this can help police easily determine the true ownership of goods; if the police apprehend D with property they suspect is stolen, markings on the property could help them validate (or not) those suspicions in very little time. As a practical matter, these precautions increase the probability of detection (p) for crimes committed against the victims who take them.[20]

To some extent, victim precautions are a substitute for government (police) protection. By taking precautions, victims reduce the need for government protection; and by providing protection, government reduces the need for victim precautions. However, victim precautions can also supplement government protection. Government can provide a baseline level of protection and victims can add more protection to suit their needs.

Indeed, inaccurate sanctions may encourage high-harm victims to take more precautions.[21] The law's shortcoming acts like an insurance policy deductible. It gives high-harm victims an incentive to buy more precautions to protect themselves. Naturally, one would expect high-harm victims to buy the most private precautions – certainly more than low-harm victims, given the comparatively high benefit of precaution taking for them. In essence, the possibility of victim precautions reduces one of the problems outlined above – the problem that law provides inadequate protection for high-harm victims.

The societal benefit of precaution-taking by high-harm victims is twofold. First, criminals may forego certain crimes altogether if they cannot target high-harm victims. Suppose D gains 80% of what his victim loses ($20,000 from robbing A and $8000 from robbing B). As discussed above, sanctions based on average harm would deter D from robbing B but not A. Suppose, however, that A took precautions, e.g., A locked up his jewelry in a safe or bought a handgun; these precautions might cause D to forego theft altogether, thereby reducing the crime rate and the harms of crime to society.[22]

Second, even if the precautions do not deter crime, they might displace it onto lower-ham victims. This, in turn, would reduce the total harm of crime to society, even if it does not affect the crime rate. Suppose D would gain $20,000 by robbing either A or B. The harms to each victim remain the same ($25,000 for A and $10,000 for B). Accurate sanctions would not deter D from robbing B, but they might deter D from robbing A; and in so doing, the sanctions would reduce the harm of the crime by $15,000. In other words, displacing crime may have economic benefits – a point that has been overlooked in the law and economics and criminology literature (Mikos 2006).

Of course, relying on victims to supplement law's protection is not a perfect solution for the problems identified above. It does not address the over-deterrence problem; low-harm victims would still be over-protected by average sanctions. What is more, victims still do not have the incentive to take the optimal level of precautions. Such precautions generate externalities that victims do not have to consider. For example, if A's precaution merely shifts the theft onto B, A will not consider the harm B suffers, only the benefit to himself (i.e., the reduction in his own crime risk). The harm B suffers would (probably) be less than the harm A would have suffered, but the savings might not exceed the cost of the precaution itself. There are various other factors that could distort the market for victim precautions. Some high-harm victims may not have enough wealth to afford precautions; some victims may not have accurate information concerning the probability of crime; and precaution-taking by high-harm victims could push low-harm victims to take precautions as well (Mikos 2006).

Nonetheless, I want to suggest that victims could help reduce the costs associated with a second-best sanctioning system constrained by information problems. Victims can supplement law's imperfect protection. In essence, they can help achieve a level of tailoring impossible for public law enforcement to accomplish. As I have argued elsewhere, "victims can do what police, prosecutors, and courts cannot; victims can finely tune the level of crime protection to achieve a more efficient [level and] distribution of crime in society" (Mikos (2006) at 341). Scholarship has overlooked this important role for victims because most criminal law and economics scholarship assumes victims are homogeneous and most law and economics scholarship concerning accuracy ignores victim-precaution taking altogether.

5.   CONCLUSION

Victims of similar criminal acts oftentimes suffer significantly different harms. In many cases, however, the law is unable to impose accurate sanctions based on actual harms because information problems pervade the criminal justice system. Criminals oftentimes do not know who the high-harm victims are *ex ante*. Courts oftentimes cannot confirm certain types of harms *ex post*. And even when they can, courts cannot always utilize the information they have in their possession. As a result, the law commonly treats dissimilar cases alike. Within large bounds, law imposes the same expected sanction on crimes inflicting different levels of harm.

There may not be anything law can do about this. The law may currently operate on an "optimal" level, given the aforementioned information constraints. But victims of crime are not so constrained. They have information that criminals and courts do not concerning the actual harms that would be suffered as the result of a crime. They can also act upon that information, by taking precautions against crime. Indeed, the law may give high-harm victims an incentive to do so, by failing to protect them adequately. To be sure, the precautions taken by high-harm victims may simply displace crime onto low-harm victims. But there is still a societal benefit to this, namely, a reduction in the harmfulness of the crime. Victim incentives are far from optimal; but victims may play a useful – and heretofore largely neglected – role in supplementing an imperfect criminal justice system.

NOTES

1. The law and economics literature defines "accurate sanctions" as sanctions that reflect the harms caused in an individual case. Cf. Kaplow and Shavell (1996). To my mind, it would be more apt to say that such sanctions are individualized; after all, a sanction could be accurate on average, even if it did not reflect the harms of the particular case in which it was imposed. However, this chapter generally uses the more common definition of accuracy used in the literature.
2. Accurate sanctions also reflect the precise probability that the particular criminal act would be detected and punished (p_i). In the final section, I consider how manipulating the probability of detection in individual cases could improve the accuracy of criminal sanctions; otherwise, I assume the probability of detection is identical across all cases (= p).
3. In Mikos (2006), I criticize the assumption of victim homogeneity on two grounds. First, on a theoretical level, the assumption fails to explain why homogeneous victims purchase heterogeneous levels of precaution. Second, it ignores the fact that crime definitions are quite broad and thus allow (and perhaps even require) courts to impose identical sanctions, even when cases involve different levels of harm. This chapter builds on and extends Mikos (2006).
4. Clearance rates provide one rough metric of the probability of detection (p). The clearance rate refers to the percentage of reported crimes for which law enforcement officials arrest, charge, and prosecute a suspect. The clearance rate, however, overstates the probability of detection. First, some crimes are never reported and are thus not included in the denominator used to calculate clearance rates. Second, some prosecutions do not result in convictions (or sanctions), but are nonetheless included in the numerator.
5. A's death would not necessarily go unpunished in a utilitarian system. Rather, punishment for A's death would be distributed among all robbers, as long as it is incorporated as part of the average harm of robbery.
6. The felony murder rule (FMR) represents an exception. In general, the FMR holds defendants criminally liable for any death that occurs in the course of a felony, even if that death is not foreseeable *ex ante*. The FMR does not, however, undermine the general point that criminal law ignores unforeseeable harms. Not all jurisdictions recognize the FMR, and, in any event, the FMR does not apply to non-lethal harms that are unforeseeable.

7. U.S.S.G. § 1A.1 cmt. 3 (2005).
8. D might gain less than the market value because, e.g., he cannot use the goods openly or because he must pay a fence to dispose of the property.
9. At the very least, the law is highly unlikely to punish D 2.5× as much for robbing A as opposed to B.
10. As I discuss in Mikos (2006), the law and economics literature has completely overlooked the prospect of efficient displacement of crime.
11. Suppose, e.g., that D gleans 72% of the market value of the stolen jewelry, but also attaches $11,000 in sentimental value to B's jewelry.
12. I assume that D would choose his victim randomly if the law did not give him an incentive to consider victim harms. The robbery of A would result in a societal loss of $7,000 more than the robbery of B.
13. The notion of efficient crime is controversial in law. For present purposes, I simply assume (without endorsing) that law values a criminal's gains from crime and thus that law should not deter all crimes, only those crimes for which a criminal's gains are exceeded by her victim's losses.
14. I say only "arguably" because I have ignored the indirect costs of theft. For a discussion of the societal cost of theft, see Hasen and McAdams (1997).
15. Obviously, I do not claim that imposing accurate sanctions is feasible; nor do I claim that criminals are perfectly informed about victim harms. I merely set up the construct to highlight the costs of the information constraints discussed earlier.
16. Legal scholars characterize sentencing systems as real or charge based. In a charge offense system, cases are graded and sentenced based on the elements of the offense, rather than on any special circumstances of the incident that occurred. In other words, the categories of criminal offenses are limited, largely in order to cabin the discretion of sanctioning judges and promote (at least superficial) uniformity across cases. In a real offense system, by contrast, judges are empowered to adjust sanctions according to the circumstances of each case, including idiosyncratic harms.
17. *United States v. Booker*, 543 U.S. 220 (2005). Of course, judges may also use their freedom to adjust sanctions based on other factors as well, such as the characteristics of the defendant.
18. To illustrate, suppose the law imposed the same nominal sanction $(\bar{S})$ in all cases involving a particular type of crime; $\bar{S}$ would be based on the average harm $(\bar{H})$ for the crime, divided by the average probability of detection $(\bar{p})$. Suppose $\bar{p} = .10$ Suppose further that law enforcement officials know how much harm prospective victims would suffer *ex ante*; what is more, they can raise the actual probability of detection for high-harm victims to p_h (e.g., by shifting police patrols) and correspondingly lower it for low-harm victims to p_l, whereby $p_h > \bar{p} > p_l$. In our robbery example, where A would lose $25,000 and B would lose $10,000 from theft, the nominal sanction in both cases would be $175,000 ($17,500 / .10). However, the expected sanction would be accurate if $p_h = 14.3\%$ and $p_l = 5.7\%$.
19. One might assume that victims would be largely indifferent to catching a criminal, since much of the benefit goes to society at large, and not the victim. After all, as long as a victim is chosen at random, it seems unlikely the criminal would target the same victim twice. Putting the criminal behind bars (incapacitation) would thus benefit the general population, and not just the victim. However, victims do gain something extra when a criminal is caught. They might be compensated by the criminal (that is a benefit which is not shared generally). And in the case of someone who loses an article that has sentimental value, the return of that article could undo the harm.
20. Some unobservable precautions would also increase p for all victims. LoJack is a prime example (Ayres and Levitt 1998).
21. This point builds on the work of Ben-Shahar and Harel (1995) and Hylton (1996), who suggest that criminal law could manipulate victim incentives to self-protect. Hylton assumes that victims take too few precautions; he suggests that law could encourage them to take more precautions by lowering the legal sanction for crime. Ben-Shahar and Harel (1995) suggest that law could adopt a comparative fault approach to imposing sanctions; namely, courts could adjust criminal sanctions based on the optimality of the precautions the victim took. The authors, however, do not consider variations in the level of harm across victims; hence, they do not recognize that law may already incentivize precaution-taking by some victims imposing sanctions based on average harms.
22. The benefit to society would depend, of course, on the cost of the precautions as well as the reduction in crime harms.

REFERENCES

Ayres, Ian and Levitt, Steven (1998) "Measuring Positive Externalities from Unobservable Victim Precaution: An Empirical Analysis of LoJack," 113 *Quarterly Journal of Economics* 43

Becker, Gary (1968) "Crime and Punishment: An Economic Approach," 76 *Journal of Political Economy* 169

Ben-Shahar, Omri and Harel, Alon (1995) "Blaming the Victim: Optimal Incentives for Private Precautions against Crime," 11 *Journal of Law, Economics and Organization* 435

— (1996) "The Economics of the Law of Criminal Attempts: A Victim-Centered Perspective," 145 *Pennsylvania Law Review* 299

Clotfelter, Charles (1977) "Public Services, Private Substitutes, and the Demand for Protection Against Crime," 67 *American Economic Review* 867

Hasen, Richard and McAdams, Richard (1997) "The Surprisingly Complex Case Against Theft," 16 *International Review of Law and Economics*

Hylton, Keith (1996) "Optimal Law Enforcement and Victim Precaution," 27 *Rand Journal of Economics* 197

Kaplow, Louis (1994) "The Value of Accuracy in Adjudication: An Economic Analysis," 23 *Journal of Legal Studies* 307

Kaplow, Louis and Shavell, Steven (1994) "Accuracy in the Determination of Liability," 37 *Journal of Law and Economics* 1

— (1996) "Accuracy in the Assessment of Damages," 39 *Journal of Law and Economics* 191

Mikos, Robert (2006) "'Eggshell' Victims, Private Precautions, and the Societal Benefits of Shifting Crime," 105 *Michigan Law Review* 307

NCSC (National Center for State Courts) (2007) *Examining the Work of State Courts: An Analysis of State Court Caseloads*

Shavell, S. (2004) *Foundations of Economic Analysis of Law*

5 Wealth redistribution and the social costs of crime and law enforcement
*Avraham D. Tabbach**

1. INTRODUCTION

Redistributing wealth from the rich to the poor is an exercise in balancing marginal social costs and benefits. The social benefits derive from the idea that people have decreasing marginal utilities of wealth (poor individuals value the marginal dollar more than do rich individuals) or that the social welfare function exhibits aversion to inequality (individuals in a given society tend to prefer equality). The social costs involved are associated with the administration of the wealth redistribution and the use of distortionary, rather than lump sum, taxes.

This chapter argues that redistribution generates additional social benefits or costs of a completely different kind, namely, its impact on the social costs of crime and law enforcement. I show that, in a broad range/set of circumstances, redistribution reduces these costs and (back-of-the-envelope calculations suggest) to a significant extent. This serves as an additional justification for progressive taxation, indicating that the scope of redistribution should be greater than what is usually recommended in the public finance literature.

The kernel of the argument put forth here is grounded in the notion that it is generally cheaper to enforce the law on the rich than on the poor, for two cumulative reasons: first, because monetary sanctions are less costly than enforcement efforts in achieving any particular level of deterrence, and, second, because, for obvious reasons, monetary sanctions cannot exceed offenders' level of wealth. Thus, the greater offenders' level of wealth, more deterrence can be achieved at no additional cost or the same level of deterrence can be maintained at a lower cost through appropriate reduction of the enforcement efforts. A redistribution of wealth from the rich to the poor would increase the possible fine for the latter, thereby reducing the social costs of enforcing the law on them, and reduce it for the former, thereby increasing the social costs with regard to them. Whether or not redistribution is socially desirable becomes, then, a question of the relative magnitudes of these benefits and costs, a question of the trade-off between the social costs of enforcing the law on the rich and the social costs vis-à-vis the poor.

As this chapter will demonstrate, this trade-off depends, amongst other things, on how the benefits from the harmful act are distributed (the shape and range of the distribution function, which is assumed to be the same for all individuals), whether the probability of punishment can vary across poor and rich individuals (the technology of law enforcement), and how wealthy the given society is in general. While I show that redistribution of wealth towards greater equality is socially desirable in a wide set of circumstances, there are certain circumstances in which the reverse is true and greater inequality is socially preferable. These latter circumstances, presumably less common, are more likely to arise in poorer societies. Thus, a pattern may emerge in which greater equality generates in richer countries additional social benefits in the form of reduced social costs of crime and law enforcement, while in poorer countries, it is more likely to be associated with additional social costs.[1]

As an illustration of the argument that redistribution may reduce the social costs of crime and law enforcement, let us consider Example 1.

> *Example 1*: Suppose that rich individuals and poor individuals have monetary resources of $12,000 and $6000, respectively, and can both engage in a certain harmful act from which they obtain benefits that range uniformly from $0 to $2000 and that causes harm of $1500. Further suppose that given the costs of law enforcement, optimal enforcement requires setting the probability of punishment, which we will assume to be identical for all, at 0.2 and the fine at $7500.

Under these circumstances, poor offenders will pay, if apprehended, their entire wealth ($6000). They face an expected sanction of $1200 ($6000 × 0.2) and therefore are under-deterred, in the sense that some of the poor will commit the harmful act even though the harm exceeds the benefits they obtain (1500 > 1200). Wealthy offenders, in contrast, if apprehended, will pay less than their entire wealth ($7500); their expected sanction is $1500 ($7500 × 0.2), and accordingly, they are "perfectly" deterred, in the sense that no rich individual who commits (refrains from) the harmful act will derive benefits that are less (greater) than the harm generated. Now, say we redistribute $1000 from the rich to the poor so that, respectively, they have monetary resources of $11,000 and $7000. This will have no impact on the level of deterrence for the rich, because they will still face an expected sanction of $1500 ($7500 × 0.2); it will, however, enhance the deterrence of the poor, as they now will face the higher expected sanction of $1400 ($7000 × 0.2). The latter increase in deterrence will reduce social harm because poor individuals were previously under-deterred, and moreover, this outcome would entail no social costs, because enforcement efforts have not been changed. Thus, redistribution increases social welfare.[2] In this simple illustration redistribution was socially desirable because, amongst other things, poor individuals were under-deterred, while rich individuals were perfectly deterred, but, as will be shown in this chapter, the point holds under broad circumstances.

As already mentioned, redistribution is not always socially desirable and there are certain circumstances in which inequality may be preferable. One possible reason (discussed in section 5.3) is that the benefits from harmful acts for *all* individuals are sufficiently high relative to wealth. Example 2 illustrates this point:

> *Example 2*: Suppose that rich individuals and poor individuals have monetary resources of $12,000 and $6000, respectively, and they can engage in some harmful act from which they will obtain benefits that range from $12,000 to $14,000 and that causes harm of $13,000.

Under these circumstances, there is no point in investing any resources in law enforcement, even if it is very cheap, because all individuals would commit the harmful act regardless (the minimum benefits are equal to or greater than the maximum expected sanction). Redistributing wealth from the rich to the poor is obviously pointless. However, suppose that $1000 were redistributed from the poor to the rich, giving the latter $13,000 while the former remain with $5000. Under this scenario, rich potential offenders could be perfectly deterred by setting the probability of punishment at 1, assuming, for simplicity, that enforcement efforts are virtually costless, and the magnitudes of the fines at $13,000, so that the expected sanction for the rich ($13,000 × 1) is equal to the harm, $13,000. Under the same scheme, poor individuals would be completely undeterred as their expected sanction ($5000 × 1) would be less than their minimum expected benefit ($12,000). Since, with redistribution, deterrence of the rich is increased from zero to perfect deterrence, while deterrence of the poor remains unchanged, social welfare is enhanced. In this example, more unequal wealth distribution is socially desirable because, amongst other things, the original distribution of wealth results in no deterrence at all. However, the point that unequal distribution may be socially beneficial holds more generally and in different circumstances, as discussed in sections 4, 5.3, and 5.4.

The arguments in this chapter are not founded on the notion that the poor are more likely to break the law because they derive greater utility from doing so (i.e., the poor have greater needs), or because the opportunity costs of crime are lower for them (i.e., the poor derive less utility from legitimate alternatives), or because they suffer less from imprisonment (i.e., the opportunity costs of time are lower for them), or because the greater the level of inequality, the greater the benefits of criminal behavior and thus the greater the likelihood of its occurrence (i.e., the potential pay-off from theft or burglary is higher). Rather, this chapter assumes identical distribution of the benefits and harm resulting from a given harmful act across all individuals, rich or poor.[3] These premises are roughly applicable with regard to many types of harmful acts, such as leisure-related offenses (littering the beach, double-parking, and so on) and certain violent crimes. However, the framework and analysis I present in this chapter can be extended to more traditional property crimes and can incorporate the observations pointed out above as well.

This chapter is motivated in part by the existing literature on crime and law enforcement, which examines extensively the theoretical and empirical relationships between deterrence and income distribution in society.[4] Both theory and empirical evidence suggest a positive correlation between crime and wealth inequality, but the effects are not clear-cut.[5] However, very few works have explored the *normative* question of the social desirability of redistributing wealth from the perspective of crime and law enforcement. These questions, it should be stressed, are different, because social welfare may be greater as a result of redistribution even if the crime rate remains the same or even rises, as demonstrated in this chapter.

The literature on crime and law enforcement which explores the normative rather than the positive effects of redistribution includes, amongst others,[6] papers by Benoit and Osborne (1995) and Demougin and Schwager (2000). Both papers, however, differ significantly from the inquiry undertaken here in several aspects. In particular, both focus on the political mechanism by which wealthy individuals would seek to finance welfare transfers to the poor in order to "purchase" security, whereas this chapter adopts the standard of social welfare maximization. In addition, the forces that drive the results in these papers are markedly different from those in the present chapter. For example, under the Demougin and Schwager (2000) model, only the poor are potential criminals and the rich are classified as the victims, whereas in Benoit and Osborne (1995), the possibility that innocent people will be punished is included as an important explanatory variable for the results. None of these parameters are present in the model set forth.

This chapter builds on the work of Polinsky and Shavell (1984, 1991) and of Garoupa (2001), which explore the optimal probability and severity of punishment when wealth varies across individuals. However, these authors did not consider either the possibility or the social desirability of wealth redistribution in reducing the social costs of crime and law enforcement, which is the focus of this chapter.

The chapter is organized as follows. Section 2 unfolds the general model, and section 3 demonstrates that greater or even perfect equality is socially desirable if, amongst other things, the probability of punishment is uniform for all offenders. Section 4 shows that greater equality in wealth distribution is also generally desirable if the probability of punishment can vary across individuals but that there are circumstances in which greater or even perfect inequality is socially preferable. Section 5 refines the basic model presented in section 2 and examines the robustness of the results. It too points to circumstances in which perfect equality is socially undesirable, even if the probability of punishment is uniform for all individuals. Section 6 concludes and the Appendix contains the formal proofs.

2.   THE MODEL[7]

Risk-neutral individuals contemplate whether to commit a harmful act causing harm of h. Each individual obtains benefits b which are assumed to be distributed uniformly on the support $[0, \hat{b}]$.[8] Assume that, for some individuals, the benefits exceed the harm, $\hat{b} > h$, implying that some harmful acts are socially desirable. This, however, is not crucial for the results. Following Polinsky and Shavell (1984, 1991), further assume that the benefits and harm resulting from the harmful act are not contingent on the level of wealth of individuals or the distribution of wealth among individuals.[9]

If an individual does commit the harmful act, he will face some probability of being caught and fined. Assume that the fine may depend on offenders' wealth or, alternatively, that it is set regardless of wealth, but those offenders who lack the resources to pay the fine in full pay all that they have. The maximum feasible fine f is, therefore, constrained to the level of wealth of offenders, which, in turn, depends on how all the wealth in society is distributed amongst all individuals. If wealth is distributed equally, the level of wealth and, hence, the maximum feasible fine for each individual will be $\overline{w}$. However, wealth is generally not distributed equally in most societies. For simplicity, assume that the total population, which is normalized and set at 1, is divided into two equally-sized groups,[10] Rich, R, and Poor, P. Poor individuals have a wealth level of $w_P(\geq 0)$, and rich individuals $w_R(>0)$, where $w_P \leq w_R$ and $w_P + w_R = 2\overline{w}$.

The social planner can affect the distribution of wealth in society by transferring wealth from rich individuals to poor individuals or vice versa. Without loss of generality, it is assumed that the rich individuals are at least as rich as the poor individuals following the redistribution. Together, these imply that the amount of wealth redistributed from the rich to the poor, x, should satisfy $-w_P \leq x \leq w_R - w_P/2$.[11] To abstract from other issues commonly related to redistribution, it is assumed that wealth redistribution is costless, entailing neither administrative costs nor incentive effects beyond those associated with engaging in the harmful act. Coupled with the assumption that all individuals have identical, linear utility functions, this assumption implies that redistribution is relevant if and only if it affects the social costs of crime and law enforcement. It also suggests an alternative interpretation of the model, developed in the Appendix, according to which the social planner sets directly the wealth levels of the poor and rich, $w_P(\geq 0)$ and $w_R(>0)$ subject to $w_P \leq w_R$ and $w_P + w_R = 2\overline{w}$. Thus, the notions of greater or less wealth equality and redistribution are treated as equivalent and used interchangeably in this chapter.

The enforcement technology is assumed at the outset to be "general" in nature or "non-discriminatory," so that the probability of punishment must be identical for all individuals. This is justified if it is difficult to adjust enforcement efforts in accordance with wealth, for example, if poor and rich individuals offend in the same area and it is hard to identify whether offenders are rich or poor prior to resources being spent on enforcement. The alternative, that enforcement efforts are "specific" in nature or "discriminatory" so that the probability of punishment can vary across individuals, emerges as significant and will be analysed in section 4.[12] Assume that the costs of enforcement, which are given by the function $c(p)$, are not contingent on the distribution of wealth in society, but, rather, are identical for all offenders, and that this cost function exhibits decreasing or constant marginal returns, so that $c'(p) > 0$ and $c''(p) \geq 0$.

Social welfare or, equivalently, the social costs of crime and law enforcement, amount to the sum of benefits obtained by individuals who commit the harmful act, less the harm done, and less the enforcement costs. To determine social welfare, observe that all individuals, rich or poor, will commit the harmful act if and only if the benefits they derive exceed the expected sanction they face, that is, if $b > pf_i$, $i = P, R$. Hence, social welfare before redistribution can be expressed as:

$$SW = \frac{1}{2} \int_{pf_P}^{b} (b - h)g(b)db + \frac{1}{2} \int_{pf_R}^{b} (b - h)g(b)db - c(p) \qquad (1)$$

The usual social problem is to choose the probability and severity of punishment that maximize social welfare. The main purpose of this chapter is to consider the conditions under which redistributing wealth increases or reduces social welfare or, more generally, the optimal level of redistribution (i.e., the optimal distribution of wealth).

3. GENERAL ENFORCEMENT

Our analysis of the social desirability of redistributing wealth will be conducted in two steps. First, we will depict the optimal law enforcement scheme (the optimal probability and severity of punishment) given some unequal distribution of wealth, and then we will analyse whether social welfare can be augmented by way of wealth redistribution. The optimal distribution of wealth is directly derived in the Appendix.

3.1 Optimal Enforcement Scheme

The optimal probability and optimal severity of punishment for a certain unequal distribution of wealth are arrived at by solving the constrained maximization problem (1), which is characterized by the following lemma (see Polinsky and Shavell 1984):

Lemma 1:   (1) The optimal fine for poor offenders is equal to their entire wealth, $f_P^* = w_P$. (2) The optimal fine for rich offenders is equal to their entire wealth or is set according to the multiplier principle, whichever is less, $f_R^* = \min [w_R, h/p^*]$. (3) The optimal probability of punishment gives rise to two scenarios: (a) under-deterrence of poor individuals but perfect deterrence of rich individuals, that is, $p^*f_P^* < h = p^*f_R^*$, which occurs if $f_R^* = h/p^* < w_R$, or (b) under-deterrence of both poor and rich individuals, that is, $p^*f_P^* < p^*f_R^* < h$, which occurs if $f_R^* = w_R$. (4) Poor individuals inevitably face a lower expected sanction and, therefore, are less deterred than rich individuals, $p^*f_P^* < p^*f_R^*$.[13]

Proof: See Polinsky and Shavell (1984).

The explanation of Lemma 1 is roughly as follows. If enforcement efforts were costless and offenders' wealth sufficiently large, the optimal expected sanction would equal harm for both the rich and the poor. This would guarantee that individuals would commit the harmful act if and only if the benefits they derive were to exceed the harm. However, since enforcement efforts are costly while fines are socially costless, the optimal fine for *poor* individuals should amount to their entire wealth; otherwise social welfare could be increased by raising the fine to its maximum level and possibly reducing the probability of punishment without affecting deterrence. This is Becker's (1968) argument. A certain degree of under-deterrence with respect to the *poor* is socially optimal, because at the starting point of perfect deterrence (i.e., the expected sanction equals the harm) the net harm imposed by the marginal poor offenders is virtually zero. Therefore, a slight reduction in the probability of punishment saves enforcement costs at no cost. This is Polinsky and Shavell's point. Since the probability of punishment is the same for all offenders, rich individuals cannot optimally face a lower expected sanction than poor individuals do, for otherwise, social welfare could be increased at no cost by increasing the sanction imposed on the rich, which would be feasible. The rich can be optimally under-deterred, but then the fine imposed on them must be equal to their entire wealth. The rich can also be perfectly deterred, but then they should not face a fine that is equal to their entire wealth but rather one that is set according to the multiplier principle, i.e., equal to the harm divided by the probability of punishment, so that the expected sanction will equal the harm. As Polinsky and Shavell emphasize, Becker's argument for increasing the fine to its maximum and reducing the probability of punishment appropriately is no longer valid, because it comes at the expense of increasing under-deterrence of the poor, since the probability of punishment must be the same for all. This completes the explanation of Lemma 1.

Having described the optimal enforcement scheme, let us now prove that greater equality increases social welfare, first for situations in which the poor are under-deterred and the rich perfectly deterred (Scenario (a)) and then for situations in which the poor and rich are both under-deterred (Scenario (b)).

3.2   Poor Individuals Under-deterred; Rich Individuals Perfectly Deterred

Suppose first that the optimal enforcement scheme is characterized by Scenario (a) as illustrated in Figure 5.1.

This implies that the fine imposed on the poor is equal to their total wealth (they face

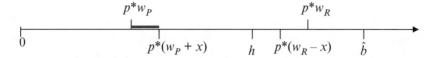

Figure 5.1   Redistribution, levels of deterrence and expected sanctions (Scenario (a))

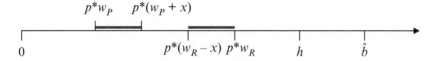

Figure 5.2   Redistribution, levels of deterrence and expected sanctions (Scenario (b))

an expected sanction of p^*w_P), while the fine imposed on the rich is less than their entire wealth, i.e., it is set according to the multiplier principle (they face an expected sanction of h rather than p^*w_R). Therefore, redistributing a sufficiently small amount of wealth x (satisfying $0 < x < w_R - h/p^*$) from the rich to the poor will not affect the feasibility of the fine imposed on the rich, but it will enable an increase in the fine imposed on the poor by x. If the probability of punishment is unchanged, the expected sanction for the poor will be increased to $p^*(w_P + x)$, that is, by p^*x, while the expected sanction for the rich will remain at h (Figure 5.1). Therefore, redistribution will increase deterrence of the poor without compromising deterrence of the rich. Since, under the original distribution, poor individuals are under-deterred (Lemma 1(3)), social welfare will necessarily increase following redistribution. Example 1 in the Introduction illustrates this situation precisely.

3.3   Poor and Rich Individuals Under-Deterred

Now suppose that both poor and rich individuals are under-deterred, $p^*w_P < p^*w_R < h$, as illustrated in Figure 5.2 (Scenario (b)).

This means that the fines imposed on rich and poor individuals are at the maximal level. Here, redistributing wealth from the rich to the poor will come at a cost: deterrence of the rich will necessarily drop. Nevertheless, say we redistribute x from the rich to the poor, adjust fines accordingly to $f_R = w_R - x$ and $f_P = w_P + x$, and keep the probability of punishment at its original level. The third move entails that the costs of enforcement are unaffected. The second move entails that the expected sanction that poor (rich) offenders face increases (decreases) by exactly p^*x (Figure 5.2). Thus, poor individuals are deterred more and rich individuals deterred less. Since the benefits from the harmful act are distributed uniformly, an equal change in the expected sanction increases (decreases) the number of offenders by exactly the same amount. This means that there are fewer poor individuals who commit the harmful act but an increase in exactly the same amount of rich individuals committing the act.[14] Nevertheless, social welfare is increased, because the net harm generated by the additional rich offenders amounts to less than the savings in net harm that would have been created by the additional deterred poor individuals.

The reason for this is that the benefits derived by the additional rich offenders are greater than the benefits forgone by the now-deterred poor offenders. This stems from the fact that rich offenders face a greater optimal expected sanction than do poor individuals (Lemma 1(4)). Thus, net harm is reduced and social welfare is increased.[15]

To illustrate this result numerically, consider Example 3, a variation on Example 1 from the Introduction that assumes that, because enforcement efforts are higher, both the poor and rich are under-deterred.

> *Example 3*: Suppose that rich individuals and poor individuals have monetary resources of $12,000 and $6000, respectively, and that they can engage in some harmful act from which they obtain benefits that range uniformly from $0 to $2000 and that causes harm of $1500. Further suppose that, given the costs of law enforcement, optimal enforcement requires setting the probability of punishment at $p^* = 0.1$ and the fine at $f = $12,000$.

Under these conditions, poor individuals face an expected sanction of $600 ($6000 × 0.1) and rich individuals a sanction of $1200 ($12,000 × 0.1), and both are therefore under-deterred. Suppose we now redistribute $1000 from the rich to the poor, so that the latter will have $11,000 and the former $7000. Poor individuals now face an expected sanction of $700 ($7000 × 0.1) and rich offenders an expected sanction of $1100 ($11,000 × 0.1). The expected sanctions for the poor (rich) have thereby increased (decreased) by exactly $100. Since the benefits are distributed uniformly, this means that there is exactly the same amount of additional rich offenders as there are fewer poor offenders.[16] The overall rate of crime (the combined deterrence of poor and rich individuals) has not changed. However, although the same harm of $1500 is imposed per offender from either group, the additional rich offenders derive benefits that range from $1100 to $1200 (or, on average, $1150) per offender; in contrast, the additional deterred poor individuals derive benefits ranging from $600 to $700 (or, on average, $650) per individual. In other words, the additional rich offenders impose, on average, a net harm of $350 ($1500 − $1150) per offender, while the additional deterred poor individuals impose, on average, a net harm of $850 ($1500 − $650) per individual. Thus, redistributing $1000 from rich individuals to poor individuals increases social welfare by $500 ($850 − $350) on average per each rich offender who replaces a poor offender, which is socially desirable.[17]

3.4 Summary

It was shown above that regardless of the optimal enforcement scheme, redistribution (greater equality) increases social welfare. This leads to the following proposition:

Proposition 1:   If the enforcement technology is general, then perfect equality in the distribution of wealth is socially desirable.

The explanation of Proposition 1 is twofold (a direct proof can be found in the Appendix): first, redistributing wealth from rich to poor individuals causes the overall rate of crime to drop, as deterrence of the rich is unaffected, whereas deterrence of the poor increases (Scenario (a)). Second, even if the overall rate of crime is unaffected, since the increase in deterrence of the poor is completely offset by the decrease in deterrence of the rich, the shift in the composition of the group of offenders is socially desirable, since marginal poor offenders impose greater net harm than do marginal rich ones.[18] This is the case not because poor individuals cause greater harm or because rich individuals derive greater benefits from the harmful act (by assumption, harm and benefits are the same across offenders regardless of wealth), rather because *marginal* rich offenders derive greater benefits than do *marginal* poor offenders, as the expected sanction the former face is higher. This explanation hints at the factors that may impact the validity of Proposition 1, for example, how the benefits from the harmful act are distributed. These factors will be discussed in section 5, where the model is refined.

4. SPECIFIC ENFORCEMENT

The previous section showed that redistribution is socially desirable if, amongst other things, the enforcement technology is general. This section examines how this outcome changes when enforcement efforts are specific, in the sense that the probability of punishment can vary between rich individuals and poor individuals. This is justified, for example, if the poor and rich live and commit offenses in different areas or if offenders can be identified as poor or rich prior to the decision as to how much to invest in enforcement efforts, for example, tax auditors can audit rich individuals more frequently than poor ones. Now, the social planner has another tool at its disposal for maximizing social welfare: the enforcement efforts vis-à-vis the poor can be fine-tuned separately from the measures taken against the rich. This turns out to be critical for the social desirability of wealth redistribution.

4.1 Optimal Enforcement Scheme

Let us begin again by depicting the optimal enforcement scheme given a certain wealth inequality. To simplify things, the enforcement costs are assumed to be proportional to the probability of punishment, but this is not qualitatively crucial. Social welfare (1) is adjusted to account for the nature of the enforcement technology and can be formulated as follows:

$$SW = \frac{1}{2} \int_{p_P f_P}^{b} bg(b)\,db - h[1 - G(p_P f_P)] - \frac{1}{2}c(p_P) + \tag{2}$$

$$+ \frac{1}{2} \int_{p_R f_R}^{b} bg(b)\,db - h[1 - G(p_R f_R)] - \frac{1}{2}c(p_R)$$

Since the probability and severity of punishment can vary across individuals, the optimal enforcement schemes for the poor and rich are determined independently. These schemes are represented by the following Lemma 2 (see Polinsky and Shavell 1984, Garoupa 2001):

Lemma 2:   (1) The optimal fine for poor and rich individuals is the maximal fine, $f_i^* = w_i$. (2) The optimal probability of punishment for each gives rise to under-deterrence, $p^*(w_i)w_i < h$. (3) The optimal expected sanction for the rich is greater than the optimal expected sanction for the poor, $p^*(w_P)w_P < p^*(w_R)w_R$.[19]
Proof: See Garoupa (2001).

The explanation of Lemma 2 is straightforward. Since fines are socially costless whereas enforcement efforts are socially costly, *fines should be set at their maximum level.* Otherwise, social welfare could be increased by raising fines to their maximum level and reducing the probability of enforcement with no impact on deterrence. This is Becker's argument. *Some degree of under-deterrence is socially optimal,* because under first best deterrence, i.e., the expected sanction equals the harm, the net harm imposed by the marginal offenders stands at virtually zero. Therefore, reducing the probability of punishment slightly saves enforcement costs at virtually no cost. This is Polinsky and Shavell's point. The reason why *the expected sanction is greater for the rich than for the poor* is as follows: as wealth increases, the same optimal level of deterrence can be achieved by increasing the fine and reducing the probability of punishment, so that the optimal expected sanction remains constant. However, as the fine increases the deterrent effect of enforcement efforts are higher.[20] Therefore, since optimality is characterized by some degree of under-deterrence, it is not optimal to reduce the probability of punishment all the way down. Rather, it is desirable to achieve greater deterrence. Accordingly, as wealth increases, the optimal expected sanction increases, indicating that the expected sanction for the rich is greater than the expected sanction for the poor. This is Garoupa's point.

As the above explanation makes clear, it is cheaper to enforce the law against the rich than against the poor. This means that redistributing wealth from rich individuals to poor individuals reduces the social costs of crime and law enforcement associated with the poor but, at the same time, increases the social costs of crime and law enforcement associated with the rich. Whether redistribution is socially desirable depends, then, on the relative magnitudes of these costs, i.e., on the trade-off between the social costs entailed with the poor and those entailed with the rich. Since the two groups are distinguished only in terms of their wealth, this trade-off can be partly determined by inquiring into the properties of the value function of the social problem at hand, to which we now turn.[21]

4.2   Value Function

Value function, $V(w, p(w)) = \max_p \int_{pw}^{\hat{b}} (b - h)g(b)db - c(p)$, renders the maximum social welfare attainable under our model as a function of the wealth of a group of identical individuals. It is obtained by solving the maximization problem time and again for different levels of wealth of a group of identical individuals. Since the optimal fine is the entire wealth of offenders, regardless of their level of wealth, the value function can be determined solely with respect to the probability of punishment. The value function increases with wealth, because it is cheaper to enforce the law upon richer individuals. Using the envelope theorem, this can be understood by observing that

$$\frac{dV(w, p(w))}{dw} = \frac{\partial V(w, p(w))}{\partial w} = p^*(h - p^*w)g(p^*w) > 0 \qquad (3)$$

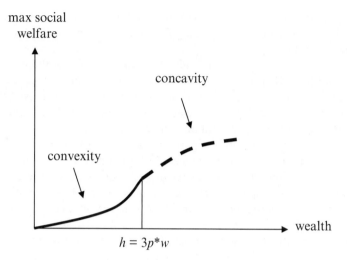

Figure 5.3   Maximum social welfare as a function of wealth

In determining the trade-off between the social costs of crime and law enforcement associated with the rich and those associated with the poor, one critical question is whether the value function increases with wealth at increasing or decreasing rates. Namely, does increasing the wealth of individuals by, say, $1000 increase social welfare by more or by less than the decrease in social welfare resulting from an equivalent reduction of $1000 in the wealth of individuals? Graphically, the shape of the value function is of great importance, in particular either its concavity or convexity. If, for example, the value function were concave (convex) throughout its support, then greater or, indeed, perfect equality (inequality) in the distribution of wealth would be socially desirable. The reason for this is that redistributing wealth from rich (poor) individuals to poor (rich) individuals would always increase the social welfare associated with the poor (rich) by more than the decrease in social welfare associated with the rich (poor). If, however, the value function is partly convex and partly concave – as is, indeed, the case – another important matter must be determined: the positions of the poor and rich, given their wealth levels, on the function. For example, if both the poor and rich are positioned on the concave (convex) interval of the value function, then greater equality (inequality) will be socially desirable.

The shape of the value function is determined by the sign of its second derivative with respect to wealth,

$$sign\left[\frac{d^2 V(w, p(w))}{dw^2}\right] = sign[(h - 2p*w)^2 - (p*w)^2] \qquad (4)$$

and is illustrated in Figure 5.3.

As evident from Figure 5.3, the value function can be partitioned into two intervals: one where it is convex (the unbroken line) and one where it is concave (the broken line). As can be easily verified from equation 4, the inflection point occurs exactly at $w = h/3p*(w)$ or, equivalently, at $h = 3p*(w)w$. The partition of the value function is based on the magnitude of offenders' wealth, w, relative to the optimal multiplier principle, $h/p^*(w)$ or, equivalently, on the magnitude of the harm, h, relative to the optimal expected sanction, $p^*(w)w$.

The explanation for the shape of the value function (its convex and concave intervals) is roughly as follows. If harm is large relative to the optimal expected sanction that prevails for a given level of wealth, then the social gains from increased deterrence are enormous. As wealth increases, these social gains can be achieved not only by maintaining the probability of punishment, but actually by increasing it even further. As a result, at low levels of wealth, social welfare increases rapidly. However, as wealth climbs, the optimal expected sanction becomes sufficiently large relative to the harm (although it never equals the harm, because some degree of under-deterrence is always optimal), and the social gain from increasing deterrence is relatively small. At sufficiently moderate levels of wealth, social welfare increases mainly due to the savings in enforcement efforts, and it therefore increases only gradually.

The shape of the value function clarifies that the social desirability of redistributing wealth depends on the positions of the poor and the rich along the function curve. This is a matter of the relative magnitude of wealth and the optimal multiplier principle or, equivalently, of the relative magnitude of the harm and the optimal expected sanctions associated with the poor and rich, respectively. This leads to the following results.[22]

4.3   Results

The first result stands in sharp contrast to the social desirability of perfect equality (Proposition 1).

> *Proposition 2(1):*   If the enforcement technology is specific, then perfect equality in the distribution of wealth is not socially desirable if the harm is sufficiently large relative to the optimal expected sanction associated with perfect equality, i.e., if $h > 3p^*(\overline{w})\overline{w}$.

The proof for this Proposition is straightforward. If $h > 3p^*(\overline{w})\overline{w}$, then the value function is convex at $\overline{w}$. Therefore, redistributing wealth from those designated *poor* to those designated *rich* will increase the social welfare associated with the rich by more than the decrease in the social welfare associated with the poor. The combined social welfare will increase, indicating that perfect equality is not optimal. The following numerical Example 4 illustrates this.

> *Example 4:* Suppose that all individuals, rich and poor, have $900 in monetary resources and can engage in some harmful act from which they obtain benefits that are distributed uniformly, ranging from $0 to $2000, and that causes social harm of $1500. Suppose also that optimal law enforcement requires setting the probability of punishment at 0.4 and the fine at $900. Thus all individuals face an expected sanction of $360 ($900 × 0.4), which is less than one-third of the harm ($360 × 3 < 1500).[23]

Consider now redistributing $100 from those designated *poor* to those designated *rich*, so that rich individuals and poor individuals have monetary resources of $1000 and $800, respectively. Say we adjust the fines accordingly as well as the probability of punishment so that for rich individuals $p_R = 0.45$ and for poor individuals $p_P = 0.35$. Since enforcement efforts are assumed to be proportionate to the probability of punishment, the increased costs of enforcement associated with the rich are entirely offset by the decrease in the enforcement costs associated with the poor. The expected sanction for the rich increases to $450 ($1000 × 0.45), or by $90 ($450 − $360), and, for the poor, decreases to $280 ($800 × 0.35), or by $80 ($280 − $360). Since the benefits from the harmful act are distributed uniformly from $0 to $2000, the increase in deterrence of the rich indicates that there is an additional 2.25% (50 × 90/2000) of the population that is deterred. The decrease in deterrence of the poor suggests that there is an additional 2% (50 × 80/2000) of the population that commits the harmful act. In total, deterrence has therefore increased by 0.25%.[24] The additional rich individuals who are deterred have derived benefits that range from $360 to $450, or, on average, $405 per offender, and have imposed harm of $1500. Therefore, the net harm imposed by these individuals is $1095 ($1500 − $405) per offender and $2463.75 ($1095 × 2.25) in total. The additional poor offenders derive benefits that range from $280 to $360, or, on average, $320 per offender, and likewise impose a harm of $1500. Therefore, the net harm imposed by these offenders is $1180 ($1500 − $320) per offender and $2360 ($1180 × 2) in total. By redistributing $100 from poor individuals to rich individuals, the social costs of crime and law enforcement associated with the rich has decreased by $2463.75, which is greater than the $2360 increase in the social costs of crime and law enforcement associated with the poor. Social welfare has thus increased by $103.75, which contradicts the presumed optimality of equal distribution of wealth.[25]

While Proposition 2(1) suggests that *some* inequality in the distribution of wealth may be socially desirable, the shape of the value function leads to an even stronger and more intriguing result.

Proposition 2(2): If the enforcement technology is specific, greater inequality in the distribution of wealth is socially desirable if the harm is sufficiently large relative to the optimal expected sanction associated with the rich, that is, if $h > 3p^*(w_R)w_R$. Perfect inequality is socially desirable if this condition holds for $w_R = 2\overline{w}$.

The proof for Proposition 2(2) is also straightforward. It rests on the observation that the optimal expected sanction for the rich is greater than for the poor, that is, $p^*(w_P)w_P < p^*(w_R)w_R$ (Lemma 2(3)). If the optimal expected sanction for the rich is sufficiently small relative to the harm, then, both the rich and poor are positioned on the convex interval of the value function (see Figure 5.3). Therefore, increasing inequality reduces the social costs of crime and law enforcement associated with the rich by more than the increase in those costs associated with the poor. The second part of the Proposition implies that this process will continue to hold if, for any possible unequal distribution of wealth, both the poor and the rich are positioned on the convex interval of the value function.[26] Therefore, perfect inequality is socially desirable.

We demonstrated that some or even perfect inequality in wealth distribution may be socially desirable if the enforcement technology is specific in nature. The conditions presented, however, were quite extreme in that the optimal expected sanctions relative to harm are very small and, accordingly, under-deterrence is very substantial. These conditions *ceteris paribus* are more likely to occur in poorer countries, which suggest that redistribution is more likely to impose additional costs in those countries. We will now seek to show that under ordinary conditions, conditions that, *ceteris paribus*, are more likely to arise in richer countries, greater equality of wealth distribution is socially desirable.

> *Proposition 2(3):*   If the enforcement technology is specific, greater equality in the distribution of wealth is socially desirable if the harm from the harmful act is sufficiently moderate relative to the optimal expected sanction associated with the poor, that is, if $h < 3p^*(w_P)w_P$.

The proof for this Proposition is essentially the mirror-image of the proof for Proposition 2(2), using the observation that $p^*(w_P)w_P < p^*(w_R)w_R$. If the optimal expected sanction associated with the poor is sufficiently moderate relative to the harm, then both the poor and the rich, given their wealth levels, are positioned on the concave interval of the value function (see Figure 5.3). Therefore, redistributing wealth from the rich to the poor will increase the social welfare associated with the poor by more than it decreases the social welfare associated with the rich, after the appropriate adjustments to the respective enforcement schemes have been made. Thus, greater equality increases social welfare and is, accordingly, socially desirable.

4.4   Greater Equality is Socially Desirable if $p_R^* < p_P^*$

Thus far, we have analysed the social desirability of redistributing wealth on the basis of the *shape* of the value function. However, this line of inquiry is not helpful if the poor are positioned on the convex interval of the value function and the rich on its concave interval. This scenario is possible if the harm from the harmful act is sufficiently great relative to the optimal expected sanction associated with the poor and sufficiently moderate relative to the optimal expected sanction associated with the rich, that is, if $3p^*(w_P)w_P < h < 3p^*(w_R)w_R$.[27] In such a case, a direct analysis of the trade-off between the social costs of crime and law enforcement associated with the poor and the same social costs associated with the rich is required and leads to the following simple yet compelling result.

> *Proposition 2(4):*   If the enforcement technology is specific, greater equality in the distribution of wealth is socially desirable if the optimal probability of punishment associated with the rich is less than that associated with the poor, i.e., if $p_R^* < p_P^*$.

Proposition 2(4) can be proved easily by using equation (3),[28] but for uniformity, we will use a similar method to that used in section 3. The optimal enforcement scheme, given that rich individuals receive w_R and poor individuals receive w_P, is set forth in Lemma 2. Suppose we redistribute x from the rich to the poor and alter their respective fines accordingly, to $f_P = w_P + x$ and $f_R = w_R - x$. We will hold the respective probabilities of punishment at their original levels, so that the costs of enforcement remain unaffected. Assume that x is a sufficiently small amount, so that $p_P^*(w_P + x) < p_R^*(w_R - x)$, i.e., $0 < x < p_R^*w_R - p_P^*w_P/p_R^* + p_P^*$, as illustrated in Figure 5.4.

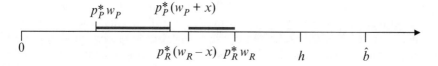

Figure 5.4 *Redistribution, levels of deterrence and expected sanctions: specific enforcement*

The expected sanction that rich individuals face, $p_R^*(w_R - x)$, is decreased by p_R^*x, while the expected sanction that poor individuals face, $p_P^*(w_P + x)$, is increased by p_P^*x. Since p_P^* is assumed to be greater than p_R^*, the expected sanction for the poor increased by more than the parallel decrease in the expected sanction for the rich, that is, $p_P^*x > p_R^*x$. This implies that the deterrence of the poor increased by more than the deterrence of the rich decreased (since the benefits from the harmful act are distributed uniformly). Thus, the overall rate of crime necessarily falls. In addition, since poor individuals face a lower expected sanction than that faced by rich individuals, the *marginal* poor individuals who are now deterred have created greater net harm than generated by the *marginal* rich individuals who now commit the harmful act. Social welfare is therefore clearly increased, which contradicts the presumed optimality of the original unequal distribution of wealth. The following Example 5 illustrates this numerically.

> *Example 5*: Suppose that rich and poor individuals have monetary resources of $12,000 and $6000 respectively and they can engage in some harmful act from which they obtain benefits that range uniformly from $0 to $2000 and that causes a harm of $1500. Suppose that, given the costs of law enforcement, optimal enforcement requires setting the probability and severity of punishment at 0.1 and $12,000 for the rich and at 0.15 and $6000 for the poor.

Thus, poor individuals face an expected sanction of $900 ($6,000 × 0.15) and rich individuals face $1200 ($12,000 × 0.1); both are under-deterred. Let us now redistribute $1000 from the rich to the poor, so that the former have $11,000 and the latter $7000, and adjust the fines accordingly. Poor individuals now face an expected sanction of $1050 ($7000 × 0.15), that is, an increase of $150 ($1050 − $900), and rich offenders face an expected sanction of $1100 ($11,000 × 0.1), a decrease of $100 ($1200 − $1100). Since benefits are distributed uniformly, the increase in deterrence of the poor reduces the crime rate by 3.75% (0.5 × 150/2000) and the decrease in deterrence of the rich raises it by 2.5% (0.5 × 100/2000). In total, the crime rate drops by 1.25% (3.75% − 2.5%). Note that the additional rich offenders derive benefits ranging from $1100 to $1200, or an average of $1150 per offender, and impose a harm of $1500 per offender. Thus, the additional rich offenders impose a net harm of $350 ($1500 − $1150) per offender and $875 (350 × 2.5) in total. In contrast, the additional deterred poor individuals derive benefits ranging from $900 to $1050, or an average of $975 per offender. They, too, impose a harm of $1500 per offender. Thus, the additional deterred poor individuals impose a net harm of $525 ($1500 − $975) per offender and $1968.75 (525 × 3.75) in total. Consequently, social welfare increases by $1093.75 ($1968.75 − $875).[29] This contradicts the presumed optimality of the original unequal distribution of wealth and shows that greater equality is socially desirable.

Proposition 2(4) holds as long as $p_R^* < p_P^*$. However, since perfect equality is not always socially desirable, as proved by Proposition 2(1), it follows that the optimal enforcement scheme can be also characterized by $p_P^* < p_R^*$.[30] In the present model, the optimal probability of punishment as a function of wealth increases as long as $h > 2p^*(w)w$ and decreases when $h < 2p^*(w)w$.[31] This implies that the reverse of Proposition 2(4) is not true: greater equality may be socially desirable even if $p_P^* < p_R^*$.

5.   REFINING THE MODEL

The previous sections analysed the social desirability of redistributing wealth under the alternative assumptions of general enforcement efforts and specific enforcement technology. This section relaxes certain other assumptions underlying the model. For the purpose of simplicity, the analysis relates only to general enforcement efforts (section 3). This however is not crucial for the analysis to hold.

5.1   Socially Non-desirable Crimes

The model thus far has assumed the harmful act to be socially desirable for some potential offenders in the sense that the benefits they derive are greater than the harm. This accords with many regulatory offenses such as speeding, double-parking, polluting, and sometimes even theft.[32] However, many other harmful acts, which likely constitute the core of the criminal law, such as violent crimes, are presumably never socially desirable, i.e., the harm always exceeds the benefits. Nevertheless, the social desirability of redistributing wealth is not contingent on this question.

If the harmful act is never socially desirable, then complete deterrence is what we would strive for but for the costs of enforcement. This implies that, ideally, the expected sanction should be equal to the maximum benefits that can be derived from the harmful act rather than the harm created. The optimal enforcement scheme, given some unequal distribution of wealth, is set forth in the following Lemma 3.

Lemma 3:   (1) The optimal fine is equal to the entire wealth of offenders, $f_i^* = w_i$. (2) The optimal probability of punishment gives rise to three possibilities: (a) complete deterrence of poor and rich individuals, $p^*w_P = \hat{b} < p^*w_R$; (b) complete deterrence of rich individuals but under-deterrence of poor ones, $p^*w_P < \hat{b} < p^*w_R$; or (c) under-deterrence of poor and rich individuals, $p^*w_P < p^*w_R < \hat{b}$. (3) Poor individuals are (weakly) less deterred than rich individuals.
Proof: Omitted.

If the harmful act is never socially desirable, then the fines for both the poor and the rich will amount to their entire wealth, which is obvious. Note that Scenarios (b) and (c) in Lemma 3 are analogous to those discussed in section 3. Therefore, the arguments applied there can be applied here to show that greater equality increases social welfare. In particular, under Scenario (b) (poor individuals are under-deterred but the rich are completely deterred), greater equality increases social welfare, because greater deterrence of the poor can be achieved without affecting the deterrence of the rich. Similarly, under Scenario (c) (both poor and rich individuals are under-deterred), greater equality increases social welfare, because the additional rich offenders impose less net harm than do the additional deterred poor individuals.

Scenario (a), in which both poor and rich individuals are completely deterred, arises when the enforcement efforts are sufficiently cheap. Nevertheless, to save on enforcement efforts, the expected sanction for the poor should amount to only the maximum benefits. Greater equality still increases social welfare, because by increasing the wealth of the poor, complete deterrence can be achieved at lower enforcement costs.[33] Thus, perfect equality is socially desirable even if the harmful act is always socially undesirable.

5.2   Benefits from the Harmful Act have No Social Value

We have assumed that the benefits from the harmful act are taken into account in the social welfare calculus. While this is valid for minor offenses such as speeding, double-parking, and even theft, some argue that the illicit benefits offenders derive from major offenses should be given little if any weight in the social calculus. If this is the case, the harmful act is obviously never socially desirable (i.e., the harm always exceeds the social benefits). Indeed, the harmful act imposes the same *net* harm, regardless of who commits it. This *should* affect the results, since the argument for redistribution was based on the observation that the marginal rich offenders impose less net harm than the marginal poor offenders impose. Nevertheless, perfect equality is at least as good as any unequal distribution of wealth and therefore (weakly) superior.

Although the benefits derived from the harmful major offenses are given no social weight, they still determine who commits the harmful act. Therefore the optimal expected sanction should ideally be equal to the maximum benefits. The optimal enforcement scheme in these circumstances is also depicted by Lemma 3.

Under Scenario (a) (both poor and rich individuals are completely deterred), greater equality remains socially desirable, because, as argued above, complete deterrence can be achieved at lower enforcement costs. Under Scenario (b) (the poor are under-deterred but the rich are perfectly deterred), greater equality is also socially desirable, because greater deterrence of the poor can be achieved without compromising deterrence of the rich. However, under Scenario (c) (both the poor and the rich are under-deterred), greater equality does not increase social welfare, because the gain in deterrence of the poor is completely offset by the loss in deterrence of the rich. Since the benefits are not included in the social calculus, the change in the composition of offenders is of no consequence. This suggests that greater equality neither increases nor reduces social welfare in this scenario. Since greater equality sometimes increases social welfare, but never reduces it, it is weakly superior to any unequal distribution of wealth.

5.3   Minimum Benefits from the Harmful Act are Substantial

The assumption that the benefits from the harmful act are distributed uniformly on the support $[0, \hat{b}]$ may be crucial for the results of this chapter. Suppose, instead, that the benefits are still distributed uniformly but on the support $[\bar{b}, \hat{b}]$, so that the harmful act confers a positive benefit $\bar{b}$ on all offenders. This seemingly technical change *might* mean

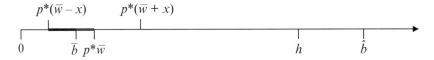

Figure 5.5   Redistribution, levels of deterrence and expected sanctions: perfect equality results in positive deterrence

that perfect equality is no longer socially desirable or, worse, that perfect inequality is preferable.

To illustrate this, suppose that, with perfect equality, the wealth of individuals is less than the minimum benefits they derive from the given harmful act, $\overline{w} < \overline{b}$, which is, of course, impossible if $\overline{b} = 0$. In this case, there is no point in investing any resources in enforcement, even if very cheap, since all individuals will in any event commit the harmful act. The optimal enforcement scheme thus results in no deterrence at all.[34] However, if some resources x were redistributed from those designated poor to those designated rich, the wealth of the latter might then exceed the minimum benefits, $\overline{w} + x > \overline{b}$ (this requires that $2\overline{w} > \overline{b}$). It might therefore be socially desirable to expend resources on enforcement, so that the expected sanction for the rich exceeds the minimum benefits, $p^*(\overline{w} + x) > \overline{b}$. This would create some deterrence for the rich, without affecting the deterrence of the poor, which is already non-existent. Social welfare would increase, implying that inequality in wealth distribution is socially desirable. Example 2 in the Introduction illustrated precisely this possibility.

Note that if *some* redistribution from poor to rich individuals increases social welfare, then *more* redistribution will accomplish the same. The reason is that deterrence of the poor is not impacted, whereas deterrence of the rich is either increased at no additional cost or the same level of deterrence is achieved but at lower enforcement cost.

Wealth inequality may be socially desirable even if perfect equality results in positive but relatively little deterrence. The explanation is as follows (see Figure 5.5): since $p^*\overline{w} > \overline{b}$, it is true that redistributing x from those designated poor to those designated rich (and keeping p^* constant) unequivocally reduces social welfare, as long as $p^*(\overline{w} - x) \geq \overline{b}$, for the same reason explained in section 3.3: the additional poor offenders impose greater net harm than do the additional deterred rich individuals.[35] However, at $p^*(\overline{w} - x) = \overline{b}$, *further* redistribution of wealth from the poor to the rich increases social welfare (creates social gains), because it saves the social costs of enforcing the law upon the rich, at no social cost to the poor who are already completely undeterred. Therefore, wealth inequality is socially desirable if these social gains are greater than the social loss.[36]

Note that the likelihood of perfect equality being socially desirable is contingent on, amongst other things, how rich the given society is as a whole. The reason for this is that, all things equal, optimal expected sanctions increase as (total) wealth increases (see Lemma 1(4)). As is clear from the previous discussion, the social losses and social gains associated with wealth inequality are contingent on the magnitude of the optimal expected sanction relative to the minimum benefits deriving from the harmful act. If, for example, the optimal expected sanction is sufficiently large relative to the minimum benefits, $p^*\overline{w} \gg \overline{b}$,[37] then there is a greater likelihood that perfect equality is the socially desirable option, since the social losses are relatively large and are likely to outweigh the potential social gains. In contrast, if the optimal expected sanction is not sufficiently large relative to the minimum benefits, then there is a greater likelihood of the social desirability of greater inequality, for the opposite reason. This roughly suggests that, all else being equal, in poorer countries, redistribution might entail additional costs in that it increases the social costs of crime and law enforcement, whereas in relatively richer countries, redistribution entails additional benefits, because it reduces the social costs of enforcing the law.

5.4 Non-uniform Distribution of Benefits from the Harmful Act

The assumption that the benefits from the harmful act are distributed uniformly across all individuals may also be crucial for our results. To see this, recall the argument in favor of redistribution when both the poor and the rich are under-deterred (section 3.3). There, it was explained that redistributing wealth from rich to poor individuals (and keeping the enforcement efforts constant) would result in an increased expected sanction for the poor but a lower expected sanction for the rich reduced by the exact same amount. Since the benefits from the harmful act were assumed to be uniformly distributed, the corresponding changes in the expected sanctions would mean that the overall rate of crime would be unaffected. There would be fewer poor individuals committing the harmful act, but the same amount of additional rich offenders. Redistribution was nevertheless shown to be socially desirable, because the additional deterred poor individuals would impose greater net harm (derive less benefit) than would the additional rich offenders.

If the benefits from the harmful act are distributed non-uniformly, then an equal change in the respective expected sanctions of the poor and the rich could affect deterrence of the former to a greater or lesser extent than it affects deterrence of the latter. If, for example, there are more additional deterred poor individuals than additional rich offenders, then the social desirability of redistributing wealth gains additional force, since the overall rate of crime actually falls. However, if the reverse is true and there are more additional rich offenders than additional poor non-offenders, then redistributing wealth from the rich to the poor is not necessarily socially desirable, because the overall rate of crime actually rises. The additional deterred poor individuals will have imposed greater net harm (derived less benefit) than the additional rich offenders *per offender*, but the former are fewer in number.

Unfortunately, how the benefits from harmful acts are distributed in reality is unknown. However, two general observations can be made. First, several common density functions decrease throughout their support.[38] This roughly implies that there are many individuals who obtain few benefits and a relatively small number of individuals who obtain great benefits. If the benefits from the harmful act were characterized by these density functions, then the marginal rich offenders, who always face higher expected sanctions than their poor counterparts and therefore derive greater benefit, would always be less affected than the marginal poor offenders from any corresponding change in the expected sanction. Therefore, greater equality would be socially desirable. Second, even those density functions that do not monotonically decrease, such as the density function of the normal distribution, which has the usual bell shape, tend to first increase and then decrease. This suggests, again, that if a given society has a relatively large total wealth, it is more likely that the marginal offenders will be positioned on the decreasing interval of the density function (because their expected sanction and, therefore, their benefits are greater). In contrast, if a given society's overall wealth is relatively small, it is more likely that the marginal offenders will be positioned at the increasing interval of the density function.[39] This also roughly indicates that greater equality tends to be socially desirable in richer countries, whereas some inequality may be socially preferable in poorer countries.

6.   CONCLUSION

This chapter has explored how the distribution of wealth affects the social costs of crime and law enforcement. The key insight of the analysis is that the social desirability of wealth redistribution is contingent on a trade-off between the social costs of enforcing the law upon the poor and those costs vis-à-vis the rich. This trade-off is not trivial. It depends, among other things, on how benefits from harmful acts are distributed (the shape and range of the distribution function), on the enforcement technology (whether it is general or specific), and on society's total wealth.

Two general conclusions emerge from the analysis: (1) Redistribution under a broad set of circumstances reduces the social costs of crime and law enforcement and, in this respect, is socially desirable. (2) All things equal, there is a greater likelihood that greater equality will be socially desirable in richer countries, while inequality is more likely to be socially desirable in poorer countries. Put differently, in richer countries, greater equality is more likely to confer additional benefits in the form of reduced social costs of crime and law enforcement, whereas in poorer countries, it is more likely to entail additional costs.[40]

The analysis intentionally omitted the well-known and extremely important social benefits and costs associated with wealth redistribution. First, it was assumed that redistribution is of no welfare consequence in and of itself. In reality, of course, redistribution confers social benefits because individuals have decreasing marginal utility of wealth (the poor values the marginal dollar by more than the rich), or because individuals might have a preference in favor of equality (the social welfare function may exhibit aversion to inequality). Second, redistribution was assumed to be costless. In reality, again, redistribution certainly bears social costs; it involves administrative costs and imposes deadweight loss (distorts behavior) due to the use of distortionary rather than lump sum taxes. These social benefits and costs, however, should not affect the qualitative results of this chapter, i.e., the direction of redistribution, with ramifications only for their magnitude.

The framework and analysis in this chapter can be extended in several directions, two of which are particularly noteworthy. First, it was assumed that the benefits from the harmful act are independent of the wealth of offenders or distribution of wealth in society. However, the benefits derived from different types of offenses can differ for the poor and the rich or can depend on the level of wealth inequality. For example, property crimes might confer more benefits to the poor than to the rich and might be more beneficial to potential offenders the greater the wealth inequality. In contrast, offenses that save in time resources, such as speeding, might be of greater benefit to the rich than to the poor, because time may be more valuable to the former. These possibilities can be easily incorporated into the model, and they might either reinforce or weaken the results.

Second, the analysis assumed monetary sanctions to be the sole form of punishment. However, many types of offenses are punished by way of imprisonment, and the principal economic justification for this is the limited wealth of poor offenders. This suggests that deterrence of the poor can be achieved by supplementing fines with imprisonment. Generally speaking, the availability of imprisonment should not affect the fundamental results of this chapter, because imprisonment bears lower social costs than fines. Therefore, it should be generally desirable to redistribute resources from the rich to the poor in order to save on a socially costlier instrument. However, further inquiry would be required to establish this formally.

NOTES

*   I would like to thank Ariel Porat for his tremendous help and support, as well as Oren Bar Gill, Massimo Dantoni, Sharon Hannes, Jacob Nussim, and the participants at the Seina-Tel-Aviv-Toronto conference in law and economics (2007) and the American Law and Economics Association Annual Meeting (2008) for their helpful comments and suggestions.
1. Or, from another perspective, this chapter suggests that all else being equal, rich (poor) countries tend to be wealthier the more (or less) equally their wealth is distributed, because the costs of enforcing the law correspondingly decrease.
2. Alternatively, social welfare could be increased by a saving in enforcement efforts without affecting deterrence. To understand this, let us redistribute again $1000 from the rich to the poor, increase the fine to $8750, and reduce the probability of punishment to approximately 0.171. These changes would maintain the same levels of deterrence for the poor and rich (the rich would face an expected sanction of $8750 × 0.171 = $1500 and the poor would face $7000 × 0.171 = $1200), but also would reduce enforcement efforts. Thus, social welfare would increase.
3. Compare with Polinsky and Shavell (1984, 1991) and Bar-Niv and Safra (2002), who make a similar assumption.
4. See, e.g., Fleisher (1966), Ehrlich (1973), Heineke (1978), Zhang (1997), Chiu and Madden (1998), Kelly (2000).
5. For example, Zhang (1997) found that certain welfare programs have a negative and often significant effect on property crime, but no significant effect on violent crime. Kelly (2000) found that income inequality has no effect on property crime, but has a significant and robust effect on violent crime, while poverty and police activity have a significant effect on property crime, though little impact on violent crime.
6. See also Cassone and Marchese (2006), who expand the work of Demougin and Schwager (2000) to consider risk aversion and continuous labor supply. Also noteworthy is Eaton and White's (1991) work, which explores the effect on economic efficiency of the distribution of wealth and systems for enforcing property rights.
7. The model follows and expands on the general model found in Polinsky and Shavell (1984).
8. Section 5 briefly analyses: (1) non-uniform distribution functions and (2) uniform distribution functions whose support is $[\bar{b}, \hat{b}]$, where $\bar{b} > 0$. These may affect the results.
9. Section 6 points out how the model can be modified to account for other possibilities.
10. This, however, is not crucial. See *infra* note 15. In addition, in the Appendix the main results are proven for any two groups not necessarily of equal size.
11. Negative amounts of x represent mathematically the possibility of redistributing wealth from the poor to the rich. It is therefore bounded by $-w_P$.
12. The terms "general enforcement" and "specific enforcement" are borrowed from Shavell (1991).
13. Lemma 1 can be summarized as $f_P^* = w_P$, $f_R^* = \min [h/p^*, w_R]$, $p^* f_P^* < p^* f_R^* \leq h$
14. Since the population is normalized to 1, an increase (decrease) of the expected sanction for the poor (rich) by $p^* x$ implies that there are additional $p^* x / 2\bar{b}$ poor individuals who are deterred (rich offenders). This follows from the definition of a uniform distribution function: there is the same number of individuals in any given interval as there are in any other interval of the same length.
15. Note that this result does not depend on the assumption that the two groups are equal in size. Assume,

for example, that the Rich group is of size μ and the Poor group of size $1 - \mu$. Now transfer x from the Rich to the Poor, giving the Rich offenders $w_R - x$ and the Poor offenders $w_p + \mu x/1 - \mu$. Since benefits are distributed uniformly, the reduction in deterrence of the Rich, $\mu p * x$, is exactly equal to the increase in deterrence of the Poor, $(1 - \mu)p*\mu x/(1 - \mu) = \mu p*x$. Thus the argument follows accordingly.

16.   Again, under the definition of a uniform distribution function, there are as many individuals in any given interval as there are in any other interval of the same length. In the present example, the number of rich individuals who derive benefits that range from $1100 to $1200 is the same as the number of poor individuals who derive benefits that range from $600 to $700. In percentage terms, we are dealing with 2.5% ($0.5 \times 100/2000$) of the overall population of poor/rich individuals.

17.   A back-of-the-envelope calculation of the total savings in social costs (reduced net harm) can be made based on the above redistribution. Since the change in the composition of offenders is 2.5% of the total population ($0.5 \times 100/2000 = 0.025$) and the savings per offenders amount to $500, the total savings add up to $12.5 ($0.025 \times 500 = 12.5$). Compared with the total net harm associated with crime before the redistribution takes place – $50 ($0.5 \times 1400/2000[1500 - 1300] + 0.5 \times 800/2000[1500 - 1600]$) – this is a reduction of 25%(!) in net harm ($12.5 \times 100/50$). Furthermore, if redistribution were complete (i.e., $x = 3000$), the net harm associated with crime would be reduced to $27.5 ($1100/2000[1500 - 1450]$), which would be a reduction of 45% in net harm!

18.   This shows that the normative question concerning the social desirability of wealth inequality is different from the positive question concerning the effects of the distribution of wealth on deterrence.

19.   The notation terms p_i and $p(w_i)$ will be used interchangeably.

20.   To illustrate, if the optimal fine is $1000 then any 1% increase in the probability of punishment has an impact on the level of deterrence of $10 ($1000 \times 1\%$). However, if the optimal fine is $2000, then any 1% increase in the probability of punishment generates an impact of $20 ($2000 \times 1\%$) on the level of deterrence.

21.   A more direct approach shows that the trade-off depends on the "shadow prices" of wealth for the rich and poor. This is the approach taken in section 4.4.

22.   To minimize repetition, the following results are stated in terms of the relation between harm and the optimal expected sanctions. However, they could be stated and understood in terms of the relation between wealth and the optimal multiplier principle.

23.   Indeed, individuals are substantially under-deterred: the crime rate is 82% ($100 \times 1640/2000$).

24.   The crime rate therefore falls to 81.75%.

25.   Observe that the net harm associated with the harmful act when wealth is distributed equally is $262.4 (($1180 - $1500)$1640/$2000). Therefore, increased inequality will reduce net harm by almost 40% ($103.75 \times 100/262.4$).

26.   Stated mathematically, if $h > 3p*(2\overline{w})2\overline{w}$, then for any i, $h > 3p*(w_i)w_i$, which indicates that the value function is convex at the interval $[0, 2\overline{w}]$.

27.   The opposite, however, is impossible because the value function is first convex and then concave.

28.   The proof is as follows: a small redistribution decreases the social costs associated with the poor by $p_P^*(h - p_P^*w_P)g(p_P^*w_P)$ and increases those costs associated with the rich by $p_R^*(h - p_R^*w_R)g(p_R^*w_R)$. Since $p_P^*w_P < p_R^*w_R$ (Lemma 2(3)) and $g(p_P^*w_P) = g(p_R^*w_R)$, total social welfare increases if $p_P^* > p_R^*$.

29.   Illustrated differently, the reduction in the crime rate translates into a saving of $1875 ($1500 \times 1.25$). However, rich offenders derive benefits that amount to $2875 ($1150 \times 2.5$), while poor offenders derive benefits that amount to $3656.25 ($975 \times 3.75$). Social welfare therefore increases by $1093.75 ($1875 + $2875 - 3656.25).

30.   Garoupa (2001) proved this possibility.

31.   By the implicit function theorem: $sign dp*(w)/dw = sign[h - 2p*(w)w]$.

32.   The well-known example is that of a man who loses his way in the woods and, as an alternative to starving, enters an unoccupied cabin and steals a negligible amount of food.

33.   To illustrate this formally, let us redistribute x from rich to poor individuals, adjust fines accordingly, and lower the probability of punishment so that $p'(w_P + x) = \hat{b} < p'(w_R - x)$. This move, which is always feasible, indicates that complete deterrence can be achieved with less enforcement efforts.

34.   No deterrence, i.e., $p* = 0$, can result under the basic model, as a corner solution, if, at that point, $w_P/2\hat{b}(h - p*w_P) + w_R/2\hat{b}(h - p*w_R) < c'(p*)$. But this condition holds for any choice of w_P and w_R, so our results are not actually affected.

35.   Indeed, the social loss equals $p*x/2\hat{b}p*x$.

36.   The following example illustrates this numerically. Suppose that $\overline{w} = 9000$ and the benefits from the harmful act are distributed uniformly ranging from $1500 to $3500, with the social harm from the act at $3000. Suppose also that optimal law enforcement requires setting $p* = 0.2$ and $f = 9000$ for an expected sanction of $1800 ($9000 \times 0.2$). Deterrence is positive but low ($1800 > $1500). The crime rate is 85% ($100 \times 1700/2000$). Say we redistribute $3000 from those designated poor to those designated rich, so that the rich have $12,000 and the poor have $6000; we adjust the fines accordingly and hold $p*$ at its original

level. The expected sanction of the poor will decrease to $1200 ($6000 × 0.2). Since the minimum benefit from committing the harmful act is $1500, all poor individuals commit the harmful act. Therefore, the decrease in the deterrence of the poor accounts for 7.5% of the total population (50 × 300/2000). The net harm associated with those additional poor offenders is on average $1350 per offender ($3000 − $1650) or, in total, $101.25 ($1350 × 7.5%). The expected sanction of the rich has increased to $2400 ($12,000 × 0.2). This amounts to an additional 15% (50 × 600/2000) of the population who are now deterred. These additional rich non-offenders impose a net harm of $900 per offender ($3000 − $2100) or a total of $135 ($900 × 15%). Social welfare is increased by $33.75 ($135 − $101.25).

37. As in section 4, this condition can be restated in terms of wealth relative to the (modified) optimal multiplier.
38. These distribution functions include, for example, exponential distribution, log-normal distribution (for some parameters of σ), and the F distribution.
39. Of course, poor and rich offenders may be positioned at different parts of the density function.
40. Viewed from a different perspective, this chapter raises the possibility that societies with more equal distributions of wealth tend to be wealthier than societies with less equal distribution, if, from the outset, all these societies are sufficiently wealthy, and vice versa if all are sufficiently poor.

REFERENCES

Bar Niv, Moshe and Zvi Safra (2002) "On the Social Desirability of Wealth Dependent Fine Policies," 22 *International Review of Law and Economics* 53

Becker, Gary S. (1968) "Crime and Punishment: An Economic Approach," 76 *Journal of Political Economy* 169

Benoit, Jean-Pierre and Martin J. Osborne (1995) "Crime, Punishment, and Social Expenditure," 151(2) *Journal of Institutional and Theoretical Economics* 326

Cassone, Alberto and Carla Marchese (2006) "Redistribution and crime when agents have limited liability: A note," 2 *Review of Law and Economics* 56

Chiu, W. Henry and Paul Madden (1998) "Burglary and Income Inequality," 69 *Journal of Public Economics* 123

Demougin, Dominique and Robert Schwager (2000) "Excess Burden of Criminality and Redistribution," 20 *International Review of Law and Economics* 329

Eaton, B. Curtis and William D. White (1991) "The Distribution of Wealth and the Efficiency of Institutions," *Economic Inquiry* 336

Ehrlich, Isaac (1973) "Participation in Illegitimate Activities: A Theoretical and Empirical Investigation," 81 *Journal of Political Economy* 521

Fleisher, M. Belton (1966) "The Effect of Income on Delinquency," 56 *American Economic Review* 118

Garoupa, Nuno (2001) "Optimal Magnitude and Probability of Fines," 45 *European Economic Review* 1765

Heineke, John M. (1978) "Economic Models of Criminal Behavior: An Overview," in *Economic Models of Criminal Behavior*, J.M. Heineke, ed., North Holland, 1–33

Kelly, Morgan (2000) "Inequality and Crime," 82(4) *Review of Economics and Statistics* 530

Polinsky, A. Mitchell and Steven Shavell (1984) "The Optimal Use of Fines and Imprisonment," 24 *Journal of Public Economics* 89

— (1991) "A Note on Optimal Fines When Wealth Varies Among Individuals," 81 *American Economic Review* 618

Shavell, Steven (1991) "Specific versus General Enforcement of Law," 99 *Journal of Political Economy* 1088

Zhang, Junsen (1997) "The Effect of Welfare Programs on Criminal Behavior: A Theoretical and Empirical Analysis," *Economic Inquiry* 120

APPENDIX

Here a formal and direct proof of Proposition 1 is provided for the case in which the fraction of rich (poor) individuals in the population is μ $(1 - \mu)$.

The social problem is to choose p, f_P, f_R, w_P and w_R to maximize:

(1B) $$SW = (1 - \mu) \int_{pf_P}^{\hat{b}} (b - h)g(b)db + \mu \int_{pf_R}^{\hat{b}} (b - h)g(b)db - c(p)$$

Subject to $f_i \leq w_i$ $i = P, R,$

$$(1 - \mu)w_P + \mu w_R = \overline{w}$$

$$w_P \leq w_R$$

$$w_P \geq 0$$

Define the Lagrangian function as:

(2B) $$L = SW + \lambda_1(w_P - f_P) + \lambda_2(w_R - f_R) + \lambda_3(\overline{w} - (1 - \mu)w_P - \mu w_R)$$

$$+ \lambda_4(w_R - w_P) + \lambda_5 w_P$$

The optimal solution to the problem p^*, f_P^*, f_R^*, w_P^* and w_R^* should satisfy the Kuhn-Tucker conditions (second order conditions are assumed to be satisfied):

(3B) $$L_{f_P} = (1 - \mu)p(h - pf_P)g(pf_P) - \lambda_1 = 0$$

(4B) $$L_{f_R} = \mu p(h - pf_R)g(pf_R) - \lambda_2 = 0$$

(5B) $$L_P = (1 - \mu)f_P(h - pf_P)g(pf_P) + \mu f_R(h - pf_R)g(pf_R) - c'(p) = 0$$

(6B) $$L_{w_P} = \lambda_1 - \lambda_3(1 - \mu) - \lambda_4 + \lambda_5 = 0$$

(7B) $$L_{w_R} = \lambda_2 - \lambda_3\mu + \lambda_4 = 0$$

(8B) $$L_{\lambda_1} = (w_P - f_P) \geq 0, \lambda_1 \geq 0 \text{ and } \lambda_1(w_P - f_P) = 0$$

(9B) $$L_{\lambda_2} = (w_R - f_R) \geq 0, \lambda_2 \geq 0 \text{ and } \lambda_2(w_R - f_R) = 0$$

(10B) $$L_{\lambda_3} = \overline{w} - (1 - \mu)w_P - \mu w_R = 0$$

(11B) $$L_{\lambda_4} = w_R - w_P \geq 0 \, \lambda_4 \geq 0 \text{ and } \lambda_4(w_R - w_P) = 0$$

(12B) $$L_{\lambda_5} = w_P \geq 0 \quad \lambda_5 \geq 0 \text{ and } \lambda_5 w_P = 0$$

Suppose that $w_P^* = 0$. Then, from (10B), $w_R^* = \overline{w}/\mu > 0$, and from (11B), $\lambda_4 = 0$. From (8B), we have $f_R^* = 0$, and from (3B) $\lambda_1 = (1 - \mu)phg(0) > 0$. Suppose $\lambda_2 = 0$. Then, from (4B) $p^*f_R^* = h$. But then $L_P = -c'(p) < 0$, which contradicts (5B). Therefore $\lambda_2 > 0$, which implies that $f_R^* = w_R^*$. From (7B), we have $\lambda_2 = \mu\lambda_3$. Substituting this into (4B), we get that: $\lambda_3 = p^*(h - p^*f_R^*)g(p^*f_R^*)$. Similarly, from (6B), it follows that $\lambda_1 = (1 - \mu)\lambda_3 - \lambda_5$.

Substituting this into (3B), we get that: $\lambda_3 = p^*hg(0) + \lambda_5/1 - \mu$

But since $p^*(h - p^*f_R^*)g(p^*f_R^*) < p^*hg(0) + \lambda_5/1 - \mu$, we get a contradiction. Therefore, $w_P^* > 0$ (and $\lambda_5 = 0$).

Suppose that $w_R^* > w_P^*$. Then from (11B) $\lambda_4 = 0$. From (7B) we get: $\lambda_2 = \mu\lambda_3$, and from (6B) $\lambda_1 = (1 - \mu)\lambda_3$ (recalling that $\lambda_5 = 0$). Suppose now that $\lambda_3 = 0$, which implies that $\lambda_1 = \lambda_2 = 0$ as well. From (3B) and (4B) we get that $h = p^*f_P^* = p^*f_R^*$, but this leads to $L_P < 0$, which ontradicts (5B). Thus, $\lambda_P, \lambda_R, \lambda > 0$, which implies (from (8B) and (9B)) that the wealth constraints are binding: $f_P^* = w_P$ and $f_R^* = w_R$. Substituting $\lambda_1 = (1 - \mu)\lambda_3$ and $\lambda_2 = \mu\lambda_3$ to (3B) and (4B) respectively and rearranging, we get: $(h - pw_P) = (h - pw_R)$, which is impossible if $w_R^* > w_P^*$. Therefore, $\lambda_4 > 0$, which implies that $w_P^* = w_R^* = \overline{w}$ (the last equality follows from (10B)).

This completes the proof of Proposition 1.

Given that $w_P^* = w_R^* = \overline{w}$, straightforward reasoning leads also to $f_P^* = f_R^* = \overline{w}$, and p^* satisfying: $\overline{w}(h - p^*\overline{w})g(p^*\overline{w}) = c'(p)$, such that $p^*\overline{w} < h$.

6 Deterrence and incapacitation models of criminal punishment: can the twain meet?
Thomas J. Miceli

1. INTRODUCTION

Economic models of law enforcement beginning with Becker (1968) have primarily focused on the role of criminal punishment in deterring crime. This approach to the determination of optimal criminal penalties relies on the *rational offender assumption*, which maintains that potential offenders decide whether or not to commit an illegal act by comparing the gain from commission to the expected punishment. Although some may doubt the validity of this assumption, there is a growing body of empirical evidence to support it (as reviewed in the next section).

One of the clearest policy implications emerging from this model is that fines should be relied upon to the maximum extent possible before imprisonment is used. The obvious reason is that, while fines and prison are equally capable of deterring rational offenders, fines are costless to impose while prison is costly. The use of prison should therefore be limited to those offenders whose lack of wealth makes the threat of a heavy fine ineffective as a deterrent (Polinsky and Shavell 1984). The extensive use of prison in actual punishment schemes, however, appears to be inconsistent with this prescription.

One explanation for this practice is the desire for equal treatment of rich and poor offenders, given that the economically efficient punishment scheme would essentially allow rich offenders to "buy their way out of jail" (Lott 1987). Another explanation is that prison serves an incapacitation function; that is, it allows the state to detain those offenders who are expected to commit further harmful acts if released. Recent three-strikes laws enacted by many states, which imprison certain repeat offenders for life, appear to be motivated primarily by this rationale (Shepherd 2002). Economists have devoted relatively little attention to incapacitation as a basis for criminal punishment. An exception is Shavell (1987), who shows that the optimal incapacitation policy involves holding an offender in prison as long as the harm he is expected to impose if free exceeds the cost of imprisonment. The incapacitation model is silent, however, about why offenders choose to commit crimes in the first place.

As the literature stands, therefore, the deterrence and incapacitation models exist as separate theories of criminal punishment. The deterrence theory is the more refined and elegant of the two, and it clearly occupies the predominant position in the literature, but its inability to provide an adequate explanation for the actual use of prison undermines its status as a positive theory of law enforcement. The incapacitation theory, in contrast, is more ad hoc from a theoretical perspective, but it offers a more convincing explanation for certain imprisonment policies. Clearly, what is needed is a model of law enforcement that integrates the best of both theories. The purpose of this chapter is to outline such a model.

The resulting unified (or hybrid) model of criminal punishment retains the theoretical rigor of the deterrence model by assuming that offenders are fully rational. Thus, potential offenders make crime decisions based on the expected punishment, including the possibility of imprisonment. A role for incapacitation is introduced into this setting by allowing potential offenders to face repeated criminal opportunities over an infinite lifetime. The threat of imprisonment therefore deters some offenders from committing crimes in the first place, while the detention of previously convicted offenders prevents them from committing further crimes by depriving them of future criminal opportunities. In this way, the model embodies both the deterrence and incapacitation functions of imprisonment within a single, coherent framework.

The remainder of the chapter is organized as follows. Section 2 reviews the empirical evidence on the relationship between imprisonment policy and crime. While the evidence clearly shows that prison has a crime-reducing effect, this result is consistent with both the deterrence and incapacitation theories. By employing methods for disentangling the two effects, however, econometricians have shown that both are relevant. Section 3 reviews the standard economic models of deterrence and incapacitation, and discusses their compatibility. Section 4 then lays out the basic hybrid model, and shows that the pure deterrence and pure incapacitation models emerge as special cases. It goes on to show that, when prison is the only form of punishment, adding incapacitation can result in either a longer or a shorter prison term compared to the pure deterrence model. Intuitively, if there is under-deterrence in the pure deterrence model, then introducing incapacitation will cause the optimal prison term to be longer because it prevents offenders from committing further inefficient acts. Conversely, if there is over-deterrence, incapacitation will cause the optimal prison term to be shorter so that offenders are able to commit further efficient acts. When a fine is combined with prison and the fine is not constrained by the offender's wealth, then, as in the pure deterrence model, it is never optimal to use prison either for deterrence or incapacitation. The reason is that the optimal fine achieves the efficient (first-best) level of crime, so only efficient crimes are ever committed. Thus, there is no social gain from incapacitation. However, when the fine is limited by the offender's wealth, the optimal prison term is determined by the same factors as in the prison-only version of the model.

Section 5 extends the model in two ways. First, it allows the probability of apprehension to be endogenous. Second, it examines a version of the model in which the offender's utility is not counted as part of social welfare. This case is of interest because most crimes for which incapacitation is relevant are harmful to society and hence are not likely to be socially desirable. In the prison-only version of this model, the optimal prison term is either finite (with deterrence and incapacitation offsetting each other), or infinite (with deterrence and incapacitation reinforcing each other). This last case seems most descriptive of the rationale for three-strikes laws. Finally, Section 6 offers concluding comments.

2. EMPIRICAL EVIDENCE ON THE IMPACT OF IMPRISONMENT ON CRIME

Empirical analyses of the impact of imprisonment policies have focused on measuring their effects in reducing crime.[1] In particular, they ask whether increases in the use of

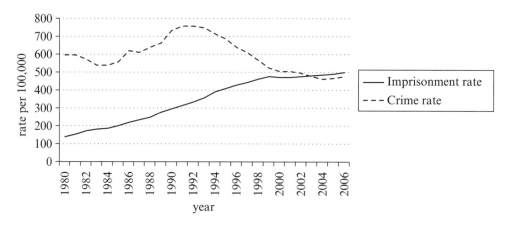

Figure 6.1   Crime and imprisonment rates (per 100,000) 1980–2006

prison as a criminal sanction, as reflected by more frequent use of prison and/or longer prison terms, are associated with a reduction in the crime rate, as predicted by both the deterrence and incapacitation models of crime. Although the hypothesis is a straightforward one, uncovering such a causal effect from aggregate crime data presents significant empirical problems. One of the difficulties is illustrated by Figure 6.1, which graphs the rate of violent crimes and the imprisonment rate in the United States from 1980–2006.[2] Depending on the particular time interval, one can observe either a positive or a negative correlation between the variables. Thus, by focusing on a particular time period, one can either conclude that an increase in the use of prison has not reduced the crime rate (and may actually have increased it), or that it has had the desired crime-reducing effect. The problem stems from a failure to account for multiple causal influences on the crime rate besides imprisonment, as well as the likely feedback effect of the observed crime rate on prison policy (i.e., the tendency for policy-makers to respond to rising crime rates by enacting more stringent criminal policies, resulting in a reverse-causal effect).

Recent studies have employed sophisticated empirical techniques to overcome these challenges. The results suggest that increases in the rate of imprisonment do in fact cause a decline in the crime rate. Recall, however, that this conclusion is consistent with both the deterrence and incapacitation models. In other words, the mere establishment of a causal connection between increased use of imprisonment and lower crime rates does not tell us whether this is due to a behavioral response of rational offenders who choose to commit fewer crimes for fear of punishment, or whether it is because offenders who otherwise would have committed crimes are deprived of the opportunity to do so because they are held in prison longer. In addition to its theoretical relevance, this distinction is important from a policy perspective because, as we will see, the specific prescriptions from the two models are different.

Fortunately, economists have found ways of disentangling the two effects. For example, Kessler and Levitt (1999) looked for changes in the crime rate immediately after California enacted Proposition 8, which provided for enhanced prison sentences for certain serious crimes. Since the incapacitating effect of the new law could only take effect after the standard prison term had run, any observed reduction in the crime rate before that time would have had to be solely due to deterrence. The authors in fact found that the crime rate fell more for affected offenses than for non-affected offenses in the year after adoption, showing that deterrence mattered. However, they also found that the crime rate fell twice as much in the three years after adoption as it did in the first year, suggesting that incapacitation had also contributed to the overall decline in the crime rate. Other studies have yielded similar results, confirming that deterrence and incapacitation effects are both relevant factors in assessing the impact of prison policies.

3. ECONOMIC THEORY OF CRIME AND PUNISHMENT

The empirical finding that both deterrence and incapacitation effects matter sets the agenda for theoretical models seeking to explain the observed relationship between crime and punishment. This section reviews the basic versions of both the pure deterrence and pure incapacitation models by way of providing a context for the hybrid model to be developed in the next section.

3.1 Economic Theory of Deterrence

As noted, the economic theory of criminal punishment is primarily based on the goal of deterrence. Although such a theory was discussed as early as the eighteenth century by Beccaria (1767) and Bentham (1789), the modern mathematical version was first developed by Becker (1968) and elaborated on by Polinsky and Shavell (2000, 2007). I will hereafter refer to this as the BPS model of deterrence. The key behavioral assumption underlying this model is the rational offender assumption, which maintains that would-be criminals decide whether or not to commit illegal acts in the same way that they would make any other economic decision; namely, by comparing the expected gain from committing the act to the expected punishment, where the latter consists of the probability of apprehension and conviction multiplied by the sanction (a fine and/or imprisonment term). If the expected gain exceeds the expected sanction, the offender commits the act; otherwise, he is deterred.

Summing over all offenders who choose to commit illegal acts yields the aggregate crime rate, which, by virtue of the rationality assumption, is decreasing in the severity of the expected sanction. In other words, increases in both the likelihood of apprehension and the severity of the sanction have the effect of reducing the crime rate. Based on this relationship, policy-makers can choose the law enforcement policy that achieves the socially optimal crime rate. This is usually taken to be the crime rate that maximizes a social welfare function that depends on the net cost of crime to society (consisting of the harm to victims less any acceptable benefits to offenders) and the cost of enforcement.

To see this formally, let

g = monetary gain from committing a criminal act
$z(g)$ = density function reflecting the distribution of gains across offenders
h = harm caused by a criminal act (assumed to be fixed)
p = probability of apprehension and conviction[3]

$k(p)$ = cost of maintaining an apprehension rate of p, $k' > 0$, $k'' \geq 0$
f = fine imposed on conviction
s = length of the prison term imposed on conviction
δ = unit cost of prison to the offender
c = unit cost of prison to society

In the case where the sanction consists of a fine and imprisonment, the expected sanction from the offender's perspective is given by $p(f + \delta s)$. After observing the gain, g, he will therefore commit the crime if and only if

$$g \geq p(f + \delta s) \equiv \hat{g} \tag{1}$$

where $\hat{g}$ is the threshold gain separating those offenders who commit crimes from those who are deterred. Thus, condition (1) is the embodiment of the rational offender assumption. Since the gain is distributed by $z(g)$ across potential offenders, the aggregate crime rate is given by $1 - Z(\hat{g})$, where Z is the distribution function associated with z (i.e., $Z' \equiv z > 0$). It follows that the crime rate is decreasing in p, f, and s, reflecting the deterrent effect of increases in both the likelihood of apprehension and the severity of sanctions.

Social welfare in the BPS model consists of the net gain to offenders from committing illegal acts, minus the harm and enforcement costs. It is typically assumed in deterrence models that the gain to offender should count as part of social welfare, making the net social gain from a given crime $g - h$. This assumption is questioned by some (see, e.g., Stigler 1970[4] and Lewin and Trumbull 1990), and clearly is more reasonable for some types of crime (e.g., speeding, double-parking) than for others (e.g., violent crimes). Rather than debate this point, however, I will maintain the standard assumption for most of the analysis. (However, section 5.2 examines the effect of excluding the offender's gains from welfare in the context of the hybrid model.)

Formally, welfare in the BPS model is given by

$$W = \int_{\hat{g}}^{\infty} (g - h - p(c + \delta)s)z(g)dg - k(p) \tag{2}$$

where the integral represents offender's gain minus the harm and expected punishment costs, summed over all offenses (where $\hat{g}$ is defined by (1)), while $k(p)$ represents apprehension costs. The enforcement authority is assumed to maximize this expression by its choice of the policy variables f, s, and p. It is easiest to see the optimum by first supposing that the probability of apprehension, and hence apprehension costs, are fixed.[5] In this case, we first consider punishment by a fine alone ($s \equiv 0$), and then by prison alone ($f \equiv 0$).

In the fine-only punishment scheme, we set the derivative of (2) with respect to f equal to zero and solve for f to obtain

$$f^* = h/p \tag{3}$$

Thus, the optimal fine equals the harm per crime, appropriately adjusted to reflect the uncertainty of apprehension. In this case, only efficient crimes (those for which $g > h$)

are committed. To illustrate, suppose that the harm imposed per criminal act is $500. Thus, only those offenders who expect a gain of more than $500 should commit the act. Optimal deterrence therefore requires the expected fine, pf, to be set equal to $500. If the probability of apprehension is ½, this requires the *actual* fine to be set at $1000.

Obviously, the above policy is limited by the wealth of the offender, w, which will prevent the attainment of the first-best outcome for those offenders whose wealth is less than h/p. As will be shown below, this problem provides the economic rationale for the use of imprisonment.

Before considering the combined use of fines and prison, however, we consider the optimal prison term when it is the only possible sanction. This is found by maximizing (2) with respect to s with $f = 0$. Assuming an interior solution, the resulting first order condition is given by

$$(h + pcs)z(\hat{g})\delta = [1 - Z(\hat{g})](c + \delta) \tag{4}$$

The left-hand side of this condition represents the marginal benefit of a longer prison term in the form of the avoided harm plus the expected savings in punishment costs. The right-hand side is the marginal cost of punishment, consisting of the number of crimes multiplied by the incremental cost to society and the offender of lengthening the prison term. Unlike the case of a fine, there is no simple formula for the optimal prison term.

Now suppose that fines and prison can be combined. One of the key prescriptions of the BPS model of crime is that when both sanctions are available, prison should never be used unless the offender's wealth precludes setting the fine at the level prescribed by (3) (Polinsky and Shavell 1984). This is easily proved by supposing initially that $f < w$ and $s > 0$. Now raise f and lower s so that the critical gain, $\hat{g}$, remains constant. According to (1), the crime rate will remain unchanged, but expected punishment costs, $p(c + \delta)s$, will fall, implying that welfare must increase. Thus, the original scheme with $f < w$ could not have been optimal. Intuitively, it is never optimal in the BPS model to impose a prison term rather than a fine for deterrence purposes for the simple reason that the two sanctions are equally capable of deterring crimes, but fines are costless to impose while prison is costly. Thus, only when the offender's wealth does not allow the fine to be set at the first-best level in (3) is it possibly desirable to impose a prison term. In this case, the optimal prison term is found by maximizing (2) with respect to s with $f = w$. Since prison is costly, this may or may not result in a positive prison term, depending on the magnitude of the marginal deterrence benefits compared to the marginal cost of imprisonment.

As an example, suppose that the social optimum entails a level of offender gains, $\hat{g}$, equal to $4000, meaning that it is only efficient for those offenders who receive a benefit of more than $4000 to commit crimes. Also, let the probability of apprehension be ½, let the unit cost of prison to the offender be $500 per month, and let the offender's wealth be $2000. Then from (1) we have $\hat{g} = p(f + \delta s) = $4000. After substituting $p = 1/2$, we obtain $f + \delta s = $8000. Since this amount exceeds the offender's wealth, the optimal fine is maximal, or $f = $2000, while the optimal prison term solves $2000 + ($500)s = $8000, or $s = 12$ months. The socially optimal punishment scheme thus involves a fine of $2000 and one year in prison.

Finally, consider the effect of allowing the enforcement authority to choose the probability of apprehension along with the severity of sanctions. In this case, the optimal sanction, in both the fine-only and the prison-only schemes, is maximal.[6] The proof of this proposition proceeds as above. Specifically, suppose initially that the sanction (the fine or the prison term) is less than maximal. Now raise the sanction and lower p so as to hold the critical gain, $\hat{g}$, fixed. Since this lowers $k(p)$ while holding the integral term in (2) fixed, welfare must increase. Thus, the initial punishment scheme could not have been optimal. This conclusion makes intuitive sense in the fine-only case since, as before, increasing the fine is costless while increasing p is costly. It is less obvious, however, why the prison term should be maximal. The reason is that only those offenders who are caught are imprisoned. Thus, by lowering p, fewer offenders are caught and imprisoned, thereby lowering (or at least not raising) expected punishment costs.

When fines and imprisonment are combined, the optimal fine is still maximal, but the optimal prison term may not be maximal. This is true because, when the fine is set equal to the offender's wealth, simultaneously raising the prison term and lowering the probability of apprehension so as to hold the expected cost of prison fixed will *reduce* deterrence because the expected fine, pw, falls. Thus, it is not necessarily welfare-enhancing to continue to raise s while proportionately lowering p. The optimal prison term in this case depends, as before, on the particular relationship between the marginal deterrence benefits and the marginal cost of imprisonment.

3.2   Economic Theory of Incapacitation

Incapacitation protects society from the harm caused by criminals, not by deterring them, but by depriving them of the opportunity to commit crimes. Imprisonment is therefore the primary form of incapacitation. Unlike the deterrence model, however, incapacitation is not concerned with an offender's decision about whether or not to commit a crime. Instead, it takes the crime rate as given and asks whether social costs are lower if an offender, once apprehended, is detained or released. Specifically, the comparison is between c, the cost of holding the criminal in prison, and h, the expected harm that he would impose if released, where both are defined per unit of time. If $c > h$, the offender should be released, but if $c < h$, he should be imprisoned and detained for as long as the inequality continues to hold, possibly for the remainder of his life. In the likely case where the harm an offender would impose declines with his age, the optimal policy is therefore to release him as soon as the threatened harm falls below the cost of holding him in prison (Shavell 1987).

3.3   Are the Economic Models of Deterrence and Incapacitation Compatible?

At present, the deterrence (BPS) and incapacitation models represent distinct strands in the economics of crime literature, with the BPS model being the predominant paradigm. As noted, however, there is a somewhat troubling disconnect between the prescriptions of the BPS model and actual criminal policy, especially as regards the use of prison. In particular, actual practice seems to involve a significantly greater reliance on prison than the BPS model prescribes, especially as exemplified by the recent spate of three-strikes laws that impose life sentences on repeat offenders for certain crimes. The goal of incapacitation would seem to be a better explanation for such a policy.

In principle, however, there is no reason why deterrence and incapacitation cannot co-exist as complementary economic theories of criminal punishment. From a deterrence perspective, the threat of punishment should prevent some offenders from committing dangerous acts in the first place, while from an incapacitation perspective, the imprisonment of those offenders who are not deterred, or who are not deterrable (for whatever reason), will prevent them from committing further harmful acts. The literature, however, has yet to offer a fully integrated model that captures both of these approaches to crime prevention (though Ehrlich 1981 represents an early effort).

A necessary first step in developing such an integrated model is to make the BPS model dynamic so as to introduce the time dimension that is inherent in the incapacitation motive. Several recent efforts along these lines have been made by way of investigating the pervasiveness of escalating penalty schemes for repeat offenders (Polinsky and Rubenfeld 1991; Polinsky and Shavell 1998; Miceli and Bucci 2005), but none of these models has explicitly addressed the question of incapacitation. Still, these studies have revealed an important insight that sheds light on the compatibility of deterrence and incapacitation models. In particular, they have shown that escalating penalties can never be optimal in a pure deterrence model when penalties are structured so as to achieve efficient (first-best) deterrence. The reason is that, in such a regime, only efficient crimes are committed, so there would be no social gain from increasing the punishment on those offenders who commit them repeatedly. Doing so would be like charging a higher price for repeat customers (Polinsky and Shavell 2000). By the same logic, there would seem to be no social gain from incapacitating offenders who are expected to commit further efficient crimes once they are released.

The foregoing argument suggests that, in order to accept incapacitation as a basis for imprisoning offenders, one must either believe that some offenders are undeterrable and hence can only be prevented from committing inefficient crimes by detaining them, or that the optimal punishment policy involves some under-deterrence. Regarding the first of these possibilities, while it is likely that some offenders are in fact undeterrable, this does not provide a very satisfying answer to the compatibility question because it suggests that incapacitation can never be relevant for rational offenders. (It also requires the court to be able to distinguish deterrable and undeterrable offenders at the time of sentencing.)

Regarding the second possibility, it turns out that the BPS model does generally result in imperfect deterrence when punishment is costly (i.e., when it takes the form of prison). In particular, the socially optimal prison term as defined by Equation (4) above may entail either over-deterrence or under-deterrence (Polinsky and Shavell (2000) at 50). In other words, the gain enjoyed by the marginal offender may be larger or smaller than the harm caused by the act (i.e., $\hat{g}$ may be larger or smaller than h at the optimum). This is true because the optimal prison term must account for the expected cost of punishment, which depends both on the number of offenders punished and the length of the prison term. Thus, adjusting the prison term downward, for example, will reduce the cost per offender but will raise the number of offenders. And since the effect on expected costs is ambiguous, this may or may not be socially desirable.

The model to be developed in the next section exploits the fact that there is imperfect deterrence in the BPS model to develop a fully rational, dynamic model of law enforcement in which both deterrence and incapacitation arise naturally as rationales for possibly imprisoning convicted offenders.

4. DETERRENCE AND INCAPACITATION: A HYBRID MODEL

This section lays out the hybrid model of criminal punishment. It first shows that the pure deterrence and pure incapacitation models emerge as special cases, and then examines the optimal enforcement policy in the general version.

4.1 The Basic Model

The model to be developed in this section retains the rational offender assumption, but extends the standard BPS model to make it dynamic. In particular, offenders are assumed to have infinite life spans and potentially to commit crimes throughout their lives when not imprisoned. As in the BPS model, offenders decide whether or not to become criminals by comparing the gain from an illegal act to the expected punishment. If an offender chooses to commit a crime, he does so continuously until he is apprehended. Then, after serving his prison term, he confronts another criminal opportunity immediately upon release and makes a new calculation. This sequence of crime and punishment repeats itself throughout the offender's infinite lifetime.

To model this formally, we again let g be the gain from a criminal act, which continues to be distributed across offenders by the density function $z(g)$. For simplicity, we will assume that the value of g that an offender draws at time zero (his first criminal opportunity) defines his "type" throughout the remainder of his life (i.e., whenever he encounters a criminal opportunity).[7] Also, since time is continuous, we now define g to be the gain per instant of time up to the date when the offender is apprehended. Thus, if t is the date of apprehension, the present value of the gain from committing the initial crime, as of time zero (the commission date), is given by

$$\int_0^t ge^{-r\tau}d\tau = \frac{g}{r}(1 - e^{-rt}) \tag{5}$$

where r is the instantaneous discount rate. If we normalize the gain from not committing crimes to be zero, then expression (5) represents the gross gain from commission of a single criminal act as a function of the apprehension date, t.

We model the apprehension technology in a manner first suggested by Davis (1988) in his intertemporal model of crime.[8] In particular, let the apprehension date, t, be a random variable that is distributed exponentially with density function

$$v(t) = pe^{-pt} \tag{6}$$

where p is the instantaneous probability of apprehension. The corresponding distribution function is given by $V(t) = e^{-pt}$, and the expected time until apprehension is $1/p$.

Since we are interested in incapacitation, we focus on prison as the form of punishment, possibly combined with a fine. Thus, at the time of apprehension, the offender is assessed a fine (if any), denoted by f, and is imprisoned for a length of time s. Then, at the

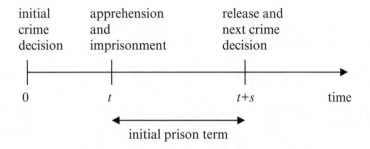

Figure 6.2   Time line of crime and punishment over an infinite horizon

date of release, which occurs at time $t + s$, the offender immediately confronts another criminal opportunity, and the process begins again. Given the above assumption that the offender's type remains fixed throughout his life, and assuming a time-invariant punishment policy,[9] the offender will make the same decision at each opportunity. Thus, those offenders who find crime profitable at time zero will become repeat (habitual) criminals, while those who are initially deterred will never commit crimes. Figure 6.2 depicts the time sequence of events as just described.

Following Polinsky and Shavell (2000, 2007), we first examine the optimal punishment scheme assuming a fixed probability of apprehension. We begin with a prison-only scheme, and then introduce the possibility of a fine combined with prison. In section 5, we extend the model to allow an endogenous probability of apprehension.

4.2   Punishment by Prison Only

We have already derived the gross gain for an individual who chooses to commit a crime. We now need to combine that with the expected punishment cost. In the prison-only scheme, this involves the expected present value of the cost of imprisonment from the date of apprehension, t, up to the date of release, $t + s$. Proceeding as above, we calculate the punishment cost for the offender's initial crime as a function of t and s to be

$$\int_t^{t+s} \delta e^{-r\tau} d\tau = \frac{\delta}{r}(e^{-rt} - e^{-r(t+s)}) \tag{7}$$

where, recall, δ is the unit cost of imprisonment to the offender. The net benefit for the initial offense is thus given by the difference between (5) and (7), or

$$\frac{g}{r}(1 - e^{-rt}) - \frac{\delta}{r}(e^{-rt} - e^{-r(t+s)}) \tag{8}$$

Since the apprehension date is a random variable, we need to compute the expected value of this expression. Thus, weighting (8) by the density function in (6) and integrating over all values of t, we obtain

$$G(g, s, p) = \int_0^\infty \left[\frac{g}{r}(1 - e^{-rt}) - \frac{\delta}{r}(e^{-rt} - e^{-r(t+s)})pe^{-pt}dt \right]$$

$$= \frac{1}{p + r}\left[g - \frac{p\delta}{r}(1 - e^{-rs}) \right] \tag{9}$$

This expression represents the net expected gain to the offender from committing the first criminal act. If the opportunity were one-time, he would choose to commit the act if and only if this expression is positive, or if and only if

$$g \geq \frac{p\delta}{r}(1 - e^{-rs}) \tag{10}$$

where the right-hand side is the critical gain. As in the standard BPS model, this condition indicates that the offender is less likely to commit a crime as the length of the prison term and the likelihood of apprehension are increased. The only difference here is that the cost of imprisonment is expressed in present value terms.[10]

For purposes of integrating deterrence and incapacitation, the crucial extension of the standard model is the assumption that offenders face repeated criminal opportunities over an infinite horizon. This is captured in the above framework by computing the present value of lifetime net benefits, given the assumption of time invariance. Formally, this is done by forming the recursive equation

$$\Gamma(g, s, p) = G(g, s, p) + \beta(s)\Gamma(g, s, p) \tag{11}$$

where $\beta(s)$ is the expected discount factor. According to this expression, the offender expects to receive a net gain of G from every episode of crime and punishment over an infinite number of periods. The discount factor is in expected terms because it depends on the random date of apprehension. The expected value of this factor is thus computed as follows:

$$\beta(s) = \int_0^\infty e^{-r(t+s)}pe^{-pt}dt = \frac{pe^{-rs}}{p + r} \tag{12}$$

Substituting this expression into (11) and solving for $\Gamma(g, s, p)$ yields:

$$\Gamma(g, s, p) = \frac{1}{p(1 - e^{-rs}) + r}\left[g - \frac{p\delta}{r}(1 - e^{-rs}) \right] \tag{13}$$

A potential criminal at time zero will commit the initial crime if this expression, which represents the present value of his expected income from a life of crime, is positive. Note that the condition for (13) to be positive is given by (10), which was the condition for the first crime to be profitable. This makes sense since, given time invariance, if the first crime is profitable, all subsequent crimes will be profitable as well. The threshold level of g separating criminals and non-criminals is thus given by the right-hand side of (10), or

$$\tilde{g}(s, p) \equiv \frac{p\delta}{r}(1 - e^{-rs}) \tag{14}$$

which, as noted, is decreasing in s, reflecting the deterrence function of prison.

Now consider the social cost of crime. This consists of three components, (1) the harm suffered by victims, (2) the cost to society of imprisoning offenders, and (3) the cost of apprehension. In the current version of the model where p is treated as a parameter, apprehension costs, $k(p)$, are fixed. The harm suffered by victims is again denoted by h, but, like the gain enjoyed by offenders, this cost is now measured per unit of time that the offender is free and committing crimes. Similarly, the cost of imprisonment, c, is defined to be the cost society incurs per unit of time that the offender is incarcerated. The harm plus imprisonment costs for the offender's first episode of crime and punishment are thus computed as follows:

$$\int_0^t he^{-r\tau}d\tau + \int_t^{t+s} ce^{-r\tau}d\tau = \frac{h}{r}(1 - e^{-rt}) + \frac{c}{r}(e^{-rt} - e^{-r(t+s)})$$

Proceeding as above, we compute the expected value of this expression to obtain

$$C(s, p) = \int_0^\infty \left[\frac{h}{r}(1 - e^{-rt}) + \frac{c}{r}(e^{-rt} - e^{-r(t+s)}) \right] pe^{-pt}dt$$

$$= \frac{1}{p + r}\left[h + \frac{pc}{r}(1 - e^{-rt}) \right] \tag{15}$$

Finally, we can convert this to the present value of social costs over the lifetime of the offender by again using the recursive equation

$$\Psi(s, p) = C(s, p) + \beta(s)\Psi(s, p) \tag{16}$$

Substituting from (12) and solving yields the present value of harm plus punishment costs

$$\Psi(s, p) = \frac{1}{p(1 - e^{-rs}) + r}\left[h + \frac{pc}{r}(1 - e^{-rs}) \right] \tag{17}$$

Total social costs consist of this expression plus the fixed costs of apprehension, or $\Psi(s, p) + k(p)$.

Before proceeding with the analysis of the hybrid model, we note that the pure deterrence (BPS) and pure incapacitation models emerge from this general model as special cases.

4.2.1 Pure deterrence model

The pure deterrence model emerges from the above formulation by considering only the initial episode of crime and punishment. In other words, instead of assuming that the offender commits repeated crimes throughout his life, we assume his crime decision is one-time. Obviously, imprisonment cannot serve an incapacitation function in this case because there is no threat that the offender will commit further harmful acts. Thus, the only possible function of prison is to deter the initial crime.

Social welfare in this case consists of the net benefits to the offender from the first criminal act, given by (9), minus the corresponding social costs, given by (15), summed over those offenders who choose to commit the crime (i.e., those for whom $g \geq \tilde{g}$), minus the fixed cost of apprehension. The resulting welfare function is

$$W_d = \int_{\tilde{g}(s,p)}^{\infty} [G(g, s, p) - C(s, p)]z(g)dg - k(p)$$

$$= \int_{\tilde{g}(s,p)}^{\infty} \frac{1}{p+r}\left[g - h - \frac{p(c+\delta)}{r}(1 - e^{-rs})\right]z(g)dg - k(p) \tag{18}$$

Note that this expression corresponds closely to the welfare function for the BPS model in (2). The resulting first order condition for the optimal prison term is given by

$$\left[h + \frac{pc}{r}(1 - e^{-rs})\right]z(\tilde{g})\delta = [1 - Z(\tilde{g})](c + \delta) \tag{19}$$

which has the same interpretation as (4) and only differs by the fact that the punishment cost savings on the left-hand side of (19) are in present value terms.

4.2.2   Pure incapacitation model

The pure incapacitation model of Shavell (1987) also emerges from the above formulation by choosing the prison term that minimizes the present value of harm plus imprisonment costs, holding the crime rate fixed. In this case, the repeated-offense model is relevant. Thus, the problem is to choose s to minimize (17). The derivative of this expression with respect to s is given by

$$\frac{\partial \Psi}{\partial s} = \frac{pre^{-rs}(c - h)}{[p(1 - e^{-rs}) + r]^2} \tag{20}$$

the sign of which depends on a comparison of c and h. If $c > h$, (20) is positive, implying that costs are increasing in the length of the prison term. In this case, the optimal prison term is zero; that is, offenders should face no prison time. Intuitively, if the cost of imprisonment exceeds the harm that the offender would impose on society if free, then it is inefficient to detain them. In contrast, if $c < h$, (20) is negative, implying that the optimal prison term is infinite. In this case, the cost of imprisonment is less than the harm that offenders would impose if free, so they should be imprisoned for life.

The simple model involves a corner solution (a zero or infinite prison sentence) because h and c are both assumed to be constant. More generally, if the offender's danger to society declines over time, either because a criminal's propensity to commit crime naturally declines with age, or because prison has a rehabilitative effect, then it becomes optimal to release the offender at the point where h falls below c (Shavell 1987).

4.2.3 Hybrid model

Finally, consider the general model that encompasses both deterrence and incapacitation. Social welfare in this case consists of the present value of net gains to offenders over their infinite lifetimes, given by (13), minus the present value of social costs, given by (17), both summed over those crimes that are committed, minus fixed apprehension costs. The resulting welfare function is given by

$$W_h = \int_{\tilde{g}(s,p)}^{\infty} [\Gamma(g,s,p) - \Psi(s,p)]z(g)\,dg - k(p)$$

$$= \int_{\tilde{g}(s,p)}^{\infty} \frac{1}{p(1 - e^{-rs}) + r}\left[g - h - \frac{p(c+\delta)}{r}(1 - e^{-rs})\right]z(g)\,dg - k(p) \qquad (21)$$

The optimal prison term maximizes this expression. The relevant first order condition, assuming an interior solution, is given by

$$\left[h + \frac{pc}{r}(1 - e^{-rs})\right]z(\tilde{g})\delta = \frac{1}{p(1 - e^{-rs}) + r} \int_{\tilde{g}(s,p)}^{\infty} (c + \delta + g - h)z(g)\,dg \qquad (22)$$

The left-hand side of this condition is identical to the left-hand side of (19) and again represents the marginal deterrence benefit of increasing the length of the prison term. However, the right-hand side of (22), the marginal cost of a longer prison sentence, is different. As in the pure deterrence model, it includes the marginal cost to society and to the offender of a longer sentence, captured by the $c + \delta$ term in the integral, appropriately adjusted to reflect the repeated nature of crime and punishments. But in addition, the marginal cost of punishment includes a term to reflect the incapacitation effects of imprisonment. Specifically, the $g - h$ term in the integral represents the foregone net social benefits of those crimes that the offender is unable to commit because he is detained in prison for a longer period of time, conditional on the fact that he would continue to commit crimes if set free, given $g \geq \tilde{g}$. Notice, however, that this incapacitation term may be positive or negative, depending on whether the expected value of g for those offenders who find crime profitable is larger or smaller that h. If it is positive, the marginal cost of imprisonment is larger compared to the pure deterrence model, implying that the optimal prison term should be shorter. In contrast, if it is negative, the marginal cost of imprisonment is smaller compared to the pure deterrence model, implying that the optimal prison term should be longer.

The intuitive explanation for these results is as follows. Suppose that the prison sentence is initially set at the length that would be optimal from a pure deterrence perspective. Then, if the expected gain for offenders who commit crimes is less than the social harm that they cause, then on average they are committing *inefficient crimes*. That is, $E[g - h|g \geq \tilde{g}] < 0$. In this case, there is a net social gain from detaining them longer in prison to prevent them from committing additional crimes at the margin. In other words, incapacitation dictates that the optimal prison sentence should be longer than would be indicated by a pure deterrence model. In contrast, if the expected gain for those offenders who commit crimes is larger than the harm they impose (i.e., if $E[g - h|g \geq \tilde{g}] > 0$), then on average they are committing *efficient crimes*. In this case, there would be a social loss from detaining them for a longer period of time because it deprives them of the opportunity to commit further efficient crimes. In other words, holding offenders in prison for purposes of incapacitation actually results in a net social loss. The optimal prison term is therefore shorter than would be prescribed under a policy of pure deterrence.

As a general rule, it is not possible to tell from (22) whether crimes are efficient or inefficient at the optimum. All we can say is that the right-hand side of (22) must be positive, which requires that

$$c + \delta > h - E[g|g \geq \tilde{g}] \tag{23}$$

Note that this condition necessarily holds if crimes are on average efficient (i.e., if the right-hand side is negative), but it can also hold if crimes are inefficient (i.e., if the right-hand side is positive). Thus, we can only conclude that incapacitation can either raise or lower the optimal prison term compared to a regime based on deterrence alone.

This possibility that incapacitation can actually lower the optimal prison term is obviously a consequence of the assumption that the offender's benefit from crime counts in social welfare. Given the controversial nature of this assumption (especially for violent crimes), section 5.2 will therefore examine the implications of relaxing it.

4.3   Prison and Fines

In the prison-only model analysed in the previous section, the optimal prison term had to balance deterrence and incapacitation. We now extend the model to allow the use of fines along with prison. Fines obviously can have no incapacitation effect, but they can deter offenders, thus allowing the use of prison solely for incapacitation purposes. We noted above that in the pure deterrence (BPS) model, when fines and prison are both available, fines should be maximal (i.e., equal to the offender's wealth) before the use of prison is considered. The question is whether this conclusion continues to hold in the hybrid model. To provide an answer, we assume initially that there is no limit on the offender's ability to pay the fine.

Assume that the fine, f, is imposed as a lump sum amount at the instant the offender is apprehended. For the initial crime, the present value of the fine as of time zero is therefore $e^{-rt}f$, which is subtracted from the offender's net benefit in (8). Calculating the expected value of this expression as above yields

$$G(g, f, s, p) = \frac{1}{p + r}\left[g - pf - \frac{p\delta}{r}(1 - e^{-rs})\right] \tag{24}$$

Converting this to the present value of gains over the offender's infinite lifetime yields

$$\Gamma(g, f, s, p) = \frac{1}{p(1 - e^{-rs}) + r}\left[g - pf - \frac{p\delta}{r}(1 - e^{-rs})\right] \tag{25}$$

As in the prison-only model, the offender commits the first crime if and only if this expression is positive, or if and only if

$$g \geq pf + \frac{p\delta}{r}(1 - e^{-rs}) \equiv \tilde{g}(f, s, p) \tag{26}$$

which differs from the threshold in (14) by the addition of the expected fine, pf, on the right-hand side.

The social cost of crime also needs to be amended to account for the fine revenue received by the government. Proceeding as above, we obtain the following expression for the present value of expected social costs over the offender's lifetime:

$$\Psi(f, s, p) = \frac{1}{p(1 - e^{-rs}) + r}\left[h + \frac{pc}{r}(1 - e^{-rs}) - pf\right] \tag{27}$$

Finally, we form the social welfare function by subtracting social costs in (27) from offender gains in (25), integrating over the set of offenders who commit crimes, and subtracting fixed apprehension costs:

$$W_h^f = \int_{\tilde{g}(f, s, p)}^{\infty} \frac{1}{p(1 - e^{-rs}) + r}\left[g - h - \frac{p(c + \delta)}{r}(1 - e^{-rs})\right]z(g)\,dg - k(p) \tag{28}$$

Note that the fine revenue drops out of this expression since it is simply a transfer payment. Thus, welfare in this case differs from the expression in the prison-only case in (21) only by the lower limit of the integration, which here depends on the expected fine as well as the prison term. This reflects the fact, noted above, that the fine only affects deterrence (i.e., the number of crimes committed).

Consider first the optimal fine, which is found by maximizing (28) with respect to f. Under the assumption that there is no limit on the offender's ability to pay, we obtain

$$f^* = h/p + \frac{c}{r}(1 - e^{-rs}) \tag{29}$$

which says that the optimal fine equals the harm suffered by victims, appropriately inflated to reflect uncertain apprehension, plus the present value of imprisonment costs that the offender imposes on society. In the special case where there is no imprisonment, this expression reduces to the optimal fine in the fine-only version of the BPS model, as shown in (3). If deterrence were the only consideration, there would be no reason to impose a prison term since the fine achieves perfect deterrence. The question is whether there is a role for prison in the hybrid model for purposes of incapacitation.

To answer this question, we set $f = f^*$ in (28) and take the derivative with respect to s. The result is

$$\left.\frac{\partial W_h^f}{\partial s}\right|_{f=f^*} = \frac{pre^{-rs}}{[p(1 - e^{-rs}) + r]^2}\int_{\tilde{g}(f^*, s, p)}^{\infty} (-g - \delta - c + h)z(g)\,dg \tag{30}$$

where

$$\tilde{g}(f^*, s, p) = h + \frac{p(c + \delta)}{r}(1 - e^{-rs})$$

Now evaluate this derivative at $s = 0$:

$$\frac{\partial W_h^f}{\partial s}\bigg|_{f=f^*, s=0} = \frac{p}{r} \int_h^{\infty} (-g - \delta - c + h)z(g)\,dg < 0 \tag{31}$$

where the sign follows from the fact that the integration is over the range where $g \geq h$, which implies that the entire term inside the integral must be negative. It follows that $s^* = 0$; that is, no prison term should be imposed. Since the fine is unconstrained by the offender's wealth, it can be set to achieve the efficient (first-best) level of deterrence. Thus, although offenders will continue to commit crimes continuously throughout their lifetimes (since they are never imprisoned), those crimes are socially efficient, so there is no social gain from incapacitating them.

Note that this conclusion is consistent with the results in the previous section, where the gain from incapacitation (if any) arose from the possibility of under-deterrence when prison was the only available sanction. In other words, because prison alone cannot generally achieve first-best deterrence due to the cost of punishment, there is a potential gain from adjusting the prison term for purposes of incapacitation when criminals are known to be repeat offenders. In contrast, when the fine can be adjusted at no cost to achieve perfect deterrence, there is no gain from incapacitation.

Of course, this conclusion would be different if the fine were constrained by the offender's wealth. In that case, it is easy to show that the optimal fine is maximal, or $f = w$ (as in the BPS model), and prison may now be desirable for purposes of both deterrence and incapacitation. The trade-off is identical to that in the prison-only model. That is, a positive prison term is optimal if the expected deterrence benefits exceed the expected punishment costs.

5.   EXTENSIONS OF THE MODEL

This section examines two extensions of the above model. First, we consider the case where the probability of apprehension is endogenous, and second, we consider the implications of not counting the offender's gains as part of social welfare.

5.1   Endogenous Probability of Apprehension

Consider first the case where prison is the only available sanction. Recall that in the BPS model, the optimal prison term is maximal in this case. It turns out that this result continues to hold in the hybrid model. To see why, consider the welfare function in (21) and suppose initially that s is less than maximal. Now raise s and lower p so as to hold the term $p(1 - e^{-rs})$ constant. Since the integral term is unchanged but apprehension costs fall, welfare must rise, implying that welfare could not have been maximized under the initial policy. Thus, for any $p > 0$, welfare cannot be maximized if s is less than maximal. The fact that offenders (potentially) commit an infinite number of crimes in the hybrid model does not affect this conclusion because each crime is an exact replay of the previous one, and the optimal policy with respect to the first crime remains the optimal policy throughout time. Besides, a maximal prison term implies that the offender would be imprisoned for life on the first offense, so he would have no opportunity to commit further crimes.

When the threatened prison term is infinite, the threshold gain in (26) reduces to $\tilde{g} = p\delta/r$. Thus, the threat of life imprisonment does not generally result in complete deterrence in the hybrid model. In this case, the welfare function in (21) becomes

$$W_h = \int_{p\delta/r}^{\infty} \frac{1}{p+r} \left[g - h - \frac{p(c+\delta)}{r} \right] z(g)\,dg - k(p) \tag{32}$$

The optimal apprehension rate is found by maximizing this expression with respect to p. Assuming an interior solution, we obtain the following first order condition

$$\frac{1}{p+r}\left(h + \frac{pc}{r}\right)z(\tilde{g})\frac{\delta}{r} = k'(p) + \frac{1}{(p+r)^2}\int_{p\delta/r}^{\infty} (c + \delta + g - h)z(g)\,dg \tag{33}$$

The left-hand side is the marginal deterrence benefit of a higher apprehension rate in the form of the reduced harm to victims and saved punishment costs. The right-hand side is the marginal cost of increasing p (the cost of hiring more police officers, for example), plus the increased punishment costs incurred as more offenders are caught and imprisoned. Note that the marginal punishment cost term (the second term on the right-hand side) includes the incapacitation effect described above (represented by the $g - h$ term in the integral), reflecting the foregone net gains from those crimes that offenders are unable to commit due to the higher apprehension rate. As before, this may be positive or negative at the optimum, and so may increase or decrease the marginal cost of raising p.

Finally, consider the case where both fines and prison are available when p is endogenous. As was true in the case where p was fixed, it is never optimal to use prison unless the fine is first set at its maximal level. Thus, after setting $f = w$, the prison term and probability of apprehension are chosen simultaneously to maximize welfare in (28). In this case, the prison term is not necessarily maximal. To see why this is true, suppose that s is less than maximal, and then proceed as above to raise s and lower p so as to hold $p(1 - e^{-rs})$ fixed. In this case, apprehension costs fall, but so does deterrence because the expected fine (given by pw) falls. Thus, welfare is not necessarily increased. As usual, the desirability of imposing a prison term in this case depends on the marginal deterrence benefits compared to the marginal cost.

The basic conclusions in this section are qualitatively similar to those in the standard BPS model. They differ only by the inclusion of the incapacitation effect in the marginal cost of imprisonment, as discussed above.

5.2   Effect of Excluding the Offender's Gain from Social Welfare

To this point we have maintained the standard practice of counting the offender's gain as a component of social welfare. Early on, however, Stigler ((1970) at 527) questioned the propriety of this practice when he asked, "What evidence is there that society sets a positive value upon the utility derived from murder, rape, or arson? In fact, the society had branded the utility from such activities as illicit." But the issue is not a simple one since some acts that society labels as "crimes" can yield benefits to the offender that most people would consider a valid component of social welfare. Consider, for example, a man who exceeds the speed limit to get his pregnant wife to the hospital, or a lost hiker who breaks into a cabin for food and shelter. Further, as Friedman ((2000) at 230) observes, once we start sorting criminals into "the deserving and the undeserving," we make the error of "assuming our conclusions" about the appropriate treatment of criminals. For these reasons, economists have for the most part retained the standard assumption of counting the offender's utility in welfare.

Still, it is almost certainly the case that for those offenses where incapacitation is a relevant consideration, like dangerous crimes, Stigler's point is a valid one. Thus, in order to get a true sense of the interaction between deterrence and incapacitation, it would seem worthwhile to consider a version of the above model in which the offender's gain is excluded from welfare. For this purpose, it is sufficient to focus on the prison-only version of the model and to assume a fixed probability of apprehension. (Thus, in this section we ignore the fixed cost of apprehension.)

The measure of social welfare in this case simply consists of the harm suffered by victims plus the present value of expected punishment costs, summed over the range of offenders.[11] The relevant cost expression is thus given by (17), integrated over $g \geq \tilde{g}(s)$, where $\tilde{g}(s)$ is defined by (14). Thus, the optimal prison term in this case is chosen to minimize the following cost expression:

$$SC = \int_{\tilde{g}(s)}^{\infty} \frac{1}{p(1 - e^{-rs}) + r}\left[h + \frac{pc}{r}(1 - e^{-rs})\right]z(g)\,dg \qquad (34)$$

Note that this choice problem differs from that in the pure incapacitation model described in section 4.2.2 only by the endogeneity of the crime rate, as embodied by the threshold gain, $\tilde{g}(s)$.

The derivative of (34) with respect to s is given by

$$\frac{\partial SC}{\partial s} =$$

$$\frac{-rpe^{-rs}}{p(1 - e^{-rs}) + r}\left\{\left[h + \frac{pc}{r}(1 - e^{-rs})\right]z(\tilde{g})\frac{\delta}{r} + \frac{1}{p(1 - e^{-rs}) + r}\int_{\tilde{g}}^{\infty}(h - c)z(g)\,dg\right\} \quad (35)$$

Note that the first term in braces is identical to the left-hand side of (22) and again represents the marginal deterrence benefit of increasing the prison term. However, the second term in braces, the marginal cost of increasing s, is different from the right-hand side of (22). Note in particular that it may be positive or negative, depending on the relationship between the harm suffered by victims, h, and the cost of imprisonment, c. Thus, this term reflects the pure net benefit (cost) of incapacitation.

Suppose initially that $h < c$, or that the cost of imprisonment exceeds the harm from crime. In this case, the second term in (35) is negative, meaning that increasing the prison term imposes a net cost on society. The optimal prison term will therefore occur at the point where the derivative in (35) equals zero, or where the marginal deterrence benefit equals the marginal incapacitation cost. The resulting prison term will therefore generally be of finite length. Although imprisonment is undesirable from a pure incapacitation perspective because the cost of holding the offender in prison exceeds the harm that he would impose if free, it is still socially desirable to impose some prison time on offenders because of the deterrence benefits.[12] The optimal prison term in this case thus represents a trade-off between deterrence and incapacitation.

Suppose in contrast that $h > c$, or that the harm caused by the offender exceeds the cost of holding him in prison. In this case, the second term in (35) is positive, implying that the entire derivative is negative. Thus, social costs are strictly decreasing in s. As a result, the optimal prison term is infinite (maximal). (Note that there is no possibility of "over-deterrence" in this case because all crimes are assumed to be inefficient.) In this case, incapacitation and deterrence reinforce each other and indicate that the prison term should be as long as possible.

In terms of policy relevance, this last outcome seems to be most descriptive of the prototypical case where deterrence and incapacitation serve as complementary reasons for imprisoning dangerous offenders. Specifically, the threat of imprisonment deters some offenders from committing dangerous crimes in the first place, while those offenders who reveal their predilection to commit crimes in spite of the threatened punishment should be imprisoned for life on their first apprehension in order to prevent them from having further criminal opportunities. This logic seems to be the motivation underlying three-strikes laws, though the current model, with its assumption of a time-invariant policy, does not account for the gradual progression in such policies toward a maximal prison term. Indeed, the current model with fully rational offenders provides no basis at all for waiting until the third (or even the second) offense to impose the maximal sentence. Explaining this provision of the law therefore requires further elaboration of the basic model.

6. CONCLUSION

The economic theory of law enforcement has traditionally focused on deterrence as the primary motivation for criminal punishment. Since fines and imprisonment are equally capable of deterring crime under this theory, the model prescribes that prison should never be used unless the limited wealth of offenders prevents the attainment of the desired level of deterrence. To the extent that the actual use of prison seems to be more extensive than is warranted by this prescription, however, the economic model falls short as a positive theory of criminal policy. In addition, the economic model offers no rationale for punishing offenders who are undeterrable. The theory of incapacitation, on the other hand, addresses both of these shortcomings, but it offers no theory of criminal behavior. Unfortunately, the law and economics literature has yet to find a way to incorporate these two theories into a coherent model. Filling that gap has been the goal of this chapter.

The hybrid model outlined herein showed that, in a dynamic setting where fully rational offenders face recurrent criminal opportunities throughout their lifetimes, deterrence and incapacitation emerge naturally as complementary motives for criminal punishment. In particular, the threat of imprisonment (and/or a fine) deters some potential offenders from ever committing crimes, while the actual imposition of a prison sentence on convicted offenders prevents them from committing further, inefficient crimes by detaining them in jail. The optimal prison sentence thus embodies both approaches to harm prevention. In most respects, the hybrid model does not prescribe fundamentally different policies as compared to the pure deterrence model. Still, by combining the two motives for punishment into a coherent framework, the hybrid model provides a more compelling theory of actual punishment policies without having to abandon the theoretical appeal of the standard economic model.

NOTES

1. See the survey by Levitt and Miles (2007), on which the current section is based.
2. The data were obtained from the Statistical Abstract of the United States, various years. Statistical Abstract of the United States, Crime and Imprisonment Rates 1980–2006 (Govt. Publishing Office).
3. The model abstracts from the adjudication of guilt by assuming that all offenders who are apprehended are convicted. This, of course, ignores the possibility that some guilty defendants will be acquitted at trial, and some innocent defendants convicted. For a model that incorporates these errors, see Miceli (1991).
4. Stigler (1970) at 527.
5. This is the approach adopted by Polinsky and Shavell (2000, 2007).
6. In the case of prison, a maximal sanction might be life imprisonment, or some other statutorily determined maximum term.
7. This reflects the idea that the group of individuals who become criminals and those who refrain from criminal acts are distinct and remain constant over time. The results would be unaffected if individuals took a new draw of g at each criminal opportunity, in which case the identity of criminals would change over time.
8. For earlier approaches in this style, see Loury (1979) and T Mortensen (1982) who use a similar approach to model the uncertain discovery of a technological innovation.
9. To keep the model simple, we do not consider enforcement policies that condition an offender's punishment on his offense history. For models that do allow such a policy, see the references *supra* p. 129.
10. As a result, proportionally raising s and lowering p (or vice versa) will *not* leave deterrence unaffected, as was true in the BPS model (Davis 1988).
11. For consistency, we do not count the offender's disutility from imprisonment as part of punishment costs.
12. Even if fines were available, some prison time might still be desirable, given that optimal deterrence in this case is complete deterrence. Thus, any finite level of wealth would be a binding constraint.

REFERENCES

Beccaria, Cesare (1767) [1995] *On Crimes and Punishments, and Other Writings*, R. Bellamy, ed., Cambridge, MA: Cambridge University Press
Becker, Gary (1968) "Crime and Punishment: An Economic Approach," 76 *Journal of Political Economy* 169

Bentham, Jeremy (1789) [1973] *An Introduction to the Principles of Morals and Legislation,* in *The Utilitarians,* Garden City, NJ: Anchor Books

Davis, Michael (1988) "Time and Punishment: An Intertemporal Model of Crime," 96 *Journal of Political Economy* 383

Ehrlich, Isaac (1981) "On the Usefulness of Controlling Individuals: An Economic Analysis of Rehabilitation, Incapacitation and Deterrence," 71 *American Economic Review* 307

Emons, Winand (2004) "Subgame Perfect Punishment for Repeat Offenders," 42 *Economic Inquiry* 496

Friedman, David (2000) *Law's Order: What Economics has to Do with Law and Why it Matters,* Princeton, NJ: Princeton University Press

Kessler, Daniel and Steven Levitt (1999) "Using Sentence Enhancements to Distinguish Between Deterrence and Incapacitation," 17 *Journal of Law and Economics* 343

Levitt, Steven and Thomas Miles (2007) "Empirical Study of Criminal Punishment," in *Handbook of Law and Economics,* A. Mitchell Polinsky and Steven Shavell, eds., Amsterdam: North-Holland, vol. I, 455–95

Lewin, Jeffrey and William Trumbull (1990) "The Social Value of Crime?"10 *International Review of Law and Economics* 271

Lott, John (1987) "Should the Wealthy be Able to Buy Justice?" 95 *Journal of Political Economy* 1307

Loury, Glenn (1979) "Market Structure and Innovation," 93 *Quarterly Journal of Economics* 295

Miceli, Thomas (1991) "Optimal Criminal Procedure: Fairness and Deterrence," 11 *International Review of Law and Economics* 3

Miceli, Thomas and Catherine Bucci (2005) "A Simple Theory of Increasing Penalties for Repeat Offenders," 1 *Review of Law and Economics* 71

Mortensen, Dale (1982) "Property Rights in Mating, Racing, and Related Games," 72 *American Economic Review* 968

Polinsky, A. Mitchell and Daniel Rubinfeld (1991) "A Model of Optimal Fines for Repeat Offenders," 46 *Journal of Public Economics* 291

Polinsky, A. Mitchell and Steven Shavell (1984) "The Optimal Use of Fines and Imprisonment," 24 *Journal of Public Economics* 89

— (1998) "On Offense History and the Theory of Public Law Enforcement," 18 *International Review of Law and Economics* 305–324

— (2000) "The Economic Theory of Public Law Enforcement," 38 *Journal of Economic Literature* 45–76

— (2007) "The Theory of Public Enforcement of Law," in *Handbook of Law and Economics,* A. Mitchell Polinsky and Steven Shavell, eds., Amsterdam: North-Holland, vol. I, 403–54

Posner, Richard (2003) *Economic Analysis of Law,* 6th ed., New York: Aspen Law and Business

Shavell, Steven (1987) "A Model of Optimal Incapacitation," 77 *American Economic Review* 107

Shepherd, Joanna (2002) "Fear of the First Strike: The Full Deterrence Effect of California's Two- and Three-Strikes Legislation," 31 *Journal of Legal Studies* 159

Stigler, George (1970) "The Optimum Enforcement of Laws," 78 *Journal of Political Economy* 526

7 Corporate criminal liability: theory and evidence
*Jennifer Arlen**

1. INTRODUCTION

Corporations are subject to a host of laws that criminalize acts that are potentially profitable for the firm but harm society. Some of these laws, such as those prohibiting securities and health care fraud, criminalize intentional wrongdoing. Others, such as many environmental regulations, use criminal law to encourage firms to invest in measures to prevent harms that otherwise would naturally occur as part of their operations. Almost all of these laws are enforced through a combination of individual and corporate liability imposed on people who commit the wrong. The central policy question facing enforcement authorities is how to structure individual and corporate civil and criminal sanctions to optimally deter such crimes.

This chapter employs economic analysis to examine the optimal structure of individual and corporate criminal liability for corporate crimes.[1] It shows that, in order to optimally deter corporate crime, the state generally needs to impose both individual and corporate criminal liability. It also shows that, for most important crimes, the optimal structure of corporate liability differs from classic optimal individual criminal liability for purely individual crimes, as expressed in Becker (1968).[2] Optimal corporate liability also differs in structure from optimal corporate liability considered in the classic economic models of corporate vicarious liability (Kornhauser 1982; Sykes 1984; Polinsky and Shavell 1993).

Pure individual crimes generally involve an individual seeking to benefit from imposing harm on a third party. The central goal of individual liability is to deter all crimes which impose social costs greater than the benefit of the crime. Individual criminal liability can achieve this goal by imposing sanctions directly on the individual wrongdoer whose expected cost equals the social cost of crime. When individual actors have limited assets, the state may need to spend resources on detection or on non-monetary sanctions such as prison (Becker 1968).

Corporate crimes differ from these simple individual crimes because they involve an additional actor, the firm, which can intervene to deter (or encourage) crime both *ex ante* and *ex post*.[3] Firms can deter crime *ex ante* by adopting measures that lower the expected benefit of crime to employees or increase the direct costs of its commission. Corporations have direct control over the expected benefit of crime – control that even the state does not have – because the wrongdoers generally benefit from corporate crimes indirectly, through the compensation and other benefits they obtain from actions that increase the firm's profits. Firms thus are uniquely positioned to intervene *ex ante* to deter crime through their ability to structure compensation and promotion policies so as to make crime less profitable. Firms also can intervene *ex ante* in other ways that increase the direct costs of committing crimes, interventions we refer to as "prevention measures" (Arlen and Kraakman 1997). Corporations also can help deter crime by intervening to increase the probability that the government detects and sanctions wrongdoers. Firms can do this by undertaking *ex ante* monitoring, *ex post* investigation, and cooperation to increase the probability that the government detects the wrong, identifies the individuals responsible, and obtains the evidence needed to convict them. We refer to interventions that increase the probability of sanction as "policing measures" (Arlen and Kraakman 1997).

Corporations not only can deter crime, but they generally are the most cost-effective providers of many vital forms of prevention and policing. This implies that, in the case of corporate crime, the state has an extra instrument available to it when (as is usually the case) it cannot rely entirely on maximal individual monetary sanctions (with minimal enforcement) (Becker 1968). In the corporate context, the state can, and generally should, deter crime by inducing firms to undertake optimal prevention and policing measures. To achieve this goal, the state usually must impose corporate liability structured to induce both optimal corporate policing and prevention (Arlen and Kraakman 1997).[4]

In contrast with individual liability, the state cannot induce optimal corporate behavior by holding the firm criminally liable whenever a crime occurs, subject to a fine of *F*. Thus, the state cannot use strict corporate *respondeat superior* liability (with a fixed penalty) to optimally deter corporate crime (Arlen 1994; Arlen and Kraakman 1997). Firms held strictly liable for employee wrongdoing will invest in optimal prevention when the expected sanction equals the social cost of the crime.[5] Yet the state cannot use strict corporate liability with a fixed fine to produce an equilibrium where the firm undertakes optimal prevention and policing because the fixed sanction that induces optimal prevention would not induce optimal policing. Strict corporate liability is inefficient because under this rule a firm that undertakes effective policing increases its own expected liability by helping the government detect and sanction wrongdoing. Strict corporate liability thus imposes a private cost on firms that police that exceeds the social cost of policing. Thus, it cannot simultaneously induce optimal prevention and policing. Indeed, *respondeat superior* may deter corporate policing under some circumstances (Arlen 1994; Arlen and Kraakman 1997).[6]

To induce corporate policing, the government should employ a "duty-based" regime under which firms are obligated to undertake optimal monitoring, self-reporting, and cooperation, and are subject to a special sanction for violating any one (and each) of these duties (Arlen 1994). Firms that satisfy all policing duties should escape criminal sanction. Nevertheless, they generally should face "residual" civil liability designed to ensure that they adopt optimal prevention measures (Arlen and Kraakman 1997) – unless market forces ensure the firm internalizes the social cost of employees' wrongs.

This chapter then examines whether the current US enforcement practice is consistent with optimal corporate liability, focusing on four distinctive features of US corporate criminal enforcement. First, the United States imposes criminal liability on both individual wrongdoers and their corporate employers. Second, although corporations formally are subject to strict corporate liability for employees' crimes, the Department of Justice (DOJ) regularly exempts firms from indictment if they self-report wrongdoing and/or cooperate with government efforts to convict individual wrongdoers. Third, firms that report and cooperate nevertheless are subject to some form of expected monetary sanction, whether imposed by the DOJ or civil enforcement authorities. Finally, firms avoiding conviction increasingly are subject to monetary and non-monetary sanctions; the latter include mandates requiring firms to adopt government-approved compliance programs, corporate governance reforms, and corporate monitors. This chapter shows that each of these features is consistent with optimal corporate liability when liability is needed to induce both corporate prevention and policing.[7]

The chapter is organized as follows. Section 2 discusses the current structure of individual and corporate criminal liability for business crimes. It also presents empirical evidence on federal criminal enforcement, including evidence on the effect of the DOJ's leniency program on sanctions imposed on publicly-held firms. Section 3 summarizes the traditional economic model of corporate crime, which applies in a perfect world where the state can optimally deter crime without spending resources on enforcement. Section 4 examines optimal deterrence when the state cannot optimally deter wrongs without incurring marginal expenditures on enforcement, and shows that in this situation a state seeking to optimally deter crimes by large firms needs to induce corporate prevention and policing. Section 5 shows why, in this situation, the state generally must impose both individual and corporate liability. Section 6 examines the optimal structure of corporate criminal liability and shows that the government cannot rely on strict corporate liability to induce optimal corporate policing, but instead must employ a duty-based corporate criminal liability regime under which firms avoid liability if they self-report and fully cooperate. Section 7 explains why the state must couple duty-based liability for suboptimal policing with residual strict corporate liability, and considers the situations where this liability can be reduced or eliminated. Sections 6 and 7 also compare the existing enforcement regime with an optimal system. Section 8 considers briefly the choice between corporate criminal and civil liability.

2.   CORPORATE CRIMINAL ENFORCEMENT IN THE UNITED STATES

The United States has an unusual approach to corporate criminal liability which differs from the approach taken by most other countries. The five most important features of the current system, particularly as applied to publicly-held firms, are: (1) joint individual and corporate liability for business crimes; (2) strict *de jure* corporate criminal and civil liability for crimes by employees committed in the scope of employment; (3) substantial corporate criminal penalties; (4) duty-based *de facto* criminal liability, under which firms can avoid criminal indictment or conviction by assisting federal enforcement efforts; and (5) prosecutors' use of deferred and non-prosecution agreements to impose monetary sanctions and structural reforms on firms that avoid conviction (DPAs and NPAs, respectively). This section describes these features of the US system and presents recent evidence on the federal corporate criminal enforcement practice.

2.1   *De Jure* Individual and Corporate Criminal Liability for Corporate Crimes

Under US law, both corporations and individual wrongdoers are potentially criminally liable for corporate crimes committed in the scope of employment. Any employee who commits a crime can be held criminally liable, even if the firm is also convicted.

Table 7.1   Organizations sentenced under the Organizational Sentencing Guidelines[8]

Fiscal year (Oct. 1–Sept. 30)	2006	2007	2008	2009
Total organizations convicted	217	197	199	177
Public firms	4	7	3	14
Closely-held/Private	135	127	58	35
Partnerships	7	4	28	41
Sole proprietorships	10	3	38	45
Other	9	6	7	6
Missing data on firm type	52	50	65	36

Moreover, individuals can be liable even if they commit the crime in their agency capacity in order to benefit the firm, or were following orders, as long as they had the requisite *mens rea*. Prior to the 1990s, prosecutors often focused on convicting corporations for corporate crimes while individuals escaped conviction (Cohen, (1991) at 268).[9] Today, the DOJ encourages prosecutors to focus on obtaining individual convictions.[10]

Corporations can be held strictly criminally liable for crimes by employees committed in the scope of employment through the doctrine of criminal *respondeat superior*.[11] The firm can be held criminally liable so long as the employee committed the crime in the scope of employment ostensibly to benefit the firm;[12] it also faces civil *respondeat superior* liability. The scope of corporate *respondeat superior* liability in the United States is very broad – significantly broader than the scope of corporate liability in other jurisdictions.[13] In the United States, corporations can be criminally liable for crimes committed by all of their employees in the scope of employment; liability is not limited to wrongs of senior management.[14] Moreover, firms can be held criminally liable even when senior management ordered employees not to commit any crimes.[15] Similarly, the fact that a firm adopted and maintained an effective compliance program, self-reported detected wrongdoing, and fully cooperated with federal authorities' efforts to investigate wrongdoing is not a defense to *de jure* corporate criminal liability.[16]

2.2   Corporate Sanctions

Corporations convicted of federal crimes can be subject to substantial penalties, including criminal fines, other criminal monetary sanctions (such as restitution and remediation), non-monetary criminal penalties, collateral penalties tied to conviction (including the loss of business licenses), civil and administrative sanctions imposed by the government, private civil liability, and, in some cases, reputational penalties.

2.2.1   Criminal fines
Corporations convicted of federal crimes face substantially larger monetary sanctions than they did 20 years ago. In the mid-1980s, average and median fines imposed on firms convicted of a federal crime were $108,000 and $10,000, respectively (Cohen (1996) at 401). By contrast, in 2006–2008, the average fine imposed on an organization convicted of a federal crime ranged from $5.7 to $17.3 million.

By contrast, the median organizational criminal fine is quite small (Table 7.2).[17]

Table 7.2   Organizations sentenced under the Organizational Sentencing Guidelines[18]
            (dollars in thousands)

Fiscal year (Oct. 1–Sept. 30)	2006	2007	2008	2009
Total organizations convicted	217	197	199	177
Guilty plea	91%	85%	91%	96%
Mean fine	$5890	$7329	$5736	$17,293
Median fine	$50	$132	$60	$119
Firm unable to pay entire fine	42%	33%	37%	43%
Compliance program ordered	20%	24%	6%	5%

Notes: Mean and median fines are based on the subset of convictions with non-zero fines for which data was available. The percentages are based on convictions where we have data.

Table 7.3   Sanctions imposed on corporations (public and private)[19]
            (dollars in thousands)

Fiscal year (Oct. 1–Sept. 30)	2006	2007	2008	2009
Total corporate convictions	139	134	61	49
Median fine	$138	$1145	$375	$1800
Corporation unable to pay entire fine	57	50	17	14
	56%	55%	40%	34%

Notes: Median fines and percentages are based on the subset of convictions sentenced under the Organizational Guidelines with non-zero fines and where the data was available on fines and firm type.

Nevertheless, criminal fines often exceed the firm's ability to pay because most convicted corporations are small and/or thinly capitalized. Thus, more than one-third of all convicted organizations do not have sufficient assets to pay the entire criminal fine imposed. Most convicted *corporations* also are small.[20] Many (and in some years most) convicted corporations also are unable to pay the entire fine imposed (Table 7.3).

Publicly-held firms face substantially larger mean and median fines than those imposed on firms generally. Reforms adopted in the mid-1980s and early 1990s, including the Organizational Sentencing Guidelines, had a large impact on sanctions imposed on publicly-held firms. A comparison of fines imposed on publicly-held corporations immediately before and after (and under) the Organizational Sentencing Guidelines found that mean and median criminal fines imposed on publicly-held corporations went from $1.9 million and $633,000, respectively, in the years prior to the Organizational Guidelines to $19 million and $3 million, respectively, for firms sentenced under the Organizational Guidelines in the years immediately after their adoption (1996 dollars) (Alexander, Arlen, and Cohen 1999a). More recently, the Sentencing Commission's data suggests that average criminal fines imposed on publicly-held firms are lower than they were in the early 1990s (see Table 7.4). Yet this is the result of changes in enforcement practices. Today, publicly-held firms usually are sanctioned for employees' crimes without a formal criminal conviction through the use of DPAs and NPAs, as is discussed below. These sanctions are not included in the Sentencing Commission's data. Annual

Table 7.4   Publicly-held firms sentenced under the Organizational Sentencing Guidelines[21]
(dollars in thousands)

Fiscal year (Oct. 1–Sept. 30)	2006	2007	2008	2009
Total convictions	4	7	3	14
Mean fine	$114	$29,564	$300	$9451
Median fine	$88	$1070	$300	$1500
Firm cannot pay entire fine	1	0	1	3
Compliance program ordered	33%	29%	33%	10%

Notes: Mean, median fines, and percentages are based on the subset of convictions with non-zero fines and data available on firm type and fines. Other percentages are based on convictions where we have data.

mean sanctions imposed by the DOJ through those agreements range from $1.1 million to $46 million (Arlen and Kahan 2012; see Table 7.5). These DOJ-imposed penalties provide a good measure of the expected "criminal" penalty for larger firms.

2.2.2   Additional criminal and civil sanctions

In addition to criminal fines, convicted corporations often are subject to additional penalties, including non-fine criminal penalties (such as restitution, remediation, and community service payments), government-imposed civil penalties, administrative sanctions, and state-imposed penalties. They also can face private civil liability. These additional penalties can be significant. For example, publicly-held firms sentenced after the adoption of the Organizational Sentencing Guidelines faced an average total sanction of more than $49 million. This average total sanction exceeded the mean criminal fine by more than $30 million (1996 dollars) (Alexander, Arlen, and Cohen (1999a) at 410).[22]

Convicted firms also can be subject to non-monetary sanctions.[23] Non-monetary penalties normally take the form of corporate probation, which prohibits the firm from committing another criminal violation and enhances the firm's sanctions if it does. Probation orders also can be used to impose additional non-monetary sanctions, such as a court-mandated compliance program or adverse publicity. Finally, convicted firms also may face serious collateral penalties, generally imposed through administrative regulations. These penalties include loss of licenses and orders precluding the firm from contracting with certain agencies, such as Health and Human Services or the Defense Department, for some period of time (Cohen (1996) at 409). For firms in some industries, the collateral penalties may be more damaging than the monetary penalties.

2.2.3   Reputational and market penalties

Convicted corporations also may suffer a reputational penalty that reduces firm value. The claim is that customers, lenders, shareholders, and other market participants may be less likely to deal with a "criminal" firm on favorable terms. The firm's stock price falls as a result of the market's anticipation that it will earn less revenue, have higher costs, and/or face a market that does not give full weight to any positive financial information (Karpoff and Lott 1993).

Three important features of the reputational penalty are worth noting. First, firms do not always bear a reputational penalty as a result of employee wrongdoing. Market participants react negatively to some crimes but not others. Second, evidence suggests that the penalty is triggered when the market receives credible information that the crime occurred. Formal conviction does not appear to be necessary. Finally, while the initial market sanction appears to act as a kind of strict corporate liability for employee wrongdoing, it does appear that there are steps firms can take to reduce the reputational penalty.

Economic theory suggests that market participants should have a negative view of firms that commit some crimes but not others. Specifically, parties that contract with a firm can be expected to respond negatively to news that the firm committed a crime that harms them or other contracting parties, such as fraud. But contracting parties have little reason to fear harm from a firm that commits other types of wrongs, such as environmental harms that injure third parties (Karpoff and Lott 1993; Alexander 1999). Evidence appears to support this hypothesis. Studies find that corporate market value declines sharply on news that the government is investigating a firm for fraud, or has instituted proceeding against it, and that the decline exceeds the amount properly attributable to the sanctions imposed and also to the earnings restatement and/or loss of criminal profits (Karpoff and Lott 1993; see Karpoff *et al.* 2008a). By contrast, firms do not suffer a market sanction when they are either sanctioned for regulatory violations involving non-contracting third-parties (Karpoff and Lott 1993) or convicted of an environmental violation (Karpoff *et al.* 2005). Consistent with theory, the evidence also reveals that markets penalize firms for corporate crime even when the firm is not convicted. Market players respond negatively to credible evidence of fraud (such as evidence that a government agency is pursuing a civil enforcement action against the firm) even when the firm is not subject to a criminal investigation (Karpoff and Lott 1993; Alexander 1999; Karpoff *et al.* 2008a).

Although the evidence supports the hypothesis that firms with certain types of detected wrongdoing are subject to a market penalty, the magnitude of the penalty may be less than some studies have suggested. Empirical measures of reputational penalties tend to obtain the reputational penalty by comparing stock price movements following the announcement of a crime with the adjustment that would result from the financial penalties eventually imposed on the firm as well as the adjustment justified by the magnitude of the crime. This measure overstates the reputational sanction in several situations. First, it overstates the reputational penalty when the financial cost of the formal penalties imposed on the firm exceeds the costs of the monetary sanctions reported publicly. For example, firms indicted or convicted of certain crimes, such as fraud, face substantial collateral consequences, such as delicensing or an inability to contract with the federal government (Alexander 1999; Baer (2008a) at 1062 and n. 145). Any analysis that does not incorporate these sanctions into the expected government-imposed penalty will obtain an artificially high measure of the reputational penalty (Alexander 1999).

Beyond this, studies that measure the reputational penalty based on initial stock price reaction to news of the crime will over-estimate the reputational penalty in situations where information about one crime provides a strong signal that the firm either is in serious financial trouble or likely committed other crimes. For example, disclosed securities fraud often signals that the firm is in serious financial trouble since many securities frauds are committed by managers who fear they are in a last period because the firm is in financial trouble (Arlen and Carney 1992; see Karpoff *et al.* 2008a (finding that many firms with financial misstatements delisted or went bankrupt during the enforcement period)). Given this, market participants should discount the share price by more than is justified by the magnitude of the disclosed fraud alone in anticipation of future bad news relating to past conduct (e.g., additional earnings restatements or additional criminal conduct). Under many reputational studies, this additional discount is categorized as a market penalty if the firm neither later restates earnings nor is found liable for another crime even though it might simply reflect uncertainty about the magnitude of the wrong at the time the news first reaches the market.

Finally, firms under investigation for certain crimes may experience a decline in future earnings – unrelated to any reputational penalty – as they abandon profitable activities, beyond those specifically under investigation, that are either illegal or potentially illegal. The anticipation of these lost profits should depress share price but these lost profits are not a reputational penalty.[24] Nevertheless, while the magnitude of the claimed market penalty likely exceeds the true market penalty for many firms, the market does penalize firms for committing certain types of crimes (e.g., fraud), especially if the crime is announced by a credible source, such as a government agency.

2.3 *De Facto* Scope of Corporate Criminal Liability

Although all firms are formally subject to strict *respondeat superior* liability for their employees' crimes, this rule is not the actual *de facto* regime that is applied in practice for some firms. In particular, while closely-held firms generally are held strictly criminally liable for employees' crimes (especially when the crime is committed by owner-managers), in practice larger firms (those characterized by a separation of ownership and day-to-day management) are not held strictly criminally liable for their employees' crimes. Instead, the *de facto* regime governing larger firms closely approximates a "duty-based" liability regime under which the government expects firms to assist in its enforcement efforts by monitoring for crime, self-reporting, and cooperating with the government's efforts to prosecute individual wrongdoers, and reserves criminal liability for firms that do not satisfy any of these duties (at least for certain crimes).[25]

In 1999, the DOJ formally adopted a policy governing corporate criminal liability under which corporations can avoid criminal liability for employees' crimes by engaging in particular types of good corporate conduct, such as self-reporting the wrong or cooperating with federal enforcement efforts. This change in the corporate liability regime was not adopted through an act of Congress. Instead, then-Deputy Attorney General Eric Holder initiated the new policy by issuing guidelines to federal prosecutors on when prosecutors should indict corporations for employees' crimes committed during the scope of employment. The Holder memo encouraged prosecutors to focus on convicting the individuals responsible for the crime.[26] The Holder memo also recognized that prosecutors can best detect and prosecute individuals if firms help detect, report, and investigate crimes and that firms may be reluctant to help prosecutors if they are held strictly liable for their employees' crimes.[27] Accordingly, the Holder memo encouraged prosecutors not to indict firms for employees' crimes if the firm had engaged in particular good acts, such as (1) adopting and maintaining a compliance program, (2) self-reporting the wrong promptly, and/or (3) fully cooperating with the federal investigation.[28] The Holder memo in effect replaced strict corporate liability with a quasi "duty-based" corporate liability regime by encouraging prosecutors not to impose corporate criminal liability for firms that adopted an effective compliance program, promptly reported detected wrongdoing, and/or fully cooperated with federal authorities.[29]

The current policy governing corporate prosecution retains the core structure of the Holder memo, but introduced some modifications. In particular, the Holder memo treated the decision not to indict as, in effect, criminal amnesty for firms engaging in desired conduct. Firms that were not indicted thus generally left the prosecutors' jurisdiction,[30] although they could be, and often were, subject to government-imposed civil and administrative sanctions. This changed in 2003 when then-Deputy Attorney General Larry Thompson issued his memo to prosecutors governing corporate liability. The Thompson memo encouraged prosecutors to insist that firms adopt "effective" compliance programs. It also encouraged them to exert more authority over firms eligible for non-prosecution through the use of DPAs and NPAs, which require the firm to comply with a series of conditions to avoid indictment or prosecution.[31] From 2003–2010, federal prosecutors entered into at least 163 D/NPAs.

Standard conditions include payment of monetary penalties (e.g., to the DOJ, other federal authorities or state authorities) (Arlen and Kahan 2012), and corporate acceptance of a description of the wrong sufficient to establish the firm's criminal liability (Garrett 2007). Prosecutors also regularly use these agreements to impose non-monetary performance mandates on the firm. For example, most agreements require firms to adopt prosecutor-approved compliance programs (Garrett 2007; Arlen and Kahan 2012). Many also require firms to appoint an outside corporate monitor who reports to federal authorities (Garrett 2007; Khanna and Dickinson 2007). Some require firms to make other structural changes, including changes to the structure or composition of management or boards of directors, as well as to business practices (Garrett 2007; Arlen and Kahan 2012). These conditions transform corporate criminal liability into a form of duty-based monetary criminal liability coupled with prosecutorial authority to engage in firm-specific regulation of corporate practices relating to deterring and investigating corporate crime (Arlen and Kahan 2012).

The formal conditions governing leniency are quite broad and could potentially apply to all firms in many circumstances.[32] Conversations with prosecutors and the available evidence suggest that a firm's willingness to cooperate with federal prosecutors is the most important factor in determining whether a firm avoids prosecution. This hypothesis would predict that almost all firms with a DPA or NPA would have cooperated with authorities and that few firms convicted will have cooperated (since cooperating firms get leniency). If we examine the Sentencing Commission's data on convictions we see that few publicly-held firms sentenced under the Organizational Guidelines received credit for cooperation; convicted firms also rarely self-reported crime (Table 7.6).[33] By contrast, almost all firms that escape conviction by agreeing to a DPA or NPA cooperated with federal authorities (Arlen and Kahan 2012) (Table 7.5).

Theory and evidence also suggest that the DOJ's non-prosecution policy affects firms where the owners are not directly involved in day-to-day management (e.g., publicly-held firms) more than owner-managed closely-held firms. Firms generally are not eligible for non-prosecution unless they fully cooperate with federal authorities to bring the individuals responsible for the crime to justice. Often managers are potentially liable for the crime. In such cases, owner-managed closely-held firms can be expected to forgo the offer

Table 7.5   Federal criminal DPAs and NPAs[34] (dollars in millions)

Year	2003	2004	2005	2006	2007	2008	2009	2010
Total	5	9	14	20	39	19	19	38
Publicly-held	4	8	10	15	27	13	16	33
Mean DOJ Penalty	$6	$16	$12	$26	$8	$17	$1	$46
Mean total monetary penalty	$60	$116	$155	$137	$51	$14	$149	$126
Compliance program	3	7	9	9	23	15	11	27
	(60%)	(80%)	(65%)	(45%)	(60%)	(80%)	(60%)	(70%)
Monitor mandated	3	6	7	6	13	6	2	11
	(60%)	(65%)	(50%)	(25%)	(35%)	(30%)	(10%)	(30%)

Source: Arlen and Kahan 2012.

Table 7.6   Self-reporting and cooperation by corporations sentenced under the Organizational Sentencing Guidelines[35]

Fiscal year (Oct.–Sept.)	2003	2004	2005	2006	2007	2008	2009
Accept responsibility and cooperate (all corporations)	35	20	19	27	22	9	5
Self-reported crime	1	2	1	1	2	0	1
Public firms that accepted responsibility/cooperated	0	1	0	1	2	1	3
Public firm self-reporting	0	0	0	0	0	0	1

Notes: Based on a subset of the cases where the data was available.

of corporate leniency in order to protect their owner/managers. By contrast, publicly-held firms face strong pressure to delegate the leniency decision to outside directors, who in turn face strong pressure to cooperate in return for leniency, even when senior managers are implicated. Consistent with this hypothesis, we find that approximately 142 publicly-held firms were convicted in the five years following the adoption of the Organizational Guidelines (Alexander, Arlen, and Cohen (1999a) at 408). By contrast, since 2003, only a handful of publicly-held firms were convicted according to the Sentencing Commission's data (Table 7.4), yet 126 publicly-held firms were subject to DPAs and NPAs (Arlen and Kahan 2012). This suggests that when the DOJ sanctions a publicly-held firm for a corporate crime it now tends to do so through a DPA and NPA and closely-held owner-managed firms rarely avoid prosecution through these agreements.[36]

2.4   Summary

Accordingly, US corporate criminal enforcement policy has several core features: first, joint individual and corporate liability for employee crimes committed in the scope of employment; second, strict *respondeat superior* liability for owner-managed firms; third, "duty-based" corporate criminal liability (generally coupled with strict civil liability) for larger non-owner managed firms; and fourth, prosecutors' use of DPAs and NPAs to impose firm-specific mandates on firms potentially eligible for conviction, including government-mandated compliance programs, corporate monitors, and reforms to the composition or structure of management or boards. A central question for the economic analysis of corporate crime is whether these features are consistent with optimal deterrence. This chapter considers each of these in turn.

3. LIABILITY FOR CORPORATE CRIME IN THE CLASSIC MODEL

This section presents the classic economic analysis of corporate liability for crime, focusing on the optimal individual and corporate liability in a "perfect world" in which (i) corporations and employees have no wealth constraints; (ii) sanctions can be costlessly imposed; (iii) all parties (including courts) are rational and fully informed; (iv) firms and employees engage in costless contracting; and (v) the probability that the government sanctions a committed crime is positive (P > 0) even if it does not spend marginal resources on enforcement.[37] We analyze this case, in which the state need not spend money on enforcement, to provide a foundation for the analysis of corporate liability under the more realistic assumption that optimal deterrence requires marginal enforcement expenditures.[38]

This section shows that, in this perfect world, the government can optimally deter corporate crime using a simple regime of strict criminal liability, with liability imposed on either individual wrongdoers or the firm. Accordingly, under the assumptions of this model, there is no economic justification for the current practice of imposing joint individual and corporate liability, composite duty-based corporate liability, and non-monetary structural reform, as these corporate sanctions are either unnecessary (in the former case) or welfare reducing (in the latter two).

3.1 Optimal Individual Deterrence in the Simple Model

Corporate crimes involve wrongdoing by an employee acting in the scope of employment. The crime may be intentional or accidental. For our purposes, an employee commits an intentional crime when he knowingly decides to commit a crime. By contrast, accidental crimes can occur when an employee engages in a lawful activity that creates a risk of a negative outcome (e.g., environmental harm) that has been criminalized, and where employee care-taking reduces the risk of a violation but does not eliminate it. In either case, both the employee and the firm can affect the probability that a crime occurs, the former doing so directly and the latter only indirectly. The central economic issue is to determine what individual and corporate liability rules provide optimal incentives to both individual wrongdoers and their corporate employers.

To address these issues, we begin by discussing the classic model of individual criminal liability when there is no corporate employer (and no need to spend additional resources to obtain a conviction). It is useful to start with this framework because economic theory implies that corporate crimes are really crimes committed by individuals who happen to be working for firms.[39] Thus, employees only commit intentional crimes when the benefit of the crime exceeds the expected cost (Becker 1968). Similarly, they only allow acciden-tal crimes to happen when the cost of the additional precautions needed to prevent the crime exceed the expected benefit of precaution (Segerson and Tietenberg 1992; Polinsky and Shavell 1993). This implies that to induce the optimal amount of crime (or its pre-vention) society needs to use the tools available to it to ensure that individual wrongdo-ers want to avoid suboptimal crimes.

Individual criminal liability is a particularly effective mechanism for deterring indi-viduals from committing crimes. To determine the optimal level of individual criminal liability we must first determine the optimal level of crime. To do this, we first consider individual liability for intentional crimes through the use of a simple model.

3.1.1   Intentional crimes

The standard model of intentional crimes considers a perfectly informed, rational, risk-neutral individual who can commit a crime which gives him a benefit of b (which is also a social benefit), but imposes a social cost on society of H. In most cases, society is better off when the crime does not happen, $H > b$. Social welfare is maximized when individuals refrain from any crime where the social cost of the crime, H, exceeds the social benefit of the crime (given here by b). Society gains, however, when individuals commit crimes where the social benefit exceeds the social cost of the crime: $b > H$ (Becker 1968).[40]

Society cannot rely on individuals to make optimal decisions regarding crime because individuals act in their own self-interest. Thus, individuals will commit a crime whenever the private benefit of the crime, given by b, exceeds the expected cost of crime. Given this, society will be burdened by too many crimes if it does not impose criminal liability on wrongdoers. Individuals maximize their own welfare. Thus, absent liability, they will commit all crimes which provide them a positive benefit, without regard for the social cost ($b > 0$) (Becker 1968).

Society can deter socially harmful crimes by imposing a criminal fine, f, that ensures that wrongdoers face expected liability equal to the harm they cause, H. In this situation, wrongdoers (who only commit crimes when the benefit of crime exceeds the expected sanctions) will in turn only commit crimes when the benefit of crime exceeds the social cost of crime, H. Thus, they will eschew socially costly crimes ($b \leq H$), but will continue to commit crimes which benefit society ($b > H$). This implies that, when the state always detects and sanctions crime, the optimal fine, f^*, equals H. In general, the state cannot detect and sanction all crimes; instead the probability of crime being detected and sanc-tioned in given by, P, which is less than 1. In this case, each wrongdoer faces an expected sanction equal to Pf. To optimally deter crime, this expected sanction must equal the social cost of crime to society, H, which in turn implies that the optimal individual fine is given by:[41]

$$f^* = \frac{H}{P} \tag{1}$$

(Becker 1968).

The preceding discussion assumed that P is fixed. In reality, the probability of sanction is not fixed. Instead, the state can increase the probability that wrongs are detected and sanctioned by spending resources on enforcement, E: i.e., $P'(E) > 0$. The higher the probability of sanction, the lower the optimal fine. Questions thus arise about whether the state should increase enforcement expenditures in order to lower the sanction. In a seminal article, Gary Becker showed that the state minimizes the cost of deterring crime by minimizing enforcement costs, as long as individuals are not wealth constrained, sanctioning costs are zero and individuals are risk neutral (Becker 1968). Given this, under these circumstances, it is efficient for the state to minimize costs by spending as little as possible on enforcement, $\underline{E}$, and then impose a fine equal to:

$$f^* = \frac{H}{P(E)} \tag{2}$$

In those situations where the state can still detect wrongs without any marginal enforcement expenditures ($E = 0$), the optimal sanction equals $H/P(0)$, which far exceeds the social cost of the crime, H (Becker 1968). So long as the state can feasibly impose this sanction, there is no need for anyone, the state or the firm, to spend resources on enforcement.

3.1.2   Unintentional crimes

The classic economic analysis of unintentional (or accidental) crimes yields similar results. To see this, consider the situation where each individual engages in an activity that may cause a crime that imposes social costs of H, the probability of which, $p(e)$, depends on the individual's level of effort to avoid the crime, e, which the individual undertakes at cost $c(e)$. In this situation, social welfare is maximized when individuals invest in the level of effort to prevent crime that minimizes the expected total social cost of crime and its prevention, as given by:[42]

$$c(e) + p(e)H \tag{3}$$

(Segerson and Tietenberg 1992; Polinsky and Shavell 1993). Absent liability, individuals will not invest optimally in crime prevention because they will minimize their own costs, $c(e)$, without considering the cost of crime to others. The state can induce optimal effort by holding risk neutral individuals strictly liable for crimes subject to an expected sanction equal to the social cost of crime. In this case, the expected sanction is given by $Pp(e)f$ and the expected social cost of crime is given by $p(e)H$. Accordingly, the optimal sanction f equals $H/P(E)$, just as in the case of intentional crimes (Polinsky and Shavell (1993) at 254; Kornhauser 1982; Sykes 1984).[43] Also, as in the case of intentional crimes, when individuals are risk neutral and can pay the optimal fine, monetary sanctions are costless to impose, and enforcement is costly, then the optimal enforcement strategy is to minimize enforcement while setting the fine equal to $H/P(0)$, where $P(0)$ is the probability of sanction when enforcement is minimized at $\underline{E}$ (Becker 1968).

3.2   Optimal Deterrence in the Simple Model when Wrongdoers Work for Firms

We now expand the model to consider corporate crime: defined as crimes committed by employees in the scope of their employment with some intent to benefit the firm. Corporate crimes differ from purely individual crimes because corporations affect the social costs and benefits of crime as potential inducers, or enforcers of crime and, in some cases, victims of corporate crimes.[44] Firms can induce crimes because they directly control the compensation, promotion, and retention policies that often determine the degree to which employees benefit from crimes committed in the scope of employment. Firms are potential enforcers because they can intervene to help the government detect and investigate crime and identify and convict individual wrongdoers (Arlen 1994; Arlen and Kraakman 1997). Firms are potential victims of crime to the extent that crimes committed for an ostensible short-run gain in fact harm the firm in the long-run (as when managers use crime to hide their poor performance from shareholders) (Arlen and Carney 1992).

As this section shows, these differences can affect both the individual sanction and the optimal scope of corporate liability for employees' crimes. The extent to which these differences matter, however, depends on the type of firm: owner-managed or not. It also depends on whether we remain within the simple model. As we shall see, when we remain in the simple model, the firm's ability to spend resources to deter crime has no effect on the optimal individual sanction or the structure of liability, because the state optimally deters crime (at lowest cost) through individual liability alone, without any expenditure on enforcement or prevention. Corporate intervention and liability become essential to optimal deterrence only once we explore the more realistic situation where the state cannot optimally deter crime by imposing an individual sanction of $H/P(0)$.

3.2.1 Crimes by owner-managers of closely-held firms

Corporate crimes can be divided into two categories. The first are crimes where individual wrongdoers are truly acting on behalf of the firm, in that the individual committing (or orchestrating) the crime only benefits if the firm benefits, both in the short and long run, and also fully suffers any liability costs (including those imposed on the firm) proportionate with his share of the benefit. The second category is crimes committed for private benefit, often at the long-run expense of the firm.

Crimes by owner-managers of closely-held firms generally fall into the first category. Owner-managers tend to commit corporate crimes to increase the firm's profits and benefit from the crime only through the effect of the crime on the value of their shares. In this situation, the social benefit of crime is given by the benefit of the crime to the firm, b. The individual wrongdoer's private benefit of crime equals his equity share in the firm's benefit, as given by αb, where α is the portion of the firm that he owns.

In this situation, as before, the state maximizes social welfare by using liability to ensure that wrongdoers do not benefit from socially costly crimes. The state should impose a sanction of H/P on the individual wrongdoer whenever private contracting between owners would ensure that he commits a crime whenever the firm as a whole benefits. When there is no contracting over benefits between owners, then optimal expected individual sanction equals αH, which implies that the optimal fine equals $\alpha H/P$.

The state also can use corporate liability to optimally deter crime. In this context, corporate liability directly deters crimes by eliminating the benefit to the firm of socially costs crimes. This directly eliminates the benefit to individual wrongdoers of committing a socially costly crime. Accordingly, in this context, the state can optimally deter crime by imposing strict *respondeat superior* liability on the firm for crimes by its owner-managers, accompanied by a fine equal to H/P. This ensures that neither the firm nor its owners benefit from any crime for which the social benefit of crime is less than the social cost of the crime. Observe that, in this context, there is no need for joint individual and corporate liability, because either form of liability is sufficient to eliminate the wrong-doer's incentive to commit socially harmful crimes.[45]

Moreover, in the case of crimes by controlling owner-managers, the state need not adjust the corporate liability rule to induce firms to help detect or investigate crimes (even if enforcement is needed) because controlling owner-managers will not help convict themselves. Moreover, in this context, we need not consider the firm's ability to reduce incentives to commit the crime because the state can use corporate or individual liability to eliminate the expected benefit of socially costly crimes.

3.2.2   Crimes by employees of publicly-held firms
The story is quite different when crimes are committed by employees who are not con-trolling owners and managers of the firm, as is the case with managers and other employ-ees of publicly-held firms. In this situation, the private benefit of crime often differs from both the corporate benefit of crime (if any) and the social benefit of crime. In addition, in this context firms can materially affect wrongdoers' expected benefit of crime and the expected cost of liability (a consideration we explore in full in section 4).

When crimes are committed by employees of publicly-held firms, the private benefit of crime to individual wrongdoers rarely equals the social benefit of the crime. Nor is it equal (or proportionately equal) to the benefit of crime to the firm, given by B. Corporate crimes generally directly benefit the firm (at least in the short run), for example through higher revenues, lower costs, or higher share price (a benefit we denote, B). This benefit is the social benefit of crime. Yet individual wrongdoers (including managers) of publicly-held firms do not obtain a substantial portion of this benefit directly because they rarely own a substantial share of the firm. Instead, indi-vidual wrongdoers expect to benefit indirectly, through the increase in compensation, job security, or job status resulting from actions that benefit the firm. These benefits need not be proportionately tied to the firm's benefit. Indeed, wrongdoers can obtain a long-run expected benefit from crime even when the firm does not. For example, managers benefit from crimes that enable them to avert termination by making the firm appear financially healthier than it is, even when the firm itself does not obtain a long-run expected benefit once one takes account of (1) the cost to shareholders of mistakenly retaining managers that they should have fired, and (2) the expected cost of the reputational penalty that the firm will bear should the wrong be detected (Arlen and Carney 1992; see Karpoff *et al.* 2008a).[46]

In this situation, we must adjust the individual sanction. A sanction that ensures that an individual wrongdoer expects to bear the full social cost of crime will not optimally deter wrongdoing when the individual benefit of crime does not equal the social benefit of crime. Thus, we must adjust the sanction to account for the difference between the social benefit of crime and the private benefit of crime. In addition, we may need to adjust the social cost of crime to reflect any net costs imposed by the crime on the firm, H_c. The state need not do this, however, if the firm sanctions its employees privately. This implies that the state should impose a sanction equal to $(H + H_c)/P$, unless the firm sanctions its employees.[47]

Corporate crime by publicly-held firms also differs from owner-manager crime and purely individual crimes because they involve firms that can, and will, intervene to deter crime, either by reducing the benefit to wrongdoers of crime or increasing its expected cost, or both. Corporations can directly affect the benefit to employees of corporate crime because most non-owner employees only benefit from corporate crimes indirectly through the expectation that they will obtain increased compensation, promotion, or job retention – expected benefits which are in the firm's control (Arlen and Kraakman 1997; see Arlen and Carney 1992). Corporations also can affect the direct benefit of crime through measures that make crimes more difficult (costly) to commit either *ex ante* or *ex post* (for example, by sanctioning wrongful employees). These interventions that reduce the net benefit of crime (without affecting the probability of sanction) are referred to here as "prevention measures" (Arlen and Kraakman 1997; see Kornhauser 1982; Sykes 1984; Polinsky and Shavell 1993). Corporations also can increase the expected sanctions associated with crime by helping the government detect and sanction the wrong (Arlen 1994; Arlen and Kraakman 1997). These interventions, referred to here as "policing" measures, include (i) *ex ante* monitoring to increase the probability of detection; (ii) *ex post* investigation of suspected wrongdoing; (iii) self-reporting of wrongs to government authorities; and (iv) fully cooperating with the government's efforts to obtain the information needed to identify and convict the individuals responsible for the wrong (Arlen 1994; Arlen and Kraakman 1997). Corporations also can affect the expected social cost of crime, H, through their control over their own activity levels (Polinsky and Shavell 1993; Arlen and Kraakman 1997), as well as their control over the scope of authority granted to their employees.

Although firms can intervene in many ways to deter corporate crime, most of these interventions are not part of an optimal enforcement strategy as long as we remain within the simple model. In the simple model, the state can optimally deter individual wrongdoers, at minimal cost, by holding individual wrongdoers liable for any crimes they commit, subject to an expected penalty (Pf) equal to the harm caused (H). The state gains nothing from inducing the firm to spend unnecessary resources to reduce the benefit of crime or increase the probability of sanction. Indeed, any such corporate intervention only increases the social cost of deterrence relative to a world in which the state relies entirely on individual liability. In this model, corporate intervention is only welfare enhancing when the state does not impose individual criminal liability, and even then, the state only benefits from one form of corporate prevention: the imposition by the firm of sanctions on individuals who commit corporate crime. Accordingly, in this model, the state can optimally deter crime through *either* individual liability or optimal corporate sanctions provided that the social costs of sanctioning are the same whether sanctions are imposed by the state or the firm (see Kornhauser 1982; Sykes 1984; Polinsky and Shavell 1993).

In some cases, a state seeking to maximize social welfare must be concerned about one additional aspect of corporate behavior: corporate activity levels. In some situations (e.g., accidental crimes), corporate operations give rise to a positive risk of welfare-reducing crime even when individuals face optimal sanctions. In many of these situations, the expected social cost of these "unavoidable" crimes is higher the greater the firm's activity level. For example, the expected cost of environmental harm often is greater the more a firm produces because increased production generally increases the probability of an accidental violation and/or the magnitude of the violation. In this situation, a state seeking to maximize social welfare must not only optimally deter crime, but also must ensure that firms' activity levels are optimal. Thus, firms should engage in the level of activity that would maximize their profits if they internalized all the social benefits and bore all the social costs (including expected crime costs) of their activities. Moreover, when the state imposes corporate liability, it can rely on strict *respondeat superior* liability (Polinsky and Shavell 1993).

Accordingly, in the simple model, the economic analysis of corporate crime is very similar to the economic analysis of purely individual crime. In both cases, the core goal is to induce individuals to refrain from all social welfare reducing crimes, and the state can optimally deter through individual liability alone. Moreover, in this context, corporate liability is needed only when the state does not impose individual liability, and then only to induce the firm to act as a perfect substitute for the state by sanctioning its own employees. The only genuine divergence between the individual and corporate context in the simple model is that in the corporate context the state also needs to ensure that firms' activity levels are optimal whenever corporate activity levels affect the expected social cost of crime.

3.3   Is Corporate Liability Necessary: The Neutrality Principle

This section considers whether there is any justification for joint individual and corporate liability assuming that we remain in the simple model. Specifically, we consider whether a state needs to use both individual and corporate liability to achieve its two core efficiency goals under the simple model: imposing optimal sanctions on individual wrongdoers and inducing optimal corporate activity levels. We show that in this context, the state can optimally deter crime through either individual or corporate liability and thus does not need to employ joint individual liability and corporate liability. Moreover, as long as the social cost of public and private sanctions are the same, the state is indifferent (neutral) between individual and corporate liability (Kornhauser 1982; Sykes 1984; Segerson and Tietenberg 1992; Polinsky and Shavell 1993).[48] This result (that the state can optimally deter through either individual or corporate liability) is known as the neutrality principle.

The neutrality principle can be demonstrated using the following simple analysis. Consider a firm that has one employee who makes one unit of the product each time he works. The product is valued by consumers and sold in a competitive market. The benefit to society of the last unit produced equals the marginal consumer's willingness to pay for the product. Although the product does benefit society, its production imposes a social cost in the form of a risk of a crime, which imposes a social cost of H. The probability of the accident, $p(e)$, depends on the employee's effort to avoid the accident, given by e; effort is unobservable. The cost to the employee of this effort is given by $c(e)$. Given that the market is competitive, the product price equals the marginal cost to the firm of making the product, which includes both the direct cost of crime prevention, wages, and the firm's expected liability (if any).

Social welfare is maximized when (i) the employee takes the level of effort that minimizes the social cost of crime and its prevention, $c(e) + p(e)H$ and (ii) the firm only produces a unit when the total social expected cost of the product, as given here by $c(e) + p(e)H$, equals or exceeds the benefit to the marginal consumer of that product. We know that employees will take due care if they bear the full social cost of crime. Corporate activity level (production levels) is efficient when firms bear the full social marginal cost of each unit produced, including costs associated with crime and its prevention, $c(e) + p(e)H$. Activity levels are optimal in this circumstance because firms will incorporate these costs into product prices. The firm thus will be unable to sell the product if its social cost of production (including crime costs) exceeds consumers' willingness to pay (see Shavell, 1980).

We now show that the state can both optimally deter crime and induce optimal activity levels through either individual or corporate liability, so long as the sanction equals H/P, where P is the (exogenously given) probability that wrongs are detected and sanctioned (Kornhauser 1982; Sykes 1984; Segerson and Tietenberg 1992; Polinsky and Shavell 1993).[49] Consider first individual liability. We know from section 3.1.2 that if the state imposes individual liability (with $f = H/P$), potential wrongdoers will invest optimally in effort to avert the crime because they will invest in the effort that minimizes $c(e) + p(e)Pf = c(e) + p(e)H$. Optimal individual liability also induces optimal activity levels because firms internalize the expected cost of accidental crime and its prevention, even when only employees are held liable, because each firm must pay wages that compensate employees for their expected effort costs and their expected liability (when effort is optimal). Wages must compensate employees for these costs because both effort and liability for accidental crime (when effort is optimal) constitute costs to the employee of working for the firm. Thus, even when only individuals are liable, firms bear the expected cost of both effort and crime through their obligation to pay wages equal to their employees' expected costs when they act optimally: $c(e^*) + p(e^*)H$. Accordingly, activity levels are optimal (Kornhauser 1982; Sykes 1984; Segerson and Tietenberg 1992; Polinsky and Shavell 1993).[50]

Now consider corporate liability. Corporate liability also can induce optimal activity levels and optimal effort by employees if the firm faces a sanction of H/P. Under corporate liability, firms bear the cost of expected effort and criminal liability *ex ante* through wages (as we will see). Firms operating in competitive markets will seek to minimize these costs in order to reduce the product price. To do this, the firm will intervene to induce its employees to invest optimally in effort. It can do this by imposing a sanction equal to H/P on each employee who commits a crime (section 3.1.2). Thus, corporate liability induces optimal employee effort. Corporate liability also will induce optimal activity levels, even when firms shift the *ex post* sanction to employees. As with individual liability, firms must pay wages to each employee equal to the employee's expected effort costs and his expected liability when they invest optimally in effort. Thus, the firm internalizes both expected effort and expected liability through its wages payments (Kornhauser 1982; Sykes 1984; Segerson and Tietenberg 1992; Polinsky and Shavell 1993). Thus, both corporate and individual liability optimally deter crime and induce optimal activity levels in the simple model.

3.4 Summary

The simple model yields several conclusions relevant to the debate over corporate liability, at least in those situations where the assumptions of this model apply. First, in this context, the state can have simple goals. Social welfare is maximized when the state seeks to optimally deter individual wrongdoers and induce optimal corporate activity levels.

The state need not induce firms to deter crime through policing or prevention because the state can optimally deter crime using individual liability. Second, the state can both optimally deter wrongdoing and induce optimal activity levels using either individual liability or corporate liability, so long as the expected sanction equals the social cost of the crime. The two forms of liability are complete substitutes in this model. Moreover, the state need not, and indeed should not, impose both forms of liability if doing so entails any additional cost. Finally, should the state employ corporate liability, it can use strict *respondeat superior* liability, as this induces both optimal sanctioning by firms and optimal activity levels.

This analysis might seem to suggest that US law governing corporate enforcement is inefficient because we currently impose both individual and corporate liability and use duty-based liability intended to induce corporate policing. This simple analysis does not in fact undermine the validity of the current system because it only applies when the core assumptions of the simple model are satisfied. Specifically (1) the state and the firm each can impose optimal sanctions on wrongdoers at zero marginal cost because employees have unlimited wealth and $P(E)$ is positive; (2) firms and employees contract costlessly; (3) labor markets ensure that firms bear their employees' expected costs of working for the firm (including liability); and (4) all parties are perfectly informed about the expected costs and benefits of each other's actions. In practice, these assumptions are rarely, if ever, satisfied in the corporate context. Of particular importance, for any important corporate crime, employees rarely have sufficient assets to pay the sanction that is optimal when neither the state nor the firm incurs marginal enforcement costs, $H/P(0)$. This dramatically changes the analysis because once the state cannot optimally deter crimes unless resources are spent to deter crime, a state seeking to maximize social welfare must use the most cost-effective tools available to it. These tools tend to include the prevention and policing measures under firms' control. Accordingly, this seemingly minor modification transforms the state's goals from inducing optimal behavior by individual wrongdoers and optimal corporate activity levels, to include the additional goals of inducing optimal corporate prevention and optimal corporate policing. As we shall see, satisfying these goals materially alters the analysis of optimal corporate liability, rendering invalid the conclusions that joint liability is unnecessary, that the neutrality rule holds, and that the state can use strict corporate liability to deter crime (Arlen 1994; Arlen and Kraakman 1997).

4.   CORPORATE LIABILITY BEYOND THE SIMPLE MODEL

In most cases, employees have limited assets and thus the state cannot optimally deter crime unless someone, the state and/or the firm, spends resources on prevention and enforcement. Often, the firm is the least cost provider of prevention, detection, and initial investigation. This expands the goals of liability and in turn alters its optimal structure.

This section identifies the purposes of corporate liability in those situations when optimal deterrence requires expenditures on prevention and enforcement. It explains why firms must play a greater role in deterring crime when employees have limited assets and, in turn, why this expands the goals of criminal liability. Section 5 shows that, in this situation the neutrality principle, does not hold. Section 6 shows that strict *respondeat superior* corporate liability is inefficient (Arlen and Kraakman 1997; see Arlen 1994).

4.1 When Does Optimal Deterrence Require Prevention and Policing?

Corporations do not have a vital deterrence role to play in the simple model because this model assumes that the state can optimally deter crime at zero marginal cost by imposing liability directly on individual wrongdoers, as long as the sanction equals $H/P(0)$, where $P(0)$ is the probability that a wrongdoer will be detected and sanctioned when no one undertakes any *ex ante* or *ex post* policing (Becker 1968). The state gains nothing from inducing corporate prevention or policing.

In the real world, however, states cannot costlessly optimally deter corporate crime through monetary sanctions alone. Individuals wrongdoers usually do not have sufficient wealth to pay the fine that is optimal when enforcement costs are minimized, $f = H/P(0)$.[51] Individuals committing corporate crimes are particularly likely to be unable to pay the optimal negligible-enforcement fine because the social cost of corporate crimes tends to be high and the probability of sanction (absent enforcement) is very low. The social cost of organizational crimes tends to be high because individuals committing crimes through large firms often reach (and harm) far more people than they would if acting alone.[52] The low-enforcement probability of sanction is low (and thus the sanction multiplier, $1/P$, is high) because corporate crimes often are hard to detect and prove. Many corporate crimes (such as frauds) do not cause obvious harms and thus can remain undetected for years, even indefinitely.[53] In addition, absent expenditures on enforcement, the state often cannot determine which individuals were responsible for the crime because often so many people are directly or indirectly involved in committing the harmful act (Arlen and Kraakman 1997; Buell 2006). Moreover, the state often cannot establish the requisite *mens rea* absent expenditures to investigate the crime. Thus, absent enforcement, the probability of sanction often will be so small that the optimal zero-enforcement sanction, $H/P(0)$, is infeasible. Thus, the state cannot optimally deter corporate crime through individual liability with a monetary sanction equal to $H/P(0)$ and a probability of sanction equal to $P(0)$.

It might seem that the state can optimally use the threat of imprisonment to remedy the asset insufficiency problem, without resorting to prevention or policing expenditures. This is not generally the case. First, when the optimal low-enforcement sanction, $H/P(0)$, is very high, the state may be unable to impose sufficient imprisonment to ensure that the sanction equals $H/P(0)$. For, even when the state can impose life in prison, the duration of this penalty is limited by the defendant's age and health. The maximum duration of imprisonment for many corporate crimes is lower than many street crimes because corporate wrongdoers tend to be substantially older.[54]

Beyond this, even when the state can use prison to impose a sanction of $H/P(0)$, it often is not optimal for it to do so. First, this approach creates marginal deterrence concerns if the state employs long prison terms for non-violent offenses (with a low probability of sanction), leaving it little room for sanction enhancement for violent offences. Second, imprisonment is very costly; the costs can be especially high in corporate crime cases. The social costs of prison include the direct cost of incarceration, the cost of removing an otherwise productive individual from society, and the *ex ante* social costs of threatening risk averse individuals with imprisonment for crimes they cannot be confident of avoiding. Imprisonment (and the low-enforcement/high sanction strategy in general) imposes particularly large social costs when employees are risk averse and face a risk of being found criminally liable even when they behave optimally (as can occur when employees can violate the law unintentionally).[55] In this case, the *threat* of criminal liability imposes costs on *each* risk averse employee even if he never commits a crime. Thus, the larger the sanction imposed on wrongdoers, the larger the social cost associated with deterrence. The state often can lower the social cost of enforcement, without sacrificing deterrence, by lowering the magnitude of the monetary sanction while using other mechanisms to deter crime (Polinsky and Shavell 1979; Polinsky and Shavell 1992). These alternative measures include "prevention measures" that reduce the benefit of crime or increase the direct cost of its commission and "policing measures" that increase the expected cost of crime by increasing the likelihood that wrongdoing is detected and sanctioned (Arlen and Kraakman 1997).[56]

4.2   How Corporations Can Deter Crime

In the case of corporate crime, firms often are the most cost-effective providers of many (if not most) forms of prevention and policing (at least in the context of wrongdoing by non-owner/managers) (Arlen and Kraakman 1997; see Arlen 1994). Indeed, corporations are unusually well positioned to help deter corporate crime because they can affect (1) the benefit individuals obtain from a crime, b, as well as the *ex ante* direct costs of committing the crime (Arlen and Kraakman 1997; see Kraakman 1986); (2) the likelihood that the crime will be detected and the wrongdoer sanctioned for his crimes, $P(E)$ (Arlen 1994; Arlen and Kraakman 1997); and (3) the magnitude of the sanction imposed, f (Kornhauser 1982; Sykes 1984; Polinsky and Shavell 1993; Arlen and Kraakman 1997).[57] Moreover, firms often can intervene to prevent crime and enhance its probability of sanction more effectively than can the state acting alone (Arlen and Kraakman 1997). Because these claims for corporate intervention rest on the assertion that corporate prevention and policing often is more cost-effective than pure state enforcement measures, we now consider these mechanisms in more detail, focusing on prevention and policing by larger firms.[58]

4.2.1   Corporate prevention
Corporations can deter crime by reducing the direct benefit to employees of committing crime or making crimes more costly to commit.

Corporations can make it harder for its employees to commit crimes through policies that increase the number of people the perpetrator would need to involve to accomplish the crime. Firms also can increase the cost of crime by creating a genuine corporate culture of legal compliance that imposes either direct psychological costs on those who commit crimes or increase the likelihood that fellow employees will report suspected wrongdoing (Tyler and Blader (2005) at 1153; Conley and O'Barr 1997).

Corporations can reduce the expected benefit of corporate crime by altering their compensation, promotion, and retention policies. As previously explained, the direct effect of corporate crimes generally falls on the firm, which benefits (at least in the short run) from the effect of crime on corporate profits, sales or reported earnings. Non-owner employees derive little direct gain from this effect. Instead, employees benefit from crime through the operation of corporate employment and retention policies, which may confer an increase in compensation or job security when the firm (or the employee's division) has good results. Of course, this reveals that firms directly influence the degree to which their employees can expect to benefit from crime. In turn, firms can reduce the employees' expected benefits of corporate crime by altering their compensation, promotion, and tenure policies (Arlen and Kraakman 1997).

For example, many corporate crimes (such as securities fraud) confer apparent short-run benefits on the firm, and yet harm the firm in the long run (Macey 1991; Arlen and Carney 1992; Arlen and Kraakman 1997). Compensation policies that tie employee rewards to short-run results encourage such crimes because employees can benefit from committing such crimes (and can leave before the firm suffers any long-run costs). By contrast, firms that tie employee welfare to long-run performance measures deter such crimes that impose a long-run cost on the firm, even if there is a short-run benefit.[59] When it is socially costly to invest in the resources needed to detect and sanction corporate crime, it often will be more socially cost-effective for the firm to restructure its compensation policies to reduce employees' incentives to commit crime, rather than to rely entirely on *ex post* sanctions (Arlen and Kraakman 1997).

In some cases, firms' pursuit of profit is sufficient to induce firms to structure employee compensation optimally. Yet in many other situations, firms may benefit from using high-powered short-run compensation policies to increase employee productivity, even when this is suboptimal because it creates an excessive risk of corporate crime.[60] Corporate liability can deter this practice by forcing firms to internalize the social costs of crime, thereby giving them an incentive to deter crime.

Given that firms generally have better information than the state on the expected social costs and benefits of prevention,[61] the state often can most effectively induce optimal corporate prevention by using strict corporate liability (with optimal sanctions) to ensure that firms bear the full expected cost of their employees' crimes. Firms subject to this liability will adopt the prevention measures that minimize both their expected costs and total social costs. This liability need not (and probably should not) be criminal (Arlen and Kraakman 1997) (see section 7).

4.2.2   Corporate policing

Corporations also can deter crime by implementing policing measures that increase the probability that the government detects crimes, identifies the individual wrongdoers, and obtains sufficient evidence to sanction them. Policing deters by increasing the expected cost to individuals of government sanctions for crime, Pf (Arlen 1994).[62] Firms can intervene in a variety of ways to increase the probability that wrongdoers are criminally sanctioned. They can adopt *ex ante* monitoring programs (compliance programs) designed to both detect crime and collect evidence to obtain a conviction (Arlen 1994; Arlen and Kraakman 1997). They also can intervene *ex post*, after a wrong is committed, to investigate suspicious activities, report detected crimes, and cooperate with the government effort to identify and convict the individual wrongdoers (Arlen and Kraakman 1997).

The social costs of enforcement often are lower when firms assist the state by undertaking corporate policing because firms generally are the lowest marginal cost providers of many types of *ex ante* and *ex post* policing. Large corporations can monitor for crime more effectively and at lower marginal cost than can the state. Firms, in the daily course of operations, already collect and assess massive amounts of information regarding their own operations. As much of its existing information can be used to detect wrong-doing, the marginal cost to the firm of adopting an optimal compliance program often is lower than the marginal cost to the state of a similar program (Arlen (1994) at 839–40). Corporations also are better able to analyze the information obtained because they have expertise concerning their own operations. They can use this expertise to identify areas of opportunity for crime and distinguish normal activities from activities associated with criminal conduct.[63]

In addition, firms often can intervene *ex post* to investigate suspected wrongdoing more cost-effectively than can the state on its own.[64] First, whereas the state must spend resources to determine who to interview, firms know their own chains of authority and have better information on the character of their employees (Arlen and Kraakman (1997) at 691–93, 699; see Buell 2007).[65] Thus, they can more cost-effectively determine with whom to speak and can better identify the individuals responsible for crimes. Firms also know their own operations and are better able to distinguish legitimate from illegitimate activities. Finally, firms often can obtain evidence of wrongdoing (including documents, emails, and employee interviews) at lower cost than the state because they know where to look, what to look for, and can access information and employees (e.g., foreign-based employees) more effectively than can the state (Arlen and Kraakman 1997).

Accordingly, unlike in the context of purely individual crimes where it generally is appropriate to treat the state as the primary enforcement authority, in the corporate crime context optimal deterrence generally requires the intervention of a second enforcer in addition to the state – the firm. Thus, when we move beyond the simple model, we see that in order to optimally deter corporate crime the state must not only attempt to deter individual wrongdoers directly and induce optimal corporate prevention, it also must induce firms to adopt optimal policing measures, in the form of corporate monitoring, investigation, self-reporting and cooperation with authorities to identify and prosecute the individuals responsible for the crime. To achieve this goal, the state needs to induce firms to implement all policing measures where the social cost of the policing is less than or equal to the social benefit as measured by the benefit to society of the wrongs deterred by the corporate policing (or threat thereof) (Arlen and Kraakman 1997).[66] As we will see, this goal alters the optimal structure of corporate liability (Arlen 1994).

4.2.3 Corporate sanctioning

Although we see that corporations can deter through ways not relevant in the simple model, firms also can deter crime by sanctioning individuals caught committing crimes. While corporate monetary sanctions often are simply substitutes for government-imposed sanctions, corporations can impose sanctions, such as termination, that differ in their consequences or cost from the sanctions the government imposes.[67] Moreover, firms may be able to impose higher expected sanctions on wealth-constrained employees than can the state because firms can sanction more frequently and thus with higher probability. The government can only sanction employee neglect that results in a crime. By contrast, firms may be able to sanction employees for conduct (such as suboptimal effort) that increases the probability of a crime, even if the crime does not occur. Where employee neglect occurs more frequently than crime, corporate sanctions can increase deterrence because the expected sanction the firm can impose exceeds the expected sanction the government can impose when the feasible sanction is limited by employee wealth constraints (Kornhauser 1982; Sykes 1984; see Arlen and MacLeod 2005a).[68]

4.3 Optimal Deterrence of Corporate Crime

Accordingly, optimal deterrence of corporate crimes differs significantly from optimal deterrence of individual crimes once we move beyond the simple model. In the case of purely individual crimes, criminal liability serves a simple goal: provide optimal incentives to individuals to not commit crimes. By contrast, in the corporate context, the state must not only provide optimal incentives to potential individual wrongdoers, it also must provide optimal incentives to their corporate employers. Specifically, the state generally needs to use corporate liability to induce firms to undertake optimal prevention and policing because corporate prevention and policing generally is more cost-effective than the substitute measures the state would employ. This implies that the state must not only impose optimal individual sanctions and invest optimally in enforcement, it also must ensure that firms have optimal incentives to prevent wrongdoing, undertake optimal policing measures (monitoring, self-reporting, and cooperation), and optimally impose private sanctions (Arlen and Kraakman 1997). Activity levels also should be optimal (Polinsky and Shavell 1993; Arlen and Kraakman 1997).

To induce optimal corporate prevention the state often must impose liability that ensures that firms bear the expected social cost of their employees' crimes (see section 7). To induce optimal policing, the state must ensure that firms are better off when they police optimally than when they do not. Thus, firms must face higher expected costs if they do *not* police optimally than if they do, even though policing increases the probability that wrongdoing will be detected and sanctioned (Arlen and Kraakman 1997).[69] We now turn to the issue of whether the state must use corporate liability to achieve these goals or whether instead the state can continue to rely on individual liability to optimally deter corporate crime, as the neutrality principle would predict.

5. OPTIMALITY OF JOINT INDIVIDUAL AND CORPORATE LIABILITY

This section considers the question of whether the state needs to use both corporate and individual liability, assuming that the assumptions of the simple model do not hold, and that the state cannot optimally deter crime through low-enforcement/high-sanction individual liability ($f = H/P(0)$). We assume instead that, as in section 4, the state needs to spend resources on enforcement and induce firms to undertake optimal prevention and policing. This section shows that once we move beyond the simple model, the neutrality principle generally does not hold. To optimally deter crime the state generally needs to impose liability on both individuals and corporations. Thus, this section provides an economic justification for the current US practice of imposing liability for corporate crimes on both individuals and their corporate employers. Throughout this section, we assume that the employees do not have sufficient assets to pay the optimal low-enforcement-cost fine of $H/P(0)$ and that optimal deterrence requires corporate expenditures on prevention and policing.

5.1   Need for Corporate Liability

Under the simple model, we saw that the state can induce firms and individuals to behave optimally through *either* individual liability or corporate liability. There is no need to use joint liability (Kornhauser 1982; Sykes 1984; Polinsky and Shavell 1993 (replicating this result in the corporate crime context); Arlen and MacLeod 2005a (extending the analysis to authority relationships)). Corporate liability is not needed under the simple model of accidental crime, even when the state needs to provide firms incentives to deter wrong-doing because, in this framework, individual liability can ensure that firms bear the full social cost of crime. This is because employees bear the full social cost of crime and firms' wage payments equal their employees' expected liability.

Individual liability only provides firms with optimal incentives if two conditions are met: (1) individual liability forces employees to bear the full expected cost of their crimes, even if firms under-invest in policing,[70] and (2) firms expect to bear the full expected cost of their employees' expected liability through *ex ante* wage payments (Kornhauser 1982; Sykes 1984; Polinsky and Shavell 1993). When we look beyond the simple model of accidental crimes to the context facing most large firms we see that these conditions rarely hold.

5.1.1   Employee asset insufficiency

The state cannot rely on individual liability to provide firms with optimal incentives unless employees face expected sanctions equal to the social cost of crime even when firms under-invest in policing. This implies that the state cannot rely entirely on individual liability to induce optimal corporate behavior if employees do not have sufficient assets to pay a fine of $H/P(E_g^*,0)$, where $P(E_g^*,0)$ is the probability of sanction when the state engages in optimal enforcement but the firm does not undertake any policing.[71]

Under pure individual liability, firms may not behave optimally when their employees have insufficient assets to pay the optimal low-enforcement fine because firms only have incentives to deter crime to the extent that they bear the social cost of crime through wage payments. Since firms only need to compensate employees for liability costs their employees expect to incur, firms' expected wage payments will be less than the social cost of crime when employees cannot pay the optimal sanction when the firm under-invests in policing. Given this, the private benefit to the firm of increasing its policing to the optimal level is less than the social benefit of the crimes deterred. Similarly, in this situation, the firm also does not obtain the full social benefit of prevention either. Thus, the firm will not invest optimally in deterrence measures such as prevention and policing (Arlen 1994; Arlen and Kraakman 1997).[72] Activity levels also will be inefficient (Polinsky and Shavell 1993; Arlen and Kraakman 1997).

Note that if employees do not have sufficient assets to pay the optimal sanction when firms do not police optimally, the state may be unable to rely on individual liability to induce optimal firm behavior even when employees have sufficient assets to bear the optimal sanction when firms police optimally. To see this, consider the situation where employee wealth just equals the optimal sanction when firms police optimally

($H/P(E^*)$). Now assume that optimal policing triples the probability of sanction compared to the situation where the firm does not police, and that employees subject to optimal policing exert optimal effort to deter the crime (thereby decreasing the probability of crime to $p(e^*)$). The social benefit of policing is the resulting decrease in the probability of crime multiplied by the social cost of crime, H. Yet the private benefit to the firm of policing is less than this. The firm does not obtain the full social benefit of the crimes deterred because its expected costs per crime would have been less than H had it not policed optimally (because employees are asset constrained). Moreover, the firm incurs a private cost of policing in this situation: when the firm increases its employees' expected sanction per crime by increasing the probability of sanction, it also increases the wages it must pay them for each crime committed. Accordingly, the firm has suboptimal incentives to police. Moreover, when the magnitude of the per-crime expected sanction enhancement effect exceeds the deterrence benefit to the firm of the crimes deterred by policing, a firm subject to only individual liability may not police at all. As a result, neither employees nor the firm bear optimal expected sanctions and both behave suboptimally.

In these situations, the state cannot optimally deter crime through individual liability. In order to provide firms with optimal incentives to undertake prevention and policing, the state must impose liability directly on firms (Arlen and Kraakman 1997; see Kornhauser 1982; Sykes 1984). Thus, states seeking to optimally deter most significant corporate crimes need to impose liability directly on firms, since these crimes generally impose high social costs (relative to agents' wealth) and have a low probability of sanction (absent corporate intervention).

5.1.2   Intentional wrongdoing by employees of large firms

In addition, the state cannot rely on individual liability to provide firms with optimal incentives if firms do not internalize their employees' expected liability costs through wage payments or otherwise.[73] This implies that corporate liability may be needed for willful misconduct, when the standard of liability is sufficiently clear that employees can costlessly avoid the risk of liability by not intentionally committing a crime. Firms will not compensate employees for liability associated with these crimes because employees can avoid the risk of liability by not doing the illegal act (which we assume that the firm would prefer not be committed). Given this, these crimes are not an intrinsic cost of working for the firm and employees will be willing to work for the firm even if they do not receive any wage compensation for expected liability for acts that they should not commit (and can costlessly avoid). Corporations will only compensate employees for the risk of liability for willful crimes resulting from court error. Thus, whenever optimal deterrence of intentional crimes requires corporate intervention,[74] the state will often need to impose liability directly on firms.

5.1.3   Summary

Accordingly, we see that corporate liability is an essential component of an optimal deterrence regime whenever employees are asset constrained. Corporate liability is particularly important in the case of intentional wrongdoing. Moreover, we see that in these situations corporate liability is needed even when firms face the same constraints as the state in sanctioning employees because it is needed to induce firms to take other actions, such as prevention and policing, which reduce employees' expected benefit or increase their expected cost of wrongdoing.[75]

5.2   When is Individual Liability Necessary?

This section examines whether individual liability is needed even when corporations are liable for their employees' crimes. Contrary to the neutrality result of the simple model, this part shows that individual liability often is needed to supplement corporate liability because the state often cannot rely on firms to impose optimal sanctions on employees. Thus, to ensure that individuals face optimal sanctions (given wealth constraints) the state needs to impose liability on them directly. Pure corporate liability can be inadequate in the case of both closely-held firms and publicly-held firms.

Corporate liability will not induce firms to impose optimal sanctions on individual wrongdoers when firms do not bear the full social cost of crime because the optimal sanction exceeds the firm's ability to pay (Kraakman 1984). This problem is particularly likely to arise with closely-held firms and smaller publicly-held firms. Large publicly-held firms may fail to impose optimal sanctions on wrongdoers because of agency costs, contracting inefficiencies, and other problems. Firms also cannot impose optimal sanctions when the optimal individual sanction exceeds the maximum feasible sanction that the firm can impose; individual liability will be superior when the state can impose a higher sanction than the firm. When any of these problems is present, the state can improve social welfare by imposing individual liability in addition to corporate liability.

5.2.1   Corporate asset insufficiency

Corporate liability provides optimal individual deterrence when firms bear optimal liability and firms (and those who control them) have optimal incentives to sanction individual wrongdoers. Corporate liability will not induce firms to impose optimal sanctions on individuals if firms have (or can be made to have) insufficient assets to pay the optimal corporate sanction. Corporate asset insufficiency is an important consideration given that many organizations (33–43%) and corporations (34–56%) are unable to pay the criminal fines imposed on them (see Tables 7.2 and 7.3), even though current fines tend to be less than optimal.[76] Many more firms could be rendered unable to pay optimal fines if owners were so inclined, as many would be under pure corporate liability (see below).

Under corporate liability, firms use sanctions to induce employees to invest in the level of effort, e, that minimizes effort costs plus the firm's expected liability costs, $c(e) + p(e) PF$, where here F is the feasible sanction. If the firm is asset constrained, then PF is less than the social cost of crime, H. In this case, the firm does not want employees to invest in optimal effort (given a crime cost of H) but would prefer that they invest in suboptimal effort. The firm can achieve this by imposing a suboptimal sanction on employees (Kornhauser 1982; Kraakman 1984; Sykes 1984). Accordingly, in this situation the state must impose liability directly on individuals.

Individual liability serves another purpose beyond simply ensuring that individual wrongdoers bear optimal sanctions when firms do not have sufficient assets to pay the optimal sanction: it enhances the deterrent effect of corporate liability by eliminating the incentives produced by pure corporate liability to under-capitalize the firm (Kraakman

1984). Under pure corporate liability, firms are harmed by crime only to the extent that they can pay the sanction imposed. As a result, under pure corporate liability, corporate owners (especially of closely-held firms)[77] can reduce the firm's expected costs by keeping their firms thinly capitalized. Individual liability reduces firms' incentives to engage in strategic judgment proofing. First, once employees are directly liable for wrongs, firms bear the expected cost of crime through *ex ante* wage payments; owners must ensure that the firm can make these payments on an ongoing basis and cannot avoid this portion of its expected liability through strategic judgment proofing. Second, the threat of individual liability also deters managers from engaging in strategic judgment proofing if managers risk being held criminally liable and managers' expected costs are lower if the firm is solvent than if it is not. This can occur when the firm pays its employees' litigation costs if it is solvent. In such situations, managers facing a threat of individual liability will endeavor to keep the firm solvent in order to reduce their own expected liability (Kraakman 1984; see Kornhauser 1982). Accordingly, joint individual and corporate liability reduces the benefit of strategic judgment proofing, thereby enhancing the effectiveness of corporate liability (Kraakman 1984; see Arlen and MacLeod 2005b).

5.2.2   Agency costs and other causes of corporate sanction insufficiency

Individual liability often is essential when firms cannot be relied upon to impose sanctions on individual wrongdoers because of agency costs and other problems.

Agency costs are particularly likely to result in firms imposing suboptimal sanctions when the corporation is characterized by a separation of ownership and control, and corporate managers either committed or were complicit in the crime. Absent active shareholder oversight, these managers may be able to ensure that the board decides not to pursue sanctions against individual wrongdoers (Arlen and Kahan 2012; see also Arlen and Carney 1992 (discussing securities fraud)).[78] Individual liability can be used to remedy this agency cost problem by ensuring that individual wrongdoers are sanctioned. It also can facilitate shareholder oversight of managers and the board by publicly identifying those responsible for the crime.

Corporations also may fail to impose optimal sanctions because they are unable to do so. This argues for individual liability when the state can impose higher sanctions than the firm. Corporations cannot optimally deter crime (when the state can) when the optimal sanction includes non-monetary sanctions such as imprisonment because employees have limited assets. The state also can impose a larger monetary penalty than firms can because individuals can use bankruptcy laws to obtain protection from corporate sanctions. In this situation, the state can increase social welfare by using individual liability (Segerson and Tietenberg 1992; Polinsky and Shavell 1993).

5.3   Summary

Accordingly, we see that, contrary to the predictions of the simple model, optimal deterrence of corporate crime generally requires the use of *both* individual and corporate liability. Corporate liability is needed when employees cannot pay the sanction needed to optimally deter crime when firms do not police optimally. The argument for corporate liability is strongest in the case of intentional crimes because individual liability will not provide firms with any incentive to deter those intentional crimes that employees can costlessly avoid. Individual liability is needed to ensure that individual wrongdoers face the full consequences of their crimes in those situations where the firm cannot be relied upon to optimally sanction employees. Suboptimal sanctioning may result from corporate asset insufficiency, agency costs, or other problems. Smaller firms are especially likely to have insufficient assets to pay the optimal fine (Tables 7.2 and 7.3); larger ones are likely to be plagued by agency costs. Thus, we see that, when we move outside the simple model, economic analysis provides support for the current US practice of imposing potential criminal liability on both individuals and their corporate employers.

6.   WHY CORPORATE CRIMINAL LIABILITY MUST BE DUTY-BASED

Sections 4 and 5 show that in order to optimally deter corporate crime, the state generally needs firms to undertake optimal prevention and policing (*ex ante* and *ex post*) (Arlen 1994; Arlen and Kraakman 1997). Firm activity levels also should be reduced to reflect the social cost of crime when crime is one of the social costs of producing the product (Segerson and Tietenberg 1992; Polinsky and Shavell 1993; Arlen and Kraakman 1997). Moreover, the state generally needs to impose corporate liability for employees' crimes in order to achieve these goals.

This section addresses the question of how the state should structure corporate liability to induce optimal corporate policing and prevention. More specifically, can the state achieve these goals by following the prescription of the simple model that we impose strict *respondeat superior* liability? We also examine whether corporate liability is unnecessary when market forces ensure that firms bear the full social cost of employee misconduct, as the simple model predicts.

This section begins our analysis by focusing on how to structure corporate liability to induce optimal corporate policing. It shows that the state cannot optimally rely on strict corporate vicarious liability with a fixed sanction[79] to induce both optimal policing and optimal prevention (Arlen 1994; Arlen and Kraakman 1997). When strict corporate liability is structured to induce optimal prevention it fails to induce optimal policing because firms that police optimally do not obtain a benefit from policing equal to the benefit to society of the crimes deterred (the deterrence effect). The benefit to a firm of policing is lower than this because, under *respondeat superior*, firms that police bear an inefficient cost in the form of enhanced expected liability for the crimes that the firm does not deter (Arlen 1994). Indeed, strict corporate liability fails to induce optimal corporate investment in both *ex ante* monitoring (Arlen 1994) and *ex post* policing (Arlen and Kraakman 1997).

The section shows that the state can induce optimal *ex ante* and *ex post* policing by subjecting firms to a "duty-based" corporate liability regime. Under this regime, firms that engage in optimal policing are not held criminally liable for their employees' crimes;[80] by contrast, firms that fail to police optimally are subject to a criminal sanction that ensures that firms face higher expected costs when they do not police optimally, even though failing to police reduces the probability that wrongdoing is detected and sanctioned (Arlen and Kraakman 1997). Moreover, this section shows that the state must employ duty-based liability to induce optimal policing even when firms are hit with a market sanction when crime is detected. Indeed, under plausible assumptions, the possibility of a market sanction enhances the need for duty-based liability because market sanctions can dissuade firms from undertaking efforts to detect and report crime in the absence of duty-based corporate liability. This section thus provides an economic justification for the current US practice of enabling firms to avoid formal criminal conviction by engaging in *ex post* policing (self-reporting and cooperating).[81] This section also notes reforms that could improve the current system.

6.1 Why Strict Corporate Liability Cannot Induce Optimal Corporate Policing

This part shows that the state cannot use strict corporate liability with a fixed fine to induce firms to engage optimally in either *ex ante* monitoring (Arlen 1994) or *ex post* policing (such as self-reporting and cooperation) (Arlen and Kraakman 1997) when the state also uses corporate liability to induce optimal corporate prevention. To establish this, we assume that the state sets the corporate fine equal to H/P^*, where P^* is the probability of sanction when policing is optimal. This is the sanction needed to induce optimal prevention if policing is efficient.[82] We now consider whether this sanction also can induce an equilibrium in which firms do policing optimally.

6.1.1 *Ex ante* monitoring

In order to show that there does not exist a single fixed fine that enables the state to induce both optimal policing and optimal prevention when firms are held strictly liable for all employee crimes (through *respondeat superior*), we show that firms will not engage in optimal policing if required to pay a sanction of H/P^* for each crime that the state is able to detect and sanction.

Corporate policing (such as monitoring) deters crimes by increasing the probability that crimes will be detected, thereby increasing wrongdoers' expected sanction (Pf). Corporate policing is optimal when firms invest in any policing measure for which the direct social cost of policing (as measured by the cost to the firm of the investment in policing) is less than or equal to the social benefit of policing, as measured by the social benefit of the crimes deterred. This social benefit equals the social cost of crime (H) multiplied by the expected number of crimes deterred.

It might at first seem that firms held liable through *respondeat superior* liability (and subject to a fine equal to the expected cost of crime when policing is optimal (H/P^*)) should police optimally. After all, firms already bear the direct cost of policing and this sanction ensures that firms obtain a benefit of H from each crime deterred (the deterrence benefit). This conclusion is not correct. Strict *respondeat superior* liability is not efficient because the benefit to the firm of policing is less than the social benefit of the crimes deterred. This is because, under *respondeat superior* liability, policing is a double-edged sword. It deters some crimes, to the firm's benefit. But it also increases the probability of sanction for the crimes that are committed. This increases the firm's expected liability for these crimes (the liability enhancement effect) (Arlen 1994; Arlen and Kraakman 1997). Accordingly, when strict liability imposes the fixed sanction needed to induce optimal prevention, the firm's marginal benefit of policing is less than the social benefit of policing. Instead, it equals the benefit to society of each crime deterred (H) *minus* the cost to the firm of the resulting increase in its expected liability for all undeterred crimes. As a result, firms have too little incentive to invest in policing. Indeed, if the liability enhancement penalty of policing exceeds the deterrence benefit, strict corporate liability actually deters policing rather than encouraging it (Arlen 1994; see Arlen and Kraakman 1997).

Formal analysis   We can prove this formally. Consider a firm that employs risk neutral agents to do an act that presents them with an opportunity to commit an intentional crime. For simplicity, we assume that the crime confers a benefit of b on the wrongdoer that varies across employees and is unobservable *ex ante*. Let $z(b)$ be the probability density function of gains among individuals. The benefit of the crime can be verified *ex post*. The crime imposes a social cost of H. It is assumed that, for all employees, the benefit of the crime is less than the social cost and thus the socially optimal level of crime is zero. We assume that labor markets are competitive; we also assume that the worker's reservation utility is normalized to zero. Thus, the firm pays each worker a wage of w equal to zero.[83]

The government imposes both individual and corporate liability for crimes. Under individual liability, each wrongdoer pays a sanction s if he commits a crime. The sanction is imposed with probability $P(M)$, where M is the corporation's investment in observable *ex ante* monitoring, which the firm undertakes at cost $c(M)$. It is assumed that $P'(M) > 0$, $P''(M) < 0$, $c'(M) > 0$ and $c''(M) > 0$. We assume that employees do not have sufficient wealth to pay the optimal sanction and that the maximum feasible individual sanction (given wealth constraints and other limitations) is $\hat{s}$, which is less than $b/P(M^*)$ for some agents, where M^* is the optimal level of corporate monitoring.[84]

The corporate sanction is given by F.[85] We also assume that the state wants to induce optimal activity levels and prevention, and thus imposes a fine equal to the social cost of crime divided by the expected probability of sanction. We can determine whether strict liability can induce optimal prevention, activity levels, and policing by assessing whether a firm subject to a fixed sanction of $H/P(M^*) = H/P^*$ (as is needed to induce optimal prevention) engages in optimal policing, as would be necessary for an efficient equilibrium to exist.

We first consider the socially optimal level of policing (assuming that individual employees are wealth constrained). Employees commit the crime whenever their gain, b, exceeds the expected feasible sanction, $P(M)\hat{s} < H$. This implies that social welfare is given by:[86]

$$\int_{P(M)\hat{s}}^{\infty} -Hz(b)\,d(b) - c(M) \tag{4}$$

where the integral shows the social cost of crimes committed by employees who derive a benefit of crime that exceeds the expected feasible sanction.

We can determine the optimal level of policing by differentiating with respect to M. We find that corporate monitoring is optimal when the firm invests in monitoring up to the point where the social marginal cost of monitoring, $c'(M)$, equals the marginal benefit to society of the additional crimes deterred:

$$c'(M) = H\,dZ(P(M)\hat{s})/dM \tag{5}$$

where H is the social benefit of each crime deterred, and $dZ(P(M)\hat{s})/dM$ is the expected number of crimes deterred by the marginal increase in monitoring.[87]

We now consider whether the firm will invest optimally in policing if it is held strictly liable for its employees' crimes, subject to a sanction of $H/P(M^*)$ for each crime committed.[88] Firms subject to this liability rule face expected costs of:[89]

$$\int_{P(M)\hat{s}}^{\infty} -P(M)Fz(b)d(b) - c(M) \tag{6}$$

Differentiating with respect to M, we see that the firm will select the level of monitoring at which the marginal cost of monitoring equals the marginal benefit of monitoring:

$$c'(M) = [P(M)F]dZ(P(M)\hat{s})/dM - \int_{P(M)\hat{s}}^{\infty} [P'(M)F]z(b)d(b) \tag{7}$$

Examining Equation (7), it is readily apparent that the firm will not invest optimally in monitoring when subject to the sanction that induces optimal prevention, $F = H/P(M^*)$. In this case, Equation (7) implies *respondeat superior* induces optimal policing only if Equation (8) is satisfied when the firm selects monitoring of M^*:

$$c'(M) = HdZ(P(M)\hat{s})/dM - \int_{P(M)\hat{s}}^{\infty} [P'(M)F]z(b)d(b) \tag{8}$$

Yet Equation (5) implies that this condition cannot be met. When the firm polices optimally, then the marginal cost of policing equals the deterrent effect of policing, $H\ dZ(P(M)\hat{s})/dM$. Thus, *respondeat superior* will not induce optimal policing unless the liability enhancement effect, as given by:

$$\int_{P(M)\hat{s}}^{\infty} [P'(M^*)F]z(b)d(b) \tag{9}$$

is equal to zero. Whenever it is positive, *respondeat superior* liability with a fixed fine designed to induce optimal prevention induces suboptimal policing. When the sanction is set to induce optimal prevention, the firm's private benefit of policing is less than the benefit to society of the crimes deterred and the firm will not police optimally. Indeed, if the liability enhancement effect exceeds the deterrent effect, strict corporate liability will cause the firm to refrain from policing altogether (Arlen 1994; Arlen and Kraakman 1997).

6.1.2 Post-crime policing and the credibility problem

To optimally deter crime, the state also has to induce optimal post-crime corporate policing, including *ex post* investigation of suspicious activities, reporting activities to the authorities, and cooperating with the federal investigation. It cannot do so using strict *respondeat superior* liability with a fixed fine.

Strict corporate liability provides insufficient *ex ante* incentives for firms to want to commit to optimal policing *ex post* (should a crime be detected) for the same reason given above: the benefit to firms of policing is muted by the liability enhancement effect. Yet beyond this, strict liability also undermines firms' incentives to undertake policing *ex post*, should they actually detect a crime. This undermines the deterrent effect of *ex post* policing because, even if firms announce *ex ante* that they will aggressively pursue employees who commit crimes, employees will not believe them because they know that should the firm actually detect a crime, it will not want to report it and cooperate (Arlen and Kraakman 1997).

Consider now whether strict corporate liability with a fine of H/P^* will induce optimal investigation, reporting, or cooperation. Social welfare is maximized when policing minimizes the *ex ante* costs of crime and its enforcement. This implies that firms should invest in *ex post* policing until the marginal cost of policing equals the expected marginal benefit of *ex post* policing. Because, by definition, *ex post* policing occurs after employees decide whether to commit crimes, the social benefit of *ex post* policing is best measured by the benefit to society of the crimes deterred by employees' *expectations* concerning *ex post* policing in a Perfect Bayesian Equilibrium where these expectations are correct.

Strict corporate liability induces optimal corporate policing only if it ensures that firms both want to announce that they will engage in optimal policing *ex ante* (before the crime is detected) and want to actually implement the announced optimal policing measures *ex post*, once the crime is detected. Strict corporate liability does not satisfy the latter condition: firms held liable for their employees' crimes do not benefit optimally from actually undertaking the promised *ex post* policing.[90]

Society benefits from firms' investment in *ex post* policing to the extent that firms can credibly commit to report and cooperate with respect to detected crimes. When employees believe this threat, the threat deters crimes by increasing employees' expected sanction. Yet under *respondeat superior*, this threat is not credible. The firm's threat to report detected wrongdoing and cooperate is only credible if, after employees have heard (and responded to) the threat, a firm which detects a crime is better off reporting it to authorities, even when employees already expect it to do so (a Perfect Bayesian Equilibrium). But under *respondeat superior* liability this condition is not met. If a Perfect Bayesian Equilibrium exists with self-reporting, then in equilibrium employees expect firms to self-report. Given this, firms that detect wrongdoing obtain no added deterrence benefit by self-reporting, as employees already expect them to do so. Given this, a firm that self-reports wrongdoing that otherwise might go undetected simply increases its expected liability costs, without any deterrence benefit. As a result, firms will not self-report. Thus, such an equilibrium does not exist. Given this, firms cannot benefit from the *threat* to report wrongdoing (and cooperate) because rational employees will not believe that threat (Arlen and Kraakman 1997). Thus under *respondeat superior* there does not exist an equilibrium in which (i) employees expect firms to report detected wrongs and optimally cooperate, and (ii) firms actually report detected wrongs and optimally cooperate. Thus, strict corporate liability creates a credibility problem for firms by undermining their ability to deter crimes by threatening to report them and cooperate. Thus, traditional strict liability cannot be relied upon to induce an equilibrium where firms can credibly and accurately threaten to engage in optimal post-crime policing (Arlen and Kraakman 1997).[91]

6.1.3   Summary

Thus, we see that the state cannot rely on traditional strict corporate liability to achieve two of the four central goals of optimal corporate deterrence: optimal corporate investment in *ex ante* policing (monitoring) and *ex post* policing (self-reporting, investigation, and cooperation). This suggests that the DOJ was correct to embrace a non-prosecution policy that represents an abandonment of strict *respondeat superior* corporate criminal liability, at least in those cases where optimal deterrence requires firms to monitor, investigate, self-report, and fully cooperate with government efforts to identify and convict. In situations where corporate liability cannot be relied upon to induce corporate policing (such as where owner/managers of closely-held firms are potentially criminally responsible for the wrong) then the government need not induce corporate policing. Thus, it can rely on strict corporate criminal liability, as it seems the DOJ may be doing currently with closely-held firms (see section 2).

6.2   Optimal Corporate Liability for Failure to Police Optimally

Although the state cannot use *respondeat superior* to induce optimal policing and prevention, it can induce optimal policing through "duty-based" sanctions that grant substantial mitigation (and, in some cases, exemption from corporate criminal liability) to firms that undertake optimal policing (specifically, that monitor optimally, self-report detected wrongdoing, and/or fully cooperate with the government's enforcement efforts). Specifically, in order to induce optimal behavior with respect to all forms of policing, the state needs to employ a multi-tiered duty-based sanction regime because firms make policing decisions sequentially (with monitoring preceding self-reporting, which in turn precedes cooperation). The state needs to ensure that, at each stage in the policing process, the firm is better off responding optimally (even if it failed to respond optimally in the prior period). This is particularly important with publicly-held firms because the firm might have failed to respond optimally initially because of agency costs, but later might be able to police optimally if detection of the crime produced a change in management. Thus, instead of using a single duty-based sanction that predicates mitigation on satisfaction of all policing duties, it is more effective to have a multi-tiered regime, where the firm benefits from acting optimally with respect to each independent type of policing: monitoring, self-reporting, and cooperation.

To induce optimal monitoring, the state should impose a duty to monitor optimally enforced by a penalty imposed on firms if they fail to monitor optimally, which firms can avoid by monitoring optimally (Arlen 1994). Firms with detected wrongdoing should face an additional special sanction if, *but only if*, they fail to self-report detected wrongdoing, and an additional, and very serious, sanction if, *but only if*, they fail to cooperate fully with the government's enforcement efforts. Firms that engage in optimal *ex ante* and *ex post* policing should avoid all of these sanctions for failure to satisfy their policing duties. If these sanctions are structured correctly, they will ensure that the firm wants to police optimally, even though policing increases the probability that wrongdoing is sanctioned (Arlen and Kraakman 1997).

This section demonstrates that multi-tiered liability can induce optimal policing – both *ex ante* monitoring and *ex post* reporting and cooperation. It also determines the optimal sanction for each duty violation. To do so, assumptions must be made about the magnitude of the residual sanction imposed on firms that satisfy all their policing duties by monitoring, investigating, self-reporting, and cooperating optimally. Consistent with the analysis in section 7, we assume that firms that satisfy all their policing duties nevertheless pay a monetary penalty (herein referred to as "residual liability") structured to induce optimal prevention. It is assumed that the residual sanction for any given crime magnitude is fixed *ex ante* and is given by *S*. It is implicitly assumed that this residual sanction is civil.

6.2.1　Optimal duty-based criminal sanction for suboptimal *ex post* policing

In order to ensure that firms police optimally *ex post* the state must implement a duty-based sanction such that any firm that detects a potential crime has higher expected profits if it engages in optimal *ex post* policing (including reporting) than if it does not, even though *ex post* policing may dramatically increase the probability that the crime is detected and the firm is sanctioned. Moreover, the state needs to ensure that an equilibrium can exist where (1) employees expect the firm to investigate, self-report, and cooperate should it detect a crime, and (2) each firm that detects a crime is better off if it self-reports and cooperates than if it does not, even when these actions guarantee that the firm will be sanctioned and provides no additional deterrence benefit (as employees already assume that the firm reports all detected wrongs).[92]

The state cannot ensure that firms benefit from self-reporting and cooperation unless firms that do not self-report and cooperate face a much higher sanction than those that do. The additional penalty imposed for failing to report and cooperate must ensure that the firm's *expected* liability for detected wrongdoing is lower if it self-reports and cooperates, even when post-crime policing guarantees that the firm will be sanctioned for a crime that the government otherwise might not detect (Arlen and Kraakman 1997). One effective way to do this is to offer firms leniency from criminal sanction if they report and cooperate, leaving them subject to a non-criminal penalty of *S* (*S* could be civil or imposed by DOJ through a DPA or NPA). By contrast, firms that do not report detected wrongdoing (or refuse to cooperate) should be subject to a criminal sanction (in addition to the civil penalty, *S*). The criminal penalty, *F*, should be sufficiently high that the firms' expected (probability-adjusted) sanction is lower if they report and cooperate than if they do not. When *ex post* policing is relatively low cost, the state can satisfy this condition by setting the fine imposed on firms that do not report and cooperate greater than or equal to the increase in the firm's expected residual sanction (*S*) if it self-reports and cooperates divided by the probability of sanction if it does not (Arlen and Kraakman 1997).

To see this, assume that the firm pays both fines and civil sanctions if it failed to report and cooperate (*F* + *S*), but only pays a sanction of *S* if it engages in optimal *ex post* policing. Assume further that the probability that the firm will be sanctioned if it does not cooperate is only 20% (yielding an expected sanction of $.2(S + F)$), and that the firm will definitely be sanctioned if it does report and cooperate (but will only have to pay *S*). In this case, the firm only benefits from *ex post* policing if the total sanction imposed on firms that do not report and cooperate (*S* + *F*) is at least five times higher than the sanction imposed on those who do. This implies that $F \geq (.8/.2)S = 4S$. By ensuring that firms are better off *ex post* if they report and cooperate, the criminal fine promotes optimal deterrence by enabling firms to make credible *ex ante* threats to self-report, investigate, and cooperate (Arlen and Kraakman 1997).[93]

Formal analysis The preceding simple example assumed that post-crime policing is costless. We now derive more precise conditions for the optimal sanction assuming that the cost of cooperation is given by $C(R)$, where R is the level of *ex post* corporate policing (specifically, self-reporting and cooperation). We assume that the probability that the government detects and sanctions a crime that the firm has detected is given by $\Pi(M, R)$, where M is the level of *ex ante* corporate policing. As with the example above, it is assumed that reporting and cooperation guarantees that the state can sanction the firm. Given these assumptions, a firm with detected wrongdoing faces expected cost of $\Pi(M, 0)(F + S)$ if it does not self-report and cooperate and expected costs of $C(R) + S$ if it does. The firm will engage in optimal *ex post* policing and cooperation only if the criminal fine equals or exceeds the F such that:[94]

$$C(R^*) + S < \Pi(M, 0)(S + F) \tag{10}$$

This implies that the optimal duty-based criminal fine equals or exceeds the F such that:

$$F = \frac{C(R^*) + (1 - \Pi(M, 0))S}{\Pi(M, 0)} \tag{11}$$

where $(1 - \Pi(M, 0))$ is the increase in the probability that the firm bears the residual sanction that results if the firm self-reports and cooperates.

Observe that the magnitude of the optimal fine needed to induce self-reporting and cooperation is higher the more the state benefits from these activities. Specifically, the optimal fine is larger the smaller is the probability that the state can detect the crime and sanction the firm if it does not report and cooperate.[95] The fine also is larger the greater the residual penalty imposed on firms that do report and cooperate. This suggests that when the government benefits enormously from corporate self-reporting and cooperation, and firms suffer enormously when criminal sanctions are imposed, then the state may need to reserve the threat of formal criminal conviction for firms that fail to self-report and cooperate (coupled with severe collateral consequences), and use civil penalties to induce optimal policing and prevention.

Effect of individual liability on the optimal corporate fine The question now arises whether the state should adjust the corporate fine downwards when it also sanctions individual wrongdoers for the crime, as is implied by analysis under the simple model (Shavell 1997). In the framework of the simple model, the corporate sanction should be reduced to reflect individual sanctions because feasible individual sanctions are perfect substitutes for corporate sanctions: both impose costs on firms, with firms bearing the cost of individual liability through wage payments (Shavell 1997).

The conclusion that the state should reduce the corporate fine to reflect individual fines does not hold in the case of corporate criminal penalties imposed on firms for failure to engage in optimal *ex post* policing with respect to detected crime. This is because, *ex post* when a wrong is detected, the firm's expected costs and benefits of reporting are unaffected by individual sanctions (actual or expected). This is because firms do not bear the cost of individual sanctions directly, but instead bear these costs, *ex ante*, through their obligation to pay wages equal to employees' expected liability. Employee wage compensation is determined by contracts executed *ex ante*, based on employees' expectations about the firm's post-contractual actions (such as *ex post* policing); wages are not affected by the actions the firm actually takes post-contract.[96] Thus, *ex post* when the firm decides whether to report, it only considers the effect of policing on its own expected liability (and policing costs).[97] Accordingly, the optimal duty-based criminal penalty for failure to report and cooperate is independent of any individual sanctions imposed for corporate crime.[98]

6.2.2   Duty-based sanction for failure to monitor optimally
To optimally deter corporate crime, the state also needs to impose a duty-based sanction that induces optimal *ex ante* policing (monitoring). Specifically, the state needs to impose a sufficiently large sanction on firms that fail to adopt an effective compliance program to ensure that each firm's expected costs are lower if it monitors optimally than if it does not (Arlen 1994; Arlen and Kraakman 1997).

The state can induce optimal monitoring by imposing a duty-based sanction for failure to monitor, D, that ensures that the firm's expected costs are lower if it monitors optimally than if it does not – even though monitoring imposes direct costs on the firm, $c(M)$, and also increases the firms' expected civil liability for any crimes that its employees do commit. Thus, assuming that employees can observe monitoring *ex ante* and that the firm expects to report all detected wrongs (since the state otherwise will impose a fine of F) we see that the state can induce optimal monitoring by imposing a sanction on firms that fail to monitor, given by D, such that the firm's expected costs are lower if it monitors optimally than if it does not:[99]

$$\int_{P(m,R^*)\hat{s}}^{\infty} (P(m, R^*)(S + D) + \rho(m)C(R^*))\, z(b)d(b) + c(m) >$$

$$\int_{P(M^*,R^*)\hat{s}}^{\infty} (P(M^*, R^*)(S) + \rho(M^*)C(R^*))\, z(b)d(b) + c(M^*) \tag{12}$$

where m denotes suboptimal monitoring, $\rho(M)$ is the probability that the firm detects a wrong if it monitors, and $C(R)$ is the cost to the firm of any *ex post* policing resulting from this detection. To facilitate analysis, we assume here that post-crime policing is costless and that any firm that fails to monitor optimally does not do so at all. This implies that D must be such that:

$$\int_{P(0)\hat{s}}^{\infty} (P(0)(S + D))\, z(b)d(b) > \int_{P(M^*)\hat{s}}^{\infty} (P(M^*)(S))\, z(b)d(b) + c(M^*) \tag{13}$$

where $P(M)$ is the probability of sanction, given M, assuming that the firm self-reports all detected wrongs.

Although Equation (13) is complicated, we can derive a simpler expression for damages that suffice to induce optimal monitoring. The definition of optimal monitoring implies that the cost of monitoring, $c(M^*)$, is less than the social benefit of the crimes deterred. This implies that, as long as $P(0)(S + D) \geq H$, then

$$\int_{P(0)\hat{s}}^{P(M^*)\hat{s}} (P(0)(S + D)) z(b) d(b) \geq c(M^*) \tag{14}$$

This in turn implies that firms will monitor optimally as long as the penalty for failure to do so, D, at least equals the D such that, the firm's expected liability for crimes that would not be deterred by optimal policing is higher if it does not police optimally than if it does:[100]

$$\int_{P(M^*)\hat{s}}^{\infty} (P(0)(S + D)) z(b) d(b) = \int_{P(M^*)\hat{s}}^{\infty} (P(M^*)D) z(b) d(b) \tag{15}$$

This implies that federal authorities can ensure that firms monitor optimally if the penalty imposed for failure to monitor equals or exceeds the D such that:

$$D = \frac{[P(M^*) - P(0)]S}{P(M^*)} \tag{16}$$

6.3 Corporate Liability in a World with Agency Costs

The preceding analysis reveals that corporate liability can provide firms with optimal incentives to monitor, self-report and cooperate if the government employs the multi-tiered duty-based regime described above. This sanctioning regime will induce optimal policing if firms select the policing regime that maximizes profits. Yet we know that firms may not make profit-maximizing decisions when those in control of the firm have incentives to take actions that deviate from those that benefit the firm. This is particularly likely when corporate governance is characterized by a separation of ownership and control, as is the case with publicly-held firms. Thus, the question arises whether duty-based liability can be expected to encourage corporate monitoring and *ex post* policing as applied to these firms.

Agency costs arise because the sanction for corporate crime falls on shareholders, not on managers. Optimal corporate sanctions provide shareholders with optimal incentives to want their managers to engage in optimal policing. But this may not be sufficient to induce managers to cause the firm to police optimally.

While agency costs are a serious problem for publicly-held firms, agency costs do not always undermine managers' incentives to induce optimal policing under a duty-based regime. It depends on whether agency costs afflict corporate policing decisions. Moreover, even when they do, a duty-based regime can reduce agency costs. When this is not the case, the government needs to employ additional mechanisms to ensure that firms comply with their policing duties, such as using DPAs and NPAs to impose firm-specific policing duties on firms with detected wrongs and high agency costs, often coupled with a corporate monitor to ensure that managers comply with their duties (Arlen and Kahan 2012).

First, we need to consider when the separation of ownership and control can be expected to undermine the state's ability to use corporate liability to induce optimal corporate policing. Although managers do not bear the full cost of corporate criminal liability, this does not imply that they never have optimal incentives to police under a duty-based regime. For while managers do not obtain the full benefit of policing, they also do not bear the full cost. These also generally fall disproportionately on the firm, and thus on shareholders. Accordingly, managers should police optimally as long as they have some ownership share of the firm, and their net benefit to policing is positive whenever the firm derives a net benefit from policing (Arlen and Kahan 2012).

Managerial agency costs can be expected to undermine managers' incentives to police, however, if policing imposes private costs on managers or if managers obtain private benefits from any crime committed (separate from the direct effect of the crime on the share price). Managers obtain private benefits from crimes when they expect to obtain a promotion, bonus, or other benefit as a result of the crime, as can occur when crime increases reported earnings and managers' compensation is tied to short-run earnings (Arlen and Kahan 2012).[101] Managers also can benefit from crimes, such as securities fraud, that hide poor firm performance, thereby protecting them from termination by causing shareholders to believe the firm is doing better than it is (Arlen and Carney 1992).

Agency costs also can undermine managers' incentives to ensure that the firm engages in optimal policing when policing imposes private costs on them. For example, compliance programs impose costs on managers when managers must spend additional effort on record-keeping or oversight.[102] Beyond this, managers who value autonomy and the ability to act independently also often suffer private costs if corporate compliance limits their autonomy. These private benefits of crime and costs of policing can undermine managers' incentives to adopt corporate policing (and prevention) measures, even when corporate liability is optimally structured (Arlen and Kahan 2012).

Although agency costs complicate the state's efforts to induce optimal corporate policing, the agency cost problem generally should be lower under duty-based corporate liability than under strict corporate liability. Agency costs are lower under duty-based liability because duty-based corporate liability both provides shareholders with credible information about whether managers caused the firm to police optimally and can help shareholders sanction managers who failed to do so because they were serving their own interests. First, optimal duty-based liability provides shareholders with better information about managers' policing efforts than they would get under strict corporate liability (or no liability) because shareholders cannot easily ascertain whether managers have adopted optimal policing measures. Even when shareholders know what policing program would be optimal, they rarely have enough information to determine whether managers genuinely implemented an effective program. As a result, managers can pursue their own interests at shareholders' expense. Shareholders have better information under optimal duty-based corporate liability because the government's decision to impose corporate liability for failure to monitor, report or cooperate provides shareholders with direct and clear information about whether their managers engaged in optimal *ex ante* and *ex post* policing.[103]

Second, duty-based liability can improve shareholders' ability to sanction managers who fail to satisfy their policing duties in pursuit of private benefits. First, duty-based liability may facilitate shareholder oversight through traditional measures, such as proxy contests, to the extent that shareholders are more inclined to replace directors (and to pressure directors to replace management) who fail to satisfy their policing duties, especially when their breach subjects the firm to a higher corporate sanction.[104] In addition, over time, corporate duty-based sanctions may provide managers with a direct financial incentive to engage in optimal monitoring through a potential interaction with state fiduciary duty liability. Under Delaware law, directors face direct personal liability if they fail to act in good faith to ensure that the firm has an effective compliance program or if they fail (in bad faith) to respond effectively to evidence of wrongdoing. At present, this fiduciary duty is not particularly effective because, under Delaware law, directors can determine what constitutes the right level of corporate compliance, subject to Business Judgment Rule protection. They also presumptively enjoy Business Judgment Rule protection when determining whether a crime occurred (Arlen 2009). Duty-based federal liability could enhance the deterrent effect of state law should federal law provide clearer standards governing firms' policing duties – standards which managers could not knowingly fail to comply with in good faith without triggering fiduciary duty liability (Arlen and Kahan 2012).

Nevertheless, even though duty-based corporate liability is superior to strict corporate liability, the state will not be able to induce optimal corporate policing through duty-based monetary sanctions alone when agency costs affecting corporate policing are significant. In this situation, the government often can enhance social welfare by coupling duty-based corporate monetary sanctions with firm-specific structural reform mandates that require firms with detected wrongdoing (and high agency costs) to adopt specific optimal policing measures subject to ongoing government oversight (and the threat of government sanction should the firm fail to comply, even if no subsequent crime occurs) (Arlen and Kahan 2012).

6.4 Duty-based Liability for Crimes Imposing a Reputational Penalty

We now consider whether it is optimal for the state to impose duty-based corporate liability to induce corporate policing even when firms with detected crime are subject to a market-based (or reputational) penalty, as is the case with corporate fraud (see section 2.2.3). Analysis of corporate liability employing the simple model implies that corporate market sanctions for detected crime reduce or eliminate the need for corporate liability. This section shows that this conclusion does not hold for corporate liability that is imposed to induce corporate policing. Indeed, to the contrary: duty-based corporate liability may be more vital for efforts to induce corporate policing when firms with detected wrongdoing suffer substantial market sanctions than when they do not, holding constant other sanctions.

Duty-based liability is needed even when firms bear a market sanction for detected crime because the market sanction can actually deter firms from implementing effective policing measures. Firms with certain types of detected wrongdoing (e.g., fraud) are subject to a market sanction, in the form of reduced willingness of consumers, creditors or shareholders to deal with the firm on favorable terms. Moreover the market appears to respond negatively to credible information that the firm has committed certain crimes regardless of whether the firm is formally sanctioned (see section 2.2.3). This reputational sanction operates as a form of strict corporate liability, and thus can undermine a firm's incentives to police, if the reputational penalty depends on the occurrence of the crime, and not on corporate policing. In this situation, firms do not get the full social benefit of policing that detects crimes because, in this situation, when a firm polices it increases the probability that the market will learn about the crime and punish the firm. As a result firms subject to a market penalty do not have optimal incentives to detect wrongdoing, for the same reasons discussed in section 6.1.

Nevertheless, to the extent that firms are subject to a fixed market sanction, the state must take this sanction into account in determining both the residual sanction governing prevention measures (S) and the duty-based sanctions. So long as the residual liability and market sanction combine to equal S, then all the conclusions above about the optimal duty-based sanction remain valid, however.

6.5   Summary and Assessment of the Existing Duty-based Corporate Regime

The goals and requirements of optimal corporate liability are materially different from those that emerge from the simple model. In most important cases, particularly involving large firms, corporate liability is needed to induce far more than optimal corporate sanctioning and activity levels. It also is needed to induce optimal corporate prevention and policing. This shift in goals to include corporate policing is important because it alters the structure of optimal corporate liability. The simple model finds that the state can rely on strict corporate *respondeat superior* liability (Segerson and Tietenberg 1992; Polinsky and Shavell 1993) and that corporate liability is not needed when the firm internalizes the social cost of crime through market sanctions. By contrast, the present analysis shows that when corporate liability is needed to induce optimal corporate policing, the state cannot rely on strict corporate liability with a fixed sanction. Instead, the state should subject firms to multi-tiered duty-based liability for failure to adopt optimal policing measures. Specifically, the state should impose one duty-based sanction if the firm failed to engage in optimal *ex ante* policing, D; another if the firm failed to self-report detected wrongdoing, F_1; and a third if the firm failed to cooperate fully with the government's effort to investigate and prosecute the crime, F_2 (Arlen and Kraakman 1997). Beyond this, we see that the state needs to impose duty-based sanctions even when firms are subject to market sanctions for detected wrongdoing.

The present analysis thus implies that the Department of Justice acted consistent with optimal deterrence when it adopted a formal policy of exempting firms that comply with particular policing duties from prosecution, in situations where firms can plausibly be expected to cooperate even if senior managers may be implicated (as with publicly-held firms). The apparent DOJ practice of predicating an agreement not to prosecute on the firm's willingness to fully cooperate also is consistent with optimal deterrence, as is the apparent practice of using sanctions (including civil sanctions) imposed on non-convicted firms to regulate corporate monitoring and prevention. The imposition of firm-specific policing duties (and monitoring) on firms with detected wrongdoing also promotes optimal deterrence in certain circumstances (Arlen and Kahan 2012).

Nevertheless, while the existing system is closer to an optimal composite regime than the traditional system, reforms are still needed. First, in order to induce optimal policing, the state needs to employ a multi-tiered composite duty-based liability that clearly specifies that the firm is subject to three duties (*ex ante* monitoring, self-reporting of detected wrongs, and full cooperation), and provides clear guidance on the nature of these three duties and the sanctions for violating each. By contrast, current DOJ policy simply states that all three forms of policing are *relevant* to the decision of whether to exempt a firm from indictment and to the sanction imposed, but does not provide firms with either a right or the promise that they will avoid conviction if they undertake certain actions. Moreover, while the Sentencing Commission has provided some guidance on the requirements for "effective" monitoring (compliance), neither the DOJ nor federal civil authorities provide sufficiently clear guidance on the sanction enhancements firms can expect for breach of *ex ante* monitoring duties (or failure to self-report) should they avoid conviction by fully cooperating.[105] Finally, the current system for imposing firm-specific structural reforms on firms with detected criminal wrongdoing needs reform both in terms of which federal actor has authority to impose these sanctions, as well as the type of firms affected and the nature of the sanctions imposed (Arlen and Kahan 2012; see Garrett 2007).

7.   RESIDUAL STRICT CORPORATE LIABILITY AND OPTIMAL PREVENTION

The preceding analysis provides economic support for a core feature of the current US system: the imposition of (quasi) duty-based sanctions whose magnitude is based on corporate policing. We now consider an additional core feature of the current system: the regular imposition of monetary sanctions on firms with detected wrongdoing, even when the firm had an effective compliance program, self-reported, and fully cooperated. This liability is often imposed either through government-imposed civil or administrative sanctions or through sanctions imposed by the DOJ pursuant to a DPA or NPA (Arlen and Kahan 2012). We refer to the sanction imposed on firms that satisfy all their policing duties as residual corporate liability.

This section examines the economic justifications for imposing residual strict corporate liability on firms that satisfied all their policing duties. Although some argue that firms should not be liable if they engage in optimal policing (Weissmann 2007), this section shows that this conclusion is incorrect in all but a few circumstances. Residual corporate liability generally is needed to induce firms to invest optimally in prevention measures (and activity levels). Moreover, the residual corporate sanction generally should be strict, not duty-based; it also generally should be civil and not criminal (Arlen and Kraakman 1997). Finally, this section identifies situations where the state should reduce, or eliminate, this residual corporate sanction to reflect either individual sanctions or market sanctions.

7.1   Optimal Residual Corporate Liability

To optimally deter corporate crime, the state generally needs to induce firms to adopt optimal prevention measures, in addition to optimal policing. Prevention measures are interventions that either reduce the direct benefit of crime to employees or increase its direct cost. Compensation policy design is a particularly important type of prevention measure.

To optimally deter crime, the state needs to induce firms to invest in the prevention measures that minimize the total cost of crime and its deterrence. Firms invest optimally in prevention when they select the prevention measures that maximize the net benefit of prevention, as given by the social benefit of the crimes deterred by prevention minus the social cost of prevention, where the latter generally is given by the direct and indirect cost to the firm of the prevention measure (including any effect on worker productivity). This is to say that prevention is optimal when firms increase it up to the point where the marginal cost to the firm of prevention equals the marginal benefit to the state of prevention, as given by the social benefit of using prevention to reduce the expected number of crimes (Arlen and Kraakman 1997).

Since firms bear the direct costs of prevention, the state can induce optimal prevention by ensuring that firms obtain the full social benefit of each crime deterred (and do not obtain any private transfer benefits from crime). The state can achieve this goal by imposing strict civil corporate liability on all firms that engage in optimal policing, and strict liability coupled with duty-based sanction enhancements on the others. This liability will induce optimal prevention as long as the expected sanction equals the total social cost of crime (Arlen and Kraakman 1997). For simplicity, here we denote the social cost of crime as H; where crime enforcement includes marginal crime-specific investments by the state or the firm in enforcement, these costs should be included in the measure of the social cost of crime (Polinsky and Shavell 1984).

Accordingly, in addition to imposing multi-tiered duty-based corporate sanctions, the state should impose residual strict corporate civil liability on firms with detected wrongdoing, with an expected sanction equal to all total social costs of crime that the firm does not otherwise bear through market forces. This implies that firms that engage in optimal policing should be subject to a residual sanction equal to

$$S^* = \frac{H}{P(M^*, R^*)} \tag{17}$$

where H is the social cost of the crime, and $P(M^*, R^*)$ is the probability of sanction if it engages in optimal *ex ante* and *ex post* policing. A firm subject to this sanction will bear both the full social cost of prevention and internalize the full social benefit; thus it will invest optimally in prevention (Arlen and Kraakman 1997). This sanction also induces optimal activity levels (Arlen and Kraakman 1997; Polinsky and Shavell 1993).[106]

Strict corporate liability is superior to duty-based liability as a method of regulating prevention when, as is usually the case, the firm has better information than does the state about the expected costs and benefits of prevention; the relative benefits of strict corporate liability are particularly great when the firm can (and should) employ a variety of different types of prevention measures to deter a variety of different crimes (Arlen and Kraakman 1997).

7.2 Arguments for Modifying or Eliminating the Residual Civil Sanction

The conclusion that the state must impose expected residual corporate liability equal to the social cost of crime (plus any purely private transfer benefit to the firm of crime) must be adjusted to reflect employees' expected criminal liability in some situations, and the firm's expected market sanction for corporate crime in all situations.

7.2.1 Effect of individual liability on residual corporate liability

The optimal residual sanction must be reduced to reflect employees' *expected* individual liability in those situations where firms internalize their employees' expected sanctions, generally through additional *ex ante* compensation.[107] This adjustment must be made to ensure that the firm's *total* expected costs of crime (as determined by the *ex ante* wages it must pay to compensate employees for their expected liability and its expected *ex post* liability for crimes that occur) equals, but does not exceed, the social cost of crime (Polinsky and Shavell (1993) at 249; see Shavell 1997).[108]

This adjustment should only be made if two conditions are met, however. First, firms must bear the expected cost of their employees' expected liability through wage payments (or otherwise). As we saw earlier, this is likely to occur in the case of liability for accidental crimes. By contrast, firms will not compensate workers for their expected liability for suboptimal intentional crimes when (i) firms do not benefit from the crime; and (ii) employees can avoid criminal liability by not engaging in the undesired conduct. In this situation, employees who perform their jobs in the firm's best interests do not face any risk of criminal liability; thus, firms will not pay wages that reflect an employee's expected liability because this liability is not really a cost of employment. Accordingly, the state should not reduce the residual corporate sanction to reflect employees' expected liability for these crimes.

Second, even when the firm does pay wages to reflect its employees' expected liability, the state should not adjust the sanction unless corporate prevention measures are sufficiently visible to affect employees' expected liability, and thus wages. This implies that employees must have sufficiently good information about corporate prevention measures to correctly estimate their expected liability at the moment that they contract with the firm over wages. By contrast, when employees cannot observe corporate prevention *ex ante* when wages are set, then firms cannot reduce employees' *ex ante* expected liability (thereby reducing the firm's wage payments) by adopting optimal prevention measures. In this situation, the corporate sanction that induces optimal activity levels will diverge from the sanction that induces optimal prevention measures.

7.2.2 Effect of market penalties on optimal residual corporate liability

The state also should reduce the residual corporate sanction to the extent that the firm bears a long-run market sanction for detected wrongdoing. To induce optimal prevention, the firm must bear an expected sanction equal to the total social cost of crime (Arlen and Kraakman 1997), including crime-specific costs of enforcement (Block 1991). Accordingly, the state must adjust the residual sanction when the market automatically imposes a long-run sanction on the firm, to ensure that the total sanction imposed is optimal. Accordingly, the state should set the residual sanction equal to the total social cost of crime, H, minus the long-term market sanction, θ, in those situations where the market and government sanctions are imposed with the same probability:[109]

$$S^* = \frac{H - \theta}{P(M^*, R^*)} \tag{18}$$

Securities fraud   The preceding analysis explains why it is optimal for the state to employ composite duty-based liability to deter most crimes (Arlen and Kraakman 1997). In order to deter securities fraud (defined as intentional financial misstatements by managers of publicly-held firms) the state should employ only pure duty-based corporate liability, combined with individual liability, however (Arlen and Carney 1992). As previously discussed, most pure intentional financial misreporting[110] is committed by senior managers who are hoping to use the period of the fraud to hide bad news (Arlen and Carney 1992). This fraud directly harms shareholders by (i) distorting their trading decisions; (ii) causing them to retain suboptimal managers who otherwise likely would have been fired; and (iii) imposing on them the expected reputational sanction imposed on firms with detected financial misreporting.

Given that shareholders are the primary victims of securities fraud (Arlen and Carney 1992), it should come as no surprise that the market sanction for financial misreporting appears to be substantial (Karpoff *et al.* 2008a).[111] Moreover, this penalty falls on the same shareholders who would bear the burden of residual corporate liability for securities fraud – those who own the firm's shares at the moment the fraud is revealed.[112] To the extent that this sanction ensures that shareholders bear the full social cost of fraud, the state need not also impose residual liability on firms that engaged in optimal policing (Arlen and Carney 1992).[113] Accordingly, in the case of intentional financial misrepresentation by publicly-held firms traded in informationally efficient markets, the state likely can rely on market forces to provide shareholders with incentives to encourage managers to adopt prevention measures (Arlen and Carney 1992).[114] Moreover, imposing residual liability may undermine the state's ability to use duty-based sanctions to induce optimal policing, as firms that commit securities fraud often are asset constrained, as evidence suggests (Arlen and Carney 1992; Karpoff *et al.* 2008a). This is because the state may not be able to effectively threaten the firm with a duty-based sanction for failure to police optimally (e.g., cooperate) if the firm is already subject to a residual sanction that renders it insolvent. Thus, generally the best approach to securities fraud is to impose pure duty-based corporate liability on firms that fail their policing duties and individual liability on the managers responsible for the fraud (Arlen and Carney 1992).

7.3   Comparison with the Existing Regime

Accordingly, we see that in order to induce optimal prevention and activity levels, the state needs to subject firms that engage in optimal policing to significant civil residual liability designed to provide firms with optimal incentives to prevent wrongdoing and to induce optimal activity levels. This is consistent with the existing federal enforcement practice under which firms may be required to pay sanctions even if they engaged in optimal *ex ante* and *ex post* policing. Nevertheless, current practice does not fit all the requirements of an optimal corporate liability system in that federal authorities have not adopted clear guidelines to ensure that civil regulators and the DOJ impose optimal residual sanctions on firms – sanctions that take full account of the variety of ways in which firms bear the social costs of crime.

8.   CRIMINAL VS. CIVIL CORPORATE LIABILITY

The preceding analysis shows that the state can induce optimal policing through the use of a multi-tiered duty-based sanction. We now consider whether each of these sanctions should be criminal or whether it would be better for the state to employ government-imposed civil liability to regulate most forms of policing, reserving criminal liability for situations where firms fail to engage in the penultimate form of *ex post* policing: cooperation.

The economic analysis of corporate criminal versus civil liability is complicated because the core economic distinction for firms between these forms of liability is not well understood. In the individual context, criminal liability differs from civil liability in part because only the former entails a potential loss of liberty and certain civil rights (such as voting); it also is associated with a higher reputational penalty. These differences do not appear to apply to the corporate context. Potential criminal and civil corporate sanctions are remarkably similar in form (with an important difference discussed below) and can be made similar in magnitude. Moreover, the two actions may even impose similar market sanctions on the firm, at least when the action is brought by a government enforcement agency (Khanna 1996; see Alexander 1999).

Nevertheless, there are important differences between the two types of liability that exist in practice. First, there are important procedural differences, including a higher burden of proof in criminal cases and more powerful tools of investigation. Second, there are important substantive differences in the nature of the sanction imposed. Although at first corporate civil and criminal liability appear similar because they take the form of monetary sanctions (Khanna 1996; Fischel and Sykes 1996), criminal liability differs in that firms convicted (or indicted) for certain wrongs face the substantial threat of enormous collateral sanctions, such as debarment and de-licensing. These collateral sanctions enable the state to impose an enormous, ongoing sanction on the firm that can be the equivalent of a corporate death penalty. In addition, it appears that managers and employees of firms with detected wrongdoing may feel greater disutility if the firm is convicted of a crime than if the firm is subject to a purely monetary civil penalty (Khanna 1996), which suggests that the state can treat this sanction as a more serious sanction. Finally, under existing law, the firm faces higher potential total sanctions when convicted of a crime both because criminal fines are higher than civil penalties and because criminal fines can be imposed in addition to civil penalties.[115]

We now consider how the government can best structure a duty-based composite corporate liability regime to induce optimal corporate prevention, *ex ante* policing and *ex post* policing, assuming that criminal penalties are potentially more uncertain in their effect because of either collateral consequences, reputational penalties, or the effect on private actions.[116] The core requirements for optimal corporate liability is that the government employ a form of residual liability that nevertheless enables it to impose feasible duty-based sanctions to induce *ex ante* monitoring and *ex post* reporting and cooperation. This implies that the state needs to employ sanctions for violations of policing duties that exceed the residual penalty and are sufficiently severe that the firm will want to self-report and cooperate. It also implies that the residual sanction must be such that the firm will not avoid self-reporting in order to avoid this sanction. This consideration argues in favor of criminal liability for failure to cooperate if criminal liability is much more costly for the firm than civil liability. Corporate criminal liability is a particularly effective tool for inducing reporting if crime imposes a reputational penalty on managers and directors, as they will thus have a direct incentive to take the actions needed to avoid triggering the sanction. This need to ensure that the duty-based penalty is much higher than the residual sanction argues against using formal criminal liability to impose the residual sanction whenever firms face serious collateral penalties or reputational penalties if convicted, regardless of the monetary sanction imposed. Thus, the state should consider using the threat of criminal liability to induce firms to self-report detected wrongdoing and cooperate; firms that self-report and cooperate could be exempt from formal criminal sanctions, if the state has authority to impose civil penalties.[117] The state should supplement criminal liability with duty-based composite civil liability, with a sanction enhancement for firms that fail to adopt an optimal monitoring program. These sanctions can be civil (or imposed through a DPA or NPA). In some cases, such as where agency costs are high, the state may need to subject firms with detected wrongdoing and seriously inadequate *ex ante* policing to a duty-based monetary sanction for failure to monitor coupled with a requirement that the firm adopt a government-approved compliance program (subject to oversight) (Arlen and Kahan 2012).

9.   CONCLUSION

This chapter has shown that, in order to optimally deter corporate crime, the state cannot simply take the same approach as it does with individual criminal liability. This is especially true when corporate liability is needed to induce optimal corporate policing, prevention, and activity levels. Whereas the government can optimally deter purely individual crimes by imposing a fixed fine on wrongdoers for every crime they commit, the state cannot use strict corporate liability with a fixed fine to deter corporate crime, particularly by larger firms. Instead, the state should employ a multi-tiered duty-based composite regime that uses a combination of criminal and civil liability to induce optimal *ex ante* and *ex post* policing.

Comparing the optimal regime with existing US enforcement practice, we see that the DOJ's decision to abandon strict corporate liability in favor of a more duty-based regime is consistent with optimal deterrence. The apparent practice of offering leniency from prosecution to firms that fully cooperate, coupled with residual sanctions imposed on such firms, potentially enhances deterrence by increasing corporate cooperation while still providing firms with a financial incentive to prevent wrongdoing. Deterrence is further enhanced to the extent that federal authorities ensure that firms face higher sanctions if they did not engage in optimal *ex ante* policing or did not self-report detected wrongdoing.

Nevertheless, several facets of current practice potentially undermine the federal government's ability to use corporate liability to induce optimal corporate behavior. First, federal authorities should adopt a clear policy that, in cases where optimal deterrence requires corporate policing, prosecutors should predicate the decision of whether to grant leniency from prosecution on a firm's full cooperation. Firms must be more confident that cooperation will insulate them from criminal sanctions. Second, federal authorities should adopt clear guidelines governing the sanctions imposed on firms that do cooperate to ensure that firms face multi-tiered monetary sanctions. Specifically, the state must impose a clear duty to self-report and to adopt optimal *ex ante* monitoring, provide additional guidance on the nature of the monitoring duty, and impose substantially enhanced sanctions on any firm that breaches this duty. Effectuating this system would require both stronger policy directives from the DOJ and more coordination with civil authorities and states. Finally, and critically, optimal deterrence of corporate crime requires enhanced federal and state attention to ensure that individuals who commit corporate crimes expect to be subject to significant criminal penalties and to reforms that promote improved shareholder monitoring of managers.

Finally, in examining the requirements for optimal deterrence of corporate crime, we see the importance for law and economics of situation-specific analysis of legal rules. We see that individual criminal liability differs from optimal corporate criminal liability, and the nature of optimal corporate criminal liability depends on whether liability is directed at owner-managers of closely-held firms or larger publicly-held firms.

NOTES

* I would like to thank Cindy Alexander, Miriam Baer, Oren Bar-Gill, Samuel Buell, Brandon Garrett, Marcel Kahan, Michael Klausner, Lewis Kornhauser, A. Mitchell Polinsky, Steven Shavell, and the editors for helpful comments and discussions. I also want to thank my research assistants Lu Chen, Tristan Favro, Kristy Fields, Joshua Levy, Jared Roscoe, Robert Taylor, and Donna Xu. I benefited from the financial support of the Filomen D'Agostino and Max E. Greenberg Research Fund of the New York University School of Law.

1. "Corporate crimes" are defined throughout this chapter as crimes to which corporate liability could attach under *respondeat superior*. Thus they are crimes committed in the scope of employment with some intent to benefit the firm. Crimes falling into this category include Foreign Corrupt Practices Act violations (involving payment to foreign officials designed to facilitate the firm's interests abroad), environmental and antitrust violations, fraud against the government (especially involving over-charging), and securities fraud involving materially misleading statements. White collar crimes that do not attempt to benefit the firm are not included in this definition.

2. This chapter focuses on the question of how to use corporate and individual liability to deter corporate crime, as defined by the legislature. It does not address the separate issue of what conduct should be subject to criminal liability.

3. Strictly speaking, each firm introduces a nexus of additional actors – shareholders, directors, officers, and employees – some of which often are victims of the crime in the long run (see section 3.2) and others of whom (managers) are potential enforcers. Both the harm caused by the crime and the incentive provided by corporate liability reach these actors through the firm. See section 6.3 (discussing agency costs in enforcement) and Arlen and Kahan (2012) (same).

4. See section 5 (explaining why the state usually must impose corporate liability in addition to individual liability).

5. See *infra* notes 41, 70 and 82.

6. The conclusion that strict corporate liability is inefficient stands in contrast with the conclusion of the classic model of vicarious liability that strict corporate liability is efficient (Segerson and Tietenberg 1992; Polinsky and Shavell 1993; see Kornhauser 1982). These analyses assume that the firm deters crime

primarily through monetary sanctions. They do not examine optimal liability when firms can help the state detect and investigate wrongs.

In addition, in contrast with prior analysis which finds that the state should reduce corporate sanctions to reflect expected individual liability paid (Polinsky and Shavell 1993), this chapter shows that the duty-based criminal sanction should not be reduced to reflect sanctions imposed on either individual wrong-doers or market sanctions.

7. The conclusion that these features are consistent with optimal corporate liability does not imply that current US law is efficient in all respects. For a discussion of the problems with the current US system see Arlen (2011); Arlen (2012); Arlen and Kahan (2012); Arlen and Kraakman (1997) at 742–52).

8. Data is from the US Sentencing Commission and is limited to convictions sentenced under the Organizational Guidelines that were reported to the Sentencing Commission. This data likely is incomplete. See Garrett (2011) (producing a data-set that shows that 125 publicly-held firms were convicted between 2001 and 2010, more than twice the number in the Sentencing Commission's data); see also Alexander, Arlen, and Cohen (2000) (finding that the Commission's Organizational Data for 1991–1996 was missing scores of cases).

   Table 7.1 reports the number of cases where the Commission does not have data on the type of organization convicted to highlight the magnitude of the omitted data in this dataset. Missing data is a particular problem to the extent that the omissions are not randomly distributed – a concern raised by prior analysis of the Organizational data (Alexander, Arlen, and Cohen 2000).

9. During the 1980s, most convicted firms were small, closely-held firms. Only 8% of the convicted firms had publicly traded stock (Cohen (1996) at 402). Convicting small closely-held firms can ensure that liability is imposed on owner-managers responsible for the crime when it is difficult to establish their direct personal complicity. Yet during the 1980s, prosecutors tended to focus on corporate convictions at the expense of individual convictions even in the case of publicly-held firms. Indeed, not a single individual was convicted in about half of the cases where a publicly-held firm was convicted (Cohen (1996) at 407). This practice is hard to defend in most cases.

10. See *infra* note 26.

11. See *New York Central and Hudson River Railroad Co. v. United States*, 212 U.S. 481 (1909) (establishing corporate criminal liability through the doctrine of *respondeat superior*).

12. Federal criminal law imposes a "benefit the firm" requirement for corporate liability, but this requirement is met even when the employee committed the crime primarily for his own benefit and only incidentally to benefit the firm (Arlen (2004) at 193–4; Weissmann (2007) at 1320).

13. By contrast, other countries generally restrict corporate criminal liability to crimes by senior managers or allow a formal good faith defense for firms which had an effective compliance program designed to prevent crime. See generally (Beale and Safwat (2005) at 155).

14. Corporations can be liable for crimes by lower level employees because both the acts and the *mens rea* of employees acting in the scope of employment are attributed to the firm. See e.g., *United States v. Dye Constr. Co.*, 510 F.2d 78 (10th Cir. 1975); *Tex.-Okla. Express, Inc. v. United States*, 429 F.2d 100 (10th Cir. 1975); *Riss and Co. v. United States*, 262 F.2d 245 (8th Cir. 1958); *United States v. George F. Fish, Inc.*, 154 F.2d 798 (2d Cir. 1946).

15. See e.g., *United States v. Twentieth Century Fox Film Corp.*, 882 F.2d 656, 660–1 (2d Cir. 1989); *United States v. Hilton Hotels Corp.*, 467 F.2d 1000, 1004 (9th Cir. 1973).

16. Firms that undertake certain acts of corporate policing may benefit from a reduction in the fine imposed under the Organizational Sentencing Guidelines, US Sentencing Commission, *Guidelines Manual*, ch. 8 (hereinafter "Organizational Guidelines"), but they remain criminally liable. Thus, they face the higher expected private civil sanctions, reputational penalties, and potentially ruinous collateral penalties that can attend a federal conviction.

17. Analysis of fines imposed prior to the Organizational Guidelines found that corporate fines are small relative to the harm caused (Cohen (1996) at 401 (estimating that median fines are approximately 12% of the harm caused)).

18. See *supra* note 8.

19. Care must be taken in considering these results because the Sentencing Commission's data does not provide information on organizational type for a large number of firms, many of which may be corporations.

20. Although most convicted firms are corporations, others are sole proprietorships, non-profit organizations, unions, government entities, partnerships, associations, and other non-corporate entities.

21. See *supra* note 8 (discussing limitations of the data). The category "publicly-held" is based on the subset of cases in the Sentencing Commission's data where we have data on firm type.

22. There is evidence that judges adjust criminal fines when non-fine monetary sanctions are high (Cohen (1996) at 406), and vice versa. For example, although the Organizational Guidelines required judges to impose higher fines than they otherwise would have, analysis of corporate sanctions imposed after

the Guidelines found no significant difference in the total sanctions imposed in cases where judges were bound by the Guidelines than in post-Guidelines cases where judges were not so constrained. This suggests a substitution between fine and non-fine sanctions (Alexander, Arlen and Cohen 1999a).

23. By contrast, judges rarely imposed probation or other non-monetary sanctions on convicted firms prior to the adoption of the Organizational Sentencing Guidelines (Cohen (1996) at 409).

24. These collateral sanctions are not properly viewed as a "reputational sanction" *resulting* from a conviction because the government often makes its business relationship decision prior to conviction and, moreover, often determines the extent of collateral sanction jointly with the settlement which determines the formal monetary sanction (Alexander 1999; for additional analysis see Karpoff *et al.* 1999).

25. The existing regime approximates a "duty-based" regime but does not precisely replicate it since firms are not entitled to exemption from prosecution for good behavior.

26. See Eric Holder, Deputy Attorney General, to the DOJ departments, Memorandum from Eric Holder, Deputy Attorney General, US Dep't of Justice, to Heads of Department Components and United States Attorneys (June 16, 1999) (noting that individual criminal liability "provides a strong deterrent against future corporate wrongdoing"); Thompson memo, *infra* note 31 (stating that "[b]ecause a corporation can act only through individuals, the imposition of individual criminal liability may provide the strongest deterrent against future corporate wrongdoing"); see generally First (2010).

27. See Holder memo, *supra* note 26. The Holder memo and its progeny govern most corporate crimes, but do not apply to all crimes, such as antitrust violations, which receive separate treatment. The economic support for the conclusion that strict corporate liability can deter corporate policing efforts can be found in Arlen (1994).

28. See Holder memo, *supra* note 26. To be precise, the Holder memo encouraged prosecutors to take a variety of factors into account in determining whether to prosecute, including whether the firm had an effective compliance program, self-reported the wrong, cooperated with the investigation, and accepted responsibility. In practice, prosecutors have focused on these considerations, paying particular attention to corporate cooperation and acceptance of responsibility.

29. The Holder memo is more of a true "duty-based" regime than the Organizational Guidelines (Arlen and Kraakman (1997) at 745–9). Under the Organizational Guidelines, firms that take certain policing measures can get their fines reduced, but in the case of larger firms they often do not receive enough mitigation to encourage effective policing (Arlen 2012). The Organizational Guidelines also contain many inefficient limitations on firms' abilities to get mitigation for policing (Arlen 2012; Arlen and Kraakman (1997) at 745–9). Moreover, firms eligible for mitigation remain subject to conviction, with the associated non-fine penalties, collateral consequences (in some cases), and increased expected private civil liability.

30. See *infra* note 31.

31. Prosecutors employed DPAs and NPAs prior to 2003. Nevertheless, federal prosecutors embraced the modern deferred prosecution approach, which includes the use of DPAs and NPAs to impose structural reforms, following the issuance of the "Thompson memo" by then Deputy-Attorney General Larry Thompson. Memorandum from Larry D. Thompson, Deputy Attorney General, US Dep't of Justice, to Heads of Department Components and United States Attorneys (January 20, 2003), available at www.justice.gov/dag/cftf/corporate_guidelines.htm. US DEP'T OF JUSTICE, US ATTORNEYS' MANUAL § 9-28.900 (Principles of Federal Prosecution of Business Organizations).

32. See *supra* note 31.

33. Thus, if we take into account the DOJ's lenience policy, and recognize that firms that self-report also cooperate, we realize that the low self-reporting rates of convicted corporations do not indicate, as some have suggested, "that it is rare for enterprises to self-report crimes" (Mullins and Snyder (2009) at 223). Instead, the low self-reporting rate of convicted firms is consistent with firms self-reporting wrongdoing under a DOJ policy of not convicting the firms that self-report and cooperate.

34. Table 7.5 is based on the D/NPAs that could be confirmed. This data was hand-collected and then compared with the DPAs/NPAs listed on Professor Brandon Garret's website at the University of Virginia Law School, available at http://lib.law.virginia.edu/Garrett/prosecution_agreements/home.suphp. His dataset includes the following DPA/NPAs which are not included here because he did not have the D/NPAs (or a press release) and we could not confirm them: Facility Group (2010), M.A. Angeliades (2010), Cosmetic Laboratories of America (2010), McSha Properties (2009), Unum (2008), Levlad (2008), RFK Institute (2008), Holy Spirit Organization (2007), Medicis (2006).

The designation "publicly held" is based on the firm's status at the time of agreement, and include D/NPAs involving subsidiaries that are majority-owned by a publicly-held firm (50% or more).

The term "DOJ Fine/Penalty" includes all sums described as a fine or penalty imposed by the DOJ. It excludes any guilty pleas by subsidiaries, unless expressly incorporated into the agreement as payable by the parent corporation. It also excludes restitution, disgorgement, and forfeiture.

Means and medians are based on the total number of firms subject to DPAs/NPAs in each year. The total penalty includes any separate settlements with the government that were entered into at or around the same time as the DPA/NPA, including DOJ Civil Division and the SEC settlements, but excludes any private civil settlements, such as class actions, even if incorporated into agreement.

All percentages are rounded to the nearest 5%.

35. See *supra* note 8. This Table is limited to public and private corporations and excludes non-profits, public entities, partnerships, and sole proprietorships. Data is based on the subset of cases where we have data on both firm type and whether the firm got credit for accepting responsibility or self-reporting.

Acceptance of Responsibility code in the Sentencing Commission's data is an index that measures the degree to which the organization accepted responsibility for the offense conduct as measured by self-reporting of the offence, cooperation with the investigation, or acceptance of responsibility for the offence. See USSG 8C2.5(g) for more information.

36. Firms subject to DPAs and NPAs are only a subset of the firms potentially eligible for conviction that escaped conviction. Thus, this analysis understates the implications of the DOJ's non-prosecution policy for publicly-held firms and their subsidiaries.

37. This section and the next one follow the standard literature on corporate crime in assuming that corporate managers maximize fire profits. Thus, we assume that corporations undertake the policing and prevention measures that minimize the total expected costs of crime and its deterrence.

38. Accordingly, this analysis differs from Polinsky and Shavell (1984) which examines pure individual liability when optimal deterrence requires positive expenditures on enforcement. This chapter does not consider pure individual liability in this situation because, in the corporate crime context, whenever optimal marginal enforcement is positive, optimal deterrence will generally require corporate expenditures on enforcement. In this case, optimal deterrence will require the use of both corporate liability and individual liability.

39. Scholars discussing optimal deterrence in the purely individual crime context (street crimes) have challenged this rational actor approach on the grounds that criminals often are not in a rational frame of mind when they commit crimes, and thus are not optimally deterred by the threat of sanctions. This criticism may well be valid when applied to crimes of passion or crimes committed by addicts or the insane. Yet it does not seem valid in the corporate context (Block, Nold, and Sidak 1981, finding that increasing the probability or magnitude of the criminal sanction decreases the probability of antitrust violations); Paternoster and Simpson (1996). First, unlike most street crimes, corporate crimes generally are committed by people who are employed by a firm, often at a managerial level. The previous business success of most corporate criminals suggests that they are able to make deliberative decisions. Many perpetrators of corporate crimes serve in jobs in which they regularly compare immediate costs/gains against future uncertain rewards/costs (Baer (2008b) at 313). Moreover, unlike violent crimes, corporate crimes generally are not committed in the heat of passion, but are committed in a context where deliberation is possible – during the course of the business day, often over an extended period of time, by individuals who have full control of their mental faculties. Finally, perpetrators of corporate crimes are more vulnerable to sanctions. They often have substantial wealth and a valuable reputation that they could lose if convicted. Moreover, they have families who would be hurt. Finally, evidence suggests that corporate crimes are not committed by people living outside the law, but instead are committed by people who succumbed to financial temptation or career pressures (Paternoster and Simpson (1996) at 550; Sutherland 1949 (criminal sanctions can deter corporate crime because managers are well integrated into communities and churches and thus are especially vulnerable to the reputational cost of criminal conviction)).

40. When the legislature defines crimes optimally, this latter condition will rarely if ever be met.

41. This chapter does not thoroughly analyze individual liability, and thus does not consider the variety of reasons why optimal individual sanctions may deviate from H/P even when individuals are solvent. For example, the optimal sanction must be adjusted if wrongdoers are risk averse or the crime should be deterred completely (Hylton 2005). Moreover, when the state cannot optimally deter crime without spending resources on enforcement, then the optimal individual expected sanction is less than $P(E^*)H$, where E^* is marginal enforcement expenditures because enforcement expenditures increase the social cost of deterring crime (Becker (1968) at 192; Polinsky and Shavell 1984; Block (1991) at 397–8; Polinsky and Shavell 1992; Polinsky and Shavell (2007) at 414).

42. A complete expression of the model should include marginal enforcement expenditures, as these are a component of social welfare. We simplify the exposition by setting enforcement expenditures to zero because, as we showed above, optimal enforcement is zero when fines are costless to impose and there are no wealth constraints.

43. For a discussion of optimal individual criminal liability when individuals are risk averse, see Polinsky and Shavell (1993) at 254.

44. See *supra* note 1 (defining corporate crimes).

45. We leave proof of this result for the subsequent section on the neutrality principle.

46. Thus, crimes by publicly-held firms are best characterized as an agency cost (Arlen and Carney 1992; Macey 1991; Paternoster and Simpson (1996) at 550). Consistent with the hypothesis that crimes by

publicly-held firms generally are agency costs that benefit individuals wrongdoers, not shareholders, empirical evidence finds that corporate crime is more likely the lower is management's percentage ownership stake in the firm (Alexander and Cohen 1999). Crime also is more likely the larger the firm (Alexander and Cohen 1996), the weaker the firm's internal controls (Baysinger 1991), and the greater the emphasis on short-term financial measures in setting compensation (Hill *et al.* 1992). See also Arlen and Carney 1992 (true securities fraud benefits managers at the expense of the firm's shareholders).

47. In this section, we focus on the total optimal sanction to be imposed on the individual wrongdoer, without differentiating whether the sanction is imposed by the state or the firm.

48. This conclusion, known as the neutrality principle, was developed in the context of civil liability, (Kornhauser 1982; Sykes 1984; Arlen and MacLeod 2005a (extending the analysis to authority relationships)), but holds as well for criminal liability (Segerson and Tietenberg 1992; Polinsky and Shavell 1993).

49. See *supra* notes 38 and 41.

50. Firms facing wage payments equal to the expected cost of crime have optimal incentives to invest in measures to deter crime. Thus, in this model, when the state imposes optimal individual liability, firms have optimal incentives to prevent crime. This implies that individual liability is sufficient to optimally deter crime, in this model.

51. Observe that asset insufficiency changes the goals of corporate liability whenever wrongdoers cannot pay the optimal zero-enforcement sanction, $H/P(0)$, even when wrongdoers do have sufficient wealth to pay a monetary sanction equal to $H/P(E^*)$, where E^* is optimal enforcement given employees' wealth constraints.

52. For example, an individual committing fraud through an organization often harms more people than he would if acting alone because the organizations extends his reach.

53. See (Dyck *et al.* 2010) (only 7% of corporate frauds detected at large companies between 1996 and 2004 were detected by the SEC; 13% were detected by non-financial market regulators).

54. Of course, the pecuniary and non-pecuniary cost of each month of imprisonment for a corporate wrongdoer may be higher.

55. Employees may be held criminally liable even when they behave optimally under a variety of circumstances. These include circumstances where (1) employees may commit crimes unintentionally and optimal effort to prevent crime does not eliminate the risk of a violation; (2) individual wrongdoers are imperfectly informed about which actions are criminal even when they invest optimally in information (see Arlen and MacLeod 2005a (presenting a similar model of tort)); or (3) judges err.

56. Wrongdoers are more sensitive to an increase in the probability of sanction than to an increase in the sanction magnitude (all else equal) if they are risk preferers or discount low probability events.

57. As previously noted, firms also affect the total social costs of crime through their control over their own activity levels (Polinsky and Shavell 1993; Arlen and Kraakman 1997) and their ability to affect the scope of each employee's authority to take actions that could be harmful.

58. In addition, optimal deterrence also requires that states induce firms to undertake optimal activity levels when firm activity levels affect the total expected social cost of crime, as explained in section 3.2 (Polinsky and Shavell 1993).

59. Studies show that employees (including officers) are more likely to commit certain crimes when their firms focus on short-term financial returns when evaluating the performance of a division or individual (Hill *et al.* 1992 (finding that EPA and OSHA violations are more likely when top managers focus on rate of return criteria in evaluating division performance); Cohen and Simpson 1997; see also Smith *et al.* 2007). To further exacerbate the problem, employees whose compensation is based on short-term results, and not long-term share value, obtain the full benefit of any boost in apparent profits linked to their crime, without sharing the long-run cost to the firm of any eventual sanction imposed on the firm.

The observation that compensation policies affect the probability of crime reveals that executive compensation is not a purely private matter between executives and shareholders, as compensation policies that induce crime impose external costs on third parties. Whether this external cost of compensation policies warrants direct intervention in compensation depends on whether boards of directors can be induced to prefer compensation policies that maximize social welfare.

60. In most cases, an optimal compensation policy designed to balance the concerns of effort-inducement and crime-reduction would provide employees with lower-powered incentives than the policy that firms adopt when focused primarily on productivity.

61. In the case of compensation, the social cost of prevention includes the decreased productivity associated with a move from high-powered incentive compensation to a compensation regime focused on long-run measures of firm performance and less directly tied to individual employees' efforts.

62. Corporate actions that affect the probability that crimes are detected and individuals wrongdoers are convicted, P, are hereinafter referred to as policing measures (Arlen and Kraakman 1997).

63. One reason corporate policing is needed is that government enforcers detect few corporate crimes (or

at least few corporate frauds) on their own. Information on corporate wrongdoing tends to arise from within the firm (Dyck *et al.* (2010) at 2214 (finding that 20% of detected frauds were brought to light by the firm or its employees)).

64. For a discussion of why this may not be the case, see Baer (2009) at 988.

65. Identifying the perpetrators of corporate crimes can be particularly difficult because corporate crimes often involve actions by many people. Moreover, the person ultimately responsible for causing the crime to be committed often is not the person who committed the physical act that constitutes the crime.

66. When policing provides other benefits (e.g., reduced agency costs) these should be included in the social calculus as well.

67. In theory, firms can increase the effective sanction by paying super-compensatory wages. Super-compensatory wages increase employees' wealth, thereby increasing the potential sanction that the government can impose on criminal wrongdoers (Becker and Stigler 1974; Shavell 1997). Yet super-compensatory wages are a costly deterrence mechanism because, in order to deter crime through super-compensatory wages alone (without any expenditures on enforcement), each firm would need to pay sufficient wages to all potentially wrongful employees to give each employee actionable, after-tax, *post*-consumption, wealth of $H/P(0)$. This would be expensive and would distort labor markets. Super-compensatory wages also are ineffective against certain crimes, such as intentional misconduct and crimes resulting from managers' last period concerns. Employees who expect to engage in deliberate misconduct can reduce the monetary penalty imposed on them by consuming their super-compensatory wages or disbursing them to their heirs (see Becker and Stigler 1974; Eaton and White 1982; Dickens *et al.* (1989) at 343–4 (discussing why firms prefer enforcement to super-compensatory wages)). Super-compensatory wages also often are ineffective when employees commit the crime in the hope of preserving a job that they are likely to lose if they do not commit the crime (for example, many securities frauds (Arlen and Carney (1992) at 708–9)) because the high wage payments can enhance the employees' expected *benefit* from committing crimes that preserve their jobs.

68. For a discussion of how corporate monitoring can reduce the agent insolvency problem in the liability context see Kornhauser (1982); Sykes (1984); Arlen (1994); Arlen and Kraakman (1997); see generally, Milgrom and Roberts (1991).

69. The state cannot optimally regulate prevention solely through the use of *ex ante* regulatory mandates governing all optimal prevention measures because government authorities generally lack the expertise needed to determine optimal structure of all forms of prevention, especially those relating to internal compensation policies (Arlen and Kahan 2012). Moreover, ongoing verification of firms' actual prevention efforts is costly.

70. This is a simplification of the requirement. When optimal deterrence requires positive expenditures on enforcement, the optimal sanction generally will be less than H/P^* since the net social benefit of deterrence equals the social benefit of crimes deterred (H) minus the social cost of enforcement (Polinsky and Shavell 1984). We abstract from this additional complexity here because the asset insufficiency problem can be triggered when employees' wealth is less than $H/P(\underline{E})$ even if it is not less than the optimal fine if firms engage in optimal policing.

71. See *supra* note 70.

72. Beyond this, firms have an additional reason to under-invest in policing when workers are insolvent. A firm that credibly announces that it will aggressively detect and report crimes increases its employees' expected liability by increasing the probability of sanction. This increases the firm's expected wage payments, but may not deter many crimes if the benefit to employees of crime exceeds their expected sanction, given wealth constraints. Beyond this, policing will be suboptimal because the benefit to the firm of policing necessarily is less than the social benefit of policing when either (i) employees' expected sanction is less than the social cost of the harm caused because of wealth constraints, or (ii) firms' wage obligations in effect leave the firm strictly liable for employees' crime (see Arlen 1994).

73. Wrongdoers who control the management of the firm may be able to ensure that the firm compensates them for their actual or expected liability, directly or indirectly, even for intentional crimes.

74. Corporate intervention will not be needed, however, if employees have unlimited assets, which enables the state to optimally deter crime through individual liability alone (without marginal expenditures on enforcement). Thus, this intentional wrongdoing justification for corporate liability provides an additional justification for corporate liability when individual liability is not sufficient because employees do not have sufficient assets to pay the optimal fine.

75. Thus, it is not the case that asset insufficiency justifies corporate liability only if firms are better able to sanction workers than is the state, but not otherwise.

76. In a study done prior to the Organizational Guidelines, Mark Cohen found that the corporate criminal fine was less than the harm caused (and thus substantially less than H/P) (Cohen 1991). While the criminal fine rose after the adoption of the Organizational Sentencing Guidelines (Alexander, Arlen, and Cohen 1999a), expected sanctions appeared to stay below H/P, especially when the probability of sanction is relatively low.

77. Managers of publicly-held firms also can reduce the firm's expected liability by locating risky activities in thinly-capitalized, wholly-owned subsidiaries. These subsidiaries can pursue profitable activities that have an enhanced risk of crime, channeling the profit to the parent firm through dividends, while using thin capitalization of the subsidiary to minimize expected criminal sanctions. For evidence that firms locate certain liability-generating activities outside their legal boundaries, see, e.g., Rebitzer (1995) (showing how the petrochemical firms partly insulate themselves from liability for workplace accidents by hiring contract workers and assigning all training and supervision of these workers to off-site independent contractors less capable of regulating safety).

78. Managers can undermine corporate sanctioning if they either directly influence board decisions or have sufficient control over the information reaching the board to make sure directors conclude that sanctions would be inappropriate. Indeed, the senior manager may be able to ensure that the board concludes that no crime was committed if managers control how the internal investigation is conducted. Under corporate liability, shareholders may be unable to determine when the board is being passive incorrectly, if the deal between the firm and the government does not identify the individual wrongdoers. This information vacuum may permit the board to publicly justify its decision by asserting either that no crime was committed (and the firm just pleads guilty) or that no senior manager was responsible.

79. This analysis assumes that the state cannot feasibly implement a rule under which the corporate sanction equals $(\prod + H)/(P(M,R))$, where $P(M,R)$ equals the actual probability of detection given the firm's actual investment in pre- and post-contractual policing (M and R respectively). If the state could employ a sanction that varies precisely with the probability of sanction then strict corporate liability would not create a liability enhancement effect and could be structured to induce optimal policing. This sanction would be very costly to implement as federal authorities would have to ensure that the fine varies precisely with all changes in M and R, adjusting the sanction to reflect how monitoring and post-crime policing affects the probability of sanction for that individual firm. For a discussion of the problems with sanction-adjusted strict vicarious liability, see Arlen and Kraakman (1997).

80. To be precise, the state need only reduce the sanction imposed (Arlen and Kraakman 1997). Nevertheless, non-indictment is preferred if the state can impose civil liability on the firm, especially if criminal liability is associated with substantial collateral consequences, market sanctions, or increased private civil liability.

81. Specifically, it is consistent with optimal deterrence to reduce the sanction imposed on firms that self-report and cooperate, for example, by agreeing not to indict or convict them, along with often subjecting them to lower penalties.

82. In order to induce optimal prevention, the state needs to ensure that firms bear the full social cost of each crime committed. This implies that firms must pay a sanction equal to the social cost of crime divided by the expected probability of sanction. Accordingly, in those situations where the state expects to induce optimal policing, the fixed penalty should equal the social cost of crime divided by the probability of sanction when state enforcement and corporate policing are optimal. This is H/P^*. See section 7.

    It should be noted that this statement of the optimal sanction is correct when prevention and policing are fixed costs and not marginal costs of crime, as is often the case with *ex ante* monitoring and many prevention measures. The optimal sanction must be adjusted when sanctions are needed to induce crime-specific measures that deter crime while increasing the marginal cost of each crime committed. This chapter does not explore this issue; it is addressed in the case of individual liability in Polinsky and Shavell (1984).

83. The firm does not compensate employees for any expected criminal liability because employees can work for the firm without any risk of liability if they act optimally and the firm does not want the crime committed if it is required to bear the social cost of crime. Thus, the firm need not (and will not) compensate employees for their expected criminal liability to induce employees to work for them.

84. We focus on the situation where employees are insolvent because we are considering the effect of strict corporate liability when optimal deterrence requires corporate monitoring, as is the case when employee asset insufficiency requires positive enforcement expenditures.

85. The firm bears the full sanction *ex post* and *ex ante* since the state appropriates all the collectable wealth of convicted agents.

86. Because the private gain is a pure transfer, matched by a cost to the firm, it should not constitute a social benefit of the crime.

87. Observe that when the marginal cost of monitoring is increasing, but the marginal benefit is constant or decreasing, then optimal monitoring, M^*, is less than the level needed to deter all suboptimal crimes, defined as crimes where the direct social cost of the crime equals or exceeds the social benefit. For a more general explanation of why it is not optimal to deter all socially costly crimes when optimal enforcement expenditures are positive, see Polinsky and Shavell (1984).

88. The next section shows that corporate liability induces firms to adopt optimal prevention measures and undertake optimal activity levels when sanctions ensure that the firm internalizes the expected social cost of employee wrongdoing.

89. To be precise, we should subtract wages of w and include a participation constraint. This is not necessary here, however, because we know that the participation constraint is satisfied at $w = 0$ as result of the following assumptions: (i) the benefit to individual workers of crime is unobservable; (ii) firms do not benefit from crime and so will not hire workers who accept a wage below their reservation utility (as this signals they expect to benefit from crime); and (iii) workers obtain zero reservation utility. Nevertheless, nothing would be changed were we to set the reservation utility at R and the wage at $w = R$. The incentive compatibility constraint requires that employees only commit crimes if they earn positive expected returns and is incorporated into Equation (6).

90. As it happens, firms also have suboptimal incentives to invest *ex ante* in their ability to engage in *ex post* policing for the reasons given in the prior discussion (Arlen and Kraakman 1997).

91. Moreover, traditional strict liability is not optimal even if we recognize that a firm might obtain a reputational deterrence benefit with its own employees from reporting and cooperating on crime. The reputation effect likely exists in some cases, but is muted when the penalty of detected wrongdoing is large and managers can fail to report detected wrongdoing without employees knowing. Moreover, even when there is a deterrence benefit, firms face suboptimal incentives to undertake post-crime policing because the private benefit to the firm of policing is less than the social benefit of policing to the extent post-crime policing increases the firm's expected liability. This implies that the perverse effects of strict corporate liability are most pronounced in the very situation where corporate policing is most needed: where corporate *ex post* policing substantially increases the probability that the government detects and sanctions the wrong.

92. See *infra* note 94 and accompanying text.

93. The state can both deter crime optimally while also relying on corporate reporting more easily than it can rely on individuals to self-report their own crimes. This is because the state can give the firm substantial credit for self-reporting without significant risk of undermining overall deterrence since the primary goal of criminal liability for corporate crimes is to sanction the individual, not the firm. Thus, this regime is not subject to the problems that have been identified with laws that sanction individuals for hiding information about their own crimes or for failure to self-report (Sanchirico 2006).

94. We are interested in devising a sanction that supports a Perfect Bayesian Equilibrium in which employees believe the firm will self-report and cooperate if it detects a crime, and the firm in fact maximizes its welfare by doing so should it detect a crime. Thus, we assume that employees' expected sanction is given by $P(M,E(R)) = P(M,R^*)$, where M is the actual and observable level of *ex ante* policing and $E(R)$ is employees' expectations regarding the firm's *ex post* policing should it detect a crime. Accordingly, we see that the expected amount of employee wrongdoing is independent of the firm's actual actions. What the state needs to do is to ensure that the sanction, F, is sufficiently large to ensure that, each time the firm detects a crime, its expected costs are lower if it self-reports and cooperates than if it does not.

95. Evidence suggests that evidence of fraud often reaches the government through the firm, its employees, or through media sources (which often obtain information from employees). Government authorities detect little fraud on their own (Dyck *et al.* 2010).

96. Moreover, this conclusion holds even when we consider the effect of firms' reporting decisions on future wage payments. Firms' actual reporting decisions should not affect, and thus should not be affected by, future wage payments if the duty-based sanction is optimally designed to support a Perfect Bayesian Equilibrium in which employees correctly believe that firms will always self-report and cooperate. Employee wage payments are predicated on employees' *expected* future liability given the beliefs about whether a firm that detects wrongdoing will self-report and cooperate. When liability is optimal, employees will expect firms to do so. *Ex post*, when the firm does detect and cooperate, this confirms employees' pre-existing beliefs, rather than altering them. Thus, once a firm detects a crime, it does not expect to bear any additional future wage payments should it report because employees' wages were set on the assumption that it will report. Nor can the firm obtain any reduction in wages in the future by not reporting because the firm cannot feasibly reveal to employees that it does not report detected wrongdoing without revealing this to the government as well. Thus, *ex post*, the firm's welfare with respect to the reporting decision is not affected by its wage payments. So, the duty-based sanction, F, is independent of the expected individual sanction.

97. As before, we assume that agents are insolvent with respect to the optimal (and actual) individual sanction and thus the firm does not employ a wage that depends on whether it reports any crime is committed.

98. This result stands in contrast to the conclusion of Shavell (1997) that corporate criminal sanctions should be reduced to reflect individual criminal liability. Shavell's analysis focused on strict corporate criminal liability. He did not consider the optimal relationship between individual and corporate liability when corporate criminal liability is restricted to duty-based criminal liability for failure to report.

99. The left-hand side of this equation assumes the state imposes an optimal residual sanction (see section 7). It is assumed that the state also imposes an additional duty-based sanction designed to induce optimal reporting.

100. This is not the minimum optimal sanction.
101. There is evidence that firms committing financial disclosure violations tend to have inside and outside directors who own proportionately less of the firm's stock than the boards of non-offending firms (Gerety and Lehn 1997; Beasley 1996). This suggests that shareholders can reduce the incidence of crime by ensuring that directors' compensation is tied to the long-run fate of the firm. Similarly, evidence that the incidence of corporate crime is higher the lower the stock ownership of directors and senior officers (Alexander and Cohen 1999) suggests that shareholders can also deter crime by tying senior officers' compensation to the long-run fate of the firm. In turn, this suggests that efforts to deter corporate crime may depend on whether state and federal laws facilitate shareholders influence over director and officer compensation.
102. Corporate policing also imposes private costs on managers if the managers have engaged in undetected wrongdoing that could be detected by improved policing (Baer 2008b).
103. Of course, it is difficult to ensure that the government establishes an optimal duty-based liability regime.
104. A study of the effect of SEC and DOJ enforcement actions (1978–2006) on individuals identified as responsible for financial misrepresentations sanctioned found that 93% lost their jobs by the end of the regulatory period (Karpoff *et al.* 2008b). There also is evidence that directors discipline CEOs for excessive earnings management even when there is no enforcement action (Hazarika *et al.* 2011).
105. By contrast, the Organizational Sentencing Guidelines provide precise guidance on the nature of effective compliance and precisely lay out the effect on the corporate sanction of ineffective compliance, reporting, and/or cooperation. Unfortunately, the Organizational Guidelines do not adequately encourage corporate policing (Arlen 2012). They also do not formally apply to firms that avoid conviction.
106. See *supra* note 70 (qualifying this conclusion). When corporate enforcement is costly, the amount of corporate enforcement induced by an optimal duty-based composite regime will not deter all suboptimal crimes if the sanction that agents can bear (given wealth constraints and other factors) is less than $H/P(M^*, R^*)$.
107. By contrast, the state should not reduce the duty-based sanction for *ex post* policing to reflect employees' expected liability, even when corporate wages internalize employees' *ex ante* expected liability (see section 6.2.1).
108. For a discussion of when and why firms can be expected to pay wages that reflect the cost of their employees expected individual liability see section 3.3 and Kornhauser (1982).
109. Although the residual sanction should be reduced to reflect the market sanction, the state should not reduce duty-based liability for *ex post* policing to reflect the market sanction. Indeed, duty-based liability may be even more important when market sanctions are substantial than when they are not. See section 6.4.
110. In other words, this section focuses on pure securities fraud done solely to influence share prices, which is the fraud that should be the focus of securities fraud actions, rather than frauds motivated by managers' desire to profit from insider trading, which are covered by laws governing insider trading.
111. See Karpoff *et al.* (2008a) (finding that a firm with detected securities fraud bears a market sanction of $2.71 for every dollar that it misleadingly inflates its market value, in addition to any losses associated with the market adjusting the price to reflect both the firm's true financial value and expected legal penalties).
112. These shareholders are hit with the incidence of corporate liability even when it is imposed after they sell because, at the moment fraud is revealed, the share price will fall to reflect both the news about the fraud and the firm's expected liability.
113. Moreover, the fact that some shareholders may expect that fraud has occurred and sell before it is revealed does not justify residual corporate liability. Residual corporate liability will not deter shareholders who expect to sell during the fraud from allowing it to occur because they will exit the firm before the residual sanction is imposed.
114. The present analysis focuses on optimal government-imposed corporate residual liability for securities fraud. The arguments against private civil corporate liability for securities fraud are stronger than those presented here, because allowing private civil corporate vicarious liability for securities fraud undermines the effectiveness of private liability against individual managers, because private litigants will not sanction these wrongdoers if allowed to obtain redress from the firm – redress which the firm's managers will be all too willing to allow in return for not being held liable themselves (Arlen and Carney 1992).
115. These are not the only distinctions between corporate criminal and civil liability. There also are important procedural differences between civil and criminal enforcement actions, including the grand jury (Khanna 1996).
116. This assumes that the reputational sanction associated with a criminal sanction is larger than that associated with a civil one, even if only indirectly through the reaction of the firm's managers and employees.
117. This analysis is focused on wrongdoing by publicly-held firms. The state may optimally employ residual corporate criminal liability for intentional crimes committed by controlling owner-managers of

closely-held firms as this provides the strongest deterrent to these crimes (along with individual liability) and there is little reason to expect that such firms will fully cooperate with the government's effort to convict their owner-managers.

REFERENCES

Alexander, Cindy R. (1999) "On the Nature of the Reputational Penalty for Corporate Crime: Evidence," 42 *Journal of Law and Economics* 489
— (2004) "Corporate Crime, Markets, and Enforcement: A Review," in *New Perspectives on Economic Crime*, Hans Sjogren and Goran Skogh, eds., Northampton, MA: Edward Elgar Publishing
Alexander, Cindy, Jennifer Arlen, and Mark A. Cohen (1999a) "Regulating Corporate Criminal Sanctions: Federal Guidelines and the Sentencing of Public Firms," 42 *Journal of Law and Economics* 393
— (1999b) "The Effect of Federal Sentencing Guidelines on Penalties for Public Corporations," 12 *Federal Sentencing Reporter* 20
— (2000) "Evaluating Trends in Corporate Sentencing: How Reliable are the U.S. Sentencing Commission's Data?," 13 *Federal Sentencing Reporter* 108
Alexander, Cindy R. and Mark A. Cohen (1996) "New Evidence on the Origins of Corporate Crime," 17 *Managerial and Decision Economics* 421
— (1999) "Why Do Corporations Become Criminals? Ownership, Hidden Actions, and Crime as an Agency Cost," 5 *Journal of Corporate Finance* 1
Arlen, Jennifer (1994) "The Potentially Perverse Effects of Corporate Criminal Liability," 23 *Journal of Legal Studies* 833
— (2000) "Corporate Crime and Its Control," in *New Palgrave Dictionary of Economics and the Law*, Peter Newman, ed., London: MacMillan
— (2004) "Evolution of Corporate Liability: Implication for Managers," in *Leadership and Governance from the Inside Out*, Jeffrey Sonnenfeld and Robert Gandossey, eds., Hoboken: John Wiley and Sons
— (2009) "The Story of Allis-Chalmers, Caremark, and Stone: Directors' Evolving Duty to Monitor," in *Corporate Stories*, J. Mark Ramseyer ed., New York: Foundation Press, 323
— (2011) "Removing Prosecutors from the Boardroom: Deterring Crime Without Prosecutor Interference in Corporate Governance," in *Prosecutors in the Boardroom: Using Criminal Law to Regulate Corporate Conduct*, Anthony Barkow and Rachel Barkow, eds., New York: New York University Press
— (2012) "The Failure of the Organizational Sentencing Guidelines," 66 *University of Miami Law Review* 321 (symposium issue)
Arlen, Jennifer and William Carney (1992) "Vicarious Liability for Fraud on Securities Markets: Theory and Evidence," *University of Illinois Law Review* 691
Arlen, Jennifer and Marcel Kahan (2012) "Corporate Regulation Through Non-Prosecution," working paper
Arlen, Jennifer and Reinier Kraakman (1997) "Controlling Corporate Misconduct: An Analysis of Corporate Liability Regimes," 72 *New York University Law Review* 687
Arlen, Jennifer and W. Bentley MacLeod (2005a) "Torts, Expertise, and Authority: Liability of Physicians and Managed Care Organizations," 36 *RAND Journal of Economics* 494
— (2005b) "Beyond Master-Servant: A Critique of Vicarious Liability," in *Exploring Tort Law*, M. Stuart Madden ed., New York: Cambridge University Press.
Baer, Miriam (2008a) "Insuring Corporate Crime," 83 *Indiana Law Journal* 1035
— (2008b) "Linkage and the Deterrence of Corporate Fraud," 98 *Virginia Law Review* 1295
— (2009) "Governing Corporate Compliance," 50 *Boston College Law Review* 949
Baysinger, Barry D. (1991) "Organization Theory and the Criminal Liability of Organizations," 71 *Boston University Law Review* 341
Beale, Sara Sun and Adam G. Safwat (2005) "What Developments in Western Europe Tell Us about American Critiques of Corporate Criminal Liability," 8 *Buffalo Criminal Law Review* 89
Beasley, Mark S. (1996) "An Empirical Analysis of the Relationship Between Board of Director Composition and Financial Statement Fraud," 71 *The Accounting Review* 443
Becker, Gary (1968) "Crime and Punishment: An Economic Approach," 76 *Journal of Political Economy* 169
Becker, Gary and George Stigler (1974) "Law Enforcement, Malfeasance, and the Compensation of Enforcers," 3 *Journal of Legal Studies* 1
Block, Michael (1991) "Optimal Penalties, Criminal Law, and the Control of Corporate Behavior," 71 *Boston University Law Review* 395
Block, Michael K., Frederick C. Nold, and J. Greg Sidak (1981) "The Deterrent Effects of Antitrust Enforcement," 89 *Journal of Political Economy* 429

Buccirossi, Paulo and Giancarlo Spagnolo (2007) "Optimal Fines in the Era of Whistleblowers: Should Price Fixers Still Go to Prison?," in *The Political Economy of Antitrust*, V. Goshal and J. Stennek, eds., Amsterdam: Elsevier

Buell, Samuel W. (2006) "The Blaming Function of Entity Criminal Liability," 81 *Indiana Law Journal* 473
— (2007) "Criminal Procedure Within the Firm," 59 *Stanford Law Review* 1613

Chu, C.Y. Cyrus and Yingyi Qian (1995) "Vicarious Liability under a Negligence Rule," 15 *International Review of Law and Economics* 305

Coase, Ronald (1960) "The Problem of Social Cost," 3 *Journal of Law and Economics* 1

Coffee, John C., Jr. (1981) "'No Soul to Damn, No Body to Kick:' An Unscandalized Inquiry into the Problem of Corporate Punishment," 79 *Michigan Law Review* 386
— (1991) "Does Unlawful Mean Criminal?: The Disappearing Tort/Crime Distinction in American Law," 71 *Boston University Law Review* 193

Cohen, Mark (1991) "Corporate Crime and Punishment: An Update on Sentencing Practice in the Federal Courts, 1988–1990," 71 *Boston University Law Review* 247
— (1996) "Theories of Punishment and Empirical Trends in Corporate Criminal Sanctions," 17 *Managerial and Decision Economics* 399

Cohen, Mark and Sally S. Simpson (1997) "The Origins of Corporate Criminality: Rational Individual and Organizational Actors," in *Debating Corporate Crime: An Interdisciplinary Examination of the Causes and Control of Corporate Misconduct*, William S. Lofquist, Mark A. Cohen, and Gary A. Rabe, eds., Cincinnati: Anderson Publishing

Conley, John M. and William M. O'Barr (1997) "Crimes and Custom in Corporate Society: A Cultural Perspective on Corporate Misconduct," 60 *Law and Contemporary Problems* 5

Cooter, Robert (1984) "Prices and Sanctions," 84 *Columbia Law Review* 1523

Dana, David (1996) "The Perverse Incentives of Environmental Audit Immunity," 81 *Iowa Law Review* 969

Dickens, Williams T., Lawrence Katz, Kevin Lang, and Lawrence Summers (1989) "Employee Crime and the Monitoring Puzzle," 7 *Journal of Labor Economics* 331

Dyck, Alexander, Adair Morse, and Luigi Zingales (2010) "Who Blows the Whistle on Corporate Fraud?," 65 *Journal of Finance* 2213

Eaton, B. Curtis and William D. White (1982) "Agent Compensation and the Limits of Bonding," 20 *Economic Inquiry* 330

Efendi, Jan, Anup Srivastava, and Edward P. Swanson (2007) "Why Do Corporate Managers Misstate Financial Statements? The Role of Option Compensation and Other Factors," 85 *Journal of Financial Economics* 667

Fees, Eberhard and Markus Walzl (2004) "Self-Reporting in Optimal Law Enforcement when there are Criminal Teams," 71 *Econometrica* 333

First, Harry (2010) "Branch Office of the Prosecutor: The New Role of the Corporation in Business Crime Prosecutions," 89 *North Carolina Law Review* 23

Fischel, Daniel and Alan Sykes (1996) "Corporate Crime," 25 *Journal of Legal Studies* 319

Garrett, Brandon L. (2007) "Structural Reform Prosecution," 93 *Virginia Law Review* 853
— (2011), "Globalized Corporate Prosecutions," 97 *Virginia Law Review* 1775

Gauropa, Nuno (2000) "Corporate Criminal Law and Organization Incentives: A Managerial Perspective," 21 *Managerial and Decision Economics* 243

Gerety, Mason and Kenneth Lehn (1997) "The Causes and Consequences of Accounting Fraud," 18 *Managerial and Decision Economics* 587

Hamdami, Assaf and Alon Klement (2008) "Corporate Crime and Deterrence," 61 *Stanford Law Review* 271

Hamdami, Assaf and Reinier Kraakman (2007) "Rewarding Outside Directors," 105 *Michigan Law Review* 1677

Hazarika, Sonali, Jonathan Karpoff, and Rajarishi Nahata (2012) "Internal Corporate Governance, CEO Turnover, and Earnings Management," *Journal of Financial Economics* (forthcoming)

Helland, Eric (2006) "Reputational Penalties and the Merits of Class-Action Securities Litigation," 49 *Journal of Law and Economics* 365

Hill, Charles W. L., Patricia C. Kelley, Bradley R. Agle, Michael A. Hitt, and Robert E. Hoskisson (1992) "An Empirical Examination of the Causes of Corporate Wrongdoing in the United States," 45 *Human Relations* 1055

Holder, Eric (1999) Memorandum from Eric Holder, Deputy Attorney General, US Department of Justice, to Heads of Department Components and United States Attorneys (June 16, 1999)

Holmstrom, Bengt and Paul Milgrom (1991) "Multitask Principal-Agent Analyses: Incentive Contracts, Assets Ownership, and Job Design," 7 *Journal of Law, Economics, and Organization* 24

Hylton, Keith N. (2005) "The Theory of Penalties and the Economics of Criminal Law," 1 *Review of Law and Economics* 175

Hylton, Keith N. and Lin Haishen (2012) "Optimal Antitrust Enforcement, Dynamic Competition, and Changing Economic Conditions" (forthcoming)

Innes, Robert (1999) "Remediation and Self-Reporting in Optimal Law Enforcement," 72 *Journal of Public Economics* 379

Kahan, Marcel (1992a) "Games, Lies, and Securities Laws," 67 *New York University Law Review* 750

— (1992b) "Securities Laws and the Social Costs of 'Inaccurate' Stock Prices," *Duke Law Journal* 977

Karpoff, Jonathan M., Anup Agrawal, and Jeffrey Jaffe (1999) "Management Turnover and Corporate Governance Changes Following the Revelation of Criminal Fraud," 62 *Journal of Law and Economics* 309

Karpoff, Jonathan M., D. Scott Lee and Valaria P. Vendrzyk (1999) "Defense Procurement Fraud, Penalties, and Contractor Influence," 107 *Journal of Political Economy* 809

Karpoff, Jonathan M., D. Scott Lee, and Gerald S. Martin (2008a) "Cost to Firms of Cooking the Books," 43 *Journal of Financial and Quantitative Analysis* 581

— (2008b) "The Consequences to Managers for Financial Misrepresentation," 43 *Journal of Financial Economics* 193

Karpoff, Jonathan M. and John R. Lott, Jr. (1993) "The Reputational Penalty Firms Bear from Committing Fraud," 36 *Journal of Law and Economics* 757

Karpoff, Jonathan M., John R. Lott, Jr., and Eric Wehrly (2005) "The Reputational Penalties for Environmental Violations: Empirical Evidence," 68 *Journal of Law and Economics* 653

Karpoff, Jonathan M. and Xiaoxia Lou (2009) "Short Sellers and Financial Misconduct," 65 *Journal of Finance* 1879

Khanna, Vikramaditya (1996) "Corporate Criminal Liability: What Purpose Does it Serve?" 109 *Harvard Law Review* 1477

Khanna, Vikramaditya and Timothy L. Dickinson (2007) "The Corporate Monitor: The New Corporate Czar," 105 *Michigan Law Review* 1713

Kornhauser, Lewis (1982) "An Economic Analysis of the Choice Between Enterprise and Personal Liability for Accidents," 70 *California Law Review* 1345

Kraakman, Reinier (1984) "Corporate Liability Strategies and the Costs of Legal Controls," 93 *Yale Law Journal* 857

— (1985) "The Economic Functions of Corporate Liability," in *Corporate Governance and Directors' Liabilities*, Klaus Hopt and Gunther Teubner, eds., Berlin: Walter de Gruyter & Co.

— (1986) "Gatekeepers: The Anatomy of a Third-Party Enforcement Strategy," 2 *Journal of Law, Economics and Organization* 53

Lott, Jonathan, Jr. (1996) "The Level of Optimal Fines to Prevent Fraud when Reputations Exist and Penalty Clauses are Unenforceable," 17 *Managerial and Decision Economics* 363

Macey, Jonathan (1991) "Agency Theory and the Criminal Liability of Organizations," 71 *Boston University Law Review* 315

McChesney, Fred S. (1993) "Boxed in: Economists and the Benefits from Crime," 13 *International Review of Law and Economics* 225

Milgrom, Paul and John Roberts (1991) *Economics, Organization, and Management*, Prentice Hall

Mullins, Wallace P. and Christopher M. Snyder (2009) "Corporate Crime," in *Criminal Law and Economics*, Nuno Garoupa ed., Northampton, MA: Edward Elgar Publishing

Newman, Harry A. and David W. Wright (1990) "Strict Liability in a Principal-Agent Model," 10 *International Review of Law and Economics* 219

Paternoster, Raymond and Sally Simpson (1996) "Sanctions Threats and Appeals to Morality: Testing a Rational Choice Model of Corporate Crime," 30 *Law and Society Review* 549

Polinsky, A. Mitchell and Steven Shavell (1979) "The Optimal Tradeoff Between the Probability and Magnitude of Fines," 69 *American Economics Review* 880

— (1984) "Optimal Use of Fines and Imprisonment," 24 *Journal of Public Economics* 89

— (1992) "Enforcement Costs and the Optimal Probability and Magnitude of Fines," 35 *Journal of Law and Economics* 133

— (1993) "Should Employees be Subject to Fines and Imprisonment Given the Existence of Corporate Liability?," 13 *International Review of Law and Economics* 239

— (2007) "The Theory of Public Enforcement," ch. 6 in *Handbook of Law and Economics*, A. Mitchell Polinsky and Steven Shavell, eds., North Holland, vol. I

Posner, Richard (1985) "An Economic Theory of Criminal Law," 85 *Columbia Law Review* 1193

Rebitzer, James B. (1995) "Job Safety and Contract Workers in the Petrochemical Industry," 34 *Industrial Relations* 40

Sanchirico, Chris (2006) "Detection Avoidance," 81 *New York University Law Review* 1331

Segerson, Kathleen and Tom Tietenberg (1992) "The Structure of Penalties in Environmental Enforcement: An Economic Analysis," 23 *Journal of Environmental Economics and Management* 179

Shavell, Steven (1980) "Strict Liability versus Negligence," 9 *Journal of Legal Studies* 1

— (1985) "Criminal Law and the Optimal Use of Nonmonetary Sanctions as a Deterrent," 85 *Columbia Law Review* 1232

— (1986) "The Judgment Proof Problem," 6 *International Review of Law and Economics* 45

— (1997) "The Optimal Level of Corporate Liability Given the Limited Ability of Corporations to Penalize their Employees," 17 *International Review of Law and Economics* 203

Simpson, Sally (2002) *Corporate Crime, Law, and Social Control*, Cambridge: Cambridge University Press

Smith, N. Craig, Sally S. Simpson, and Chun-Yao Huang (2007) "Why Managers Fail to do the Right Thing: An Empirical Study of Unethical and Illegal Conduct," 17 *Business Ethics Quarterly* 633

Spindler, James (2008) "Vicarious Liability for Bad Corporate Governance: Are We Wrong about 10b-5?," USC CLEO Research Paper No. CO8-3

Spivack, Peter and Sujit Raman (2008) "Regulating the 'New Regulators': Current Trends in Deferred Prosecution Agreements," 45 *American Criminal Law Review* 159

Stone, Christopher (1975) *Where the Law Ends: The Social Control of Corporate Behavior*, New York: Harper and Row

— (1980) "The Place of Enterprise Liability in the Control of Corporate Conduct," 90 *Yale Law Journal* 1

Sutherland, Edwin (1949) *White-Collar Crime*, New York: Holt Rinehart and Winston

Sykes, Alan O. (1984) "The Economics of Vicarious Liability," 93 *Yale Law Journal* 1231

Tyler, Tom R. and Steven L. Blader (2005) "Can Business Effectively Regulate Employee Conduct? The Antecedents of Rule Following in Work Settings," 48 *Academy of Management Journal* 1143

Tullock, Gordon (1967) "The Welfare Costs of Tariffs, Monopolies, and Theft," 5 *Western Economics Journal* 224

Weissmann, Andrew (2007) "A New Approach to Corporate Criminal Liability," 44 *American Criminal Law Review* 1319

8 Stumbling into crime: stochastic process models of accounting fraud
Michael D. Guttentag*

1. INTRODUCTION

Research on accounting fraud typically begins with the assumption that accounting fraud is a premeditated act. This assumption leads scholars to analyse accounting fraud in terms of the costs and benefits to the firm and the firm's managers of committing such a fraud. Seminal work by Jennifer Arlen and William Carney, "Vicarious Liability for Fraud on Securities Markets: Theory and Evidence," is an exemplar of this approach.[1] These traditional economic models of the causes of accounting fraud can be further refined by drawing upon insights from behavioral economics, as work by Donald Langevoort has elegantly shown.[2] However, even with these refinements, most research on accounting fraud still begins with the assumption that accounting fraud is premeditated.

This chapter will explore the use of stochastic process models as a fundamentally different way to explain why managers commit accounting fraud. This chapter will show how to model the possibility that accounting fraud is the unforeseen consequence of a sequence of minor and seemingly innocuous transgressions, rather than a product of planning and forethought. While prior work has described accounting frauds as involving a "slippery slope" dynamic, this chapter will, for the first time, present models that formalize and suggest how to test the hypothesis that managers stumble into committing accounting fraud.

There are at least four reasons to suspect that stochastic process models will be a useful tool to describe the dynamics within a firm that can lead to accounting fraud. Of these four reasons, one of the most compelling reasons comes from research on how people cheat. Findings from this research show that most people are willing to cheat only when they perceive their transgressions to be minor and socially acceptable. Relatively few people cheat with wanton disregard for the law. As a result, the extent to which most people cheat is often limited by self-imposed constraints rather than by a cost-benefit analysis of the consequences of committing a transgression. Research on how people cheat also shows that willingness to cheat depends, to a large extent, on the context in which the transgression is situated. The ubiquity of self-limited and situationally contingent cheating suggests that the antecedents to accounting frauds are more likely a sequence of minor and seemingly innocuous transgressions than a single, premeditated decision to commit a major infraction.

A second compelling reason to doubt the claim that most managers commit accounting fraud with premeditation comes from research on the causes of and consequences of accounting frauds. If accounting frauds were primarily the result of reasoned consideration, then changes in the expected benefits from committing accounting fraud should affect the propensity to commit these frauds. However, changes in economic incentives do not appear to have a significant effect on the propensity to commit these frauds.[3] It is also doubtful that the marginal benefit to a manager from committing accounting fraud could justify the possibility of incurring such substantial costs. The consequences to a firm's managers if an accounting fraud is uncovered include: the almost certain loss of one's job, a dramatic reduction in the value of one's human capital, and a better than one in four chance of ending up in jail.[4] This research suggests economic incentives do not explain the propensity to commit accounting fraud.

The limited explanatory power of economic models of the dynamics leading to accounting fraud is gaining attention.[5] One alternative possibility, namely that a slippery slope type of dynamic may lead to accounting fraud, is often mentioned by practitioners in this area. For example, Robert Mueller, Director of the Federal Bureau of Investigation, recollects that: "[i]n my days in private practice . . . I saw executives who did not start out intending to break the law. But they began to believe their own explanations. And it is a *slippery slope* from behavior that skirts ethical or legal boundaries to behavior that crosses the line completely."[6] A few academics, including John Darley and Langevoort, have acknowledged the possibility that a slippery slope dynamic might lead to accounting fraud.[7] Recently, Catherine Schrand and Sarah Zechman provided a mathematical model of how a slippery slope dynamic caused by manager over-optimism might lead to accounting fraud.[8] However, these discussions of a slippery slope dynamic do not provide a systematic or verifiable account of how a sequence of minor transgressions might lead to accounting fraud.[9]

This chapter shows how stochastic process modeling can address this shortcoming in previous research and thereby advance our understanding of the dynamics within a firm that may lead to accounting fraud. Stochastic process models are a mathematical tool used to analyse a phenomenon in which observable "macroscopic" behavior is produced by the cumulative effect of numerous "microscopic" events. Such a model is especially useful when the "microscopic" events cannot be easily observed. This is likely the situation if seemingly minor and inconsequential transgressions lead to accounting frauds.

Three related types of stochastic process models are well-suited to describe the dynamics within a firm that could lead to accounting fraud. The first type of model is based on the movement of a random walker. To apply a random walk stochastic process model to accounting fraud, it is helpful to assume that the illegality of behavior within a firm can be measured along a single dimension and that movement along this "illegality" dimension is determined by a sequence of minor decisions. The resulting random walk stochastic process model of accounting fraud yields testable hypotheses about when and where accounting frauds are likely to occur.

However, a simple random walk model fails to incorporate several important aspects of the process by which minor transgressions might lead to accounting fraud. For one thing, a random walk model is non-stationary, so that over time the walker wanders farther and farther away from the starting point. However, one would not expect the level of lawful or unlawful activity within a firm to become more and more extreme over time. To account for the fact that the level of misbehavior within a firm usually stays within a given range, a mean-reverting force can be added to the simple random walk stochastic process model. The resulting stochastic process model is stationary, which may better describe the dynamics within a firm that lead the level of misbehavior to only occasionally become highly aberrant.

A second limitation of the simple random walk model is that it cannot be used to model a situation in which, once a certain boundary is crossed, it is difficult to return to where one has been. There are likely many instances during the process leading to accounting fraud in which actions are taken which are difficult to undo. For example, once a firm makes a public disclosure about its financial condition, the firm's ability to restate past performance will be limited. To take into account the likelihood that certain behaviors (such as publicly reporting financial performance), once made, will be difficult to reverse, the random walk model can be supplemented with a running maximum. This is the third type of stochastic process model I consider in this chapter.

These three types of stochastic process models (a simple random walk model, a stochastic process model with a mean-reverting force, and a stochastic process model with a running maximum) provide a first step to better understanding how a sequence of minor transgressions can lead to accounting fraud.

2.   RATIONALE FOR STOCHASTIC PROCESS MODELING OF ACCOUNTING FRAUD

A stochastic process is any function that is determined by two variables, one of which is a random variable and the other of which is time.[10] Analysis of stochastic process functions generates "mathematical models that describe the evolution of random phenomena as time goes by."[11] Historically, the most significant stochastic process model is the one that describes Brownian motion. Brownian motion is the movement of a particle in a fluid produced by random impacts from adjacent molecules. Brownian motion was observed by Robert Brown,[12] and modeled as a continuous time stochastic process by Albert Einstein in 1905.[13]

Stochastic process models can be used to describe a wide variety of phenomena, including the economics of investment decisions,[14] the movement of the prices of financial assets,[15] and traffic patterns.[16] A stochastic process model is most useful when the phenomenon under study has observable output produced by numerous smaller actions that cannot be directly observed.

There are at least four reasons to suspect that stochastic process models might describe well the dynamics within a firm that lead to accounting fraud. First, as discussed in the Introduction, the way in which most people cheat involves a willingness to commit minor but not major transgressions, and, therefore, is likely to produce precisely the type of dynamics that can be well-described by a stochastic process model. Second, also as discussed in the Introduction, findings from research on the causes of and consequences from accounting frauds are more consistent with the hypothesis that managers stumble into committing these crimes than with the hypothesis that managers commit these crimes by making a single, premeditated decision. Third, stochastic process models offer a way to estimate the cumulative effects of a system in which past outcomes influence future behavior, and the events leading to accounting fraud are probably linked together in such a manner. Finally, stochastic process models offer a way to estimate the ramifications of small and unpredictable events on observable behavior, and this is likely a feature of many business "decisions", including accounting fraud. The next sections will discuss in more detail each of these four rationales for using stochastic process analysis to model accounting frauds.

2.1   Attributes of Much of the Misbehavior by Managers

Research on unlawful behavior has identified two distinctive types of cheaters.[17] First, there are what might be called "calculating cheaters". Calculating cheaters are pre-meditated in their decision to cheat, and have little compunction about wrongdoing. Calculating cheaters weigh the decision of whether or not to commit a crime in terms of personal costs and benefits. The second group of cheaters is those who are willing to cheat only to the extent that their cheating does not disrupt their image of themselves as a fundamentally honest person. Dan Ariely calls these "honest" cheaters.[18] Recent research suggests that a large minority and perhaps even a majority of people fall into this second category, whereas calculating cheaters are less common.[19]

Because the attributes of honest cheating may prove crucial to understanding the dynamics within a firm leading to accounting fraud, it is useful to highlight several of the distinctive features of how honest cheaters cheat. When honest cheaters cheat, they usually do so in a manner that is: (1) limited in magnitude, (2) widespread, (3) sensitive to context, and (4) without calculation or forethought. Each of these four attributes of honest cheating is discussed more fully below and, taken together, support the use of stochastic process models to better understand accounting fraud.

2.1.1   Limited magnitude

One distinctive aspect of honest cheating is the self-imposed constraint such cheaters typically place on how much they are willing to cheat. Dan Ariely and colleagues have carried out numerous studies on the behavior of people they characterize as honest cheaters. For example, Nina Mazar, On Amir, and Dan Ariely used six related experiments involving a total of 791 participants to determine how participants (who knew their behavior could *not* be independently verified) would behave when paid for performance. Mazar *et al.* report "that when people had the ability to cheat, they cheated, but the magnitude of dishonesty per person was relatively low (relative to the possible maximum amount)."[20] Ariely summarizes findings from these and other experiments on cheating by observing that "even when we have no chance of getting caught, we still don't become wild liars – our conscience imposes some limits."[21]

A similar finding is reported by John Evans and colleagues who carried out three experiments on fraudulent behavior in a setting constructed to resemble the types of behavior that might lead to accounting fraud.[22] In the Evans *et al.* study participants can increase their personal gains by misreporting the performance of a business unit. The participants know that their behavior is not being monitored. Evans *et al.* find that participants choose to forgo about half of the profits that they would have realized had they not limited the magnitude of their cheating.[23]

The willingness of study participants to commit minor, but not major, infractions is hypothesized by Ariely and colleagues to be the result of the participant's desire to maintain a self-image as an honest person. Ariely and his colleagues speculate that "[p]eople are often torn between two competing motivations: gaining from cheating versus maintaining a positive self-concept as honest . . . [P]eople typically solve this motivational dilemma adaptively by finding a balance or equilibrium between the two motivating forces, such that they derive some financial benefit from behaving dishonestly but still maintain their positive self-concept in terms of being honest."[24] This image self-maintenance hypothesis is consistent with scholarship suggesting that self-regulation is an important element in determining how people behave when faced with ethical choices generally.[25]

Field studies of misbehavior provide additional evidence that most transgressors do not take full advantage of opportunities to act unlawfully. For example, a study by Robert Goldstone and Calvin Chin measured the number of copies people reported making at a university copier at which copies were paid for based on self-reported usage.[26] Goldstone and Chin found that "[i]ntermediate-level dishonesty is commonplace, whereby patrons underestimate the number of copies made but refrain from profit-maximizing dishonesty even in the absence of an external monitor . . . There are strong self-imposed constraints on the level of allowed dishonesty."[27]

In another real-world setting, Stephen Dubiner and Steven Levitt report on the exploits of a bagel-selling business, which is run without any ability to enforce payment.[28] The entrepreneur running this particular bagel business drops off bags of bagels at various businesses with a money jar placed next to the food. The entrepreneur measures every day how many bagels are purchased and how many are stolen. Dubiner and Levitt note that this "accidental study provides a window onto a subject that has long stymied academics: white collar crime."[29] The bagel entrepreneur finds that at most companies at least 80% of the bagels are paid for, and on average only 1 in 7,000 of the boxes in which the money is placed are taken. This field "experiment" shows, as Dubiner and Levitt nicely observe, "the same people who routinely steal more than ten percent of his bagels almost never stoop to stealing his money box – a tribute to the nuanced social calculus of theft."[30]

In both experiments and field studies cheating by honest cheaters appears to be of limited magnitude. Later in this chapter we will examine how this attribute of honest cheating may play a role in the dynamics leading to accounting fraud.

2.1.2   Widespread

While of limited magnitude, transgressions by honest cheaters appear to be quite widespread. Both experiments and field research suggests that a substantial minority or perhaps even a majority of people will engage in some amount of misbehavior when provided the opportunity to cheat. Ariely observes, based on the various experiments carried out by he and his colleagues, "that most of us, when tempted are willing to be a little dishonest, regardless of the risks."[31] Similarly, in the experiment set in the context of managerial reporting carried out by Evans *et al.* described above, slightly more than 80% of the participants chose to misreport their firm's "earnings" to some degree.[32]

Findings from field research support experimental evidence of a widespread willingness to commit minor infractions. The study of self-reported usage of a university copy machine discussed above finds that more than half of the users under-reported the number of copies they made.[33] In a context more closely related to accounting fraud, a field study evaluated the honesty of the reports hedge funds provide to their potential sponsors.[34] This review of hedge fund reports found that even among investment opportunities that were under serious consideration misrepresentations about past legal and regulatory problems were frequent (21%), as were incorrect or unverifiable representations about other topics (28%).[35]

Finally, casual observation supports the field and experimental evidence that minor transgressions are widespread. For example, when driving on a freeway one often observes drivers willing to drive above the legal speed limit (although the extent of such violations varies widely depending upon circumstances). Similarly, an Internal Revenue Service study on the under-reporting of income for tax purposes found a widespread practice of transgression.[36]

In both experiments and field studies cheating by honest cheaters appears to be fairly widespread.

2.1.3 Sensitivity to context

A third aspect of honest cheating is that the predisposition to misbehave is highly sensitive to the context in which the transgression takes place. A situationally contingent willingness to misbehave is evident both from experiments on how people misbehave and from the larger universe of research on human behavior generally.

The experiments of Ariely and his colleagues are again informative, as the willingness of participants to cheat proves to be contingent on a wide variety of factors. These experiments highlight the extent to which perceptions about how likely it is that other participants will cheat affect participants' own willingness to cheat.[37] Research on the contextual sensitivity of willingness to cheat among honest cheaters has also shown that the introduction of seemingly irrelevant stimuli, such as whether or not the study participant had been asked in an earlier study to read a section of the Ten Commandments from the Bible, affect the level of cheating observed.[38] Ariely and colleagues conclude that study participants are "sensitive to contextual manipulations related to self-concept."[39]

The findings of Ariely and his colleagues on the situationally contingent nature of misbehavior are consistent with findings from other research on wrongdoing. For example, Zey-Ferrell and colleagues observe that among marketing executives perceptions about how one's colleagues will behave help to predict the level of self-reporting of unethical behavior.[40] Research on genocide also supports the hypothesis that morality can shift as a result of social context, permitting an individual to behave in harmful ways that were previously inconceivable.[41] Even without direct pressure, the fact that "everyone else is doing it" may be enough for individuals to believe the unethical behavior is socially acceptable.[42] The research by Philip Zimbardo and Stanley Milgram on the effects of authority similarly suggests how situational considerations can lead to unexpected levels of malevolent behavior.[43] The situationally contingent nature of honest cheating is also consistent with findings on the situationally contingent nature of human behavior in other contexts as well.[44]

In both experiments and field studies the predisposition to misbehave by honest cheaters is highly sensitive to the context in which the transgression is set.

2.1.4 Lack of calculation

Finally, honest cheaters appear to cheat without considering the potential costs and benefits of their decision to cheat. The best evidence that honest cheating is not carried out in a calculated manner is provided by the insensitivity of this type of cheating to changes in the anticipated costs and benefits of such cheating. Sensitivity to a change in price is one of the most reliable indicators that economic considerations influence a particular type of behavior. A lack of such sensitivity is reported by Ariely and his colleagues based on their experiments studying when and how "honest" people misbehave.[45]

Other experimental findings support the findings of Ariely and colleagues that honest cheating is not strongly influenced by economic considerations. In the experiment set in the context of financial statement reporting carried out by Evans *et al.* discussed above, an increase in the rewards yielded from cheating did not lead to more cheating.[46] In fact, surprisingly, the opposite occurred. As the potential rewards for cheating were increased, the amount of cheating decreases.[47]

For the honest cheater, willingness to cheat does *not* appear to be influenced by the types of economic considerations that suggest premeditation and calculation.

Each of the characteristics of honest cheating described above (limited in magnitude, widespread, sensitivity to context, and lack of calculation) is likely to produce behavior that can be well-described with a stochastic process model. The limited magnitude of honest cheating suggests that crimes committed by honest cheaters are more likely to be produced by a sequence of minor transgressions than by a single decision to commit a major infraction. A widespread practice of honest cheating creates fertile ground for accounting frauds to occur. Sensitivity to context creates the type of link between the level of past and future transgressions that can be modeled with a stochastic process, as discussed more fully below.[48] Finally, the insensitivity of honest cheaters to economic incentives provides further reason to doubt that the process leading to accounting fraud can be fully explained as the product of a cost-benefit analysis.

2.2   Evidence Suggesting Managers Stumble into Committing Accounting Fraud

A second rationale for using stochastic process models to analyse accounting frauds is the lack of evidence supporting more traditional explanations of what causes accounting frauds. A review of the factors that have and have not been found to contribute to the likelihood of accounting frauds occurring within a firm supports the hypothesis that a propensity to commit accounting fraud is *not* closely linked to the expected economic returns from accounting fraud. Furthermore, recent research suggests that the consequences to both the firm and the individual managers involved in an accounting fraud are so severe that it is unlikely these frauds are a product of reasoned consideration.

Before reviewing the relevant findings, it is helpful to separate research on the causes and consequences of accounting fraud into three broad categories: (1) research identifying the factors that contribute to the likelihood of an accounting fraud occurring; (2) research on the consequences that flow out once an accounting fraud is uncovered; and (3) research describing the dynamics within a firm that lead to accounting fraud. The first two areas of research consider *causal explanations* of accounting fraud (specifically what precedes accounting fraud and what results from accounting fraud, respectively), whereas the third area of research probes *mechanistic explanations* of accounting fraud.

Causal and mechanistic explanations are related, but distinct, modes of explanation.[49] While a causal explanation can include a description of a hypothesized mechanism linking inputs and outputs, understanding the inner workings of a process is not a prerequisite for providing a causal explanation of a phenomenon. Conversely, a mechanistic explanation "takes the form of showing how the parts of a system, thanks to their articulation and interactions, make the whole system evolve and behave as it does,"[50] or, more simply, describes "a process in terms of mechanisms that translate input into output."[51] (This chapter provides a mechanistic explanation of accounting fraud.)

A sampling of scholarship exploring *causal* explanations of accounting fraud supports the hypothesis that managers often stumble into committing accounting fraud rather than doing so with planning and forethought, because: (1) changes in potential gains do not appear to have a strong effect on the propensity to commit accounting fraud, and (2) the consequences for managers determined to have committed accounting fraud are so harsh that committing accounting fraud seems unlikely to be the product of premeditation, even granting that this premeditation may be distorted by cognitive and behavioral biases.

2.2.1   Minimal effects of changes in potential gains

A major focus of research on what causes accounting fraud is the identification of attributes within and outside of the firm associated with a higher incidence of such frauds. Among the important contributions in this area of scholarship are articles by Baucus *et al.*,[52] by Beneish,[53] and by Dechow *et al.*[54] Baucus *et al.*, published in 1991, finds that firms with abundant resources and that had been performing relatively well are more likely to engage in various kinds of illegal activity.[55] Beneish, published in 1999, identifies eight accounting variables, including gross margin, asset quality, sales growth, depreciation, SG&A expenses, leverage, indexed day's sales in receivables, and accruals to total assets, which, when combined, indicate an increased propensity for a firm to be involved in accounting fraud.[56] Dechow *et al.*, first posted online in 2008, finds that firms accused by the SEC of manipulating their financial performance have had strong performance prior to the manipulation, and concludes that most manipulations are motivated by managers' desire to hide deteriorating financial performance.[57]

Other studies on the causes of accounting frauds investigate whether specific firm characteristics are associated with a higher level of accounting fraud. Among the specific attributes investigated are: (1) the quality of corporate governance;[58] (2) the levels of contingent compensation paid to a firm's managers;[59] and (3) the levels of over-confidence among the senior managers of the firm.[60] Based both on the studies analysing which specific factors affect the propensity to commit accounting fraud, and the research of Baucus *et al.*,[61] Beneish,[62] and Dechow *et al.*[63] surveyed above, it does not appear to be the case that the propensity to commit accounting fraud is clearly linked to the potential gains a manager could receive from committing the fraud. In fact, Armstrong *et al.* recently found that a high level of CEO equity incentives may be associated with a lower, rather than a higher, likelihood of accounting irregularities.[64]

The apparent lack of connection between financial incentives and the propensity to commit accounting fraud is consistent with the findings from an experiment several colleagues and I carried out to study how to prevent accounting fraud.[65] We structured our experiment to replicate many of the salient features of accounting fraud, and manipulated several variables to see if these changes would reduce the propensity of participants to commit an experimental proxy for accounting fraud. We found that a disclosure treatment greatly reduced the extent to which participants in our study were willing to act in an unethical manner. Yet this disclosure treatment was specifically designed not to affect the cost-benefit analysis of study participants. This result is consistent with other experimental evidence that willingness to commit unlawful behavior is rarely a function of economic considerations.[66]

If accounting fraud were a product of planning and forethought, then we might expect to find a relationship between the amount of a manager's contingent compensation and the propensity to commit accounting fraud. Finding no such association supports the claim that the decision to commit accounting fraud is *not* based on rational calculation, and suggests why accounting frauds may be more effectively explained as the unanticipated consequence of a sequence of minor and seemingly inconsequential transgressions.[67]

2.2.2 Severity of penalties

Recent studies have measured the consequences to both a firm and a firm's managers when an accounting fraud is uncovered. Not surprisingly, the consequences to both the firm and the managers responsible for committing the fraud are quite negative. An analysis by Karpoff *et al.*, published in 2008, estimates that the cost to an investor when an accounting fraud is uncovered at a firm is equal to approximately 40% of the value of the investment.[68] As for managers accused of being involved in committing accounting fraud, over 90% of such managers lose their jobs, and a sizeable minority (28%) face criminal charges and penalties, including jail sentences that average 4.3 years according to a separate analysis by Karpoff *et al.*, also published in 2008.[69]

Given the severe penalties both firms and responsible managers face, it does not appear to be a sound exercise of judgment for a manager to commit accounting fraud. The apparent lack of rationality in choosing to commit accounting fraud is also suggested by the circumstances typically preceding the decision to commit these frauds. The most common circumstances in which accounting frauds occur involve an attempt to avoid disclosing a downturn in sales or profits.[70] It is difficult to conceive how the cost of making a truthful disclosure in such a circumstance would be anywhere as severe as the potential penalties imposed upon those found to have committed accounting fraud. Nor does it seem reasonable for managers to expect that an accounting fraud can go undetected for long periods of time.[71] Arlen concludes upon reviewing the consequences to a firm of having an accounting fraud discovered that committing accounting fraud is probably not in the shareholders' best interest.[72] A similar logic suggests that the cost to a manger of honestly reporting a downturn in sales or earnings is much less than the expected cost of committing accounting fraud.

One example of the apparent economic irrationality of committing accounting fraud is provided by the events leading up to the bankruptcy of Worldcom in 2002.[73] The Chief Executive Officer (CEO) of Worldcom at the time, Bernie Ebbers, was a major instigator of the accounting fraud at Worldcom, and it is reasonable to ask whether it might have been a sound personal financial decision for Bernie Ebbers to instigate this particular fraud. For Ebbers the result of committing accounting fraud is that he is likely to spend much of the remainder of his life in jail. What would have happened if he had not committed accounting fraud? In the worst case, he would now be the ex-CEO of a company that failed to continue to report higher profits. Those who point to Ebbers' potential profits from selling shares before the fraud is uncovered would have to explain the fact that Ebbers held on to almost all of his Worldcom stock, even when the valuation was based on what Ebbers knew to be falsified accounting information.[74]

There are various explanations that might be offered as to why managers regularly undertake the seemingly unwise course of action involved in committing accounting fraud. One way to explain the continued propensity to commit accounting fraud is to focus attention on those few situations where the benefits of committing accounting fraud may be greater than the costs.[75] A second way to explain why managers commit accounting fraud even when the expected value of such behavior is negative is to point to behavioral biases in manager decision-making that distort the manager's ability to accurately evaluate the personal costs and benefits of committing accounting fraud.[76] A third way to explain managers' willingness to undertake such a costly course of action is that the choice to commit accounting fraud is not premeditated. This third approach is the one modeled in this chapter.

But before proceeding to a consideration of how to use stochastic process analysis to model accounting fraud, there are two more reasons I will offer as to why the use of stochastic process analysis is justified in this context.

2.3 Links Between Past and Future Transgressions

The power of stochastic process analysis comes from its ability to account for the *cumulative* effects of relatively small changes over time. But effects of small changes over time only accumulate in a way that can be estimated with a stochastic process model if past outcomes influence future behavior. Therefore, the relevance of a stochastic process model to the dynamics leading to accounting fraud depends upon whether a history of prior transgressions influences the likelihood and magnitude of future transgressions. There are both operational and psychological reasons to expect that the extent of past transgressions within a firm will influence the level of future transgressions within that firm.

Before reviewing evidence of a link between the level of past transgressions within a firm and the likelihood of future transgressions, it may be helpful to provide a simple example of what such a link between past and future behavior might look like. Suppose the outcome of a coin toss determines which direction an object will move on a line, and then from that new position the coin is tossed again to determine the direction of the next move. In this situation the future position of the coin is determined not only by the outcome of the most recent coin toss, but also by outcomes of all of the past coin tosses. Because of this link between past outcomes and future position, the movement along a line determined by this sequence of coin flips can be modeled as the product of a stochastic process. If, however, the process always started from the same position regardless of past outcomes, then the history of previous coin tosses would not have any influence on the next position. In such a situation, a stochastic process analysis would not be helpful. Similarly, if the likelihood an executive will commit accounting fraud is not linked to the extent of previous transgressions, then stochastic process models will be of little value in understanding accounting fraud.

One of the primary reasons why the extent of past transgressions in a firm is, in fact, likely to affect the number and extent of future transgressions is operational. Inertia is a common feature of most large organizations. In setting expectations for future performance the most natural reference point will be past performance. If a firm reports selling a given number of units in a year, then the likely assumption will be that the firm will sell at least the same number of units in the next year, whether or not the number of units sold in the previous year was accurately reported.

In the context of financial reporting this assumption leads financial analysts to expect, at a minimum, that a firm will maintain a given level of performance. (Financial analysts may also expect a firm to maintain the rate of growth established in earlier periods.) The result in the context of misreporting is likely the dynamic described by Schrand and Zechman as follows:

> [e]arnings management in minor amounts in a given period is likely to go undetected. If performance does not improve in the next period, however, the manager is forced either to manage earnings in an increasing amount to cover reversals and keep up the earnings expectations he has created or reveal poor performance. Eventually, the level of earnings management required to hide a series of bad performance realizations can be obtained only if the manager 'cooks the books' and makes the kinds of accounting misstatements that are prosecuted by the SEC.[77]

This description provides a simple example of how misrepresentations about past performance may create operational pressures to commit more transgressions in the future.

Psychological dynamics also suggest why the extent of past transgressions in a firm will affect the extent of future transgressions in that firm. One psychological dynamic linking the level of past and future transgressions is the situationally contingent nature of much misbehavior, as discussed above in the context of "honest" cheating.[78] People are more likely to judge a transgression permissible, if the transgression is not significantly more pernicious than transgressions recently committed by either themselves or other members of their group.

Darley has identified three other psychological dynamics by which past transgressions might also spur on future transgressions. First, Darley observes how through a process known as "pluralistic ignorance" other members of a firm may "accept the implied definition that the first actions were ethical in nature" if untoward actions are not publicly repudiated.[79] Second, Darley notes that a sense of loyalty to the group is likely to lead other members in the management group to "allow or abet" earlier transgression.[80] Third, Darley points to research on social identity to highlight how people will attempt to "become the prototypical member of the group, and the cues around [them] are that the prototypic group members are engaging in corrupt actions."[81] Darley's conclusions are consistent with findings by other psychologists that groups tend to continue or even escalate a course of action, regardless of the propriety of the initial behavior.[82]

A management team which has carried out operations based on punctilious abidance by legal requirements is unlikely to suddenly operate in an unlawful manner for both operational and psychological reasons. Such a firm will not face pressure to meet performance expectations created by falsified reports, or to treat substantial falsifications as acceptable behavior. Conversely, a firm with a widespread practice of past infractions is likely to continue, and perhaps even escalate, this style of operation in the future. These observations suggest why the level of past transgressions within a firm will influence the level of future transgressions within that firm, and, therefore, why the dynamics within a firm leading to accounting fraud are amenable to a stochastic process analysis.

2.4   Unpredictable Events and Minor Decisions as Determinants of Business Outcomes

Stochastic process models provide a method to estimate the cumulative effects of a large number of unobservable and unpredictable events. It is generally true that uncertainty about future outcomes pervades business operations. This uncertainty provides another reason to turn to stochastic process models to better understand accounting frauds.

Previous research on accounting fraud has suggested why the path leading to accounting fraud may be marked by unpredictability. For example, in the Arlen and Carney analysis, managers recognize and hope to take advantage of the fact that future financial performance is uncertain.[83] In the Schrand and Zechman analysis, managers are motivated by the same hope for an unexpectedly positive future financial performance identified by Arlen and Carney, but the calculation made by the manager in the Schrand and Zechman analysis is based on unduly optimistic perceptions as to the probability of such an outcome.[84] Both Arlen and Carney and Schrand and Zechman observe that uncertainty surrounding future financial results can create incentives to commit accounting fraud.[85]

More generally, organizational behavior research highlights the extent to which activity within a firm is determined by a firm's complex social systems, rather than by the decisions of one or a few key decision-makers. Much corporate "behavior" is, therefore, likely produced in a manner similar to the way in which I hypothesize accounting frauds come to fruition, namely as the product of a sequence of seemingly inconsequential decisions not linked together into a purposeful plan. In fact, the social systems within large organizations have proven sufficiently difficult to study in a systematic manner that organizational behavior researchers often use small group behavior as a proxy for larger scale organizational behavior, and, even at the level of the small group, researchers find that the interactions and dynamics that produce behavior are surprisingly complex.[86]

Research on drug delivery accidents in hospitals offers an example of an area of organizational behavior research which supports the claim that stochastic process models may be useful in understanding the dynamics leading to accounting fraud.[87] Drug delivery accidents in hospitals are unfortunately quite widespread, but are rarely the result of malevolent behavior by a specific caregiver. Instead, drug delivery accidents are usually a predictable, though unintended and undesirable, outcome of the malfunctioning of systems developed for just the opposite purpose: to protect patients. Amy Edmundson compared the administration of drugs in two different urban hospitals in an attempt to understand why there was a difference between the two hospitals in drug administration error rates. To her surprise, Edmundson finds that higher error rates are reported in hospital units where there is more of a practice of open communication and information sharing.[88]

Edmundson's findings provide an example from outside the accounting fraud context of a situation in which organizational behavior is better explained as the unintended consequence of a sequence of minor decisions rather than as the consequence of a single, premeditated decision. The potential applicability of stochastic process models to the analysis of business outcomes generally provides a fourth reason to investigate stochastic process analysis as a way to model accounting fraud.

3.   PREVIOUS RESEARCH ON DYNAMICS WITHIN A FIRM LEADING TO ACCOUNTING FRAUD

This section reviews previous research on the dynamics within a firm that may lead to accounting fraud. This review identifies work by several scholars which makes claims that hint at the potential usefulness of stochastic process modeling of the dynamics within a firm leading to accounting fraud. However, no one has described the dynamics leading to accounting frauds with the specificity, flexibility, and verifiability offered by the stochastic process modeling approach explored in this chapter.

For the purposes of clarity, it is helpful to begin this review by describing a spectrum along which different types of mechanistic explanations about the dynamics within a firm leading to accounting fraud can be arrayed. At one end of such a spectrum would be mechanistic explanations based upon the assumption that accounting fraud is the product of a calculated, premeditated decision made by one or a few senior managers. At the other end of such a spectrum would be mechanistic explanations based on the assumption that accounting fraud is the unanticipated consequence of a multitude of seemingly minor and inconsequential transgressions. Thus, this spectrum of mechanistic explanations of accounting fraud ranges from explanations of accounting fraud as the product of rational choice to explanations of accounting fraud as the product of managers' stumbling. I discuss below where the various existing mechanistic explanations of the causes of accounting fraud fall along this spectrum.

Much of the best scholarship on the dynamics within a firm that may lead to accounting fraud falls at the end of the spectrum where accounting fraud is assumed to be the result of calculated, premeditated decisions made by one or a few managers. One exemplar of this approach is the article by Arlen and Carney.[89] The specific calculation that Arlen and Carney hypothesize as central to a manager's decision of whether to commit accounting fraud proceeds as follows.[90] First, Arlen and Carney hypothesize that in most circumstances, "the expected costs of committing Fraud on the Market are very high and the expected benefits are low. A manager of a healthy firm generally will not benefit substantially from fraud even if he owns shares in the firm, because the passage of time is likely to reveal that the manager's fraudulent positive statements were false."[91] There is, however, according to the Arlen and Carney account, one set of circumstances in which the manager's expected pay-off from committing accounting fraud may become positive. This situation can occur when a manager is in what may be the last period of his or her employment. Arlen and Carney argue that in the last period of employment it might be rational for managers to commit accounting fraud "in an attempt to save their jobs, by using the period of the fraud to turn the firm around."[92]

One limitation of Arlen and Carney's "last period" model is the assumption that a managers' behavior can be characterized as involving unbiased rational calculation.[93] Langevoort has offered a description of how accounting fraud may be the product of decision-making processes affected by behavioral biases. Langevoort has identified several behavioral biases, including over-confidence,[94] self-deception,[95] and perceptual filters,[96] which may lead managers to commit accounting fraud, even in circumstances where an unbiased calculation would show that the decision to commit such a fraud is unwise. Langevoort observes, for example, that "managers simply might not recognize problems or risks because of systematic perceptual filters that play crucial protective roles in the smooth functioning of the firm."[97] Elsewhere, Langevoort uses an analogy to a mechanical system, the "corporate thermostat", to describe how the culture within a firm can affect the likelihood that accounting fraud might occur.[98] With respect to the potential role of self-deception, Langevoort observes that "[w]hile some of this opportunism may well be deliberately plotted, the cognitively nimble manager will seek to legitimate the behavior, both to himself and his close associates."[99] Many of the arguments which I offer here as providing a rationale for using stochastic processes to model accounting fraud echo observations made by Langevoort about how behavioral biases may increase a manager's willingness to commit accounting fraud.

Another legal scholar who explores the decision-making distortions which may be associated with corporate wrongdoing is Manuel Utset. Utset observes that "serial offenders may not make fully informed decisions, even if they had all the information at hand, given well-known cognitive constrains faced by rational actors when making decisions in complex environments."[100] For example, Utset notes that crimes may even be carried out by people after they had "formed a long-term intention not to commit the crime."[101] Utset's research, as with Langevoort's, is parsimonious with stochastic process models of accounting fraud.

Other scholars who consider how cognitive biases may affect decision-making in a way that increases the likelihood of accounting fraud also focus their attention on the effects of over-optimism. Baruch Lev, for example, observes that "[w]hile the image of managers who feather their own nests attracts an understandably large share of attention . . . my sense is that the more common reason for earnings manipulation is that managers, *forever the optimists*, are trying to 'weather the storm' – that is to continue operations with adequate funding and customer/supplier support until better times come."[102] Schrand and Zechman also hypothesize that the propensity to commit accounting fraud is increased when managers are overly optimistic.[103]

The work on the causes of accounting fraud by Langevoort, as well as the research of Utset, Lev, and Schrand and Zechman, falls in the middle of the spectrum set out above ranging from rational choice mechanistic explanations of accounting fraud to stumbling into crime mechanistic explanations of accounting fraud. In these various accounts of the dynamics within a firm leading to accounting fraud, some amount of forethought and premeditation contributes to accounting fraud, even if such considerations are clouded by cognitive and behavioral biases.

3.1   Accounting Fraud as the Product of a Slippery Slope Dynamic

Mechanistic explanations of the dynamics leading to accounting at the end of the spectrum where managers are presumed to stumble into committing accounting fraud are less well developed. Among the limited number of discussions of accounting fraud as a crime which managers stumble into, one particular dynamic, the slippery slope, is frequently mentioned. Observations about how a slippery slope type of dynamic may lead to accounting fraud are also prevalent among anecdotal explanations of the causes of accounting frauds. For example, a survey of 45 nationally recognized white-collar crime prosecutors and defense attorneys found that most of the respondents to the survey "view white collar criminals as individuals who find themselves involved in schemes that are initially small in scale, but over which they lose control."[104]

There are also a few scholarly articles which explore the possibility that a slippery slope dynamic leads to accounting fraud. Langevoort uses the idea of a slippery slope to describe how a willingness to commit fraud is increased by both a "threat to incumbency" (echoing Arlen and Carney's analysis) and a greater willingness to commit future transgressions if past transgressions have already been committed.[105] Schrand and Zechman use the term "slippery slope" and provide a model of a simple slippery slope dynamic in their explanation of how "financial reporting fraud often represents the escalation of minor earnings management infractions." [106] The possibility of a slippery slope dynamic leading to accounting fraud is also mentioned by Darley,[107] and Sam Fraidin, Chris Porath, and myself in an earlier article, without using the slippery slope terminology, noted that "large-scale accounting frauds are frequently the result of a marginal deception evolving into a much larger deception."[108]

There are, however, limitations to the use of a slippery slope analogy to describe the dynamics within a firm that may lead to accounting fraud. First, the term slippery slope can be used to describe a host of different and even contradictory mechanisms.[109] Second, as implied by the term itself, a slippery slope dynamic refers to a mechanism that is generally deterministic and unforgiving. Thus, references to a slippery slope dynamic suggest that once a certain number of transgressions have occurred, fraud becomes almost inevitable. But such a dynamic leading to accounting fraud is inconsistent with the evidence of a large number of minor transgressions and relatively few major accounting frauds, as discussed above.[110] While it may be true that a series of minor transgressions precedes accounting fraud, the dynamics connecting antecedent transgressions to accounting fraud is almost certainly more complex than is suggested by the slippery slope analogy.

What I propose is that stochastic process models can provide a more robust framework for understanding the dynamics within a firm that may lead to accounting fraud than do references to a slippery slope.

4.   STOCHASTIC PROCESS MODELS OF ACCOUNTING FRAUD

Stochastic process models provide a method to describe mathematically the behavior of "a system that undergoes a series of relatively small changes and that does so at random."[111] To apply this type of mathematical model to the dynamics within a firm that may lead to accounting fraud it is helpful to make several simplifying assumptions. I make the following four simplifying assumptions about accounting fraud to facilitate applying a stochastic process model to this phenomenon: (1) that the illegality of a firm's behavior can be measured along a single dimension; (2) that movements along this "illegality" dimension occur through a series of small steps; (3) that one's current position on this illegality spectrum influences the illegality of one's future actions; and (4) that managers are unable to foresee the ultimate consequences of their minor transgressions. The reasons for making each of these simplifying assumptions is discussed next.

First, I assume that the illegality of the behavior within a firm can be measured along a single dimension. Assuming that firms misbehave only along one dimension simplifies the presentation of the mathematics of stochastic process analysis. A more realistic model might identify several different pathways within the same organization that could culminate in an accounting fraud, and such a scenario could be modeled by adding additional dimensions for each of these potential pathways. For the expository purposes of this chapter, such a refinement is unnecessary.

Second, I assume that movement along this "illegality" axis occurs as a series of small decisions, rather than in large jumps. The decision to model movement along the "illegality" spectrum in terms of small steps is based on the arguments presented above that accounting frauds often result from a sequence of seemingly minor transgressions unexpectedly culminating in a large-scale accounting fraud, rather than from a single decision to commit a large-scale accounting fraud.[112] If the dynamics leading to accounting fraud also involve a few major decisions, then these decisions could be included in the stochastic process model by adding the possibility of jumps occurring in the movement along the firm's illegality spectrum. The modeling of such jumps is not pursued further in this chapter, but it is a topic that is well studied in the stochastic process literature, particularly in the context of the behavior of the prices of financial assets.[113]

Third, I assume that the level of illegality within the firm has an influence on a manager's willingness to commit unlawful behavior in the future. Above I suggested why for both operational and psychological reasons the ongoing level of misbehavior within a firm is likely to affect the future level of misbehavior within that firm.[114] In the context of modeling the dynamics leading to accounting fraud, it is helpful to be more precise about the nature of the connection between the extent of past transgression and the likelihood and extent of future transgressions. The simplest way in which current behavior can influence future behavior is if a process possesses the Markov property. A process has the Markov property if all information about past behavior is fully incorporated into the current position of the system.[115] In the context of misbehavior, the Markov property would mean that the current level of misbehavior within a firm, but not the path leading to that given level of misbehavior, affects the expected future level of behavior within the firm. The Markov property is a helpful simplifying assumption in the context of modeling the dynamics leading to accounting fraud.[116]

The final assumption I make in applying stochastic process models to accounting fraud is the assumption that managers cannot foresee the ultimate consequences of committing minor infractions. If managers had sufficient foresight, then the choice to start down a path that might lead to calamitous consequences could be analysed in terms of the anticipated costs and benefits of that particular course of action. The resulting behavior would be amenable to a traditional economic analysis. However, based on the research presented earlier on the lack of foresight when honest people misbehave,[117] the absence of effects of economic incentives on the propensity to commit accounting fraud,[118] and the complexity of the processes I hypothesize may lead to accounting fraud, it seems unlikely that foresight about the potential consequences of committing seemingly minor transgressions is widespread.

With these four assumptions in place, I next consider how three different types of stochastic process models may prove helpful in describing the dynamics within a firm by which a sequence of minor and seemingly innocuous transgressions may culminate in an accounting fraud. The three types of stochastic process models I consider are: (1) simple random walk models; (2) random walk with mean reversion models; and (3) random walk with a running maximum models. The appeal of the first type of stochastic process model considered, the simple random walk model, is its simplicity. However, a random walk model with mean reversion may do a better job of capturing the shifts in behavior that probably result when managers start to act in an increasingly unlawful manner. Finally, a random walk model with a running maximum allows for the possibility that public disclosures will lock the firm's managers into a particular course of action.

Below I describe in more detail each of these three stochastic process models and how they can be applied to the dynamics leading to accounting fraud.

4.1   Accounting Fraud as the Product of a Random Walk

I start by exploring the relevance of a simple random walk to accounting fraud.[119] In a simple random walk model, there is a fixed probability of taking a step in one of two directions. Once this first step is taken, the next step starts from the place where the first step ended. In this simple way, the future action of the random walker is conditioned on the outcomes of past behavior.

A simple random walk model is consistent with each of the simplifying assumptions I discussed above to facilitate applying a stochastic process model to the dynamics within a firm that might lead to accounting fraud. First, a random walk may take place on only one dimension. Second, in a random walk model movement along a given spectrum occurs in small increments. Third, in a random walk model one's past behavior plays a central role in determining future behavior, because each step moves only a small distance away from whatever the previous location was, and the previous location was fully determined by past outcomes. Finally, in a simple random walk foresight does not affect behavior.

There are two ways to model mathematically a simple random walk. One approach is to describe the random walk as involving a series of discrete steps. With a discrete step random walk determining the probability of ending up at a given location requires comparing the various ways to reach that location with the total number of possible outcomes. Only a few variables are necessary to calculate this probability. We can let the variable t stand for the total number of steps taken, and let the total number of steps taken in the direction toward increased illegality be n. Then the probability of ending up at a given point, n, on the "illegality" spectrum after time t can be calculated as follows, if we assume the process starts at 0, and the odds of moving in a more or less unlawful direction are equal:

$$\binom{n}{t} \cdot 2^{-t}, \text{where} \binom{n}{t} = \frac{n!}{t!(n-t)!} \tag{1}$$

This formula shows that the mathematics of a discrete step random walk are closely related to the behavior of the binomial distribution, $\binom{n}{t}$ because the binomial distribution offers a way to sum up the number of various paths that can lead to a given outcome.[120]

A second mathematical approach to describing a random walk is to assume the random walk proceeds as part of a continuous process.[121] In the context of accounting fraud, it may be more realistic to describe the process within a firm that might lead to accounting fraud as involving a series of discrete steps; however, there are analytical advantages to using the mathematics of continuous steps to describe how a random walk might lead to accounting fraud. For example, the mathematics of a continuous process random walk is more amenable to refinements, such as the refinements explored below.[122]

One way to describe a continuous random walk process mathematically is to introduce the concept of a Wiener process. A function $z(t)$ is a Wiener process if each movement of $z(t)$ is determined by a random change in position of magnitude Δz, which occurs as a function of the square root of time, $\sqrt{\Delta t}$. More specifically, each of the steps in a Weiner process has the following property: $\Delta z = \varepsilon_t \sqrt{\Delta t}$, where ε_t is a normally distributed random variable with mean of zero and standard deviation of 1.[123] As the steps of the Weiner process become infinitely small, we can rewrite the movement of the Weiner process in terms of derivatives, so that $dz = \varepsilon_t \sqrt{dt}$.

With this nomenclature, the mean and variance of the Wiener process can be calculated. The mean of the Wiener process is 0, because the mean of ε_t is 0. The variance of the Wiener process is, by definition, equal to the expected value of the square of the deviations from the mean. Since the mean is 0, the variance of the Wiener process is equal to:

$$E[(dz)^2] = E[(\varepsilon_t \sqrt{dt})^2] = dt$$

In words, with the Wiener process description of the continuous step random walk, we observe not only that the variance increases with time, but, more specifically, that the variance increases linearly with increases in time.

From this equation there are several implications that can be derived if the dynamics leading to accounting fraud are correctly characterized as involving a continuous time random walk. First, as time passes, the extent of wrongdoing at the firm (measured by the variance of the distribution of wrongdoing) continues to grow. While the average level of wrongdoing remains unchanged, the number of more extreme violations steadily increases. This is due to the non-stationary nature of the random walk. A second, more general implication, which the formal model makes explicit, is that minor transgressions may have costs which go beyond their immediate consequences. Committing minor transgressions shifts the starting point from which the distribution of future transgressions will be determined. Past transgressions make it more likely that increasingly egregious transgressions will be committed in the future. This observation suggests that minor transgressions are likely to be more costly than would be suggested by an analysis which only weighs the costs of the infractions themselves.[124]

The simple random walk model offers a well-studied and plausible way to understand how a sequence of seemingly minor and inconsequential transgressions might lead to accounting fraud. But there are limitations in using a simple random walk to model the dynamics leading to accounting fraud. A first limitation has to do with the prediction of such a model that fraud will eventually occur at every company. The reason for this prediction is, as discussed above, that a random walk "spreads out" over time. The prediction that all corporations will eventually commit accounting fraud seems unduly pessimistic.

A related limitation of a simple random walk model as a model of the dynamics within a firm that may lead to accounting fraud is that this model assumes a manager's behavior is only affected by the extent of his or her past transgressions. However, it seems likely that the tendency of a manager to commit increasingly unlawful behavior would also be affected by how close he or she is to committing outright fraud. For example, managers might become more cautious as the risks of detection from committing additional transgressions increase.

These limitations of the simple random walk model of accounting fraud result from the non-stationarity of such a process. It might be more realistic to assume the probability of acting in a more or less lawful manner is determined both relative to the extent of past transgressions and by the absolute level of unlawful behavior occurring within the firm. Both of these factors can be included in the type of stochastic process model discussed next.

4.2   Accounting Fraud as the Product of a Random Walk with Mean Reversion

The mathematics of a random walk with a mean reversion may better capture the dynamics within a firm by which minor transgressions lead to accounting frauds. In addition to the attributes of a simple random walk described above, a random walk with a mean reversion includes a force that pushes the dynamic process back toward a predetermined mean. This additional force provides a way to include in a stochastic process model of accounting fraud the likelihood that the ongoing level of unlawful behavior within a firm will tend to remain within a given range.

One way to model the dynamics leading to accounting fraud as mean-reverting is to model the process as an Ornstein-Uhlenbeck process. The Ornstein-Uhlenbeck process is a well-studied type of mean-reverting stochastic process, which combines the attributes of a Wiener process with a simple mean-reverting force. Only a few modifications to the notation of a Wiener process discussed above are necessary to describe the Weiner process component of the Ornstein-Uhlenbeck process mathematically.[125] These modifications to the notation above are: (1) we introduce the idea of an x axis along which the level of illegality within the firm is measured, and (2) we introduce σ to represent the rate of diffusion of the random walk process. With this notation movement along the x-axis resulting from a random walk described by a Weiner process will be dx, which will equal $\sigma\, dz$, where $dz = \varepsilon_t\sqrt{dt}$.

We next introduce nomenclature to describe the mean-reverting force component of the Ornstein-Uhlenbeck process. We let η represent the speed with which the process reverts to the mean, and let $\bar{x}$ represent the mean position to which the system reverts. Then the following equation combines a random walk dynamic with a mean-reverting force in a manner which describes an Ornstein-Uhlenbeck process:

$$dx = -\eta(\bar{x} - x)dt + \sigma dz \tag{2}$$

The first term in this equation, $\eta(\bar{x} - x)dt$, measures the mean-reverting force, and the second term, $\sigma\, dz$, measures the effects of the random walk.

As with a continuous step random walk, the mean and variance of a mean-reverting random walk can be calculated analytically.[126] If the process starts at a point, x_0, then the expected value, or mean, of the process is:

$$E[x_t] = \bar{x} + (x\hat{o} - \bar{x})e^{-nt} \tag{3}$$

Thus, the mean of the process reverts to $\bar{x}$ over time, because e^{-nt} approaches 0. The variance of this process is:

$$V[x_t - \bar{x}] = \frac{\sigma^2}{2\eta(1 - e^{-2nt})} \tag{4}$$

This measure of the variance of the Ornstein-Uhlenbeck process shows that the Ornstein-Uhlenbeck process converges to a constant, $\sigma^2/2\eta$, because $e^{-2\eta t}$ approaches 0 over time. The constant to which the variance of the Ornstein-Uhlenbeck process converges is determined by rate of diffusion of the underlying random walk process, σ, as compared to the strength of the mean reverting force, η.

As compared with a simple random walk, the stationarity of a mean-reverting stochastic process, such as the Ornstein-Uhlenbeck process, offers a more plausible description of the relative stability one would expect over the long term in the level of unlawful behavior within most firms. The main limitation in using the Ornstein-Uhlenbeck process to model dynamics within a firm leading to accounting fraud is practical. It has proven difficult in other contexts to gather enough evidence to distinguish between a stochastic process with only a random walk component and a stochastic process that also has a mean reversion component.[127] Such difficulties are probably exacerbated in the context of estimating the parameters of a mean-reverting model of the dynamics within a firm leading to accounting fraud, given the scarcity of information about these dynamics.

Another limitation of a mean-reverting stochastic process as a model for the dynamics leading to accounting fraud within a firm is that such a model does not take into account the likelihood that certain actions once taken, such as public disclosures, may alter the future course of misbehavior within the firm.

4.3   Accounting Fraud as the Product of a Random Walk with a Running Maximum

There are a number of actions a firm may take which will be difficult to undo. One example of this type of a lock-in dynamic in the context of unlawful behavior within a firm is provided by what occurs when a firm publicly discloses information. Once such a disclosure is made, a public record is established and a public explanation of any changes in previously reported information needs to be provided. The possibility of being locked in to a certain course of action by past behavior can be incorporated into a stochastic process model in a number of ways, but not without difficulty.

One way to model the lock-in effect of making public disclosures is to include a ratchet and pawl mechanism in the characterization of the stochastic process system. Perhaps the most famous analysis of a ratchet and pawl mechanism as part of a stochastic process is provided by Richard Feynman in his "Introduction to Physics" lectures.[128] But Feynman's result is essentially negative. Feynman shows that in a closed system a ratchet and pawl need not have the unidirectional property commonly assumed. After Feynman's work, a number of physical systems involving stochastic processes have been shown to be unidirectional, but the dynamic features necessary to generate this property tend to be quite complicated.[129] Occasionally scholars outside physics have used a ratchet and pawl analogy to suggest that a particular system is unidirectional, including the application of such a dynamic to the recent financial crisis[130] and to the escalation in the length of criminal sentences.[131] However, these discussions of ratchet and pawl systems in other contexts neither offer formal models nor do they suggest how to develop testable hypotheses.

A stochastic process model combined with a running maximum provides a less familiar, but potentially more tractable, alternative to a ratchet and pawl mechanism description of the lock-in aspect of the dynamics leading to accounting fraud. The idea of a running maximum is that whenever a certain level is reached by the system, the process cannot fall below that level in the future. The prototypical example of a physical system with a running maximum is the wear on machinery. While the extent of ongoing wear on machinery is likely determined by a stochastic process, machinery never becomes less worn. The process is unidirectional. The mathematics of a stochastic process with a running maximum is developed in an article by Arthur Heinricher and Richard Stockbridge.[132]

Applying a stochastic process model with a running maximum to the dynamics within a firm leading to accounting fraud faces practical difficulties similar to those identified in the discussion above about measuring the effects of a mean-reverting stochastic process dynamic. Estimating the parameters of a stochastic process model with a running maximum in the context of accounting fraud, where data is limited, will be difficult. Therefore, from the perspective of empirical verifiability, it is unclear to what extent this refinement will lead to testable hypotheses that are different from the implications of the other two models described above, a simple random walk model and a random walk with a mean-reverting force model. However, from a descriptive perspective, a stochastic process model with a running maximum offers an elegant method to capture the likelihood that certain actions taken by a firm's managers, most notably public disclosures, once taken, cannot be easily undone.

5.   CONCLUSION

This chapter introduces the use of stochastic process modeling to the analysis of how a sequence of minor and seemingly innocuous transgressions may lead to accounting fraud. More specifically, three types of stochastic process models are identified to help better understand the dynamics within a firm which may lead to accounting fraud. These three types of stochastic process models are: simple random walk models, random walk with a mean-reverting force models, and random walk with a running maximum models.

Using stochastic processes to model the dynamics leading to accounting fraud offers an alternative to the current way in which accounting frauds are predominantly analysed. Most research on accounting fraud assumes these frauds are, at least to some degree, premeditated. Instead, the stochastic process modeling explored in this chapter is consistent with the work of scholars and commentators who have suggested that the dynamics leading to accounting fraud within a firm might resemble a type of slippery slope process. What I show here is how to use stochastic process models to develop a systematic and potentially verifiable framework for understanding the dynamics within a firm that may lead managers to stumble into committing accounting fraud.

The possibility that the dynamics within a firm leading to accounting fraud can be modeled using stochastic process analysis opens several new avenues for further research. One question to explore is how to measure the extent to which the three types of stochastic process dynamics identified here contribute to the occurrence of accounting frauds. Predictions about accounting frauds based on the assumption that these crimes are premeditated have proven of limited value. Perhaps hypotheses based on stochastic process models can improve our understanding of when and why accounting frauds occur.

The potential viability of stochastic process models as a way to analyse accounting fraud also raises important policy questions. One question that might arise from the analysis here is whether managers who stumble into committing accounting fraud in the manner described in this chapter do so with sufficient *scienter* to commit a fraud.[133] Although I suspect otherwise, one could argue that it is an oxymoron to claim managers stumble into committing a fraud.[134] A related policy question has to do with the heavy weighting courts give to the extent to which the fraud appears motivated by a desire for personal financial gain in determining whether the actions were carried out with the requisite *scienter*.[135] If the dynamics leading to accounting frauds are often as described in this chapter, then relying heavily on the presence or absence of personal gain to determine *scienter* would fail to address the most common circumstances in which accounting frauds occur.

In summary, the use of stochastic process models of accounting fraud not only provides a viable method to understand the dynamics within a firm leading to accounting fraud, but also opens new avenues of research which may, in turn, have a significant impact on important policy questions.

NOTES

* I would like to thank David Aboody, Jennifer Arlen, Carlos Berdejo, Ben Fitzpatrick, Allison Quaglino, and participants at the Loyola Law School faculty workshop for helpful comments.

1. Jennifer H. Arlen and William J. Carney, *Vicarious Liability for Fraud on Securities Markets: Theory and Evidence*, UNIV. OF ILLINOIS L. REV. 691 (1992).

2. See, e.g., Donald C. Langevoort, *On Leaving Corporate Executives "Naked, Homeless and Without Wheels": Corporate Fraud, Equitable Remedies,and the Debate over Entity and Individual Liability*, 42 WAKE FOREST L. REV. 627 (2007) (hereinafter Langevoort, *Naked, Homeless, and Without Wheels*); Donald Langevoort, *Organized Illusions: A Behavioral Theory of Why Corporations Mislead Stock Market Investors (and Cause Other Social Harms)*, 146 U. PA. L. REV. 101 (1997) (hereinafter Langevoort, *Organized Illusions*); and Donald C. Langevoort, *Resetting the Corporate Thermostat, Lessons from the Recent Financial Scandals about Self-Deception, Deceiving Others and the Design of Internal Controls* 93 GEO. L. J. 285 (2004) (hereinafter Langevoort, *Resetting the Corporate Thermostat*).

3. See, e.g., Christopher S. Armstrong *et al.*, *Chief Executive Officer Equity Incentives and Accounting Irregularities*, 48 J. ACCOUNTING RESEARCH 225 (2010); Merle Erickson *et al.*, *Is There a Link Between Executive Equity Incentives and Accounting Fraud?* 44 J. ACCOUNTING RESEARCH 113 (2006).

4. Jonathan Karpoff, D. Scott Lee, and Gerald S. Martin, *The Consequences to Managers for Financial Misrepresentation*, 88 J. FINANCIAL ECONOMICS 195 (2008) (hereinafter Karpoff *et al.*, *Consequences to Managers*).

5. See, e.g., John M. Darley, *The Cognitive and Social Psychology of Contagious Organizational Corruption*, 70 BROOK. L. REV. 1177 (2006).

6. *FBI Director Mueller Speaks to the Economic Club of New York*, US FEDERAL NEWS (June 25, 2009) (emphasis added). See also, Pamela H. Bucy *et al.*, *Why Do They Do It?: The Motives, Mores, and Character of White Collar Criminals*, 82 ST. JOHN'S L. REV. 401, 407 (2008) (reporting on a survey of 45 individuals involved in prosecuting and defending white collar criminals, and finding that over 95% of the study respondents did not believe the white collar criminals committed their crimes because they were "amoral" or "evil").

7. Darley, *supra* note 5, at 1185; Langevoort, *Resetting the Corporate Thermostat, supra* note 2, at 308.

8. Catherine M. Schrand and Sarah L. C. Zechman, Executive Overconfidence and the Slippery Slope to Fraud, Working Paper (2008) available at http://papers.ssrn.com/sol3/papers.cfm?abstract_id=1265631.

9. Schrand and Zechman, *supra* note 8, do provide a simple model connecting over-optimism and accounting fraud. However, the empirical tests Schrand and Zechman carry out identify an association between over-optimism and accounting fraud, but do not differentiate between various possible mechanisms underlying that association.

10. N. G. VAN KAMPEN, STOCHASTIC PROCESSES IN PHYSICS AND CHEMISTRY 52 (2008).

11. Jean-Francois Le Gall, *Stochastic Processes*, in THE PRINCETON COMPANION TO MATHEMATICS 647 (Timothy Gowers, ed., 2008).
12. Robert Brown, *A brief account of microscopical observations made in the months of June, July and August, 1827, on the particles contained in the pollen of plants; and on the general existence of active molecules in organic and inorganic bodies*, PHILOSOPHICAL JOURNAL 358 (1828).
13. Albert Einstein, *Über die von der molekularkinetischen Theorie der Wärme geforderte Bewegung von in ruhenden Flüssigkeiten suspendierten Teilchen*, 17 ANNALEN DER PHYSIK 549 (1905).
14. AVINASH K. DIXIT and ROBERT S. PINDYCK, INVESTMENT UNDER UNCERTAINTY (1994).
15. See, e.g., ROSARIO N. MANTEGNA and H. EUGENE STANLEY, AN INTRODUCTION TO ECONOPHYSICS: CORRELATIONS AND COMPLEXITY IN FINANCE (2000); JOHANNES VOIT, THE STATISTICAL MECHANICS OF FINANCIAL MARKETS (2005).
16. See, e.g., REINHARD MAHNKE *ET AL.*, PHYSICS OF STOCHASTIC PROCESSES: HOW RANDOMNESS ACTS IN TIME 299–349 (2009).
17. See, e.g., Dan Ariely, *How Honest People Cheat*, HARVARD BUSINESS REVIEW 24 (February, 2008).
18. See, e.g., Ariely, *supra* note 17. See also, Francesca Gino, Shahar Ayal, and Dan Ariely, *Contagion and Differentiation in Unethical Behavior: The Effect of One Bad Apple on the Barrel*, 20 PSYCHOLOGICAL SCI. 393 (2009); Nina Mazar, On Amir, and Dan Ariely, *The Dishonesty of Honest People: A Theory of Self-Concept Maintenance*, 45 J. MARKETING RESEARCH 633 (2008) (hereinafter, Mazar *et al.*, *The Dishonesty of Honest People*); Nina Mazar and Dan Ariely, *Dishonesty in Everyday Life and Its Policy Implications*, 25 J. PUBLIC POLICY & MARKETING 1 (2006) (hereinafter, Mazar *et al.*, *Dishonesty in Everyday Life*).
19. See section 2.1.2.
20. Mazar *et al.*, *The Dishonesty of Honest People*, *supra* note 18, at 642.
21. Ariely, *supra* note 17, at 24.
22. John H. Evans *et al.*, *Honesty in Managerial Reporting*, 76 ACCOUNTING REV. 537 (2001).
23. *Id.* at 543.
24. Mazar *et al.*, *The Dishonesty of Honest People*, *supra* note 18, at 634 (citations omitted).
25. See, e.g., Albert Bandura *et al.*, *Sociocognitive Self-Regulatory Mechanisms Governing Transgressive Behavior*, 80 J. PERSONALITY & SOCIAL PSYCHOLOGY 125 (2001) (describing the role of self-regulation in resisting pressure to engage in behavior that transgresses moral or legal standards); Robert G. Lord *et al.*, *Self-Regulation at Work*, 61 ANN. REV. OF PSYCHOLOGY 543 (2010) (providing a review of the different roles of self-regulation in the work context).
26. Robert Goldstone and Calvin Chin, *Dishonesty in Self-Report of Copies Made: Moral Relativity and the Copy Machine*, 14 BASIC & APPLIED SOCIAL PSYCHOLOGY 19 (1993).
27. *Id.* at 19.
28. Stephen J. Dubiner and Steven D. Levitt, *What the Bagel Man Saw*, N.Y. TIMES, June 6, 2004: M 62.
29. *Id.* at 64.
30. *Id.*
31. Ariely, *supra* note 17, at 24.
32. Evans *et al.*, *supra* note 22, at 543.
33. Goldstone and Chin, *supra* note 26, at 23.
34. Stephen Brown, *et al.*, "Trust and Delegation," available at http://papers.ssrn.com/sol3/papers. cfm?abstract_id=1456414.
35. *Id.*
36. A three-year study by the IRS found that over half of the sole proprietors who have latitude in reporting their income under-reported their income. Summary available at www.irs.gov/newsroom/article/0,,id=154496,00.html.
37. See, e.g., Gino *et al.*, *supra* note 18.
38. Mazar *et al.*, *The Dishonesty of Honest People*, *supra* note 18.
39. *Id.* at 642.
40. Mary Zey-Ferrell, Mark K. Weaver, and O. C. Ferrell, *Predicting Unethical Behavior Among Marketing Practitioners*, 32 HUMAN RELATIONS 557 (1979); Mary Zey-Ferrell and O. C. Ferrell, *Role-set Configuration and Opportunity as Predictors of Unethical Behavior in Organizations*, 35 HUMAN RELATIONS 587 (1982).
41. ERVIN STAUB, THE ROOTS OF EVIL: THE ORIGINS OF GENOCIDE AND OTHER GROUP VIOLENCE (1989).
42. ROY F. BAUMEISTER, EVIL: INSIDE HUMAN CRUELTY AND VIOLENCE (1997).
43. See, e.g., Phillip G. Zimbardo *et al.*, *The Psychology of Imprisonment: Privation, Power and Pathology*, in DOING UNTO OTHERS: EXPLORATIONS IN SOCIAL BEHAVIOR (Z. Rubin, ed., 1974); STANLEY MILGRAM, OBEDIENCE TO AUTHORITY: AN EXPERIMENTAL VIEW (1974).
44. For an authoritative review of evidence on the situational nature of much human behavior see Jon Hanson and David Yosifon, *The Situation: An Introduction to the Situational Character, Critical Realism, Power Economics, and Deep Capture*, 152 U. PA. L. REV. 129 (2003).

45. For example, Ariely and colleagues conclude from one set of experiments that "people were insensitive to the expected external costs and benefits associated with the dishonest acts." Mazar *et al.*, *The Dishonesty of Honest People*, *supra* note 18, at 642.

46. Evans *et al. supra* note 22.

47. *Id.* See also, Goldstone and Chin, *supra* note 26, at 20, reporting on another laboratory study carried out by Farrington and Kidd, which specifically measures if there is a correlation between monetary gain and likelihood of cheating by providing participants an opportunity to turn over differing amounts of "found" money. Farrington and Kidd report that the "frequency of dishonest actions was not positively related to the monetary gain anticipated by committing the dishonest act, as might be expected if the decision to engage in financial dishonesty is motivated by a rational analysis of monetary expected utilities."

48. See section 2.3

49. Findings from causal analysis of a phenomenon usually do have implications for mechanistic explanations of a phenomenon and vice versa, but maintaining the distinction between these two types of explanations has proven useful in many fields, including the study of the mind-body problem (Max Kistler, *Mechanisms and Downward Causation*, in EPSA07: 1ST CONFERENCE OF THE EUROPEAN PHILOSOPHY OF SCIENCE ASSOCIATION (Madrid, 15–17 November, 2007)), research on the origins of emotions (Agnes Moors, *Theories of Emotion Causation: A Review*, 23 COGNITION & EMOTION 625 (2009)), and work in the philosophy of science generally (Stuart S. Glennan, *Mechanisms and the Nature of Causation*, 44 ERKENNTNIS 49 (1996); Philip J. Torres, *A Modified Conception of Mechanisms*, 71 ERKENNTNIS 233 (2009)).

50. Kistler, *supra* note 49, at 2. Kistler also notes: "On closer inspection, it appears that the concept of mechanism presupposes that of causation, far from being reducible to it. Providing a mechanistic explanation means to decompose the working of a complex system into a number of simpler subsystems that interact causally with each other." Kistler, *supra* note 49, at 5.

51. Moors, *supra* note 49, at 631.

52. Melissa J. Baucus and Janet P. Near, *Can Illegal Corporate Behavior be Predicted? An Event History Analysis*, 34 ACAD. OF MGMT. J. 9 (1991).

53. Messod D. Beneish, *The Detection of Earnings Manipulation*, 55 FINANCIAL ANALYST JOURNAL 24 (1999).

54. Patricia M. Dechow *et al.*, *Predicting Material Accounting Misstatements*, CONTEMPORARY ACCOUNTING RESEARCH (forthcoming), *available at* http://papers.ssrn.com/sol3/papers.cfm?abstract_id=997483.

55. Baucus and Near, *supra* note 52.

56. Beneish, *supra* note 53.

57. Dechow *et al.*, *supra* note 54.

58. See, e.g., Anup Agrawal and Sahiba Chadha, *Corporate Governance and Accounting Scandals*, 48 J. LAW & ECON. 317 (2005); Patricia Dechow *et al.*, *Causes and Consequences of Earnings Manipulation: An Analysis of Firms Subject to Enforcement Actions by the SEC*, 13 CONTEMPORARY ACCOUNTING REVIEW 1 (1996); April Klein, *Audit Committee, Board of Director Characteristics, and Earnings Management*, 33 J. OF ACCT. & ECON. 375 (2002); Lawrence J. Abbott *et al.*, Audit Committee Characteristics and Financial Misstatement: A Study of the Efficacy of Certain Blue Ribbon Committee Recommendations (March 2002), available at http://papers.ssrn.com/sol3/papers.cfm?abstract_id=319125.

59. Armstrong *et al.*, *supra* note 3; Erickson *et al.*, *supra* note 3 (challenging implications of a relationship between contingent compensation and accounting fraud suggested by research on misreporting generally, such as in Natasha Burns and Simi Kedia, *The Impact of Performance-based Compensation on Misreporting*, 79 J. FINANCIAL ECONOMICS 35 (2006), and Jay Efendi *et al.*, *Why Do Corporate Managers Misstate Financial Statements? The Role of In-the-Money Option and Other Incentives*, 85 J. FINANCIAL ECONOMICS 667 (2007)). But see, Daniel Bergstresser and Thomas Philippon, *CEO Incentives and Earnings Management*, 80 J. FINANCIAL ECONOMICS 511 (2006) (finding use of discretionary accruals to manipulate reported earnings is positively related to the amount of CEO compensation tied to the value of stock and option holdings); Shane A. Johnson *et al.*, *Managerial Incentives and Corporate Fraud: The Sources of Incentives Matter*, 13 REVIEW OF FINANCE 115 (2009) (finding accounting fraud is positively related to incentives from unrestricted stock options).

60. Jeffrey Cohen, Yuan Ding, Cedric Lesage, and Herve Stolowy, The Role of Manager's Behavior in Corporate Fraud, available at http://papers.ssrn.com/sol3/papers.cfm?abstract_id=1160076; and Schrand and Zechman, *supra* note 8.

61. Baucus and Near, *supra* note 52.

62. Beneish, *supra* note 53.

63. Dechow *et al.*, *supra* note 54.

64. Armstrong *et al.*, *supra* note 3.

65. M. Guttentag *et al.*, *Brandeis' Policeman: Results from a Laboratory Experiment on How to Prevent Corporate Fraud*, 5 J. EMPIRICAL LEGAL STUDIES 244 (2008).

66. See *supra* notes 45 and 47 and accompanying text.

67. It is, of course, inappropriate to simply extrapolate from the failure to find an effect to the conclusion that no such effect exists. Therefore, findings from these studies can only be relied upon to show that the implications from experiments and field research about the lack of sensitivity to pay-outs observed in the context of other types of misbehavior are not contradicted by research on the causes of accounting fraud.
68. Jonathan Karpoff, D. Scott Lee, and Gerald S. Martin, *The Cost to Firms of Cooking the Books*, 43 J. Financial & Quantitative Analysis 581 (2008) (hereinafter Karpoff *et al.*, *Costs to Firms*); see also, Dechow *et al.*, *supra* note 58.
69. Karpoff, Lee, and Martin, *Consequences to Managers, supra* note 4.
70. Dechow *et al.*, *supra* note 54.
71. For a discussion of the reasons for reaching this conclusion, see *infra* note 91.
72. Jennifer Arlen, Public versus Private Enforcement of Securities Fraud, unpublished manuscript on file with author, at 27.
73. Erickson *et al.*, *supra* note 3, at 115.
74. *Id.*
75. See, e.g., discussion *infra* notes 89 to 92 and accompanying text.
76. See, e.g., discussion *infra* notes 93 to 103 and accompanying text.
77. Schrand and Zechman, *supra* note 8, at 1.
78. See section 2.1.3.
79. Darley, *supra* note 5, at 1186, citing Dale T. Miller and Cathy McFarland, *Pluralistic Ignorance: When Similarity is Interpreted as Dissimilarity*, 53 J. Personality & Social Psychol. 298 (1987).
80. Darley, *supra* note 5, at 1190.
81. Darley, *supra* note 5, at 1179.
82. See, e.g., D. Ramona Bobocel and John P. Meyer, *Escalating Commitment to a Failing Course of Action: Separating the Roles of Choice and Justification*, 79 J. Applied Psychol. 360 (1994).
83. Arlen and Carney, *supra* note 1.
84. Schrand and Zechman, *supra* note 8.
85. It may be helpful to note that these authors' interest in the relationship between uncertain future financial performance and accounting frauds is different than my own. These authors point to uncertainty about future financial performance as a way to explain how a decision to commit accounting fraud which looks irrational *ex post* may have appeared more reasonable *ex ante*. I highlight uncertainty about future financial performance to provide additional justification for using stochastic process models to understand accounting fraud.
86. For a general survey of small group research, see Joseph E. McGrath, Holly Arrow, and Jennifer L. Berdahl, *The Study of Groups: Past, Present, and Future*, 4 Personality & Soc. Psychology Rev. 95 (2000).
87. See, e.g., Amy C. Edmondson, *Learning from Mistakes is Easier Said Than Done: Group and Organizational Influences on the Detection and Correction of Human Error*, 32 J. Applied Behavioral Sci. 5 (1996) (hereinafter, Edmundson, *Learning from Mistakes*); Amy C. Edmondson, *The Local and Variegated Nature of Learning in Organizations: A Group-Level Perspective*, 13 Organizational Science 128 (2002).
88. Edmundson, *Learning from Mistakes, supra* note 87, at 17.
89. Arlen and Carney, *supra* note 1.
90. Arlen and Carney focus on incentives faced by the manager, because, as Arlen elsewhere notes, the Arlen and Carney model is an "agency cost hypothesis about the causes of accounting fraud." Arlen, *supra* note 72, at 26, note 60.
91. Arlen and Carney, *supra* note 1, at 702. According to Arlen and Carney, the reason it is likely that fraud will eventually be exposed is that it is unlikely that the "firm's subsequent operating results [will be] so positive that no one [will] have been harmed by an earlier positive statement." Arlen and Carney, *supra* note 1, at 701. Elsewhere, Arlen and Carney, *supra* note 1, at 701, elaborate that "because Fraud on the Market involves false statements made in a public way by company officials to a market populated by large, well-informed investors, ultimate detection of individual wrongdoers should be relatively certain." The hypothesis about the dynamic leading to accounting fraud developed in this chapter is consistent with this aspect of the Arlen and Carney account, in that it is assumed here, as well, that managers' likely pay-off from committing accounting fraud is highly negative.
92. Arlen and Carney, *supra* note 1, at 701.
93. Arlen herself has elsewhere observed that "[a]lthough there is considerable evidence that many frauds are a result of last period concerns, this hypothesis does not explain all frauds. The puzzle for conventional economic theory is why these other frauds occur. Employing behavioral analysis, Langevoort has suggested that perhaps some of these frauds are not actual frauds – in the sense of being intentional false statements – but rather often expressions of managers' self-serving, excessively over-optimistic view of the firm which, while lacking any reasonable basis, are nevertheless honestly held." Jennifer Arlen,

Comment: The Future of Behavioral Economic Analysis of Law, 51 VAND. L. REV. 1765, 1774–5 (1998) (citing Langevoort, *Organized Illusions, supra* note 2) (footnote omitted).

94. Langevoort, *Naked, Homeless, and Without Wheels, supra* note 2, at 635; Langevoort, *Organized Illusions, supra* note 2, at 139; Langevoort, *Resetting the Corporate Thermostat, supra* note 2, at 288.

95. Langevoort, *Naked, Homeless, and Without Wheels, supra* note 2, at 661; Langevoort, *Resetting the Corporate Thermostat, supra* note 2, at 288.

96. Langevoort, *Organized Illusions, supra* note 2, at 133–4.

97. Langevoort, *Organized Illusions, supra* note 2, at 108.

98. Langevoort, *Resetting the Corporate Thermostat, supra* note 2.

99. *Id.* at 308.

100. Manuel A. Utset, When Good People Do Bad Things: Time-Inconsistent Misconduct and Criminal Law, Working Paper (Draft: March 30, 2006) at 48, available at http://papers.ssrn.com/sol3/papers.cfm?abstract_id=895734 (hereinafter Utset, When Good People Do Bad Things) (arguing that people can "over consume misconduct in the same fashion that they over consume in other areas of their lives," at 2); see also, Manuel A. Utset, *Hyperbolic Criminals and Repeated Time-Inconsistent Misconduct*, 44 HOUS. L. REV. 610, 628 (2007); Manuel A. Utset, *Time-Inconsistent Boards and the Risk of Repeated Misconduct*, in CORPORATE BOARDS: MANGERS OF RISK (Robert W. Kolb and Donald Schwartz, eds., 2009).

101. Utset, When Good People Do Bad Things, *supra* note 100, at 19.

102. Baruch Lev, *Corporate Earnings: Facts and Fiction*, 17 J. ECON. PERSP. 27, 36 (2003) (emphasis added).

103. Schrand and Zechman, *supra* note 8, at 1 ("a manager with unrealistic (optimistic) expectations about future earnings realizations is more likely to underestimate the need for more egregious earnings management in the future periods").

104. Bucy *et al.*, *supra* note 6, at 406. Although he does not use the term "slippery slope," Harold Russell provides one of the most detailed discussions of a process which resembles a slippery slope dynamic leading to accounting fraud in HAROLD F. RUSSELL, FOOZLES AND FRAUDS (1977). See also, text accompanying *supra* note 6.

105. Langevoort, *Resetting the Corporate Thermostat, supra* note 2, at 308 (2004) ("This perspective suggests a slippery slope. Aggressiveness is mild when the threat to incumbency is distant, perhaps no more than taking advantage of norms and rules that are subject to multiple interpretations. As the threat grows, two things happen. First, there is an incentive to take even more chances (even as to illegality). It is human nature to become more aggressive when facing the risk of a loss, vis-à-vis some aspiration level, than when simply contemplating the possibility of a comparable gain. Second, the very fact of prior aggressiveness makes it more likely that a person will go a step further to prevent the loss. Gradually, the aggressiveness accumulates into a commitment to a course of action that weakens restraint. Deep into the process of concealment, deliberate falsification occurs more easily than it would at the outset.")

106. Schrand and Zechman, *supra* note 8, at 2, but see *supra* note 9 describing how the evidence they provide does not necessarily support this hypothesis.

107. Darley, *supra* note 5, at 1185.

108. Guttentag *et al.*, *supra* note 65, at 244 (footnotes omitted).

109. See, e.g., Eugene Volokh, *The Mechanisms of the Slippery Slope*, 116 HARV. L. REV. 1026, 1033 (2003) (identifying various mechanisms by which taking certain legislative action may lead down a "slippery slope" to undesirable future legislative actions).

110. See section 2.1.2.

111. JOSEPH RUDNICK and GEORGE GASPARI, ELEMENTS OF THE RANDOM WALK: AN INTRODUCTION FOR ADVANCED STUDENTS AND RESEARCHERS xi (2004).

112. See section 2.1.1.

113. See, e.g., MANTEGNA and STANLEY, *supra* note 15, at 127; VOIT, *supra* note 15, at 129.

114. See section 2.3.

115. See, e.g., RUDNICK and GASPARI, *supra* note 111, at 13.

116. However, as will be discussed below, the Markov property assumption will need to be relaxed to describe a stochastic process with a running maximum. See section 4.3.

117. See section 2.1.4.

118. See section 2.2.1.

119. The discussion of the mathematics of stochastic process analysis here largely follows the presentation in DIXIT and PINDYCK, *supra* note 14, at 59–92. Other useful references include: CRISPIN GARDNER, STOCHASTIC METHODS: A HANDBOOK FOR THE NATURAL AND SOCIAL SCIENCES (2009); MAHNKE *ET AL.*, *supra* note 16; MANTEGNA and STANLEY, *supra* note 15; RUDNICK and GASPARI, *supra* note 111; VAN KAMPEN, *supra* note 10; VOIT, *supra* note 15; and Le Gall, *supra* note 11.

120. DIXIT and PINDYCK, *supra* note 14, at 61–3; MAHNKE *ET AL.*, *supra* note 16, at 181–6; RUDNICK and GASPARI, *supra* note 111, at 1–10.

121. There is, of course, a relationship between the mathematics of a discrete step random walk and of a continuous step random walk. As the size of steps diminishes and the number of steps increases, the distribution resulting from the binomial formula approaches a normal distribution, which is the distribution for a continuous step random walk. See, e.g., MAHNKE *et al.*, *supra* note 16, at 185–6 (providing a derivation of the Gaussian structure of a continuous random walk); RUDNICK and GASPARI, *supra* note 111, at 10–12.
122. See sections 4.2. and 4.3.
123. DIXIT and PINDYCK, *supra* note 14, at 64–5.
124. In this respect, introducing a stochastic process analysis leads to parallels to the "broken windows" literature. See, e.g., James Q. Wilson and George L. Kelling, *Broken Windows: The Police and Neighborhood Safety*, ATLANTIC MONTHLY (March 1982).
125. See *supra* note 123 and accompanying text.
126. DIXIT and PINDYCK, *supra* note 14, at 74–5. For a derivation of this result see DIXIT and PINDYCK, *supra* note 14, at 90–1.
127. DIXIT and PINDYCK, *supra* note 14, at 78.
128. RICHARD FEYNMAN *ET AL.*, THE FEYNMAN LECTURES ON PHYSICS, Vol. 1, ch. 46 (1966).
129. See, e.g., R. Dean Astumian, *Thermodynamics and Kinetics of Brownian Motors*, 276 SCIENCE 917 (May 9, 1997).
130. Amir E. Khandani, Adrew W. Lo, and Robert C. Merton, *Systemic Risk and Refinancing Ratchet Effect* (September 13, 2009), available at http://papers.ssrn.com/sol3/papers.cfm?abstract_id=1472892.
131. Darryl K. Brown, *Democracy and Decriminalization*, 86 TEX. L. REV. 223 (2007).
132. Arthur C. Heinricher and Richard H. Stockbridge, *Optimal Control of the Running Max*, 29 SOCIETY FOR INDUSTRIAL AND APPLIED MATHEMATICS JOURNAL OF CONTROL AND OPTIMIZATION 936, 937 (1991).
133. By definition, the commission of a fraud requires intent to deceive. See, e.g., *Ernst & Ernst v. Hochfelder*, 425 U.S. 185, 194, note 12 (1976).
134. Stumbling into an accounting fraud in the manner described here involves a series of minor decisions, and at least some of these minor decisions are probably made with the requisite *scienter* to constitute a fraud.
135. See, e.g., *Tellabs, Inc. v. Makor Issues & Rights, Ltd.*, 551 U.S. 308, 325 (2007) ("While it is true that motive can be a relevant consideration, and personal financial gain may weigh heavily in favor of a *scienter* inference, we agree with the Seventh Circuit that the absence of a motive allegation is not fatal.")

9 The economics of prosecutors
Nuno Garoupa*

1. INTRODUCTION

The role of prosecutors in any given legal system is of critical importance in enforcing and effectively applying the law – criminal law in particular, as well as other areas of the law such as family law[1] and class action litigation.[2] The exact nature of the work performed by prosecutors and their institutional organizations varies across legal systems. Surprisingly, economists have studied prosecutors very little when compared to other legal and judicial professions.[3]

For a long time, the *efficient prosecutor model* has prevailed in law and economics, in particular since the publication of foundational works by Landes (1971) and Easterbrook (1983). Only more recently have economists started looking at prosecutors' preferences and behavior, and at their role in shaping the legal system.[4] For example, in the *efficient prosecutor model*, it only makes sense to provide full discretion to the prosecutor, particularly in the prosecution of more meritorious cases, in order to achieve efficient deterrence. Therefore, most rules of criminal procedure limiting the role of the prosecutor are inevitably inappropriate. Such was the general reasoning of the law and economics literature until recently.[5]

A more realistic economic model of prosecutors requires a deeper understanding of preferences, incentives, and institutional contexts. As with any other economic agent, we need to establish the preferences of prosecutors. At the same time, in order to explain their behavior, we must attend to the institutional incentives and constraints.

This chapter proposes that relevant differences concerning prosecutorial functions across the world deserve more serious consideration in law and economics. We start by looking at preferences and how they interact with institutional determinants. In the second part of the chapter, we offer some preliminary thoughts about advancing the economic analysis of prosecutors in a comparative perspective. The final section concludes the chapter.

2. PREFERENCES AND BEHAVIOR OF PROSECUTORS

The seminal paper by Landes (1971) proposed that prosecutors seek maximization of convictions weighted by sentence. Later, Easterbrook (1983) argued that prosecutors attempt to obtain maximum deterrence from the resources that are available. These models have nevertheless faced serious challenges and have generated empirical work that so far has not been very conclusive.[6] For instance, we still find a controversy between those who argue that prosecutors want to maximize convictions and those who argue that prosecutors are more concerned with the severity of sentences even at the expense of the number of convictions.[7]

One line of research, more European-oriented, has looked at prosecutors as a bureaucracy in which seniority is the most common criteria for promotion.[8] Incentives are for minimization of effort subject to a minimum acceptable performance. We have all the standard problems of low-powered contracts, namely moral hazard (shirking by prosecutors resulting in delays, amnesties, and procedural mistakes) and adverse selection (the career of a prosecutor does not attract the best lawyers). But even in this context, reputation matters somehow, and public recognition is certainly relevant. In a more recent paper (Garoupa 2009), we have developed a simple model to show that, due to agency costs between society and the prosecutor (such as prosecutorial insulation from her performance or risk aversion), certain rules (such as mandatory prosecution) might well be more appropriate than discretion.[9]

Prosecutors respond to monetary and non-monetary incentives. They value leisure as does everybody else. At the same time, their decisions vary with their tolerance to risk. Hence, risk preference is an important element to explain prosecutorial behavior. In Garoupa (2009), we offer three arguments to support the impression that European prosecutors could be more risk-averse and less motivated than American prosecutors: (i) the inquisitorial v. adversarial models; (ii) the relationship between the prosecutors and the enforcement agents (in general, the police forces); and (iii) the bureaucratic organization of the prosecutorial body in Europe. However, we do not know of any empirical comparative study that provides compelling evidence one way or the other; hence, our reasoning is based solely on the nature of prosecutorial bodies and their role in criminal procedure.

Different risk preference might explain why European and American prosecutors behave differently and seem to have dissimilar ways to handle, for example, criminal litigation. It might also point to different institutional palliatives to deal with possible shortcomings. Selection and performance effects cannot be fully understood without disentangling institutional context and prosecutorial preferences.

2.1   Inquisitorial vs. Adversarial Models

In the pure inquisitorial model, the prosecutor is neither the accuser nor the plaintiff's or victim's lawyer, but rather an aide to a judge who conducts the criminal trial; the prosecutor is supposed to help in the search for the facts and the truth, and she should not unilaterally represent the interests of the plaintiff (whether the plaintiff is the victim or society). By contrast, in the ideal adversarial model, the prosecutor is the plaintiff's lawyer (where the plaintiff is society or the community) and is therefore an adversary of the defendant. Obviously, none of the existing models is purely inquisitorial or purely adversarial (there is in fact an apparent trend to convergence across jurisdictions).[10] However, in the countries with a predominant inquisitorial system, the prosecutor's role is secondary to the judge; in those with a predominant adversarial system, the prosecutor has a specific role quite distinct and certainly not secondary to the judge.[11]

The inquisitorial nature of criminal procedure has consequences in terms of production of evidence, revelation of facts, type of errors, and effective functioning of adjudication.[12] Clearly, the secondary role of the prosecutor in proceedings and the non-partisan nature of the job are more attractive for risk-averse individuals. On the other hand, the distinct role of an adversarial prosecutor, not least of which its partisan nature, makes it more appealing for less risk-averse individuals.

Focusing on a possible selection effect, we should compare the risk imposed on prosecutors versus the risk imposed on lawyers (since presumably individuals can choose one legal career or the other). Within the adversarial model, it is unclear if a prosecutor bears more or less risk than a lawyer; therefore, the selection effect in this regard should not be significant. However, within the inquisitorial model, there is little doubt that a prosecutor bears less risk than a lawyer. Here, we presumably could expect a significant selection effect, with more risk-averse individuals opting for the prosecutorial career and less risk-averse individuals opting for a non-prosecutorial legal profession.

2.2 Relationship Between the Prosecutors and the Enforcement Agencies

The second aspect to consider is that the prosecutorial body obviously has to rely on enforcement agencies. The relationship between the prosecutor and the enforcement agency is important. The key elements that determine the combination between prosecution and enforcement are the benefits of specialization (monitoring and enforcement are in many cases distinct from prosecution and criminal litigation); the costs of coordination (a successful prosecution usually relies on a good, solid investigation); and the existence of hindsight bias with high social costs (a second assessment of the quality of the evidence before prosecution increases the chances of avoiding an erroneous prosecution, which is costly to society).[13]
Here we offer a brief typology:

(a) Hierarchy   The prosecutorial body has a strong possession over prosecutorial rights (eventually a monopoly) and a considerable degree of control over the agency's investigative resources and tactics (in some particular cases the prosecutorial body also plays the adjudication role of a judge).[14]

In this institutional arrangement, the costs of coordination are plausibly minimal. However, the benefits of specialization are not explored to the maximum extent. Moreover, the possibility of hindsight bias as well as a significant imbalance between plaintiff and defendant should be matters of concern. Not surprisingly, the hierarchical model requires some external forms of accountability (including procedural rules) that restrain the negative effects of hindsight bias and abuse of power.

A hierarchical model allows for riskier litigation strategies and a less conservative management of caseload because there is a better control over resources and possible outcomes.

(b) Coordination   The prosecutorial body has more prosecutorial rights than the agency but has a limited ability to influence the agency's investigative decision-making.

This is a more a balanced institutional arrangement. The coordination costs can be significant, but the approach also allows for important specialization gains. Hindsight bias is less likely, and readdressing the balance between defendant and plaintiff is presumably easier (by facilitating the defendant's direct access to the enforcement agency).

A coordination model makes riskier litigation strategies and a more aggressive management of caseload more expensive since the prosecutorial body does not have full control over the production of evidence. External costs are not fully internalized since there are two independent actors.

(c) Subordination   The prosecutorial body is weak (it only reviews the evidence provided by the agency) or ultimately fully subordinated to the agency (it is a branch of the enforcement agency).[15]

Like the hierarchical model, the subordination model has lower costs of coordination and fewer significant benefits from specialization. Hindsight bias can be significant. The difference between the subordination and hierarchical models is that the prosecutorial body is the weak party in the former model whereas it is the strong party in the latter model.

A subordination model does not provide for many options in terms of prosecutorial strategies, since prosecutors are subject to the policies designed by the enforcement agency. In this regard, more or less riskier strategies are imposed on prosecutors rather than being shaped in any fundamental way by them.

Different solutions, such as modifications to the budget or to the allocation of resources, generate distinct levels of risk as well as different incentives to prosecutors.[16] Whereas the American model is somewhat closer to the hierarchical system, the European model seems similar to a coordination system, with the United Kingdom[17] being closer to the subordination model. As the prosecutor loses control over prosecution rights and allocation of investigative resources, the risk of not achieving the prosecutorial goals is higher. Therefore, this is another reason to think that the European model should attract more risk-averse individuals than the American model. And if control over prosecution rights and allocation of investigation resources operate as an incentive device, the European model produces fewer incentives than the American model.

The relationship between prosecutors and enforcement agencies reinforces the selection effect and the asymmetric incentives we already identified in comparing the inquisitorial and adversarial models.

2.3   Organization of Prosecution

The last aspect we want to add to our argument is the ability to use discretion in order to make efficient choices over meritorious cases and available resources.[18] The sense seems to be that European prosecutors have less discretion than their American counterparts and are more controlled by heavy bureaucracy. (We should recall that in many European countries prosecutors are part of the judiciary and are subject to high judicial councils, something quite different from the American reality.) Therefore, the success or failure of prosecution is usually attributed to the prosecutorial service or bureaucracy and less so to individual prosecutors. In this context, we have the standard problem of adequate team incentives and performance evaluation. In sum, incentives seem weaker for individual European prosecutors than for individual American prosecutors in this respect.

If our arguments hold true (which ultimately requires empirical testing), our analysis indicates that prosecutors might have different preferences and risk attitudes across the world. In fact, it could be that, for example, mandatory prosecution prevailing in civil law countries is as adequate as selective prosecution prevailing in common law countries. Such an observation is independent of the historical reasons why one regime or the other has been adopted by a specific legal family. We merely point out that they might be consistent with other institutional characteristics. These institutional characteristics matter, and they might justify one regime or the other, contrary to the argument (defended by Easterbrook (1983)) for a universal *efficient prosecutor*.

The three aspects of prosecutors we have discussed explain, in our view, why the preferences exhibited by prosecutors are different. Consequently, not only does prosecutorial behavior vary, but so too does the need for different palliatives to readdress the shortcomings associated with each institutional solution. An adversarial model with a hierarchy and discretion (American prosecution) implies certain features that are different from an inquisitorial model with coordination and a lack of discretion (European prosecution).

Two points should be emphasized. First, we are not suggesting that one solution is better, in terms of efficiency, than the other solution. Both have costs and benefits. Both are likely to respond to local determinants. Second, although we point out correlation across the three aspects (criminal litigation, relationship between prosecutors and enforcement agencies, organization of prosecution), we do not suggest causation. This is certainly a point that requires further analysis, not least of which in the context of legal reform, since we know transplants in law can only be successful if we properly identify causation rather than mere correlation.

3.   PARTICULAR CASE OF PLEA-BARGAINING

Most of the economics of prosecutors has been developed in the context of a discussion about the efficiency advantages and disadvantages of plea-bargaining.[19] Evidently the role of the prosecutor in plea-bargaining depends very much on the understanding of the nature of the accuser in criminal law. Tort litigation, for example, simply aims at gaining compensation for some wrongdoing (thus assuring an efficient deterrence of accidents). We could say that the prosecutor aims at obtaining a conviction in such a way that the criminal compensates society for his crimes (hence achieving an efficient deterrence of crime). Such an approach would make the prosecutor a kind of plaintiff's lawyer in criminal cases, an interpretation that several scholars seem to have of the role of the prosecutor in adversarial systems.[20]

For reasons that are beyond the scope of this chapter, but have been discussed within the law and economics literature, the plaintiff in criminal cases should be seen not as the direct victim but as society.[21] The prosecutor is therefore the agent of society, with an aggregate perspective of the criminal justice system, whereas lawyers usually have the perspective of an individual case. How then are the interests of the agent to be aligned with those of the principal (society)?

Recently, legal economists have recognized that it is not obvious why prosecutors maximize social welfare since there is no obvious high-powered contract between prosecutors and society.[22] Some scholars argue that if prosecutors do not maximize social welfare, they will be sacked or will not be re-elected (where that is possible, i.e., in the American case). For example, in the United States, the tremendous power exerted by criminal prosecutors is counterbalanced by sentencing guidelines, the supervisory powers doctrine, the doctrine of separation of powers, professional discipline, and the political process. These mechanisms help lower agency costs between prosecutors and society. In a sense, contrary to the typical short-term relationship between the defendant and his lawyer, the prosecutor has a long-term relationship with society (her entire career) and hence there is a repeated game. Badly behaved prosecutors are likely to be punished at some point, and this should be enough to align the general interests of society with those of the prosecutor. This is the essence of the *efficient prosecutor model.*

We take the view that there are several reasons to think that agency costs between society and prosecutors are usually quite high. With institutional arrangements in place, even direct elections do not guarantee that inefficient prosecutors are punished, and hence private interests might prevail over the maximization of social welfare. Those who monitor prosecutorial behaviour – either the electorate that votes every four years or the bureaucratic bodies that prevail in most countries – have their own agenda that is usually not social welfare maximizing. Moreover, we are faced with the usual problem of specialization versus capture. The larger and less specialized the monitoring body is (e.g., the electorate), the less they are able to evaluate properly the decisions taken by the prosecutor. The smaller and more specialized the monitoring body (e.g., a supervisory body composed of senior and former prosecutors), the more likely it is to be captured.

Once we recognize that prosecutors are quite unconstrained by a powerful monitoring body that assures efficient selection of cases and allocation of effort, two important questions arise: (1) the preferences or goals of the prosecutors, and (2) how certain constraints on prosecutorial decision-making (e.g., mandatory prosecution, prosecutorial guidelines, judicial scrutiny of prosecutorial decisions, rules concerning the consideration of alternative sanctions and cautioning measures, regulation of prosecutor fines, sentencing recommendation, rules of appeal, mode of trial, charging rules, etc.) are actually weak substitutes for effective monitoring. It is clear that any kind of constraint on prosecutors only makes sense if we think that the *efficient prosecutor model* does not exist. We should emphasize that the choice of cases by the prosecutor guarantees neither efficient deterrence of crime nor the maximization of external effects of going to trial (further development of the law or jurisprudence and testing of doctrines) when the goals are different from social welfare.

The efficiency of plea-bargaining could be seriously compromised when prosecutors do not maximize social welfare. Although there is a tendency to think that inefficient prosecutors are closer to the European model than the American model, we should be careful. First, obtaining more severe sanctions at the expense of low rates of conviction is not necessarily efficient (on average, we increase the severity but reduce the probability of punishment; the overall effect is quite ambiguous). Second, precisely because prosecutors in inquisitorial systems such as France and Italy are essentially bureaucrats, their powers are more limited; however, in adversarial systems, prosecutors have more latitude, which is quite problematic if their goals are not sufficiently aligned with those of society.

Whereas common law countries have selective prosecution systems, civil law countries usually have mandatory prosecution (usually subject to the opportunity principle, which gives the prosecutor some degree of discretion).[23] Obviously, the efficient prosecutor should operate in a system of selective prosecution in order to implement successful screening. Plea-bargaining is a process that induces such an outcome. However, as we move away from the efficient prosecutor, the selection of cases is less likely to be an appropriate focus, and mandatory prosecution starts making sense. The problem with mandatory prosecution is not the lack of screening, but the allocation of the prosecutor's effort across the volume of cases. In a mandatory prosecution system, not only can shirking be a serious problem but also workload can become grave. Therefore, plea-bargaining could be a useful mechanism not for screening cases but for improving the allocation of effort and for solving congestion in criminal trials.

In sum, plea-bargaining may be seen as a transaction arrived at by two agents whose interests are not perfectly aligned with those of their principals.[24] On the other hand, it could be that rather than discussing plea-bargaining, we should look for the appropriate criminal procedure reforms in order to mitigate the problems we have encountered if plea-bargaining is to be appropriately implemented.

4.   THE INSTITUTIONAL ARRANGEMENT

We have established that the performance of prosecutors varies significantly with institutional incentives. We have also argued that the preferences exhibited by prosecutors are not the same across the world in response to institutional constraints. We turn now to how different jurisdictions have addressed these incentives and constraints.

Table 9.1 summarizes the main institutional arrangements. We start by distinguishing three types of prosecutorial agencies, depending on the branch of government into which they are integrated. In the United States, prosecutors belong to the executive branch. In the United Kingdom, the Crown Prosecution Service responds directly to the Parliament – hence, it is part of the legislative branch, broadly defined.[25] In most European countries, under different formulations, prosecutors belong to the judicial branch and might enjoy the same constitutional privileges as the judiciary.[26] Each of these three arrangements creates different behavioral incentives and responds in a particular way to the relevant constraints.

One way in which jurisdictions differ is the independence of prosecutors to decide who to prosecute, how to prosecute, how to allocate resources and how to address criminal procedure (in other words, how prosecutors use their discretion). In particular, the extent to which prosecutors are insulated from political pressure and can assess the merits of criminal cases without a particular political agenda, is important. Clearly, the possibility

Table 9.1   Institutional arrangements

	Independence from external pressure	Accountability	Available resources	Adversarial role	Interaction with police and other enforcement authorities
Executive branch (US)	Low	High	High	High	High
Legislative branch (UK)	Medium	Medium	Medium	Medium	Low
Judicial branch (Europe)	High	Low	Low	Low	High

of capture by government interests is highest when the prosecutors belong to the executive branch and is minimal when the prosecutors belong to the judicial branch.

The other side of the coin is accountability. Capture by private interests, professional interests, or even one's own agenda is more likely when accountability is weak. Inevitably, accountability is highest when prosecutors are under the tutelage of the executive branch. It is minimal when they belong to the judiciary.[27] As to the case of the legislative branch, given the serious asymmetry of information, agency control might not be so effective.

A third relevant dimension is the access to appropriate resources that allow prosecutors to perform their function. Under the executive branch, the control of the budget and resources can be more directly exercised by the prosecutors. The government does not need to use the budget and the resources to manipulate prosecution, since prosecutors are directly monitored. Under the judicial branch, usually prosecutors have little control over their budget (which is generally directed by the executive branch under the Ministry of Justice or the Ministry of Interior). The ability to manage resources shapes the strategies prosecutors can follow, the capacity to model incentives within the agency, and even the type of individuals willing to perform such jobs. Locating the prosecutors within the executive or judicial branch has significant consequences to the type of prosecutors we find. Not surprisingly, the inquisitorial system is usually correlated with prosecutors located in the judicial branch, whereas the adversarial system seems more appropriate with prosecutors located in the other branches of government. This leads us to the fourth and final dimension we should consider.

The last dimension we include in our analysis has already been discussed in section 2: the interaction between prosecutors and enforcement agencies (including police and other specialized agencies). When both enforcement agencies and prosecutors are under the same branch of government, the interaction is easier and presumably more productive. When they belong to different branches of government, the coordination is relatively more problematic since they serve different principals. Clashes of jurisdiction can happen. Nevertheless, when prosecutors belongs to the judiciary, they are still in a strong position to influence and exercise control by making use of the privileges of the judicial branch.

Looking at Table 9.1, we can easily conclude that prosecutors' position in the executive branch (largely speaking, the American solution) essentially raises questions concerning their political independence. In terms of incentives and resources, this solution is likely to be closer to high-powered contracts than to any other alternative, but the legal policy agenda might be too clouded by short-run political goals, thus raising doubts concerning social welfare maximization. In this context, judicial review plays a fundamental role in keeping prosecution under the standard rules of law. The evolution of many rules of criminal procedure can also be understood in the context of developing palliatives to address these possible shortcomings.

On the other side, we have prosecutors under the judicial branch (broadly, the European model).[28] Such a solution minimizes political dependence but also raises other concerns, as summarized in Table 9.1. This solution is dominated by low-powered contracts, possible capture by professional self-interests, and a more general problem concerning access to necessary resources. The most acute problems in this setting are the funding of prosecutorial services (which are generally controlled by the executive branch) and the blurred line between court judges and prosecutors. Jurisdictions with this institutional model tend to struggle with designing incentives to promote performance and accountability.

There is a third solution, prosecutors under the legislative branch, that seems to balance the independence and accountability concerns (largely the current British model). However, the most serious drawback seems to be the weak position of this solution vis-à-vis other enforcement agencies.[29] In fact, in Britain, recent legislative reforms have tried to address this weakness by allocating more effective powers to the prosecutors.[30]

Each institutional arrangement seems to respond to specific concerns. The implications in terms of incentives, risk preferences, and potential selection effects in explaining prosecutorial behavior are significant. The transplant of particular rules or institutions of criminal procedure (such as plea-bargaining) cannot be understood without taking into account how these different arrangements shape the prosecution.

5.   CONCLUSION

The economics of prosecutors is largely under-developed. The literature necessarily must look at preferences and incentives in a more sophisticated way than the traditional *efficient prosecutor model*. We have argued that particular institutional arrangements shape the behavior of the prosecutors, not only by providing certain incentives but also by inducing a selection effect that attracts different human capital.

A more macro-oriented analysis can identify three different loci of institutional design. Prosecutors can be under each of the three branches of government: executive, legislative, and judicial. Each solution raises different concerns in terms of (political) independence and accountability. Inevitably, the way each institutional design responds to the appropriate balance between independence (including prosecutorial discretion) and accountability has serious implications for the use of prosecutorial resources, the quality of prosecution, and the coordination between prosecution and other enforcement agencies.

Our chapter suggests a line of research by which the economics of prosecutors should consider how these three different institutional designs influence the fundamentals of an economic model (preferences and incentives). Such assessment might be more appropriate for discussing the effects of transplanting rules of criminal procedure, such as plea-bargaining, rather than persisting with the *efficient prosecutor model* that largely ignores institutional differences.

NOTES

*   I am grateful to Alon Harel and Keith Hylton for helpful comments and to Roya Samarghandi for excellent research assistance. The usual disclaimers apply.

1.   Many civil law jurisdictions have specialized prosecutors in family law working in family courts.
2.   Prosecutors take a leading role in class action litigation in Brazil; see Gidi (2003).
3.   This is a criticism already echoed more than 30 years ago by Forst and Brosi (1977).
4.   See the references cited by Garoupa and Stephen (2008) and discussion thereafter.
5.   *Id*. See also Hylton and Khanna (2007).

6. See the discussion by Richman (1996 and 1997).
7. See, among others, Glaeser *et al.* (2000); Saxonhouse (2001); Shepherd (2002); Huber and Sanford (2002); Boylan (2004 and 2005); Boylan and Long (2005); and Raghav *et al.* (2009).
8. See, among others, Boari and Fiorentini (2001); van Aaken *et al.* (2004); and Voigt *et al.* (2010).
9. Pakes (2004) distinguishes the principle of legality (if there is sufficient evidence, the individual should be prosecuted; hence there is discretion to determine not to prosecute) and the principle of opportunity (prosecution should be brought if it serves public interest; hence there is discretion to determine to prosecute; and public interest might be defined by guidelines such as in Britain).
10. See Jörg *et al.* (1995).
11. See Fonda (1995), characterizing the inquisitorial system as one where the role of the prosecutor is more neutral while the trial judge has an active duty in the investigation and examination of evidence. Also see Jörg *et al.* (1995), characterizing an inquisitorial system as one where the fact-collecting prosecutor and an independent and impartial trial judge are involved in truth-seeking. However, while truth emerges from competition in adversarial systems, it will be derived from judicial checking of fact gathering in the inquisitorial system.
12. See, among others, Shin (1998); Froeb and Kobayashi (2001); Block *et al.* (2000); Parisi (2002); Block and Parker (2004); Palumbo (2006).
13. See Garoupa *et al.* (2011) for a more general discussion.
14. See, for example, the discussion by Coate and Kleit (1998).
15. For example, prosecution by the police as in the traditional common law. See Pakes (2004).
16. See, among others, Richman (2003); Garoupa *et al.* (2011).
17. See Fonda (1995) looking at the restricted powers of the Crown Prosecution Service.
18. See, among others, Reinganum (1988); Bjerk (2005); Garoupa and Stephen (2008).
19. See, e.g., Garoupa and Stephen (2008); Gazal-Ayal and Riza (2009); Miceli (2009).
20. See, for example, Boari and Fiorentini (2001); Garoupa and Stephen (2008).
21. See Bowles *et al.* (2008).
22. See Garoupa and Stephen (2008).
23. Fonda (1995) distinguishes the common law expediency principle (which might differ depending on the duty to justify whether to prosecute or whether not to prosecute) and the civil law legality principle (prosecution is mandatory as long as there is sufficient evidence of guilt, and public interest criteria are irrelevant to determine the decision to prosecute).
24. An alternative conceptualisation is that it is a bargain that has an external effect on parties nominally but not directly involved in the bargain.
25. For example, the public interest criteria for the Crown Prosecution Service are defined by parliamentary guidelines (Code for Crown Prosecutors); see Fonda (1995). The codification of police rules enhances control of abuses but also promotes a traditionally weak prosecution; see Field *et al.* (1995).
26. As Pakes (2004) argues, prosecutors are sitting magistrates in most civil law systems.
27. Even judicial review of decisions by prosecutors is more problematic under this solution since both judges and prosecutors belong to the same branch of government. For a general discussion concerning the importance of judicial review of prosecutorial decisions, see Brants and Field (1995).
28. Largely the French and Italian models. For example, in the Netherlands and in Spain, the prosecutors are accountable to the Ministry of Justice. Political independence is assured by statutory safeguards and mandatory written justifications. See Fonda (1995). Other authors emphasize judicial review as the mechanism to constrain the Dutch prosecutors. See Field *et al.* (1995).
29. Under current English law, the neutrality of the prosecutor is a statutory principle, including independence from the police; the prosecution is only accountable to Parliament for general conduct of prosecution policy (a much weaker principle is adopted in the Scottish case). See Fonda (1995) at 89.
30. See Garoupa *et al.* (2011).

REFERENCES

Aaken, Anne van, Eli Salzberger and Stefan Voigt (2004) "The Prosecution of Public Figures and the Separation of Powers: Confusion Within the Executive Branch – A Conceptual Framework," 15 *Constitutional Political Economy* 261

Bjerk, David (2005) "Making the Crime Fit the Penalty: The Role of Prosecutorial Discretion under Mandatory Minimum Sentencing," 48 *Journal of Law and Economics* 591

Block, Michael K., Libor Dusek, Jeffrey S. Parker, and O. Vyborna (2000) "An Experimental Comparison of Adversarial versus Inquisitorial Procedural Regimes," 2 *American Law and Economics Review* 170

Block, Michael K. and Jeffrey S. Parker (2004) "Decision Making in the Absence of Successful Fact Finding: Theory and Experimental Evidence on Adversarial versus Inquisitorial Systems of Adjudication," 24 *International Review of Law and Economics* 89

Boari, Nicola and Gianluca Fiorentini (2001) "An Economic Analysis of Plea Bargaining: The Incentives of the Parties in a Mixed Penal System," 21 *International Review of Law and Economics* 213

Bowles, Roger Michael Faure, and Nuno Garoupa (2008) "The Scope of Criminal Law and Criminal Sanctions: An Economic View and Policy Implications," 35 *Journal of Law and Society* 389

Boylan, Richard (2004) "Salaries, Turnover, and Performance in the Federal Criminal Justice System," 47 *Journal of Law and Economics* 75

— (2005) "What do Prosecutors Maximize? Evidence from the Careers of US Attorneys," 7 *American Law and Economics Review* 379

Boylan, Richard and Cheryl Long (2005) "Salaries, Plea Rates, and the Career Objectives of Federal Prosecutors," 48 *Journal of Law and Economics* 627

Brants, Chrisje and Stewart Field (1995) "Discretion and Accountability in Prosecution: A Comparative Perspective on Keeping Crime out of Court," in *Criminal Justice in Europe: A Comparative Study*, Christopher Harding, Phil Fennell, Nico Jörg and Bert Swart, eds., Oxford: Clarendon Press

Coate, Malcolm B. and Andrew N. Kleit (1998) "Does it Matter that the Prosecutor is also the Judge? The Administrative Complaint Process at the Federal Trade Commission," 19 *Managerial Decision and Economics* 1

Easterbrook, Frank (1983) "Criminal Procedure as a Market System," 12 *Journal of Legal Studies* 289

Field, Stewart, Peter Alldridge, and Nico Jörg (1995) "Prosecutors, Examining Judges, and Control of Police Investigations," in *Criminal Justice in Europe: A Comparative Study*, Christopher Harding, Phil Fennell, Nico Jörg and Bert Swart, eds., Oxford: Clarendon Press

Fonda, Julia (1995) *Public Prosecutors and Discretion: A Comparative Study*, Oxford: Clarendon Press

Forst, Brian and Kathleen B. Brosi (1977) "A Theoretical and Empirical Analysis of the Prosecutor," 6 *Journal of Legal Studies* 177

Froeb, Luke M. and Bruce H. Kobayashi (2001) "Evidence Production in Adversarial vs. Inquisitorial Regimes," 70 *Economic Letters* 267

Garoupa, Nuno (2009) "Some Reflections on the Economics of Prosecutors: Mandatory v. Selective Prosecution," 29 *International Review of Law and Economics* 25

Garoupa, Nuno, Anthony Ogus and Andrew Sanders (2011) "The Investigation and Prosecution of Regulatory Offences: Is There an Economic Case for Integration?," 70 *Cambridge Law Journal* 229

Garoupa, Nuno and Frank Stephen (2008) "Why Plea-Bargaining Fails to Achieve Results in So Many Criminal Justice Systems: A New Framework for Assessment," 15 *Maastricht Journal of European and Comparative Law* 319

Gazal-Ayal, Oren and Limor Riza (2009) "Plea-bargaining and Prosecution," in *Criminal Law and Economics*, Nuno Garoupa, ed., Edward Elgar, 145–70

Gidi, Antonio (2003) "Class Actions in Brazil: A Model for Civil Law Countries," 51 *American Journal of Comparative Law* 311

Glaeser, Edward, Daniel Kessler, and Ann Piehl (2000) "What Do Prosecutors Maximize? An Analysis of the Federalization of Drug Crimes," 2 *American Law and Economics Review* 259

Hylton, Keith N. and Vikramaditya S. Khanna (2007) "A Public Choice Theory of Criminal Prosecution," 15 *Supreme Court Economic Review* 61

Huber, Gregory and Gordon Sanford (2002) "Information, Evaluation, and the Electoral Incentives of Criminal Prosecutors," 46 *American Journal of Political Science* 334

Jörg, Nico, Stewart Field and Chrisje Brants (1995) "Are Inquisitorial and Adversarial Systems Converging?," in *Criminal Justice in Europe: A Comparative Study*, Christopher Harding, Phil Fennell, Nico Jörg and Bert Swart, eds., Oxford: Clarendon Press

Landes, William (1971) "An Economic Analysis of the Courts," 14 *Journal of Law and Economics* 61

Miceli, Thomas J. (2009) "Criminal Procedure," in *Criminal Law and Economics*, Nuno Garoupa, ed., Edward Elgar, 125–44.

Palumbo, Giuliana (2006) "Optimal Duplication of Effort in Advocacy Systems," 60 *Journal of Economic Behavior and Organization* 112

Pakes, Francis (2004) *Comparative Criminal Justice*, Willan Publishing

Parisi, Francesco (2002) "Rent-Seeking Through Litigation: Adversarial and Inquisitorial Systems Compared," 22 *International Review of Law and Economics* 193

Raghav, Manu, Mark Ramseyer, and Eric Rasmusen (2009) "Convictions versus Conviction Rates: The Prosecutor's Choice," 11 *American Law and Economics Review* 47

Reinganum, Jennifer (1988) "Plea Bargaining and Prosecutorial Discretion," 78 *American Economic Review* 713

Richman, Daniel C. (1996) "Bargaining about Future Jeopardy," 49 *Vanderbilt Law Review* 1181

— (1997) "Old Chief v. United States: Stipulating Away Prosecutorial Accountability?" 83 *Virginia Law Review* 939

— (2003) "Prosecutors and their Agents, Agents and their Prosecutors," 103 *Columbia Law Review* 749

Saxonhouse, Gary (2001) "How to Explain Japan's Legal System," 3 *American Law and Economics Review* 376

Shepherd, Joanna M. (2002) "Police, Prosecutors, Criminals and Determinate Sentencing: The Truth about Truth-in-Sentencing Laws," 45 *Journal of Law and Economics* 509

Shin, Hyun Song (1998) "Adversarial and Inquisitorial Procedures in Arbitration," 29 *Rand Journal of Economics* 378

Voigt, Stefan Lars Feld, and Anne van Aaken (2010) "Do Independent Prosecutors deter Political Corruption? An Empirical Evaluation Across 78 Countries," 12 *American Law and Economics Review* 204

10 Mobile phones and crime deterrence: an underappreciated link

Jonathan Klick, John MacDonald, and Thomas Stratmann

1. INTRODUCTION

The crime decline observed in the 1990s is remarkable. Between 1991 and 2001, crime rates dropped by about a one-third across all crime categories. Perhaps more notable, this decline was almost completely unforeseen. Given the sheer magnitude of this unpredicted decline, it is not surprising that finding explanations for it is a central focus of modern empirical crime scholarship.

Explanations range from the intuitive – more cops equal less crime (e.g., Evans and Owens 2007) as does the greater use of prison (Spelman 2006), to the provocative – legalized abortion culls the population of potential criminals (Donohue and Levitt 2001), and everything in between. In an influential review of the topic, Levitt (2004) suggests that four factors, abortion legalization, increases in police forces, changes in the market for crack cocaine, and rising prison populations, account for virtually all the crime decline. Of these factors, Levitt and other scholars suggest prisons provide the largest contribution to the crime drop (Blumstein and Wallman 2000).

However, Levitt notes a puzzle. Prison populations increased during the period 1973–1991. Based on the calculations he uses to analyse the 1991–2001 period, he would have predicted large crime rate declines in the earlier period too when, in fact, reported crime increased significantly in the 1970s and 1980s according to the FBI's Uniform Crime Report (UCR) data. To some extent, concerns about reported property crime are mitigated when alternate self-report data are used. Crime rates documented using the National Crime Victimization Survey (NCVS) data show that property crime rates appear to decline by the magnitude Levitt predicts. The NCVS data do not support Levitt's violent crime estimates. This leads Levitt to suggest that there was something different occurring in the earlier period, rather than leading him to revise the confidence he has in his 1991–2001 analysis.[1]

Cook and Laub (2002) also note that these cohort and period explanations for the crime decline in the 1990s do not account for the fact that the sharpest drop in violent crime rates occurred among older adults. Rising violence rates among young adults from the 1980s and 1990s have remained fairly stable in the post-crime drop period, suggesting that shifting cohorts from legalized abortion aren't likely the cause of the crime drop. Cook and MacDonald (2010) also note that sharp period effects are less evident for property crimes, where the data from NCVS suggest that property crime rates began dropping significantly in the late 1970s. Residential burglaries (break-ins and attempts) in particular have declined by 70% between 1976 and 2007.

While it is reasonable to suggest that effects may change over time, thus explaining the discrepancy in fit of explanations between periods, another approach is to look for unaccounted factors that may bias the estimates used for these calculations, focusing especially on factors that might have been at work in the later period of the 1990s but not during the earlier decades. Some possibilities include the effect of declining lead exposure levels for children in the 1970s and 1980s as discussed in Reyes (2007), and changes in fetal alcohol exposure occurring after this was identified as a harm to children in the medical literature in 1973. The desegregation of schools in states through court orders to enforce *Brown v. Board of Education* is another example (Weiner, Lutz, and Ludwig 2010). The growth in private security in public spaces through the expansion of business improvement districts in the 1990s also appears to be associated with significant reductions in crime in a few case studies (Brooks 2008; Cook and MacDonald 2011a).

The expansion of new crime prevention technologies is another set of factors that might be at work during the crime drop of the 1990s. Technologies for motor vehicle theft prevention, including the installation of immobilizers and vehicle-tracking systems like Lojack (Ayres and Levitt 1998) and OnStar appear to be associated with dramatic reductions in theft rates in the United Kingdom and the United States (Cook and MacDonald 2011b).

Along those lines, in this chapter, we present a novel suggestion that the introduction and growth of mobile phone technology may have contributed to the crime decline in the 1990s, specifically in the areas of rape and assault. While mobile phone data availability precludes us from directly investigating this link, examination of later data suggests that such a link is plausible and could be an important missing element in understanding what happened in the 1990s. Given that mobile phones increase surveillance and the risks of apprehension when committing crimes against strangers, an expansion of this technology would increase the costs of crime as perceived by forward-looking criminals.

Although official sources do not document mobile phone subscriptions before 1999, general impressions do match up with many of the stylized facts concerning the crime decline in the 1990s. The first commercially available mobile phone was introduced in 1983, but it wasn't until the mid-1990s that more than a trivial share of the US population used the technology, as seen in Figure 10.1. This coincides with the beginning of the crime decline.

Other facts about the crime decline highlighted by Levitt (2004), such as the concentration of the effect in urban areas and the fact that the decline was greatest in the Northeast, appear to match the stylized facts regarding the growth of the mobile phone market as well.

In this chapter, we present the intuition behind a connection between mobile phones and crime. We then use the available mobile phone data to show that there is a strongly negative association between mobile phones and violent crimes, although data limitations preclude us from being able to make any claims about causality. We show how the intuition about mobile phones providing crime deterrence fits in nicely with modern discussions in the crime literature regarding optimal policy and the expanding use of private security precautions in crime prevention.

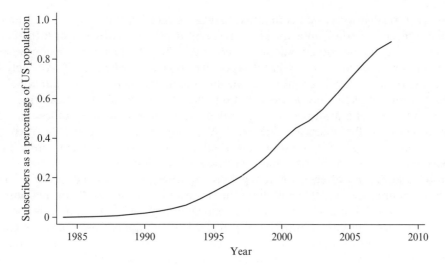

Source: FCC (2010): Local Telephone Competition available at http://transition.fcc.gov/web/iatd/comp. html

Figure 10.1   Mobile phone subscribers in the United States

2.   MOBILE PHONES AND CRIME

In the standard Becker framework, an individual commits a crime if the expected benefits of the crime exceed the costs. The expected benefits include any pecuniary or psychic benefits the individual receives from the crime. These benefits are adjusted by the individual's perceived likelihood of success. The expected cost side of the inequality includes the likelihood the individual will be punished and the individual's utility loss from the punishment.

The likelihood of punishment includes a number of factors, including the likelihood the individual will be identified, apprehended, prosecuted, convicted, and punished, as well as extra-legal factors such as the likelihood the victim or bystanders will mete out punishments defensively or as vigilantes. Most public policy interventions focus on this side of the equation, attempting to increase either the likelihood of punishment or the utility loss arising from the punishment.

Cook (1986) notes that opportunities for crime vary substantially by the attractiveness of potential victims and their level of investment in their own protection. A routine activities theory of crime is also consistent with a Becker framework (Cohen and Felson 1979). Routine activities theory suggests that crime on the aggregate increases with an increasing convergence between suitable targets of crime, potential offenders, and the lack of capable guardians against a violation. Mobile phones provide additional surveillance of motivated offenders, which is a form of increased guardianship for suitable targets of crime.

The presence of mobile phones increases the likelihood of punishment along a number of different margins. Unless law enforcement personnel happen to be located in close proximity to a crime, the first step toward punishment involves reporting the crime. Historically, for crimes committed between strangers, this involved seeking out a police officer or finding an available residential or pay phone from which the police could be called. These costs, no doubt, discouraged the reporting of some crimes, and, at a minimum, introduced delay in the reporting process. Further, this delay likely led to the loss of some details about the crime and the individual committing it which, in turn, lowered the likelihood of identification and apprehension. Data from the 1980s in the United States indicates that the police made an immediate arrest in less than 3% of serious crime calls for service (Sherman 1995). Delayed reporting and the attendant information loss might increase sources of doubt, leading to more difficulty in building an effective prosecution and reducing the chances of convictions.

Mobile phones, however, allow for quicker reporting of crimes and, in some cases, real time communication of details about the crime and the criminal. In an environment where phones are ubiquitous, the cost of reporting approaches zero, negating all the problems of delay discussed above. The perceived risk of apprehension could increase among motivated offenders when they notice potential targets are carrying a mobile phone. As technology has improved to allow the transmission of photographic images, identification, apprehension, prosecution, and conviction all presumably become even more likely. Such technology lowers the cost victims bear in reporting crime;[2] it also allows bystanders to provide details of crimes at a very low cost.[3] In some instances, a victim's phone may inadvertently provide clues that help identify a criminal. Similarly, for some crimes, the perpetrator's mobile phone can provide evidence as well.[4]

While this effect of mobile phones would appear to unambiguously lead to a decline in violent crime in the Becker framework, things are not as clear with respect to property crime. First, mobile phones are an attractive target for thieves. At least initially, the phones themselves were high value items that could be sold easily. Their small size also makes them relatively attractive targets. Roman and Chalfin (2008) note there was a significant and short-lived uptick in reported robberies in 2005 and 2006 following the mass introduction of iPod portable media devices. Further, the phones can be used cost free for a period of time until the victim cancels the service.

Popular accounts of cell phone theft suggest that it has been a large problem ever since the technology became popular.[5] Mobile phones, especially prepaid unregistered ones, might also be helpful in the activities of gangs and other crime organizations.[6]

3.   EMPIRICAL ANALYSIS

Unfortunately, it is not possible to directly analyse the contribution of mobile phones to the 1990s crime decline. Comprehensive data below the national level are not available before 1999. Data after this period come from information filed by mobile phone service providers with the FCC.[7] Service providers must make these filings by March 1 and September 1 of each year.[8]

Another problem that hampers strong causal inferences with respect to the effect of mobile phones on crime is the lack of a strong instrument or natural experiment to isolate the true causal effect of mobile phones on crime. There are a number of reasons one may be suspicious of regression results in the absence of such clearly random variation. For example, a reverse causality problem might exist whereby individuals fearing crime may purchase phones for their protection. This particular omitted variable bias may not be particularly troubling, at least in terms of verifying a link between mobile phones and crime, since, at least in a bivariate regression framework, it would imply that any estimated deterrence relationship is under-stated. Further, this mechanism in itself would provide some supporting evidence at least regarding people's belief that mobile phones are useful for counteracting criminals.

More problematic biases might arise if there are income or wealth effects that lead to increasing mobile phone penetration rates and declining crime rates. To mitigate this source of bias, we control for real state (per capita) income below, but clearly this approach cannot rule out the possibility of bias.

Our analysis covers the period 1999–2007 at the state level. Our primary outcomes of interest are rape and aggravated assault rates recorded as part of the FBI's Uniform Crime Reports (UCR). We rely on these crime outcomes because they are likely to occur among strangers and are most plausibly deterred by mobile phones. Assaults among intimates or acquaintances are more likely to be reported as misdemeanor simple assaults. Sexual assaults among non-strangers are also less likely to be classified as rapes by the police. The FBI's UCR defines rape as "The carnal knowledge of a female forcibly and against her will." The FBI also provides law enforcement agencies with scenarios that clearly show the focus is on sexual assaults committed by strangers (Uniform Crime Reporting Handbook (2004) at 19).

1. Law enforcement received a complaint from a victim who claimed that when she was leaving work late one night, she was attacked in the company parking lot by an unidentified male and forcibly raped. The offender was not apprehended.
2. Two men lured a woman to their motel room with the promise of discussing a job opportunity. They threatened her with a knife and both forcibly raped her. On complaint by the woman, the police arrested both men.
3. Three girls were attacked, assaulted, and raped by four boys. Each boy raped each of the girls. No arrests were made.

Some policy-makers have noted the potential mobile phones have for providing evidence in rape investigations.[9] Particularly as more phones include cameras, the evidentiary possibilities grow substantially, providing better descriptions in the case of stranger rapes and possibly adding veracity to claims in "he said/she said" scenarios in acquaintance rapes. Further, a victim in these cases might be able to discourage the sexual assault simply by brandishing the phone and threatening to report. To the extent the attacker is cognizant of any of these effects, rape rates should decline on the margin. Similar arguments apply in the case of assault and perhaps even homicide, though in the case of the latter, homicide was quite rare in this time period (averaging just 5.6 per 100,000 population in the period 1999–2007), most of the substantial drop in homicide occurred in the 1990s, and it has since exhibited very little variation, as shown in Figure 10.2.

For controls, we include real per capita GDP, as well as per capita spending on corrections and police to account for changes in other policies that may affect deterrence.[10] The state GDP control should account for some of the increase in mobile phone penetration that is explained by wealth or income effects, though this control is not perfect. In some subsequent regressions, we allow the relationship between crime and income to vary state to state as a robustness test.

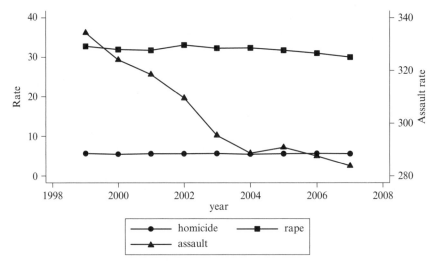

Source: BJS

Figure 10.2   Violent crime rates

For our primary measure of mobile phone penetration, we use the total number of mobile phone subscriptions in a state in a given year. An alternative would be to use this number as a fraction of total state population. We prefer the former since a number of state year cells exhibit more mobile phone subscriptions than people residing in the state.[11] Presumably, individuals with more than one subscription are much more likely to actually have a mobile phone in their possession at any given time. States with a large number of such people may project the appearance that mobile phones are ubiquitous, heightening any deterrence effect. Summary statistics are presented in Table 10.1.

Additionally, we include state and year fixed effects to account for constant idiosyncratic differences across states as well as common non-linear time trends. Because our dependent variables are rates, we use population weights in the primary regressions. Angrist and Pischke (2009) suggest that the standard approach of using weighted least squares is unwarranted on the usual justification of heteroskedasticity grounds, given that heteroskedasticity robust standard errors are easily calculated. They also warn that weighted least squares can lead to biased coefficients. We suggest, however, that the most interesting phenomena studied by social scientists exhibit treatment effect heterogeneity. If regressions are not weighted in a context like the current one, mean effects will weight what happens in Rhode Island equally with what happens in California. Such an approach is problematic. However, we do present results with equal weighting as well to demonstrate that our primary estimates are not driven by this kind of "bias".

We use standard errors that are robust to clustering both at the state and year level as discussed in Cameron, Gelbach, and Miller (2011). Clustering at the state level is used to account for the kind of serial dependence discussed in Bertrand, Duflo, and Mullainathan (2004). Clustering at the year level is used to account for measurement error related to changes in the reporting behavior of the mobile phone providers, as well as dependence arising from common technology shocks affecting the national market for mobile phones.

Table 10.1   Summary statistics

Variable	Description	Mean	SD	Source
Mobile phones	Number of mobile phone subscriptions in 1000s	7328	6923	FCC
Mobile phone rate	Number of mobile phones divided by state population	0.56	0.18	FCC
Violent crime	Number of violent crimes per 100,000 state residents	486	160	BJS
Rape	Number of rapes per 100,000 state residents	32	9	BJS
Assault	Number of assaults per 100,000 state residents	303	120	BJS
Property crime	Number of property crimes per 100,000 state residents	3529	810	BJS
GDP	Real per capita domestic product in a state (2005 dollars)	41,157	7051	BEA
Police	Per capita spending on police (state and local) in a state	231	84	BJS
Corrections	Per capita spending on corrections in state	189	55	BJS

Note: Means and standard deviations are weighted by population. Data cover 1999–2007. Police and corrections are linearly extrapolated on the basis of real per capita GDP for the years 2006 and 2007. Data sources are the Federal Communications Commission (FCC), the Bureau of Justice Statistics (BJS), and the Bureau of Economic Analysis (BEA).

In Table 10.2, we present the results for the rates of violent crime in total, rape, assault, and total property crimes with state and year fixed effects but no control variables.

As suggested, all of the violent crime measures exhibit a negative relationship with the number of mobile phones in a state, whereas the property crime rate does not. The magnitude of the effect is generally large as well. In the sample, the average increase in mobile phone subscriptions in a given year is about 1,000,000 which translates into 5 fewer violent crimes per 100,000 people (a relative effect of about 1%), 2 fewer rapes per 1,000,000 people (an effect greater than 0.5%), and 5 fewer assaults per 100,000 people (an effect greater than 1.5%). An increase of a standard deviation in mobile phone subscriptions would imply effects 7 times as large.

As suggested above, however, it would be reasonable to look at mobile phone subscriptions normalized by population. We provide the same analysis using this metric in Table 10.3.

While the results are clearly less precisely estimated, the implied effects are even larger than those presented in Table 10.2 if we use the average increase in mobile phones (normalized by population) in a given year or a one standard deviation increase as the point of evaluation. This suggests that our effect is not merely an artifact of peculiar effects observed in large states.

Table 10.4 provides the analysis where states are weighted equally.

While the precision of the rape estimate drops considerably, none of the point

Table 10.2   The relationship between mobile phones and crime rates (standard errors clustered separately on state and year in parentheses)

	Violent crime	Rape	Assault	Property crime
Mobile phones	−0.005***	−0.0002***	−0.005***	0.01
	(0.001)	(0.0001)	(0.001)	(0.01)
State effects	Yes	Yes	Yes	Yes
Year effects	Yes	Yes	Yes	Yes
Weighting	Population	Population	Population	Population

Notes:
*** $p < 0.01$ (against a two-sided test of a 0 effect)
** $p < 0.05$ (against a two-sided test of a 0 effect)
* $p < 0.10$ (against a two-sided test of a 0 effect)

Table 10.3   The relationship between mobile phones and crime rates (standard errors clustered separately on state and year in parentheses)

	Violent crime	Rape	Assault	Property crime
Mobile phone rate	−212**	−7	−169*	−42
	(90)	(5)	(87)	(612)
State effects	Yes	Yes	Yes	Yes
Year effects	Yes	Yes	Yes	Yes
Weighting	Population	Population	Population	Population

Notes:
*** $p < 0.01$ (against a two-sided test of a 0 effect)
** $p < 0.05$ (against a two-sided test of a 0 effect)
* $p < 0.10$ (against a two-sided test of a 0 effect)

estimates suggest that weighting can be generating any bias, the concern of Angrist and Pischke. In fact, the violent crime estimate appears to grow slightly in magnitude. Given our preference to use total mobile phone subscriptions and weighted least squares, combined with the evidence that these choices are not driving any of our estimates, we proceed with these choices in the tables that follow.

Table 10.5 includes our control variables described above.

Adding the covariates does very little to change our point estimates. In all four crime measures, the estimated effect of mobile phone subscriptions is stable relative to the specification that does not include the covariates. This is surprising given the hypothesized relationships between income and both crime and mobile phone penetration. Perhaps this provides some confidence that the estimated effect is not primarily driven by omitted variables bias. However, without better identification strategies, we must take these results as being merely suggestive of a deterrent effect of mobile phones on violent crime.

As one last robustness test, we allow the income effect to differ by state. We present these results in Table 10.6, suppressing the covariate estimates for presentation purposes. This specification generates more variability in the estimates, lowering confidence in

Table 10.4 The relationship between mobile phones and crime rates (standard errors clustered separately on state and year in parentheses)

	Violent crime	Rape	Assault	Property crime
Mobile phones	−0.006***	−0.0002	−0.005***	0.005
	(0.002)	(0.0002)	(0.001)	(0.014)
State effects	Yes	Yes	Yes	Yes
Year effects	Yes	Yes	Yes	Yes
Weighting	Equal	Equal	Equal	Equal

Notes:
*** p < 0.01 (against a two-sided test of a 0 effect)
** p < 0.05 (against a two-sided test of a 0 effect)
* p < 0.10 (against a two-sided test of a 0 effect)

Table 10.5 The relationship between mobile phones and crime rates (standard errors clustered separately on state and year in parentheses)

	Violent crime	Rape	Assault	Property crime
Mobile phones	−0.004***	−0.0002**	−0.005***	0.02*
	(0.001)	(0.0001)	(0.001)	(0.01)
GDP	−0.006***	−0.0002	−0.003**	−0.04***
	(0.002)	(0.0002)	(0.001)	(0.01)
Police	−0.06	0.001	−0.04	−0.56
	(0.03)	(0.004)	(0.02)	(0.42)
Corrections	0.08	−0.001	0.06	−0.55
	(0.09)	(0.006)	(0.06)	(0.62)
State effects	Yes	Yes	Yes	Yes
Year effects	Yes	Yes	Yes	Yes
Weighting	Population	Population	Population	Population

Notes:
*** p < 0.01 (against a two-sided test of a 0 effect)
** p < 0.05 (against a two-sided test of a 0 effect)
* p < 0.10 (against a two-sided test of a 0 effect)

the original analysis. Though, here too, important effects of mobile phones on crime are implied, even if only the mobile phone coefficient in the assault equation remains statistically significant at the 10% level.[12]

Another source of concern is the presence of a number of potential outliers in the sample. For example, the District of Columbia has an average violent crime rate that is almost four times the sample mean, while its mean subscriber figure normalized for population exceeds one. To examine the influence of extreme value observations in the dataset, we present the results of a leverage robust regression technique in Table 10.7.[13]

The results from the leverage robust regression estimation suggest that the results are not driven by high leverage observations. Each coefficient is as large in magnitude, and larger in the cases of violent crime and rape, in the robust regression specification as it is in the corresponding regression from Table 10.5.

Table 10.6   The relationship between mobile phones and crime rates (standard errors clustered separately on state and year in parentheses)

	Violent crime	Rape	Assault	Property crime
Mobile phones	−0.003	−0.0001**	−0.004*	0.01
	(0.003)	(0.0002)	(0.002)	(0.03)
State effects	Yes	Yes	Yes	Yes
Year effects	Yes	Yes	Yes	Yes
Weighting	Population	Population	Population	Population

Notes:
All regressions include GDP, Police, and Corrections as covariates.
*** $p < 0.01$ (against a two-sided test of a 0 effect)
** $p < 0.05$ (against a two-sided test of a 0 effect)
* $p < 0.10$ (against a two-sided test of a 0 effect)

Table 10.7   The relationship between mobile phones and crime rates (robust regression results)

	Violent crime	Rape	Assault	Property crime
Mobile phones	−0.005***	−0.0003***	−0.005***	0.01*
	(0.001)	(0.0001)	(0.001)	(0.01)
State effects	Yes	Yes	Yes	Yes
Year effects	Yes	Yes	Yes	Yes

Notes:
All regressions include GDP, Police, and Corrections as covariates.
*** $p < 0.01$ (against a two-sided test of a 0 effect)
** $p < 0.05$ (against a two-sided test of a 0 effect)
* $p < 0.10$ (against a two-sided test of a 0 effect)

Table 10.8   The relationship between mobile phones and crime rates (standard errors clustered separately on state and year in parentheses)

	Violent crime	Rape	Assault	Property crime
Mobile phones	−0.005***	−0.0002**	−0.005***	0.01
	(0.001)	(0.0001)	(0.001)	(0.01)
State effects	Yes	Yes	Yes	Yes
Region X year effects	Yes	Yes	Yes	Yes
Weighting	Population	Population	Population	Population

Notes:
All regressions include GDP, Police, and Corrections as covariates.
*** $p < 0.01$ (against a two-sided test of a 0 effect)
** $p < 0.05$ (against a two-sided test of a 0 effect)
* $p < 0.10$ (against a two-sided test of a 0 effect)

One last robustness check we perform is to allow for region specific non-linear time trends (i.e., year dummies that vary by region of the United States) to account for possible differences in the diffusion of mobile phones and coincident changes in crime patterns. We present these results in Table 10.8.

Allowing for more generality in the time effects does not affect our estimates of the effect of mobile phones on crime.

While we do not have a strong identification strategy, beyond using state and year fixed effects, our estimates exhibit a surprising degree of robustness. While it is not possible to state with confidence that there is a strongly negative effect of mobile phone penetration on violent crime rates, much less make a claim that this effect played an important role in the crime decline observed in the 1990s, the results are interesting and deserve further exploration if additional data or a better design becomes available. This effect may help to explain the puzzle of why crime rates did not begin to decline earlier since the mobile phone effect is one that is specific to the mid-1990s and beyond. Given the plausibility of the hypothesis and the robustness of our results, it is worthwhile exploring the policy implications of any mobile phone effect.

4.   POLICY IMPLICATIONS

Criminal justice policy is typically focused on the supply of public expenditures to deter offending, incapacitate active offenders, or promote rehabilitation. The primary focus in the United States has been on deterrence and incapacitation. Increased police strength (Evans and Owens 2007) and more efficiently allocating police to problematic places or crime hot spots (Weisburd and Eck 2004) are among the more promising areas of criminal justice policy with some evidence of deterrence pay-offs. Prison expansion has been credited for some measurable crime reduction through incapacitation, but there are numerous negative externalities of prison, including its effect on future labor market prospects and the direct public costs (over $20 billion a year) of detaining individuals for long periods of time in secure institutions (Spelman 2006). The focus on crime policy has underplayed the role of private efforts to prevent crime and the role that individuals play in their own risk of victimization.

The descriptive analysis of the state by year adoption of mobile phones suggests that this technology may coincide with other increases in private crime prevention that helped facilitate the crime drop of the 1990s. Our findings at least suggest some effect of mobile phones on sustaining the historically low rates of crimes of interpersonal violence between 1999 and 2007 in states.

Mobile phones provide the average citizen with the ability to effortlessly contact the police and provide exact coordinates for a crime, perhaps increasing the provision of timely reports of criminal activity to the police. The near-universal adoption of mobile phones makes these devices less likely to produce negative externalities noted in other investments in private security, like burglar alarms and security fences, that displace crime to other targets. The use of mobile phones to deter crime is also consistent with a Becker model and a routine activities theory of crime. Mobile phones increase surveillance. When motivated offenders converge in time and place with suitable targets the average level of guardianship of those targets increases with the presence of a mobile phone. This is particularly true in the case of assaults and rapes committed by strangers, where a potential victim is no longer completely isolated and can contact the police for assistance. An increased level of guardianship of potential victims raises the costs of crimes to motivated offenders. An added benefit of mobile phones is that their deterrent benefit doesn't require additional supply of public expenditures to criminal justice programs.

5.   CONCLUSION

This is the first study to posit that the introduction and adoption of cell phones led to a decrease in crime. We develop a model of this mechanism and use our framework to generate testable hypotheses. We hypothesize that cell phones had the largest negative impact for violent crimes and a lesser impact for property crimes. We test our theory using recent data and find support for our hypotheses. Our conclusions are unchanged after conducting a number of robustness tests.

Although our regressions control for state specific and year specific characteristics, and a number of other control variables, the estimates need to be interpreted with caution. In particular, if we omitted variables that are correlated with cell phone adoption rates as well as with crime, our estimates are biased.

Nonetheless, our results are consistent with our model, suggesting that cell phone adoption lowers crime. This implies that there may be relatively cheap alternatives to putting cops on the street in order to fight crime. In particular, our findings point to private solutions to deter crime. However, for the United States, many of the gains from cell phone use may have already been realized, given that a large fraction of the population already uses cell phones. However, by encouraging individuals to take cell phones with them when leaving their residences, cell phones have the potential to further reduce crime.

Future work may consider a different identification strategy to isolate the causal effect of cell phones, and determine by which mechanism cell phones lower crimes. For example, are criminals deterred by the mere possibility that potential victims will use their cell phone, are they deterred when they observe potential victims using their mobile device, or are they deterred because individuals will pull out their cell phone when they consider themselves close to an encounter with a criminal? Answers to these questions will further illuminate how cell phone adoption reduces crime.

NOTES

1. The sampling frame for the NCVS under-counts homeless and criminal offenders currently serving time in jail or prisons. This subpopulation of individuals are the most likely to be victims of violent crime.
2. See, e.g., www.nytimes.com/2008/09/19/nyregion/19arrest.html
3. See, e.g., the Swift Report Network, www.swiftreport.net/, which provides a central forum for such reports.
4. An obvious instance of this is to provide location information for tracking or verification purposes. In some cases, the evidence is even more direct. See, e.g., www.theolympian.com/2010/06/26/1285839/video-on-donated-cell-phone-leads.html

5. See, e.g., www.time.com/time/magazine/article/0,9171,214207,00.html
6. This concern is vividly portrayed in the HBO series "The Wire" (www.youtube.com/watch?v= PojAn XG 9wwU). A number of politicians in the United States and abroad have considered banning unregistered prepaid mobile phones on these grounds. See, e.g., http://schumer.senate.gov/record.cfm?id=325263
7. See "Local Telephone Competition" section of www.fcc.gov/wcb/iatd/comp.html
8. See www.fcc.gov/form477/
9. See, e.g., www.heraldscotland.com/mobile/0news/crime-courts/new-ways-to-help-rape-victims-1.1058614
10. The spending variables are linearly extrapolated based on real per capita state GDP for the years 2006 and 2007 since BJS has not yet released data for these years. Real per capita GDP was used as the pattern series rather than a simple time trend since the GDP variable explains much more variation in these spending variables than does a time trend. This is true even if level differences across states are removed from the data.
11. Results are comparable if we normalize subscriptions by population.
12. Although, it is interesting to note that if we run this regression with equal weighting, the coefficient in the violent crime equation is statistically significant at the 10% level and the coefficient in the assault equation is statistically significant at the 5% level.
13. Specifically, we use the rreg command in Stata. Note that this command does not allow for clustering of standard errors and it weights inversely according to an observation's leverage as opposed to the population weighting used above.

REFERENCES

Angrist, Josh and Jorn-Steffen Pischke (2009) *Mostly Harmless Econometrics: An Empiricist's Companion*, Princeton University Press

Ayres, Ian and Steven Levitt (1998) "Measuring Positive Externalities from Unobservable Victim Precaution: An Empirical Analysis of Lojack," 113(1) *Quarterly Journal of Economics* 43

Bertrand, Marianne, Esther Duflo, and Sendhil Mullainathan (2004) "How Much Should We Trust Differences-in-Differences Estimates?," 119(1) *Quarterly Journal of Economics* 249

Blumstein, Alfred (2000) "Disaggregating the Violence Trends," in *The Crime Drop in America*, Alfred Blumstein and Joel Wallman, eds., New York: Cambridge University Press, 13–44

Blumstein, Alfred and Joel Wallman (2000) *The Crime Drop in America*, New York: Cambridge University Press

Brooks, Leah (2008) "Volunteering to be Taxed: Business Improvement Districts and the Extra Governmental Provision of Public Safety," 92 *Journal of Public Economics* 388

Cameron, A. Colin, Jonah Gelbach, and Douglas Miller (2011) "Robust Inference with Multi-way Clustering," 29(2) *Journal of Business and Economic Statistics* 238

Cohen, Lawrence and Marcus Felson (1979) "Social Change and Crime Rate Trends: A Routine Activity Approach," 44 *American Sociological Review* 588

Cook, Philip J. (1986) "The demand and supply of criminal opportunities," VII *Crime and Justice* 1

Cook, Philip J. and John H. Laub (2002) "After the Epidemic: Recent Trends in Youth Violence in the United States," in *Crime and Justice: A Review of Research*, Michael Tonry, ed., Chicago: University of Chicago Press, 117–53

Cook, P.J. and Macdonald, J. (2010) "Public Safety Through Private Action: An Economic Assessment of BIDs, Locks, and Citizen Cooperation," NBER Working Paper No. 15877, Cambridge, MA

Cook, Philip J. and John M. MacDonald (2011a) "Public Safety through Private Action: An Economic Assessment of BIDs," 121 *Economic Journal* 445

— (2011b) "Limiting Criminal Opportunities," in *Controlling Crime: Strategies and Tradeoffs*, P. Cook, J. Ludwig, and J. McCrary, eds., Chicago: University of Chicago Press

Donohue, John and Steven Levitt (2001) "The Impact of Legalized Abortion on Crime," 116(2) *Quarterly Journal of Economics* 379

Evans, W. N. and Owens, E. G. (2007) "COPS and Crime," 91(2) *Journal of Public Economics* 181

Levitt, Steven (2004) "Understanding Why Crime Fell in the 1990s: Four Factors that Explain the Decline and Six That Do Not," 18 *Journal of Economic Perspectives* 163

Reyes, Jessica (2007) "Environmental Policy as Social Policy? The Impact of Childhood Lead Exposure on Crime," 7 *B.E. Journal of Economic Analysis and Policy* 1

Roman, J. and A. Chalfin (2008) "Has Demand for Crime Increased: Does the Increase in the Prevalence of Personal Media Devices Explain the Violent Crime Spike in 2005 and 2006?," 45(3) *American Criminal Law Review* 1149

Sherman, L.W. (1995) "The Police," in *Crime*, J.Q. Wilson and J. Petersilia, eds., San Francisco: ICS Press, 327–48
Spelman, William (2006) "The Limited Importance of Prison Expansion," in *The Crime Drop in America*, A. Blumstein and J. Wallman, eds., New York: Cambridge University Press
Weiner, David, Byron Lutz, and Jens Ludwig (2009) "The Effects of School Desegregation on Crime," NBER working paper
Weisburd, David and John E. Eck (2004) "What Can Police Do to Reduce Crime, Disorder, and Fear?," 593 *Annals of the American Academy of Political and Social Science* 42

Index